Organizational Behaviour in International

contemporary
BUSINESS SERIES

Series Editor: Professor Andrew Lock
Manchester Metropolitan University

The Contemporary Business Series is designed with the needs of business studies undergraduates and MBA students in mind, and each title is written in a straightforward, student friendly style. Though all of the books in the series reflect the individuality of their authors, you will find that you can count on certain key features in each text which maintain high standards of structure and approach:

- excellent coverage of core and option subject
- UK/international examples or case studies throughout
- full references and further reading suggestions
- written in direct, easily accessible style, for ease of use by full, part-time and self-study students

Books in the series include:

Accounting for Business
Peter Atrill, David Harvey and Edward McLaney

Information Resources Management
John R. Beaumont and Ewan Sutherland

International Business Strategy
Werner Ketelhöhn

Management Accounting for Financial Decisions
Keith Ward, Sri Srikanthan and Richard Neal

The Management and Marketing of Services
Peter Mudie and Angela Cottam

Organizational Behaviour in International Management
Terence Jackson

Quantitative Approaches to Management
Robert Ball

Organizational Behaviour in International Management

Terence Jackson

Butterworth-Heinemann Ltd
Linacre House, Jordan Hill, Oxford OX2 8DP

  A member of the Reed Elsevier group

OXFORD   LONDON   BOSTON
MUNICH   NEW DELHI   SINGAPORE   SYDNEY
TOKYO   TORONTO   WELLINGTON

First published 1993

British Library Cataloguing in Publication Data
Jackson, Terence
    Organizational Behaviour in
    International Management. –
    (Contemporary Business Series)
    I. Title II. Series
    658

ISBN 0 7506 1571 0

Composition by Genesis Typesetting, Laser Quay, Rochester, Kent ME2 4HU
Printed and bound in Great Britain

To my wife, Sheelagh

CONTENTS

Preface

The reasons for this book

The standpoint of this book is from the position of the manager in Europe. It will no longer be possible to think purely of a British manager, or a French manager. Certainly these species will exist, they will not lose their national identity. Certainly this book would not wish to presume that! The point is that managers in Britain, France, Germany, or any other European country work within an economic area which is growing in importance in the World. It is becoming more difficult just to think British, or to think French. Perhaps more importantly, it is becoming more difficult to accept uncritically, management theory drawn mainly from North America.

European managers are essentially international managers: they work across national borders. They must think cross-culturally. They must ask themselves: will this particular management theory, technique or practice work in this country? They must question how they should work with their colleagues from other countries, who have different cultures to their own.

For the European manager, potential or actual, a consideration of organizational behaviour should be made from a cross-cultural perspective. In studying essential areas such as motivation, leadership, or organizational theory, we should question whether these theories apply in the culture within which we are working, or to the foreign colleagues with whom we work.

There are now very few business schools in Europe which presume only to offer to their students a national perspective. Increasingly, they are forging links with similarly minded institutions in other parts of Europe. Courses are becoming more international in scope. Existing literature is becoming more international. It is interesting to note that existing texts in the UK on organizational behaviour are introducing European and international cases into their new editions.

Similarly, companies in Europe are becoming more internationalized. More use is being made of business schools offering an international perspective in their executive development programmes. More graduates are being recruited from schools which train their management students in more than one country. There is a need for existing managers to develop their skills in working across cultures.

This book, therefore, starts from the position of presenting concepts of organizational behaviour theory, methods and practice from the point of view of international management. The international aspects are not simply an afterthought, but an integrative part of learning about this important subject. Readers are not expected to have prior knowledge of organizational behaviour, but must be prepared to learn basic concepts through an international and cross-cultural perspective.

The aims of this book

As well as focusing on the *international* aspects of management, this text also looks at the *management* aspect of international business, and therefore sees organizational behaviour as a vehicle for the development of managers. This provides a clear emphasis on the relevance of this subject to effective management, and is written with this perspective in mind.

Perhaps one of the most important assumptions of this book is that the successful manager is a good communicator (this is a very Anglo-Saxon assumption) and that effective management is accomplished by a good understanding of human beings in organizations. Organizational behaviour is therefore regarded as a central area within management studies, and is regarded as essential for those attempting to manage across cultures. While it may be necessary for a manager to be technically proficient, without an understanding of how to deal with human beings in a multi-cultured situation, his or her technical ability may count for nothing.

The aims of this book are two-fold, representing the two parts of the book.

Part One: Theory and methods for European management

The first part of the book is intended to introduce readers to a central core of the theory and methods of organizational behaviour in order to develop an awareness and understanding of the behavioural aspects of organizational performance in the practice of European management in the global context. It introduces readers to the practical applications of the component academic subject areas such as psychology, sociology and social anthropology, drawing on both European and international sources.

Much existing theory in standard textbooks in this area is drawn from American sources and it is often impossible to ignore these sources. European management may require a different emphasis on such aspects as cross-cultural management, business leadership and management styles. There is also a growing body of European knowledge and research in this area which this book taps.

Part Two: The effective global manager

The second part of the book builds on the first in applying the core organizational behaviour theory to global and cross-cultural management practice from a European perspective. This is sometimes contrasted to prevailing American and Japanese theory and practice. This part of the book is quite focused on specific applied methods of organizational behaviour relevant to managers in international business. Readers are expected to have already grasped the basic theory in this area. Here the emphasis is on the application of specific concepts, methods, and techniques.

Part Two is therefore aimed at making readers think critically about the development of their own management competences within the global context. It explores conceptual frameworks within which the effective global manager may be developed. It considers the business and organizational context within which managers' skills are employed, particularly with regard to a changing, multi-cultured and sometimes ambiguous environment. It provides a number of techniques which readers can apply in practice.

Readership

The book is in two parts and provides a core for a one- or two-year module for advanced undergraduates or postgraduate students. It is written from a 'European' perspective and is aimed primarily at students who will be working internationally. It may also serve American management students well in gaining a different perspective, and learning more about management in the growing and dynamic marketplace of Europe.

While it is primarily a core textbook for students of management, we would also hope that it may also be useful for existing managers who wish to gain an appreciation and understanding of doing business internationally.

Part One assumes no prior knowledge of organizational behaviour or its component subjects. However, readers with such previous knowledge will find this a useful 'different perspective' and certainly a refresher.

Part Two assumes that the reader has read Part One. However, the more advanced student may like to go straight into this part of the book.

Structure

Each chapter comprises a learning unit and typically consists of:

* theoretical discussion, concept building, and outline and discussion of specific methods or techniques which may be useful to the manager operating internationally;
* case studies, which illustrate the concepts and often invite the reader to discuss particular problem areas;
* activities, which explore particular areas, either by employing a technique, or by using a questionnaire to analyse an aspect relevant to the reader;
* references, which enable the reader to follow up areas of interest.

Content of the book

As well as the two main divisions of this book, it is further divided into six broad headings which reflect the emphasis of the chapters contained within each. These are as follows.

Section 1: Theory and process of communication. This looks at the three aspects of social perception and interpersonal performance, working in teams, and the intra-personal aspects of personality and self-concept. It provides a general introduction to the main areas covered within the book, looking at why communication is important to cross-cultural management.

Section 2: Theory and process of leadership and motivation. This covers the areas of motivation, power and influence, and leadership, looking at the many cross-cultural implications of these factors in effective leadership.

Section 3: Organizational theory and process. This looks at the two main aspects of organizational structure and process, and organizational culture and its interpretations through management styles. It provides a focus on international organizations as well as on national organizational units.

Section 4: The European manager in the global marketplace. This is the first section in the second half of the book which looks at the practising manager and his or her development. The first chapter in this section discusses the nature of the European manager and the type of competences this person should be working towards. The subsequent chapters in this section then go on to look at learning, and why this is an essential feature of the adaptive manager, and then to look at career development in the interrnational context.

Section 5: Managing in a multi-national context. This explores skills which the international or global manager should develop, namely, managing cultural differences, international negotiation, and decision making or the management of uncertainty.

Section 6: Managing in a changing environment. Both Europe and the world are rapidly changing arenas. Change management is considered, as is international project management. The latter is considered as a growing management method for managing across borders. It also serves as a means for the reader to apply many of the aspects covered in this text.

Limitations of this book

It would be unfair and completely inaccurate to present this book as a comprehensive textbook on organizational behaviour. It is not! More appropriately it can be seen as a focused text providing a core element in the study of effective management in international business.

Organizational behaviour as a growing subject covers a vast area drawing on the subject areas within the social and behavioural sciences, having a plethora of conflicting theoretical positions, and seeking to provide answers to the many problems of individuals working in organizations. The many excellent tomes on this subject area bear witness to this. This book has not sought to replicate nor to replace such general textbooks.

More specifically this text has sought to provide a core element in the study of international management for non-specialists, rather than for potential or actual human resources specialists. Those seeking a more comprehensive approach would be well advised to supplement this text with one or two of the more traditional textbooks in this area. The references section after each chapter can be used as a guide.

Another limitation of this book is the lack of coverage of comparative management data. It is not the intention here to provide a detailed description of management practices in, say, the countries of Europe. Apart from the lack of space here, this approach is often counter-productive, sometimes leading to gross caricaturing and steroetyping. This text tries to provide approaches to thinking about and analysing other cultures, rather than providing a 'character sketch' on each nationality the international manager may encounter. More specifically it takes the view that in business we deal with individuals rather than nationalities. Every individual is different and may or may not be like his or her 'national cultural characteristics' (see Chapter 12, for example).

Those readers wishing to take a more detailed look at management in specific countries should consult the literature in this area. Some references are given at the end of relevant chapters.

Acknowledgements

The materials contained within this text are the result of three years development within EAP, and the interactions with management students from the many countries of Europe and beyond, and with colleagues in the four countries within which EAP works.

While every effort has been made for ethnocentrism not to creep into this text, it cannot be denied that the final result is the sole responsibility of an Englishman.

CASES

Mini cases

Case studies

Part One
Theory and Methods for European Management

Introduction to part one

This first part of the book lays the foundations for a study of organizational behaviour in international management. As such it has two main focuses: the theory of behaviour in organizations; and the problems and applications of the more familiar aspects of organizational behaviour in the cross-culture management arena.

We have used 'organizational behaviour' as a fairly generic term to embrace various disciplines within the social sciences which have an interest in how organizations work, and how individuals within them view these organizations, how they perform, and ultimately how they achieve results which are consistent with organizational objectives, group objectives and individual objectives. The main academic disciplines are:

- *Sociology*: Concerned mainly with the 'macro' aspects of organizations within society; societal influences on individuals; and, the all embracing notion of 'culture', what it constitutes, how it develops and its influences on individuals.
- *Social anthropology*: More specifically concerned with culture and its consequences in different societies, and traditionally concentrating on in-depth studies of individual cultures or society, and comparisons between different societies.
- *Psychology*: Focusing on the individual in terms of cognitive processes and behaviour; and through social psychology focusing on group processes.

We could also list more peripheral subjects such as social philosophy through which a consideration of ethical behaviour may be made; and political theory which may be applied to the growing interest in power and politics in organizations.

Through the text we refer to a general descriptive model, which really serves to remind us that in any process within organizations we must consider three broad areas:

- The *context* of the individual and group actions. This includes the organizatinal structure, the network of 'rules' which guides behaviour, the technology employed, and the general opportunity within the organization (and the wider society) to act or perform in a certain way;
- The *content* of individuals' thought processes, motivations, objectives and perceptions;
- The *conduct* of individuals within the organizations: those aspects which we can observe; their specific behaviour and performance, as well as the skills required to perform.

We have related these three areas to the three schools of thought of 'structuralism', 'phenomenology' and 'behaviourism'. Each of these theories of organizations have something to contribute and we try to provide explanations of organizational behaviour by reference to these (often diverse) schools of thought.

While this first part of the book cannot be regarded as a comprehensive coverage of the area of organizational behaviour, we have tried to concentrate on certain key areas which have a specific relevance to international managers. Hence we have started with a consideration of social perception directing this to interaction across cultures. This first chapter discusses concepts which are taken up later in the text, and introduces the descriptive model of *context–content–conduct*. Readers should therefore regard this as an introductory chapter which is important to an understanding of what follows.

When looking at cross-cultural management it is important to understand 'communication' as the key to successful management. Again, this provides a starting point to the structure and content of Part Two, which may be conceptualized in the figure below.

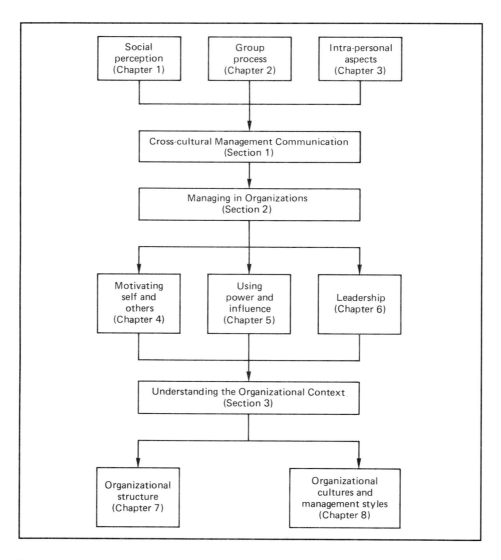

Hence, we look at some key components of communication and discuss the importance of these to cross-cultural interaction. We then focus this on management in organizations, looking at motivation, power, and leadership. We then consider this within the context of organizations, looking at both structure and organizational culture.

The relationship between theory and practice in organizational behaviour is an important one. The utility of a theory must be assessed in the light of management practice. Theory cannot be ignored because this is what gives us the flexibility of thought with a practical situation, and takes us beyond a mere pragmatic reaction to management situations. This relationship is reflected in the approach taken in Part One, where theories are illustrated where possible by short case studies and activities which the reader should endevour to tackle.

The other aspect of organizational behaviour which the current text tries to encapsulate, is the fact that the subject applies to us, as human beings. Therefore many of the suggested activities focus on how we see our own social perceptions, personality or motivation, for example.

Having worked through the first part of this book, the reader will then be well prepared to look at Part Two which in many ways takes a more practical approach, focusing on specific techniques, methods and skills.

So, Part One provides the basic theory and methods of organizational behaviour which will lay the foundations for an understanding of the requirement for effective European (that is, international) management.

Section 1
Theory and Process of Communication

In this section we argue that for the international manager communication is fundamental to success. The role of management is to communicate. Effective management across cultures can only take place if there is an understanding of the theory and processes of communication.

We look at three aspects of communication: social perception, working in teams and individual personality characteristics. While these are inter-related and there is no necessity to read one chapter before another, Chapter 1 serves also as an introductory chapter, discussing some important factors – such as 'culture', 'communication' and 'management' – which will recur throughout this text.

1

Interpersonal performance and social perception

Objectives

Following this chapter you should be able to:

1 Explain the importance of interpersonal communication to the effectiveness of management performance within organizations.
2 Describe the influence of cultural factors on the way individuals see others and their interpersonal performances.
3 Document your own cultural influences on the way you perform in an interpersonal situation.

Key concepts

- Interpersonal communication
- Social perception
- Culture
- Power
- Context, content, and conduct of communication

Introduction

Interpersonal communication is central to the effective management of a team or an organization. The communication process involves three key facets: the 'context' of the communication, the behaviour or 'conduct' of the individuals who communicate, and, arguably the most important, the different perceptions of people when they communicate: what we can call the 'content' of communication. The latter is key in this chapter and has great bearing on cross-cultural communication. This is because it involves the way people see each other and events. Perceptions, of course, may differ from one culture to another. This may considerably affect or influence both the process and outcome of the communication situation, and will have implications for the performance of a manager managing across cultures.

The subject of interpersonal communication and social perception, therefore, provides our starting point. This chapter explains why this is so important, firstly by defining the terms 'communication', 'culture' and 'power': three concepts which are important to an understanding of behaviour in international organizations. It then explores a descriptive framework for thinking about organizational behaviour which involves the three facets of 'context', 'conduct', and 'content' mentioned above. Through looking at three 'schools of thought' which provide the theoretical basis of this framework, we make clear the conceptual assumptions upon which the more practical aspects of this text are built.

We then look at social perception in relation to interpersonal performance of managers, and the cultural implications of this. The problem of ethnocentrism in the way we view the world is discussed, and illustrated by the example of American management theory and its relevance to the rest of the world. We then finish this chapter by looking at a schematic approach to self-perception and social perception: the technique of the Johari Window.

This first chapter therefore covers a lot of ground, but will provide the foundations of much of what is to come.

Communication, culture and power

We start with the premiss that communication is at the heart of successful management. This assertion will be built on and developed as we progress. For the time being we will simply say that a manager achieves results through other people. Once he or she starts to achieve direct results, then the manager ceases to 'manage'.

Mini Case 1.1 Accountants as managers

Two or three years ago I undertook a study of managers in a major UK bank's Group Accountant's Department. Qualified accountants were recruited into management grades. Depending on their seniority of grade they were put in charge of a small team of junior accountants. A questionnaire was used to try to determine the extent to which these managers were involved directly in activities concerned with their professional and technical specialism. The study found that many managers were spending up to 80 per cent of their time involved directly in technical work, whilst the rest of the time was spent in more traditional management activities such as controlling/co-ordinating, problem-solving, decision making, planning and developing staff. These 'managers' were definitely 'part-time' as they were mostly achieving their own results, rather than communicating to obtain results through others (Jackson, 1992).

However, it is difficult to see how these 'managers' would have the credibility in this type of job to manage the accountants under them if they could not show proficiency in their own technical ability!

If you are currently a manager, you may like to complete the simple questionnaire following, to give yourself an idea of time devoted to non-managerial activities.

To give an idea of what your job entails, please allocate your time between the activities below. For each activity circle the appropriate percentage.

Circle appropriate percentage

1 Technical/professional activities concerned with your specialization	10	20	30	40	50	60	70	80	90	100
2 Selling/promoting/PR	10	20	30	40	50	60	70	80	90	100
3 Planning	10	20	30	40	50	60	70	80	90	100
4 Implementing decisions	10	20	30	40	50	60	70	80	90	100
5 Developing staff	10	20	30	40	50	60	70	80	90	100
6 Controlling/co-ordinating	10	20	30	40	50	60	70	80	90	100
7 Troubleshooting/problem-solving	10	20	30	40	50	60	70	80	90	100
8 Rewarding performance	10	20	30	40	50	60	70	80	90	100
9 Obtaining direct results	10	20	30	40	50	60	70	80	90	100
10 Other (please specify)	10	20	30	40	50	60	70	80	90	100

Total should add up to 100 per cent

Items 1 and 9 are definitely not managerial tasks, but you may need them (particularly 1) to give you credibility as a manager in your own field. Item 2 could be a managerial task (particularly public relations), but if you are a sales manager and spend most of your time selling, then this definitely is not a managerial task. You can gauge for yourself what proportion of time is actually devoted to managerial duties (items 3–8), and, indeed, whether these are productive uses of your time and others.

If you are not currently a manager, you may wish to use this questionnaire to look at what other managers do. If you can investigate managers' time, what are they doing most, 'managing' or obtaining direct results through their own specialisms?

However, what should be borne in mind are cultural differences which may exist between different countries in regard to technical versus 'management' duties and expertise. Research undertaken by Derr and Laurent (for example Laurent, 1986) suggests that German and Swiss companies value technical expertise and creativity in their managers, whilst French and British companies may regard managers with such qualities as pure technicians. There may therefore be considerable differences between country cultures as well as industry, company and functional cultures in the way managers are seen in relation to their technical duties.

Elsewhere management has been defined as follows.

> A manager is someone whose main responsibility is to organize other people's time within an organization, in order to pursue the objectives of the organization, and whose primary activity is in communicating with others to achieve these ends (Jackson, 1991).

Communication is therefore paramount in the successful running of an organization, starting from interpersonal (face-to-face) communication, through inter-group and inter-organizational communication. We will in due course be dealing with all these forms of communication. Before we proceed, let us first establish a definition of what we mean by communication.

> Communication is the process whereby individuals' internalized social experiences are shared by the establishing of relationships between two or more persons within a community and whereby attitudes or behaviour are modified and through which social experience is created (Jackson, 1984).

As a result of this primary importance of communication, the problems of communicating effectively and successfully are compounded when cultural factors come into play. Again, cross-cultural communication is a central theme which we explore in various contexts. From the above definition we can see that communication is essentially a social process where people share experiences, and negotiate the reality of a situation. Individuals might bring to a situation completely different experiences. As long as they can share these experiences by finding common ground and thereby 'negotiate' an agreed meaning of what the social encounter is about, then there should not be a problem. It is only when experiences cannot be shared and agreement cannot be reached that there is a problem. This may arise through a language difficulty, or by two people coming together with such radically different prior cultural experiences. that the meaning of a situation cannot be agreed.

Why should this happen? The third concept we have introduced, 'culture', also forms a fairly central theme and must now be defined. A 'classical' definition is that of Tyler, a nineteenth century anthropologist, which we can compare with a modern definition.

> That complex whole which involves knowledge, beliefs, art, morals, law, custom and other capabilities and habits acquired by man as a member of society (Tyler, 1871).

> Culture is the commonly held and relatively stable beliefs, attitudes and values that exist within the organization (Williams *et al*, 1989)

So, whether we apply the concept to a society or an organization, we are talking about different beliefs, values or even 'rules' about how we should conduct ourselves. Certainly the most visible aspect of national culture (apart from artefacts: flags, uniforms, clothes and other objects) is the legal system where laws are usually written down. To return to our question, 'why should communication break down on the basis of different cultural experiences?', we can use the example of different legal systems.

Mini Case 1.2 Drug smugglers

Where young people from western countries have been caught with quantities of illegal 'soft' drugs in their luggage in airports in certain eastern countries, and have, through the courts, been sentenced to death (often commuted to life imprisonment), there is a sense of disbelief, incredulity and sometimes outcry from distressed family, politicians, and newspapers. While the court has the power to impose such a sentence, there is rarely agreement on the need for such a sentence and the justice of it from the people 'back home'. There is no sharing of meaning, no understanding of the values of the other culture. There would certainly be no prospect of agreement on the meaning of this situation if all parties were given a free choice.

Discussion. How do you see this situation? Cross cultural encounters often bring into play different value systems. How would you view the decision of the court in this case to impose the death sentence on an eighteen-year old girl? Does it make any difference to your views if it is a girl or whether she is young? Discuss this with your colleagues to see if you can get agreement.

We will begin to look more specifically at cultural values in Chapter 2.

It is rare for parties in an interpersonal situation to each have a completely free choice in negotiating the meaning of the situation, and 'power' relations often come into play in most organizational situations. For example, a boss–subordinate relationship might exist at the interpersonal level, or a parent–subsidiary relationship at the organizational level. Power relationships are not always as formal as this however, and may be the subject of interpersonal influence, where one party is able to persuade, influence, pressurize, or even threaten.

'Power' is therefore an important concept. We will not go into this now, but offer a short selection of definitions which will come in useful later (see Chapter 5).

A has power over B to the extent that he can get B to do something that B would not otherwise do (Dahl, 1957).

Power is that which enables A to modify the attitudes or behaviour of B (Handy, 1976).

Power is the capacity to affect people, things, situations and decisions (Lee and Lawrence, 1991).

So the use of power is one way in which the process of communication can be modified, and the influence of culture can be changed if not nullified. Take our example of the unfortunate drug smugglers. There was no need for agreement on meaning through a coming together of different cultural experiences. The court was able to impose its power over the defendants. This may often be the case where one company acquires another. Rather than trying to reach agreement on management issues, the parent company simply imposes its will.

Mini Case 1.3 The use of power in mergers and acquisitions

A study of mergers and acquisitions carried out by Rene Olie (1990) at the University of Limburg, The Netherlands, pointed to the profound post-merger problems of cultural integration citing estimated 'failure' rates of mergers and acquisitions being as high as 50 per cent over the recent years. The 'power' of an acquiring company to impose its own culture on that of the new subsidiary is a factor in the success or failure of an acquisition. This depends to a large extent on the 'strength' of the acquired culture and the value placed on this culture by the individuals in the subsidiary. The problems may be particularly acute in international mergers and acquisitions where national cultures of two countries do not coincide. Olie contrasts the success of British–Dutch mergers with the problems of German–Dutch mergers where there seems to be a lack of synergy between the two national cultures.

He gives examples at an individual level of the integration problems of 'post-merger syndrome' including simultaneous fight–flight responses of resistance to change, resentment towards new management, and a turning in towards personal security rather than organizational goals. There may also be problems of not passing information up and down, and for top management on both sides of the merger not to communicate, with conflicts increasing.

The positioning of the integration of cultures on a dimension from co-operation to domination, is determined by the power differential between the companies. This is largely defined, says Olie, by the initial negotiating power which is based on assets, resources, and access to alternative strategies.

So, although initial negotiations may be completely equal between two companies in a co-operative merger situation leading to a full integration of cultures or even an emerging third culture, this is unlikely to be the case in a hostile takeover or acquisition, where the acquirer is more powerful than the acquired company which does not have access to alternative strategies.

Olie tells us that the American managers of a Japanese banking subsidiary in the United States had great difficulty managing with no clearly stated and measurable performance targets from their Japanese top management.

The Japanese bankers were frustrated that they could not communicate their philosophy of banking, the meaning of the business to them, their responsibilities towards the local communities and relations with customers and employees, and with competitors and the role of the bank in the world at large. They felt that if the American managers could absorb this then they would understand. Then they could themselves define what their objectives should be in any situation, and they would never have to be given a target.

Similarly, a British–American merger having a board of directors consisting of both Americans and Britons continually disagreed about the amount of information needed to make a decision. The British could not understand why their American colleagues required so much data, while the Americans thought the British were 'flying blind'!

Discussion. You may recognize some of these problems if you have been involved in a merger yourself. If you have not, a useful research project would be to look at the effects of a merger or acquisition (particularly across national cultures) at the interpersonal level. What are the different perceptions of the situation, and what are the problems of communications between members of the two former companies?

Given these opening comments, we will now confine ourselves to looking in more detail at both interpersonal communication and culture.

Interpersonal performance

We now explore the process of interpersonal performance by reference to the descriptive framework of context, content and conduct and by looking at the concepts of communication, culture, and power.

In order to understand complex social and behavioural information, it is useful to construct conceptual 'models' which although having a tendency to over-simplify the variety and complexity of social and cognitive processes, none the less help us to make sense of the information which constantly bombards our senses in everyday life. The first of these 'models' which we now explore is a simple descriptive framework within which we can think about interpersonal communication and culture. We have entitled this the 3Cs model (Jackson, 1991) which consists of three interlinking and overlapping categories as shown in Figure 1.1. By using this as a simple framework we can focus on those factors which are important in interpersonal performance in organizations with regard to cultural factors and power influences.

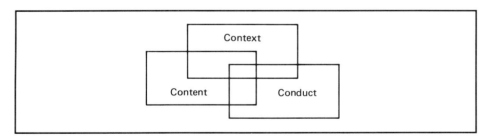

Figure 1.1 *The 3Cs Model of Communication: Context, Content and Conduct*

Conduct is what you see, the behavioural aspects of communication: what people actually do. We can also extend this to include the skills which people require in order to communicate effectively. These aspects of behaviour might be different between individuals of different cultural backgrounds.

Content is what you do not see. It includes the perceptions, motivations, attitudes and objectives of individuals, which are prerequisites to acting in a particular way. These aspects are part of the person which have been acquired or generated through the experience of living and working in a particular culture and environment, and might be quite different between people from different countries, and even from different companies or sub-cultures in the same country.

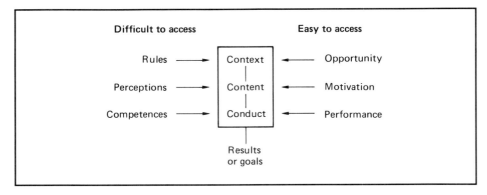

Figure 1.2 *Factors in the 3Cs model*

Context is the framework of rules, culture, social structure, and technology within which people live and work. Again, this context may be quite different from one country to another, and from one company to another.

Throughout this text we try to develop frameworks, techniques, and methods by which managers can understand different cultural situations, which might be needed when moving from one organization to another and from one country to another, rather than providing stereotypical characteristics of different national cultures. This framework now being discussed is an example.

When we analyse a communication situation, some of the aspects mentioned in the three categories above are fairly easy to determine, and some are quite difficult. However, in order to understand those factors influencing and determining management and organizational effectiveness we need to try to identify them. This can be represented by Figure 1.2.

Context and communication

We can say that the factors on the right are easier to determine than those on the left, which are often implied in a situation. The opportunities available for a manager to be able to interact and perform are possible to determine by looking at the role of the manager (what he or she is required to do), the situations which arise in the organization to allow the manager to interact with, say, a subordinate; and even the technology available (including office space, or use of computers which may prevent interaction or facilitate it). Information on the actual physical constraints and facilities, as well as the job of the manager, are reasonably easy to access. However, it is often more difficult to determine what are the rules of the situation. This is an important aspect of what we mean by context, and is fundamental to an understanding of culture and its effects on interpersonal communication.

Mini Case 1.4 The company uniform: rules of dress

When I was sitting in an airport lounge waiting for a delayed flight, I noticed a group of five or six men. They could be picked out anywhere in the airport lounge as belonging to the same party. Each wore suits, of varying styles, but all in browns, with brown shoes. This obviously constituted the 'uniform' of their profession or company, and varied from that which I was used to in the UK banking industry where men wear dark suits and black shoes. Brown shoes, and definitely brown suede shoes are not part of the uniform of bankers!

Discussion: Are there any conventions of how people dress in an organization for which you have worked?

Rules can be explicit and specified such as in a formal contract of employment which states the times when people should attend work, and may be implicit like the example above of the 'uniform'. We can use the following examples.

Explicit rules

- Rules about artefacts:
  - Parking spaces allocated by seniority
  - Managers only to use managers' toilets
- Rules about how people act and appear:
  - Should deal with customers promptly
  - Should attend early morning meetings

Implicit rules

- Rules about how people act and appear:
  - Should wear dark suit and tie
  - Should put in extra hours at home
  - Should not be a member of a trade union
- Rules about the attitudes people have
  - Be cynical towards top management
  - Regard the company as a good employer
- Rules about values people should have
  - Can deviate from the rules only if not caught doing so
  - Personal competitiveness and politics in the company is justifiable if it aids a person's promotion.

For an outsider going into a new organization, implicit rules may be difficult to determine, but is one way of finding out about how to conduct yourself. Of course rules may be legislated for within a company and used as a means of control. This may be a way of wielding power in an organization, for instance, in our mergers and acquisitions example above. This can be most manifestly seen in the structure of the organization itself which has rules about who reports to whom, and the area of responsibility of each manager. These rules may be quite loose and ambiguous, or written down and well defined, and this in itself will vary between organizational cultures and national cultures. Rules in their turn determine to a large extent the opportunities for managers to perform and to interact. So, from a cultural point of view, the actual structure of an organization in terms of opportunity and rules, may affect both the process and outcome of communication situations.

Content and communication

Returning to Figure 1.2, the second facet of communication, and indeed organizational life is 'content'. The motivation of individuals can be determined by inference from their behaviour. Motivation is important to interpersonal performance as it represents the attitudes of an individual towards a person, thing, or situation: favourable or otherwise. An employee might want to avoid a meeting with his or her boss as it will lead to a disagreement. The employee will not be motivated to confront the issue or to see his or her boss. Similarly an employee might be so demotivated in the work place that he or she is frequently late or absent. Although it is more difficult to analyse or measure motivation directly, its manifestations are often obvious, and from these we can see how motivated a person is. Nothing moves in an organization without individuals having the motivation to do something!

Not so easy to determine is the way individuals see things: their 'world view'. People from different cultures may be motivated in different ways because they see the world differently. Their values may be different.

Both perceptions and motivations of individuals are linked. From congruence theory (originated by Heider, 1947), Newcombe (1953) developed a communication model showing the 'orientation' or attitudes between two people in interaction and the subject of their communication as shown in Figure 1.3. This shows a state of disequilibrium or

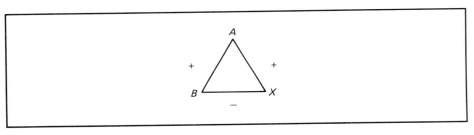

Figure 1.3 *Newcombe's communication model: disequilibrium*

incongruence in this communication situation. The reason being that person *A* is motivated and oriented positively towards the subject *X*, whereas person *B* does not have a positive orientation towards the object of communication. But because *A* and *B* have a good regard for one another there is disequilibrium. A possible outcome could be that because of the disequilibrium, *A* becomes unfavourably oriented towards *B* (for example he no longer respects his judgement or simply no longer likes him). This would then restore the equilibrium to the situation as it would not be contradictory that *A* is unfavourably disposed to the subject while being favourably disposed towards *B*, while holding fundamentally adverse views about the subject of the communication.

This example might represent the situation outlined by Olie above, where *X* represents a decision made by the British manager (*A*) on (according to the American) scant information. *A* is proud of the decision, whereas *B* (the American) does not trust the decision, is not motivated to implement the decision, and despite personally liking the British manager feels he can no longer trust him. This restores the equilibrium but is not a very favourable outcome, although just workable: they are still communicating.

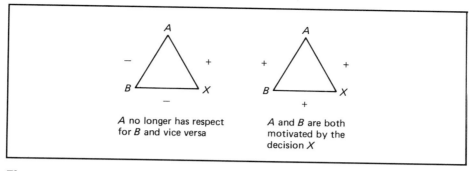

Figure 1.4 *Newcombe's model of communication: equilibrium restored*

The purpose of continued communication is to try to restore equilibrium to the situation. The two interactors both have different perceptions about the basis of the decision, because of different cultural views, and will not work well together unless the situation can be discussed, and a compromise be made by trying to understand the other's perceptions, and, through negotiation, agreeing on a way of working. So the other solution to the original state of disequilibrium is for a compromise to be met by sharing negotiated perceptions of the situation. This would definitely be the preferred solution. These restored states of equilibrium are shown in Figure 1.4.

Cultural differences, therefore, may well imply both different perceptions and different motives or motivation, and we can see this within Newcombe's congruence model of communication. Also within this model we can express a situation where A is not favourably disposed towards B because of general distrust or dislike. Between cultures this may be a product of stereotyping or prejudice where A would not respect any decision made by B. A situation of equilibrium could be represented in the model, therefore by negative signs on each side of the triangle, where there is complete distrust of the decision by at least one party and distrust towards one another. The theory of congruence tells us that the purpose of communication is to arrive at a state of equilibrium: this equilibrium may represent a positive or a negative situation.

Conduct and communication

If we now return to Figure 1.2, the last facet of communication we need to look at is 'conduct'. Performance, or the acts of communication are observable. These acts can be compared with what the manager, for example, is expected to do according to his or her role. Poor performance in an interpersonal role may lead to poor results as a manager. However, poor results may also be a consequence of lack of opportunity or lack of motivation, or both. More difficult to determine directly are the competences, skills, or capabilities of a manager to perform in an interpersonal situation. We cannot access capabilities directly. We must gain evidence by watching a manager perform: by his or her actual performance. But this is complicated by the other two factors of opportunity and motivation. Firstly the manager may not have the opportunity to use his or her capabilities to the full, and secondly, if he or she does, may not have the motivation to use the capabilities to the full.

The other complication about competences or capabilities is that what may be regarded as a competent performance in one situation, may not be so in another situation in another culture.

Mini Case 1.5 Japanese communication characteristics

Harris and Moran (1987) provide some 'cultural characteristics' of Japanese communication. The following are examples.

* Indirect and vague communication is more acceptable than direct and specific references, with ambiguity in conversation preferred.
* Sentences may be left unfinished to leave the other person to draw the conclusion in their own mind.
* The context of communication is often vague and shadowing so as not to preclude personal interpretation.
* The listener may make noises of understanding and encouragement, and 'hai' rarely means a yes of agreement, simply a 'yes, I have heard you'.
* The real business deals are often struck after the formal deliberations and while entertaining.

The more direct communication approach of the American or even the British manager may find that his or her communication skills acquired in the cut and thrust of western business do not apply in the Japanese situation.

Discussion. Can you describe the characteristics of communication in your own culture, in the same way that Harris and Moran have described Japanese characteristics?

Component of communication	Description	Easy to access	Difficult to access
Context	The structure and rules which have an impact on our communication	*Opportunities* observable through *Conduct*	*Rules* accessible only through *content* by finding out people's perceptions
Content	Own thoughts and ideas about a situation, others and self, some of which are communicated	*Motivation* is inferred by observing behaviour i.e. through *conduct*	*Perceptions* accessible through asking questions and revealing information about own thoughts, attitudes i.e. others' *content*
Conduct	Skills and behaviour of an act of communication	*Performance* can be observed through *conduct*	The competences needed to perform well cannot be accessed directly. It needs an understanding of *content*

Figure 1.5 *Communication in the context–content–conduct model*

Perhaps the best capabilities to develop, for a manager working across cultures, is an ability to be flexible and adaptable to different cultural contexts: having an ability to quickly understand the cultural situation and act accordingly. This we explore in more detail in Part Two of this text.

We summarize our discussion on the 3Cs and communication in Figure 1.5, and will meet again this basic conceptual framework in succeeding chapters.

Social perception, culture and interpersonal performance

We have seen above that the 'content' aspect is central to our view of communication, and an important part of content is the perception process, particularly how we see others, how they see us, and how we see social events and processes.

There are two ways in which perception is part of communication. Firstly, when we communicate we are communicating mainly about things, events, and people outside of us. These things we have to perceive (we have to be aware of them and understand them) before we can communicate about them. Secondly, when we communicate with other people, we are involved in a perceptual process through listening or looking, or maybe reading. We therefore perceive other people's messages and the way they communicate.

Hastorf *et al.* (1970), in dealing with perception of the outside world said that the main problem is deciding to what degree our experience of the world reflects it accurately. Although the world may seem very immediate to us, in practice we have only indirect contact with it through our senses. This physical impingement on our sensory apparatus is in fact very chaotic as stimuli of all sorts are hitting our sensory organs from every possible angle. It is from this chaos that we have to make sense of the world. Hastorf *et al.* (1970) suggest how this may happen.

Firstly we give structure to our world of experience by the highly selective nature of our sensory devices. Our senses are not passive recipients of stimuli, but highly active processors of information which sort and categorize it. The categories we use derive from our past experiences, our language, and our cultural backgrounds.

Secondly we give stability to our world of experience. A man walking towards us, for example, forms a retinal image which gets larger and larger as he approaches. If our senses did not stabilize this image by recognizing and actually seeing this man as the same size, our perceptions of the world would be very chaotic indeed.

Thirdly we give meaning to our world of experience by giving structure and stability to it, and also by relating present events to past events, and relating these to the future. This involves our past experiences and our present motivational goals for the future. We are therefore operating within a framework of purposeful activity.

Toch and MacLean (1967) took what they called a 'transactional' view of perception. Not only is perception a result of what the whole person is all about and is an outcome of past perceptions, but also the 'user' of perception is a perceptual result. He or she is constantly changing in the light of perceptual experiences, so that the person who goes to bed at night is not the same person who got up that morning. If this involves exposure to other cultures, then this would also have an influence on the person as a perceptual product.

Perceptual experiences of different individuals sharing the same experiences may be similar. For example the perceptions of common cultural objects, such as a chair, may be held in common by all those within the same culture who recognize that a chair is for sitting on. However, different experiences may create differences in the way the world is perceived: a chair may not be recognized in the same way by all people from different cultures throughout the world. Certainly the more complex the situation the more differences there will be among perceivers as it will arouse a wider spectrum of personal experiences and needs.

Although perception is a necessary component of communication, it is easy to see that it may also be a barrier to good communication. This is the view taken by Burgoon and Ruffner (1978). Taking the idea that perception is highly selective, they say that people are more sensitive to ideas and attitudes which reaffirm their own. That is, they are reinforcing their own image of themselves, what they 'know', and certainly their own cultural assumptions. This is called 'selective exposure'.

We further limit our perceptual experiences by 'selective attention'. As there is a limit to the 'bits' of information the brain can process, selection of attention is necessary. We select the most 'important' information. Familiarization to stimuli lessens attention whereas, for example, a sudden noise attracts our attention. Importance may therefore be a physical property or a subjective judgement.

Further, the way we perceive things is affected by our past experiences and expectations and our language which does not have exactly the same meaning for different people even from the same language culture. This selection device is called 'selective perception'.

Finally, 'selective retention' is a matter of our retaining information which most closely resembles our own self-image. Retention is important to perception as it colours our perceptual experience in the future as soon as the present perceptual experience has passed. However, it is difficult to distinguish perception and retention. When we communicate about an event 'inaccurately', is this a distortion of perception or retention?

Keltner (1973) looked at attention in the perceptual process dividing it into 'primary attention', 'secondary attention' and 'derived primary attention'.

Primary attention focuses on unique, strong stimuli, while secondary attention results from the selection patterns which we have learned. We consciously search for information from certain types of stimuli. Derived primary attention results from secondary attention becoming habitual and automatic, so that we are unconsciously selecting information.

Keltner (1973) looked at the perception process of listening. Listening, like any other mode of perception is a selection process where we pick out those stimuli most fitted to our needs and purposes. To a degree, therefore, what we hear has an expected meaning. This is a constantly shifting process affected by motivation and feelings surrounding a given moment, and our purpose at any particular time.

Perception is therefore an integral part of interpersonal communication as it acts as the selector of the information we communicate about, and also colours our communication by acting as a selector of feedback to our communication and a filter and organizer of what we see and hear.

World view and ethnocentrism

Our culture provides, to a great extent, a cognitive framework or world view (the German term *Weltanschauung* is often used) which influences the way we see others, events, the way we make decisions, and the way we communicate. For those who have only been exposed to their own culture there is only one world view. Even when we come into contact with other cultures we judge it through the eyes of our own culture: we apply its standards and value assumptions, even the stereotypes which that culture may hold of members from different countries. This is what is often called 'ethnocentrism'.

Triandis (1990) for example, points to studies which show that people from all cultures have a tendency to:

- think of what goes on in their own culture as natural and correct, and what goes on in other cultures as not natural or incorrect;
- perceive their own customs as universally valid;
- believe their own norms, roles, and values as being correct, particularly as concerns their immediate in-group or sub-culture;
- favour and co-operate with in-group members while feeling hostile towards out-groups.

In many languages of peoples studied by anthropologists, the word for 'human' is the same as the name of the tribe. There is therefore a tendency, to look at the world from the point of view of your own culture. Of course there is a great deal of transition, assimilation and shift in cultures. We will be looking at some of these factors in Triandis's text and the way we can analyse culture.

Mini Case 1.6 The ethnocentrism of American management theories

An example of ethnocentrism is given in an article written by Hofstede in 1980 which looked at whether American management theories apply abroad. Two concepts which are seen as almost universal in their desirability to develop in managers are 'the motivation to achieve' and 'participative management'. Much time and money has been expended in recent years in Anglo-Saxon countries in developing these aspects of management, and even 'exporting' them to other countries.

Hofstede (1980) tells us that

> The concept of the achievement motive presupposes two cultural choices – a willingness to accept risk . . . and a concern with performance. . . . This combination is found exclusively in countries in the Anglo-American group and in some former colonies. One striking thing about the concept of achievement is that the word itself is hardly translatable into any language other than English (p. 55).

A similar story is told for the concept of participative management which has little acceptance in countries such as France which have what Hofstede (1980) calls a high power distance culture (see Chapter 2 for more information on Hofstede's theories of national culture).

Discussion. Why have the Americans been such avid exporters of management theory, and why have they gained a certain popularity in many countries? Why, in recent years, has the same type of reverence been given to Japanese management practices abroad?

	Known to self	Not known to self
Known to others	*Arena* People see me the way I see myself	*Blindspot* People see these aspects of me but I do not
Not known to others	*Facade* I see these aspects of me but hide them from others	*Unknown* I do not see these aspects of me, and nor do others.

Figure 1.6   *The Johari Window*

The process of social perception starts from our self-perceptions: the way we see ourselves, and the way we believe others see us. This may be quite inaccurate, as other people may not see us in the same way that we see ourselves. This problem is depicted in the theory of Joe Luft and Harry Ingram (for example, Luft, 1961) who gave us the conceptualization called Johari Window (from Joe and Harry). This theory provides a matrix as demonstrated in Figure 1.6.

This is a dynamic model in as much as it is possible to shift the walls of each cell to include more area for, say, the arena, and less room for the facade or front we present to people. To do this requires trust and a sharing of information. To move from the blindspot to the arena requires a level of feedback which was previously not available, together with an acceptance of the information and a trusting of the sources giving that feedback. These things may be difficult to achieve in communication across cultures, unless understanding can be negotiated and agreed.

Activity 1.1 Self and social perceptions

To help you to develop an understanding of the way you see yourself, and the way you think others see you, you can complete this exercise. You may go further if you wish and discuss the outcome with colleagues (whom you trust). This is even more interesting if your colleagues are from different cultures.

First describe yourself by using as many adjectives as you can think of. Keep going until you cannot think of any more which describe you. Examples could be lazy, hardworking, studious, competent.

Next, divide these words into two separate categories: those you think are your arena (the way that you see yourself and the way others also see you), and those you think are your façade (the way you see yourself, but not the way others see you). Do you believe that people see you in the same light that you do?

If you can, ask a colleague to do the same exercise: focused on you. Ask him or her to write down as many adjectives about you which come to mind. Then check these with your list. You can quickly see that those which do not appear on your list, and are substantially different from your words about yourself, go into the category of your blindspot.

Ask your colleague also to check your list to see if he or she agrees with your words in the arena category. If he or she disagrees, then you may be wrong about the way others see you.

You may go on with this, checking with other colleagues. If you can also get them to write words on themselves, and then to check their lists, this may be useful to developing understanding between you and your colleagues.

Treat with caution, however. This is easier done in a classroom with other students, than in a commercial or office situation!

Summary

The purpose of this chapter was to introduce the process of interpersonal communication as a central factor in the success or failure of cross-cultural management, and to show why social perception is an important facet in this. Although we have raised some of the basic concepts of management, communication, culture, and power, we have simply scratched the surface of these complex phenomena. Throughout this text we will be looking in detail at various aspects of these three central concepts.

We have also described a basic descriptive framework within which we can look at the whole area of organizational behaviour: the 3Cs model of context, content, and conduct. If the manager working across cultures can remember to look at each of these three facets on entering the 'foreign culture' of a business organization, then he or she may be able to grasp the complexities of organizational life. Again, with this basic descriptive model we still have a long way to go in describing the scramble of information we have in everyday life about organizational behaviour in international business.

We have deliberately chosen to begin with the more 'subjective' aspect of people's perceptions of others and of life in general. We did this in part to show how tenuous the assumptions, beliefs, and values are about the world in which we live. Indeed, our own culture is not the centre of the universe, and there are other cultures with values and assumptions equally as valid as our own.

However, we cannot necessarily adopt a position of complete relativism. Do we have to accept that because some nations impose the death penalty for adultery, or condone bribery in business practices, that it is a valid and 'right' way to behave? Here we get into the complicated realms of comparative ethics: a valid area of study for the organizational behaviourist and an aspect we take up later in the text (see Chapter 14).

References

Burgoon, M. and Ruffner, M. (1978) *Human Communication*, New York: Holt, Rinehart and Winston.

Dahl, R. A. (1957) 'The concept of power', in *Behavioural Science*, 2, pp 201–18.

Handy, C. (1976) *Understanding Organizations*, Harmondsworth: Penguin

Harris, P. R. and Moran, R. T. (1987) *Managing Cultural Differences*, Houston: Gulf Publishing.

Hastorf, A. H., Schneider, D. J. and Polefka, J. (1970) 'The perception process' in Corner, J. and Hawthorne, J. (eds.) *Communication Studies*, (1980 edn.) London: Edward Arnold.

Heider, F. (1946) 'Attitudes and cognitive informations', *Journal of Psychology*, 21, pp. 107–12

Hofstede, G. (1980) 'Motivation, leadership and organization: do American theories apply abroad?', *Organizational Dynamics*, Summer, pp. 42–63.

Jackson, T. (1984) 'Interpersonal Communication: Education and Training in Business Studies' Unpublished Masters Thesis, Keele University.

Jackson, T. (1991) *Measuring Management Performance*, London: Kogan Page.

Jackson, T. (1992) 'Management Performance', Unpublished Doctoral Thesis, Henley the Management College, Brunel University.

Keltner, J. W. (1973) *Elements of Interpersonal Communication*, California: Wadsworth.

Laurent, A. (1986) 'The cross-cultural puzzle on international human resources management', in *Human Resources Management*, 13, 2, pp. 91–102.

Lee, R. and Lawrence, P. (1991) *Politics at Work*, Cheltenham: Stanley Thornes.

Luft, J. (1961) 'The Johari Window', *Human Relations and Training News*, January, pp. 6–7.

Newcombe, T. (1953), 'An approach to the study of communication acts', *Psychological Review*, 60.

Olie, R. (1990) 'Culture and integration problems in international mergers and acquisitions', in *European Management Journal*, 8, 2.

Toch, H. and MacLean, M. S. (1967) 'Perception and communication: a transactional view', in Sereno, K. K. and Mortensen, C. D. (eds.) *Foundations of Communication Theory*, (1970 edn.) New York: Harper and Row.

Triandis, H. C. (1990) 'Theoretical concepts that are applicable to the analysis of ethnocentrism', in Brislin, R. W. (ed.) *Applied Cross-Cultural Psychology*, Newbury Park: Sage.

Tyler, E. B. (1871) *Primitive Culture*, cited in Levi-Strauss, C. (1963) *Structural Anthropology*, Trans: Jacobson, C. and Schoel, B. G. Harmondsworth: Penguin.

Williams, A., Dobson, P. and Walters, M. (1989) *Changing Culture*, London: Institute of Personnel Management.

2

Cultural differences and working in groups

Objectives

Following this chapter you should be able to:

1 Use a conceptual framework for describing national cultural differences.
2 Explain the importance and main points of effective group working in a cross-cultural situation.
3 Document styles of group working.

Key concepts

- Cultural value systems
- Power distance
- Uncertainty avoidance
- Individualism
- 'Masculinity'
- Contingency model in group dynamics
- Task behaviour
- Maintenance behaviour
- Goal incompatibility
- Blocking behaviour

Introduction

In this chapter we explore two concepts in juxtaposition: national cultural differences and group communication. For the former aspect we look at a particular conceptual framework which was first developed over a decade ago within the multinational company IBM. We choose this framework as a starting point for looking at other ideas of cultural analysis in subsequent chapters, particularly as this, the work of Hofstede (for example, 1991) is most prominent in European cultural theory. Using this framework we then look at its implications for individuals of different cultures working in the same work group or team. We focus on group dynamics by looking at a contingency model of group leadership, and look at how we can understand the importance of task and maintenance behaviour in the context of Hofstede's cultural theory.

We then look at cross-cultural conflict in group activity through a consideration of goal incompatibility and blocking behaviour. As an example of the different values placed on goals, we look briefly at the problems of Coca-Cola in India.

In conclusion we point to ways in which groups may try to overcome some of these problems resulting in conflict. Again, this chapter, as the last, establishes some basic concepts at an early stage, which will be given further treatment throughout the remainder of the text.

Thinking about national cultural differences

Hofstede's theory is perhaps the most highly developed in terms of providing a conceptual framework for investigating national cultures. One of the approaches of looking at different nationalities which should be guarded against is the 'description' of a national culture. Such descriptions abound in a myriad of publications on how to do business in specific countries (one of the more intelligent of these being Harris and Moran, 1989). This type of approach often leads to stereotyping, and expectations about a different culture which might hamper cross-cultural communication!

Activity 2.1 Describing other cultures

When you come together with people from other countries for the first time in a working group (committee, project group, working party, etc), you may have preconceived ideas about how these people might behave, what their attitudes might be. Against each nationality below, write a few phrases on the way each nationality may be thought of. This may not be your own personal feelings but the way you think people from your own culture see different nationalities. If your own nationality is listed, write down a brief description of the way you think other nationalities see you. Blank lines are left to complete the exercise for other nationalities you may work with, or your own nationality if not included.

Your description

French   ....
English   ....
German   ....
Italian   ....
Spanish   ....
Dutch   ....
Swedish   ....
Russian   ....
Chinese   ....
American   ....
Japanese   ....

Others

_____   ....
_____   ....
_____   ....

How do you think these stereotypes are derived? Are they historical? Are they based in fact? How much truth do you think is contained within them?

Stereotyping is a common way of perceiving different nationalities, and we need to be aware of the implications of these and the difficulties which may be encountered as a result of relying too heavily on such caricatures. We do not here wish to add to these 'potted' descriptions of different nationalities, but to try to transcend such a 'common sense' approach.

So, while it may be useful to make descriptions of different nationalities based on certain dimensions, we do not take the approach of pure description, but the approach of providing managers with a way of analysing and thinking about another culture.

Mini Case 2.1 Landing on an alien planet

EAP is a European graduate business school. A French Grande Ecole, it is headquartered in Paris and also has campuses in Berlin, Madrid, and Oxford. Its main teaching programme is a pre-experience, three-year management course which takes students to three of its base countries: a different country for each year of study. For each year of study, students spend one trimester in a company in the respective country in which they are studying.

Students are being trained to operate internationally, and to cope with moving from one country to another. However, EAP does not profess to teach 'the culture' of each of the countries in which it is operating. Instead it teaches students to function effectively in any culture.

With students at EAP I use the analogy of their being suddenly landed on an alien planet. They have not got a map, and they certainly do not know anything about the people.

In these circumstances, how would you start to think about the alien culture and the way to work within it? You could start to look at the rules which are adhered to, the customs, the way people dress and address one another. You could look at the relationships between people, and so on. You have not got a detailed description of the culture, so you need conceptual frameworks, some techniques and tools, in which to place and sort the various information that you are receiving about the alien culture.

This is exactly the way in which social anthropologists have looked at a foreign culture (often of a 'primitive' culture). They may start by learning the language, by looking at relationships and the 'rules' which govern the way people relate to each other. These may be rules of kinship, of power, and authority. Institutional arrangements (churches or schools) may also be investigated as well as belief systems (religion, values, mores, morals) and how decisions are made. These interconnecting aspects, pieced together, comprise the culture of the society, often taking anthropologists years to investigate.

Unfortunately, the management student from EAP does not have this sort of time to adjust to a new culture and to be effective within it, working in three different companies (often in different industrial sectors) in three different countries, in just three years. The beginning of a career which might also involve a great deal of change and cultural adjustments in the first few years, requiring the means of rapid entry into the culture.

In some ways Hofstede provides a 'half way house' between a stereotypical description of national cultures and the tools for discovering an 'alien culture'. This is because Hofstede has already done the work in over fifty countries (albeit in one company and nearly twenty years ago) and provides a number of 'dimensions' for conceptualizing the differences. The argument here is that this work is a starting point, with sound methodology, and an idea of some of the cultural differences. We can perhaps use this methodology to develop tools for determining the nature of the 'alien culture' within the planet upon which we have just landed.

Hofstede (see for a brief synopsis, 1989) focuses on 'value systems' of national cultures which are represented by four dimensions (five in Hofstede, 1991) as follows.

- *Power distance*. This is the extent to which inequalities among people are seen as normal. This dimension stretches from equal relations being seen as normal to wide inequalities being viewed as normal.

- *Uncertainty avoidance*. This refers to a preference for structured situations versus unstructured situations. This dimension runs from being comfortable with flexibility and ambiguity to a need for extremely rigid and certain situations.

- *Individualism*. This looks at whether individuals are used to acting as individual or as part of cohesive groups. This dimension ranges from collectivism to individualism.

- *Masculinity*. Hofstede distinguishes 'hard values' such as assertiveness and competition, and the 'soft' or 'feminine' values of personal relations, quality of life and caring about others.

The other dimension which Hofstede (1991) identifies in his most recent work is that of short-term versus long-term orientation which he adapts from a Confucian idea of virtue versus truth. We do not explore this in the current chapter.

Activity 2.2 Hofstede's cultural dimensions

Before we go any further, complete the questionnaire below which is based on the dimensions above. It focuses on the educational situation, so does not require prior management experience to complete.

When you have completed the questionnaire plot your score on the following scales. Hofstede's score for some nationalities have been plotted so you can compare your results. Do not expect your results to compare directly with Hofstede's results. He in fact makes the point that the scores are statistical composites for nationalities rather than for individuals whose score may vary from the average. You should also note that this is not the questionnaire used by Hofstede, but one adapted by the current author from a proportion of the cultural factors investigated by Hofstede. You will find a copy of his questionnaire in Hofstede (1984)

Cultural dimensions questionnaire

Circle the most appropriate number from completely agree (5) to completely disagree (1).

		Disagree			Agree	
1	I much prefer the formal structure of lectures to informal group work and discussion (U).	1	2	3	4	5
2	Students should treat teachers with deference, and not as equals (P).	1	2	3	4	5
3	I expect my teacher to take all the initiatives in class (P).	1	2	3	4	5
4	I see myself as competing with other students for good marks rather than working together to achieve overall satisfactory results (I).	1	2	3	4	5
5	I like subjects where there is a right or wrong answer rather than a subject where there are differences of opinion and no conclusive answer (U).	1	2	3	4	5
6	I would prefer a job dealing with direct business problems rather than with the problems of people (M).	1	2	3	4	5
7	I prefer to work in a job where I am responsible for my own results rather than working as part of a team and supporting weaker team members (I).	1	2	3	4	5
8	I would prefer to see hard business results, rather than seeing the people I work with happy in their jobs (M)	1	2	3	4	5

Now add your scores for the following sets of statements.

Power distance		Uncertainty avoidance		Individualism		Masculinity	
Item	Score	Item	Score	Item	Score	Item	Score
2		1		4		6	
3		5		7		8	
Totals	___		___		___		___

You may now plot your scores on the following scales.

Hofstede's National Cultural Values (see 1991 for source information).

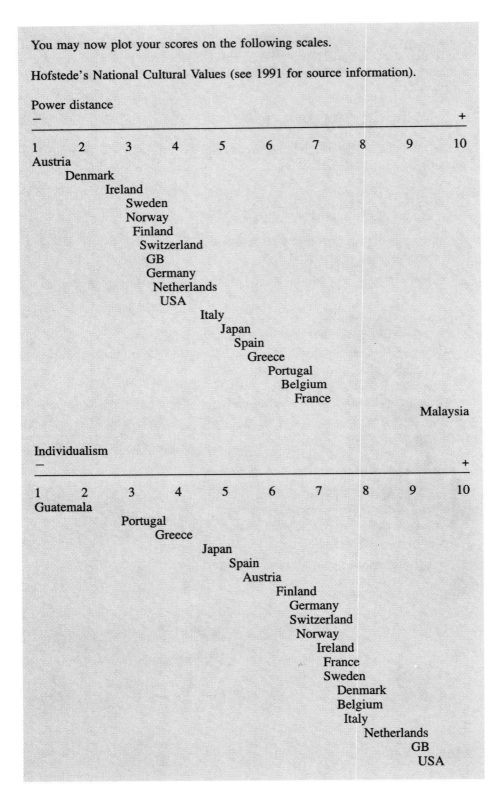

Power distance

−									+
1	2	3	4	5	6	7	8	9	10

Austria
Denmark
Ireland
Sweden
Norway
Finland
Switzerland
GB
Germany
Netherlands
USA
Italy
Japan
Spain
Greece
Portugal
Belgium
France
Malaysia

Individualism

−									+
1	2	3	4	5	6	7	8	9	10

Guatemala
Portugal
Greece
Japan
Spain
Austria
Finland
Germany
Switzerland
Norway
Ireland
France
Sweden
Denmark
Belgium
Italy
Netherlands
GB
USA

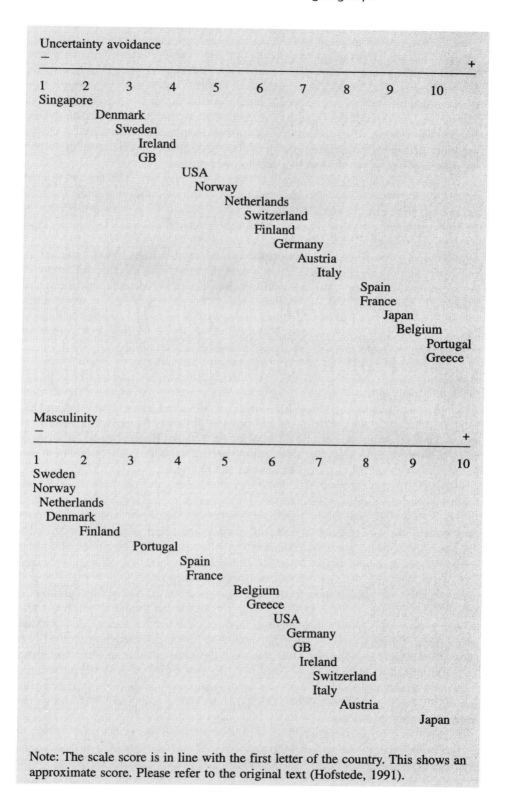

Uncertainty avoidance

−   +

1   2   3   4   5   6   7   8   9   10

Singapore
Denmark
Sweden
Ireland
GB
USA
Norway
Netherlands
Switzerland
Finland
Germany
Austria
Italy
Spain
France
Japan
Belgium
Portugal
Greece

Masculinity

−   +

1   2   3   4   5   6   7   8   9   10

Sweden
Norway
Netherlands
Denmark
Finland
Portugal
Spain
France
Belgium
Greece
USA
Germany
GB
Ireland
Switzerland
Italy
Austria
Japan

Note: The scale score is in line with the first letter of the country. This shows an approximate score. Please refer to the original text (Hofstede, 1991).

Let us look in a bit more detail at Hofstede's national cultural dimensions.

Power distance is polarized into small and large power distance and comprises attitudes which people within the culture have about the acceptable inequalities between people in the society or organization. In small power distance cultures there is a belief that inequalities among people should be minimized, that parents should treat children as equal and that teachers expect student initiative in the classroom. Hierarchies in work organizations are established as a convenience only to manage inequality of roles. Decentralization is popular, subordinates expect to be consulted, and privileges are frowned upon in a small power distance society.

Conversely, in a large power distance culture, inequalities are expected and desired, parents teach children obedience and teachers are expected to take the initiative in the classroom. Hierarchies in organizations reflect the natural order of inequalities between the higher-ups and the lower-downs, centralization is popular and subordinates expect that they are told what to do. Privilege and status symbols are expected.

Uncertainty avoidance is dichotomized weak and strong. Weak uncertainty avoidance cultures accept uncertainty as a feature of everyday life, there is generally low stress and people feel comfortable in ambiguous situations. People are curious with what is different. Students are happy with open-ended learning situations, and teachers can say 'I don't know'. Rules should only be for what is necessary, people may be lazy, and work hard only when needed. Punctuality has to be learned, and people are motivated by achievement and esteem or belonging to a group.

Strong uncertainty avoidance is characterized by the threat of uncertainty which is always present but must be fought. It is characterized by high stress and a fear of ambiguous situations and unfamiliar risk. There is a feeling that what is different must be dangerous. Students are more comfortable in a structured learning situation and like to be told the right answer: teachers are supposed to know the answers. There is an emotional need for rules, even when these may not work. There is a need to be busy, and a feeling that time is money: an inner urge to hard work. Punctuality is natural, and people are motivated by security, esteem, or belongingness.

In individualist societies people look after themselves and the immediate nuclear family. A person's identity is based on him or her as an individual. Speaking one's mind is respected. Education is aimed at learning to learn, and academic and professional diplomas increase self respect and potential economic worth. The employer–employee contract is assumed to be based on mutual advantage, and hiring decisions are supposed to be based on individual competence. Managers manage individuals, and task are more important than relationships.

In collectivistic societies people are born into and protected by extended families, to which they exchange loyalty. One's identity is based in the belongingness to a social group or network. Children are taught to think of 'we' not 'I'. Rather than speaking one's mind, harmony should be maintained and direct confrontation avoided. The purpose of education is to learn how to do, and diplomas provide an entry into higher status groups. Rather than purely a contract, the employer–employee relationship is seen as a moral one such as a family relationship, and when hiring or firing the employee's in-group is considered. Managers manage groups, and relationships are more important than tasks.

Finally, we consider the masculinity–femininity dimensions of Hofstede (1991). In a 'masculine' society values are based on material success, money and possessions. Men are expected to be assertive and ambitious, and women tender and concerned with relationships. The father deals with facts and the mother with feelings. There is sympathy for the strong and the best student is the norm: failing in school is seen as a disaster. People live in order to work. Managers are expected to be decisive and assertive, and there is a stress on competition, performance and resolution of conflict by fighting them out.

In contrast, the 'feminine' society has values of caring for others and preservation rather than progress. People and good relationships are more important than money and things, and people are expected to be modest. Both men and women are expected to be concerned with relationships, and both mother and father should deal with feelings and facts. There is sympathy for the weak, and the average student is the norm. Failing in school is a minor accident. People work in order to live. Managers use intuition and try to gain consensus. There is a stress on equality, solidarity and quality of work life. Conflicts are resolved by compromise and negotiation.

Implications for inter-cultural group work

We saw in Chapter 1 the importance of interpersonal perception to effective communication and performance. The values which people hold within a culture have implications for the way they see others, situations and solutions. Particularly when working in work teams, different perceptions may influence both the process and outcome of the group dynamic.

For example, Hofstede (1980) reports on a study of MBA students from Germany, Britain, and France, undertaken by O. J. Stevens, a former colleague at INSEAD, where the students were asked to respond to a case study of an organizational problem of conflict between the sales and production departments. The solutions given were: to refer the situation to the next higher authority in the organization (majority of French students), to establish a written policy which was clearly lacking (the German solution); and to develop a training process to overcome the problem of interpersonal performance (British students).

These solutions can be explained by reference to power distance (which equals a regard for centralization in an organization), and uncertainty avoidance (equalling formalization or a perceived need for formal rules and specialization). The French are relatively high on both uncertainty avoidance and power distance representing the high valuing of a centralized and formal organization, hence the reference of the problem to the next authority. Germans are relatively low on power distance (lack of value of centralization) and high on uncertainty avoidance, hence the perceived need for a written policy. The British are low on both uncertainty avoidance and on power distance, and therefore looked towards the relationship aspect of interpersonal communication.

Activity 2.3 Cultural preferences for organizational type

This activity can only be undertaken if you work in a group with other nationalities. It is designed to provide some insights into the different values of uncertainty avoidance, power distance, individualism, and masculinity, by addressing a group decision-making task and noting the different solutions.

1 Your first task is to construct the type of organization for which you would like to work. This should be your ideal, and you must obtain consensus from all the members of the group. If even one person disagrees, you must convince the person and arrive at a decision to which all members will subscribe. The questions you must answer are as follows.

- What type of manager/leader would you like to work with? For example, would you require him/her to have a high level of technical expertise, good people skills, etc.? How would you expect to be treated by such a person? As an equal, as mentor–mentee, etc.? What quality would you value most (one quality only)?

- What would the structure of the organization be? Pyramid, flat; highly structured; written job descriptions; codes of practice? Provide a word or a phrase to describe the nature of the organization.

- How would decisions be made and by whom? Would this be a democratic process, and if so what type of decisions would be made in what type of process? Provide a word or phrase to summarize this.

- What type of results would there be in this organization? Would they be tangible, like sales results or production output, or would they be less tangible like contributions to safeguard the future environment of the planet, or satisfaction levels of customers, and morale of staff? Would results be the responsibility of individuals or would they be group results? Would they be long or short term results? Select a suitable phrase to summarize this.

Now choose a name for your organization which will reflect both its internal identity and the image you would want it to portray to the public.

2 Once you have reached consensus look at the organization you have now constructed and analyse it in terms of the four dimensions of Hofstede.

We have so far focused on the cultural content of group work: the values which different cultures may use, the differences this may give rise to, and the outcome of group decision making. This is only part of group decision making. The other aspect is the process of group decision making, and of particular interest here, the cross-cultural aspects of this process. As a result of considering the content of such decision making, this may suggest that because of differences in approach, or values, or perceived solutions to problems, that this may give rise to conflicts in inter-cultural groups. There is therefore much overlap between the content and conduct of communication within a group decision-making process.

Group dynamics

The nature of group dynamics and the roles which people occupy may also be influenced by cultural factors. From the contingency model of leadership developed from the work of Fiedler (1967) and others, it is possible to identify two main types of behaviour in groups.

- Task behaviours: characterized by the use of one-way communication, directing, explaining and information giving.

- Maintenance (relationship) behaviours: behaviour characterized by opening two-way communication encouraging and building trust.

Figure 2.1 is a schematic reflection of these two behaviour groups and is adapted from the work of Hersey and Blanchard (1977). We may note in Hofstede's (1991) cultural theory, that in collectivist cultures there is a stress on relationships rather than on tasks, and in individualist cultures tasks are more important than relationships.

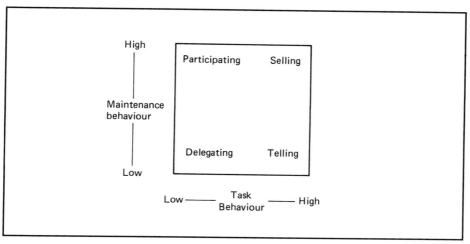

Figure 2.1 *Hersey and Blanchard (1977) schematic of situational leadership*

The labels in the quadrants are typical activities or styles of the combinations of maintenance and task behaviours. Again, we can note that in Hofstede's small power distance cultures delegating and participation may be appropriate management styles to adopt, but telling is more appropriate in a large power distance culture.

Within a group situation, a group member from a large power distance culture, say France or Malaysia, may find it difficult to work in a group where there is little direction from a recognized authority (a chairperson of the group or a senior manager in the company). Conversely, a group member from a low power distance culture (Austria, Denmark) may find it difficult to operate in a group where the chairman is using a 'telling' style rather than a consultative, or participative style. Similarly, a group member from a high uncertainty avoidance culture (Japan, Belgium) may find it difficult where the group has ill-defined terms of reference, or objectives, or procedures.

Activity 2.4 Group communication

Where you work in a multicultured group, you should do the following exercise.

The following questionnaire is adapted from Johnson and Johnson (1975) and should be used to look at the roles occupied, and the type of group communication undertaken by each member of your current group.

Rate the group participants as follows against each of the behaviours described, as follows.

Within the group the participant exhibited this behaviour: 1 = Never; 2 = Seldom; 3 = Occasionally ; 4 = Frequently; 5 = Always.

1 Gives opinions and information   ____

2. Encourages participation   ____

3 Seeks information and opinions   ____

4 Compromises and reconciles differences   ____

5 Initiates action through proposing goals and tasks   ____

6 Relieves tension by joking and relaxing others   ____

7 Provides direction on the task at hand   ____

8 Helps communication with and between others   ____

9 Summarizes by pulling together ideas   ____

10 Understands group climate by asking others how they feel   ____

11 Co-ordinates and pulls together activities of the group   ____

12 Watches the group process and feeds back information for others   ____

13 Diagnoses problems and difficulties of the group   ____

14 Sets the standards of the group   ____

15 Energizes and stimulates a higher quality of work   ____

16 Listens actively and is receptive to ideas   ____

17 Tests the practicality of ideas in real situations   ____

18 Builds trust by encouraging openness   ____

19 Evaluates the difference between goals and accomplishments   ____

20 Solves problems of interpersonal conflict   ____

Totals   ____   ____

                x y

Plot the score on the following grid on the x and y axes.

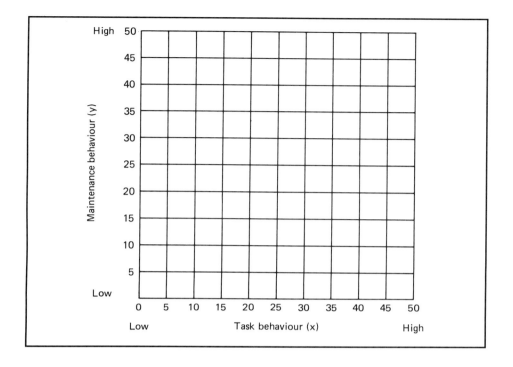

Different approaches to the process and content of group decision making may give rise to tensions, and ultimately conflict. The way conflict is handled may also be perceived differently from one culture to another.

Cross-cultural conflict

Schmidt and Kochan (1972) tell us that conflict arises through two prerequisites:

• perceived goal incompatibility
• perceived opportunity for blocking or interfering.

Goal incompatibility is simply where two people have goals which are not compatible, giving rise to a win–lose situation. For example, when two people are going for the same job, their goals are incompatible: one will get the job and one will not. Blocking is where one person's activity is intended to stop another person achieving his or her objective. So, when one person wants to sleep (his or her objective) and a neighbour plays loud music, where this is seen as an intended act, it will be seen to be blocking or interfering with the person obtaining his or her objective of sleeping.

Leung and Wu (1990) make the distinction, when looking at cross-cultural analysis of disputes, between the subjective and objective dimensions of these two prerequisites. The subjective aspects are particularly relevant when looking at cross-cultural encounters. For example, in the case above, where two people are applying for the same job, the goal incompatibility is objective: we know that only one person can get the job. However, in cross-cultural encounters, what is seen in one culture as incompatible may be regarded as compatible in another culture. So, whereas in the United States robotization of factory work was seen as incompatible with workers' well-being and job security, it was seen as compatible with getting rid of unpleasant and dangerous jobs in Japan, and a means of increasing workers' bonuses (Alston, 1985).

Similarly blocking behaviour may be either objective or subjective. Where a student in a class constantly makes a noise to disrupt the teaching, this physical interference can be objectively determined. In the subjective domain is the psychological aspect. This has implications for cross-cultural situations, where what is considered a block in one culture is not seen as such in another culture. So, in an American or Western European business situation a contract is seen as a sign of commitment. In Japanese business negotiations, a contract is seen as a sign of distrust (Sullivan *et al.*, 1981). They are seen as a block to negotiations, particularly in the early stages, when the insistence on the signing of a contract is seen as a lack of commitment to collaboration. Similarly in a negotiation, problem-solving, or group decision-making situation, Americans may be overtly argumentative and impersonal, opposing another's viewpoint but not generating animosity in a fellow American. However Malays see a strong connection between a person and his or her viewpoint or position on an issue, and may see rejection of a point of view as a rejection of the person: creating considerable interpersonal tension (Renwick, 1985).

Another factor which may increase the intensity of conflict between cultures is the value placed on a goal (Leung and Wu, 1990). The more highly valued the goal, the more intense the conflict if that goal is seen as incompatible with a fellow group member, and if it is being blocked by another group member. The differences cited in a number of studies on American and Japanese comparative practices indicate that Japanese companies take a long-term view focusing on market penetration rather than immediate profit. American companies on the other hand focus on the short term and immediate profits. This has caused problems in many US–Japanese joint ventures where the partners cannot agree on goal priority: the Japanese may want deeper market penetration, accepting a slower return on investment, whereas the American partner may want quick profits as a priority (see for example Peterson and Shimada, 1978).

Mini Case 2.2 Coca-Cola in India

In 1977 Coca-Cola withdrew its operations from India.

The government of the time had insisted that the Coca-Cola company sell its assets and technology to Indian investors. Coca-Cola agreed to reduce its interest to 40 per cent but said that it wished to maintain control over manufacturing to protect its secret beverage formula. This last point was something which Coca-Cola was not prepared to compromise. The Indian government pushed, insisting that it should acquire a majority ownership as well as the manufacturing know-how within India. Both parties insisted on their positions.

The Indian government was keen to meet its goal of reducing foreign interests. They valued nationalist ideology more than economic pragmatism. If the reverse had been true, they could have gained majority ownership of Coca-Cola in India, and have ended the conflict which finally resulted in Coca-Cola withdrawing (Gladwin and Walters, 1980).

Discussion

1 Do you not think that this story is told from the point of view of American ideology? Could we not regard Indian nationalism as a legitimate goal in view of its history? Was it not worth losing this foreign investment if Coca-Cola continued to block the Indian government's goal?

2 On the facts available, did Coca-Cola have any alternative to breaking up this joint venture in India?

Conclusions

We have therefore said that there are three main factors involved in cross-cultural conflict which have implications for international group work in organizations (or between organizations). These are:

- *Values*: cultural values which place weights on certain goals which individuals or corporations within that culture may have. We have seen one conceptual framework, that of Hofstede, which seeks to investigate the relative values cultures have which may cause individuals or organizations to respond positively or negatively towards particular goals and outcomes.

- *Perceived goal incompatibility*: goals may be set and valued according to cultural values. If a goal is highly valued, there is likely to be an increase in conflict where goals are seen to be incompatible goals from other cultures. Conflicting goals may arise through different value systems or value judgements.

- *Perceived blocking of goals*: actions which are taken by others in the group to prevent a person achieving his or her goals. Again, the more valued the goal, the more conflict will be generated by another member of the group interfering with the attainment of the goal.

So, how can we try to overcome these problems which give rise to conflict as a result of subjective judgements made by individuals from different cultures? Folberg and Taylor (1984) in discussing mediation of conflicts, may provide some of the answers. Although they talk about the objectives of mediation in managing conflict, we could also say that international working groups should have similar objectives in their working practice, to

- reduce the obstacles to communication between participants;
- maximize the exploration of alternatives;
- address the needs of everyone involved;
- provide a model for future conflict resolution.

This may involve an exploration of the group of its processes. The process described in Activity 4 above may provide a starting point. Understanding how different individuals participate in a group process may aid the reducing of obstacles to communication. This focuses on the process itself. The content of communication within the group forum should be explored by discussing different approaches and outcomes. The values of each group member should be made explicit, and a model for future work should be established.

In this chapter, we have therefore looked at some important concepts which will recur throughout this text. Principally among these is the cultural theory of Hofstede, which has had prominence in the area of cross-cultural management theory for at least a decade. This is seen here as a starting point for considering working across cultures, and provides us with broad dimensions which can usefully be built upon.

References

Alston, J. P. (1985) *The American Samurai: Blending American and Japanese Managerial Practice*, Berlin: Walter de Gruyter.

Fiedler, F. (1967) *A Theory of Leadership Effectiveness*, New York: McGraw-Hill.

Folberg, J. and Taylor, A. (1984) *Mediation: a comprehensive guide to resolving conflict without litigation*, San Francisco: Josey-Bass.

Gladwin, T. N. and Walters, I. (1980) *Multinational Under Fire: Lesson in the Management of Conflict*, New York: John Wiley.

Harris, R. P. and Moran, R. T. (1987) *Managing Cultural Differences*, Houston: Gulf Publishing.

Hersey, P. and Blanchard, K. (1977) *Organizational Behaviour: Utilizing Human Resources*, Englewood Cliffs, New Jersey: Prentice-Hall.

Hofstede, G. (1980) 'Motivation, leadership and organization: Do American Theories apply abroad?' *Organizational Dynamics*, Summer, 1980.

Hofstede, G. (1984), *Culture's Consequences: International Differences in Work-Related Values*, abridged version, Beverley-Hills, CA: Sage

Hofstede, G. (1989) 'Organising for cultural diversity', *European Management Journal*, 7, 4.

Hofstede, G. (1991) *Culture and Organizations*, London: McGraw-Hill.

Johnson, D. W. and Johnson, F. P. (1975) *Joining Together: Group Theory and Group Skills*, Englewood Cliffs, New Jersey: Prentice-Hall.

Leung, K. and Wu, P.-G. (1990) 'Dispute processes: a cross-cultural analysis', in Brislin, R. W. (ed.) *Applied Cross-Cultural Psychology*, Newbury Park: Sage

Peterson, R. B. and Shimada, J. Y. (1978) 'Sources of management problems in Japanese-American joint ventures', *Academy of Managerial Review*, 3, pp. 796–804.

Renwick, G. (1985) *Malays and Americans: Definite Differences, Unique Opportunities*, Yarmouth, ME: Intercultural Press.

Schmidt, S. M. and Kochan, T. A. (1972) 'Conflict: towards conceptual clarity', *Administrative Science Quarterly*, 17, pp. 359–70.

Sullivan, J., Peterson, R. B., Kameda, N. and Shimada, J. (1981) 'The relationship between conflict resolution approaches and trust: a cross-cultural study', *Academy of Management Journal*, 24, pp. 803–15.

3

Personality and culture: intra-personal factors in communication

Objectives

Following this chapter you should be able to:

1. Explain the importance of an understanding of individual differences in the process of interpersonal communication.
2. Explain the basic concepts and theories regarding individual personality attributes and characteristics.
3. Use some basic methods for analysing individual attributes.
4. Describe the various problems in using such theories and methods across different cultures.

Key concepts

- Personality
- Self concept
- Deep structure
- Freud's personality theory
- Jung's personality theory and its derivatives
- Factor analytical theories
- Indigenous personality theories

Introduction

One of the key factors in the way that people relate and communicate with each other is that of 'individual differences'. People are different! It is all very well generalizing about the different cultural values and attributes of peoples between different national cultures, this tells us how people are the same, but within a national culture or an organizational culture there are marked differences which simply cannot be ascribed to a particular culture. We can use the simple descriptive 3Cs model of context–content–conduct, introduced in Chapter 1 to explain why (see Figure 3.1).

Contextual influences on individuals are fundamental, yet may be quite different from individual to individual within a national culture. The influence of religion from

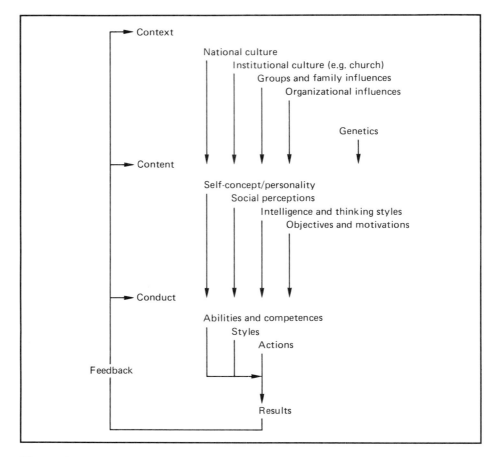

Figure 3.1 *The 3Cs model of context–content–conduct and individual differences*

one sector of a national population to another may be quite different, whether it be the outlook of Christian protestants and catholics in Ireland, or Christians and Moslems in Iraq, there may be distinct differences in social outlook and perspective from one sector to another. Also the influence that religion has from one person to another may be quite different. Family background and peer pressure from a person's social or work group, for example, may influence religious outlook. These may also influence a whole number of other aspects of a person's being: underlying values, self-esteem, objectives and motivations. Other institutions may influence attitudes from one part of the population to another.

The legal system, for example in South Africa, may have different implications and influences from one population sector to another. Work organizations may have either a big influence, or very little influence on individuals. Similarly, the influence of one organization may be completely different to the influence of another. For example, working for Bedford Trucks in England may have provided an attitude of work restricted to simply putting in the required hours and collecting your wages at the end of the week. Since the formation of IBC from a joint venture between General Motors (the former parent in the USA) and Izusi of Japan, work seems to have become more part of a way of life through taking responsibility through team working, working harder, completing the work to quality and on time. Different organizations may engender different attitudes, either across cultures as in the case of Western–Japanese joint enterprises or between large multi-national organizations to small businesses.

The second major aspect of individual differences in Figure 3.1 is that of content. Later we will look at the concept of personality and the question whether individuals are born with personality and other 'traits' or whether they acquire personality attributes through cultural and social factors. This has for a long time been a contentious issue in Western psychology and has led to some unusual conclusions, even by distinguished professors, about the attributes (such as intelligence) of different racial groups. The following is an example.

Mini Case 3.1 Intelligence of blacks and whites in the United States

Hans Eysenck was born in Berlin during the First World War, leaving Germany a few years after Hitler came to power. He studied at Dijon, Exeter, and London Universities. He later became Professor of Psychology at London University, where in the late 1960s and early 1970s he attracted a lot of attention and opposition from student and anti-racial groups. One of his many books, *Race, Intelligence and Education* was published in 1971. This explored the work of the psychologist Arthur Jensen in the United States who had 'discovered' that black Americans in general were less intelligent than white Americans. Eysenck posits a reason for this difference in intelligence which he says may be a result of genetic differences.

He says that it may be possible to consider that one racial group may have lower genetic potential than another.

If, for instance, the brighter members of the West African tribes which suffered the depredation of the slavers had managed to use their higher intelligence to escape, so that it was mostly the duller ones who got caught, then the gene pool of the slaves brought to America would have been depleted of many high-IQ genes. Alternatively, many slaves appear to have been sold by their tribal chiefs; these chiefs might have got rid of their less intelligent followers. And as far as natural selection after the shipment to America is concerned, it is quite possible that the more intelligent negroes would have contributed an undue proportion of 'uppity' slaves, as well as being much more likely to try to escape. The terrible fate of slaves falling into either of these categories is only too well known; white slavers wanted beasts of burden, ready to work themselves to death in the plantations, and under those conditions intelligence would have been counter-selective. Thus there is every reason to expect that the particular sub-sample of the negro race which is constituted of American negroes is not an unselected sample of negroes, but has been selected throughout history according to criteria which would put the highly intelligent at a disadvantage. The inevitable outcome of such selection would of course be the creation of a gene pool lacking some of the genes making for higher intelligence.

He goes on to say:

Other groups, like the Irish, probably showed the opposite tendency; it was the more intelligent members of these groups who emigrated to the USA, leaving their less intelligent brethren behind (Eysenck, 1971, pp. 46–7).

Discussion. Are you convinced by his arguments? Eysenck has always maintained that he is not racist, and you may like to take the time to read this and other books which he has written on the subject of IQ testing generally, and the balance between genetic and environmental factors on intelligence. IQ testing itself has attracted controversy, particularly when it has been linked with predominantly genetic theories. This type of theory may give rise to the possibility that some racial groups, as in the example above, may be less intelligent than others. There may therefore be problems with both this theory, and the way in which intelligence is conceptualized and tested from one culture to another.

Closely tied with intelligence and personality are those aspects which we have put under the heading of *conduct* in Figure 3.1. There is perhaps an artificial division here, but it helps to think in terms of those aspects of individuals we cannot readily see (content) and those aspects it is possible to see through people's behaviour. These are the abilities or competences to do something: to communicate well or to be manually dextrous. These competences result in products or consequences which are public and provide feedback to us, and into the community at large. Thus if we continually are good at our job, this will become known to us through the feedback of a good product or praise from others. This in its turn will affect our self esteem which might have implications for our 'personality' or 'self-concept'. Our continual interactions with others in the community will also have an affect on the community: collective activity will shape the community and culture through a continual process of negotiated meaning.

In this chapter we will be concentrating particularly on the idea of personality, and its variant concepts, and how this contributes to an understanding of individual differences between people. The aspect of culture is very much bound up with those personality factors which we look for in other individuals, the conceptualization of personality, and how (and if) this is measured. We therefore look at the methodological problems of measuring personality across different cultures. Although the whole question of personality and individual differences is important, not just for the human resources specialist involved in selection, but also for the manager generally who is doing business with individuals across different national cultures, unfortunately, we do not find simple answers. In many ways, this chapter is therefore a difficult one, and overtly a theoretical one, but will lay the foundations for many of the aspects of organizational behaviour in international management yet to be discussed.

Personality versus self theories

It is difficult to know where to start with a discussion on personality theories, simply because there are so many of them. A textbook such as Ewen (1988) describes fifteen mainstream theories, without claiming to be comprehensive. These theories are derived from psychologists working in many European countries and in the United States. There is also no accepted definition of personality, although the term has come to refer to *long-lasting and important characteristics of the individual, which may be observable or unobservable, conscious or unconscious.* The meaning favoured here is that of 'face' or 'persona' which can be seen by other people and is therefore a social perception of others which may influence ourselves in what we feel and think about ourselves (self-concept). The concept of personality as being an inherent or acquired 'trait' which pervades in all circumstances is difficult to substantiate. We may have an inclination towards certain feeling or actions in specific circumstances.

An analogy which is used by Guy and Mattock is an excellent example of what is meant here.

> Many people, when they leave home to do a day's work, put on a mask. The thickness of the mask varies from occupation to occupation: we all know, or can easily imagine, a piano tuner or a potter who is at one with his craft – maskless – and we envy such fortunates from time to time. There are certain psychometric tests, usually applied to managers, which are designed to determine how thick the subject's work mask is. The results of these tests provide valuable clues to levels of stress now and in the future. For example, the manager who travels abroad a lot, for short or long periods, is subject to stresses deeper than jet lag.
>
> Airlines understand this . . . [referring to Club Europe] A uniformed homogenized service is offered to the travelling manager to help him survive the difficult transition between home (real), work (less real), work abroad (unreal) and social life abroad (frequently quite bizarre) (Guy and Mattock, 1991, p. 15).

The 'personality' which others see may be the particular mask that we are wearing for that particular circumstance, in that particular country. The media of communication through which that personality is expressed may also be quite different from one medium to another (language to language) or through non-verbal communication which may have subtle differences from one culture to another. We have seen in Chapter 1 the Johari Window concept, and this adds another complication to the study of personality, as the 'façade' or masks in the example above may cover quite a large area in the window, the 'real you' if such exists, not being visible at all. Also the 'blindspot' in the Johari Window may cover areas which the façade or 'arena' should cover. In others words, we might have a distorted view of the way others see us. This may be particularly true when interacting with other cultures: we may not have a clue about the way they see us! In this way 'personality' can be said to be an interpersonal phenomenon. It may only be manifested through our interactions with other people.

A related concept is that of 'self-concept': the concept we have of ourselves. This focuses more on the way I see myself and how I act accordingly, rather than focusing on the way others might see me, or the mask I show to the rest of the word. The other way it differs from 'personality' is that being a social construct, and arising through interaction, the self-concept does not come from within but as a result of communication with others. 'Personality' is often deemed to come from within our psyche, rather than arising as a result of interaction.

Essentially, self-concept is the way we see ourselves in the roles we occupy. We can outline the nature of the self-concept, and its construction, as follows (see also Jackson, 1984, p. 139).

- Self-concept is a self-percept: the way we see ourselves.
- It is both descriptive and evaluative: what Argyle (1967) calls 'self-image' and 'self-esteem' respectively.
- Self-concept is an internalized social construct arising through social interaction within a particular social setting and cultural environment (Mead, 1934).

- As it arises through social interaction it is dependent on our role occupancy during that interaction and our perceptions of our enactment of that role (Goffman, 1959).
- The self-concept affects the social interaction in which we are involved as we see ourselves as we believe others see us (Cooley's, 1902, 'looking-glass self'). So, not only do we arrive at these beliefs about ourselves by interacting with others, we actually interact with them according to these beliefs.
- It is essentially an attitude. Contained within attitudes is a predisposition to respond to a social situation in some way. In other words, the attitudes we hold may affect our behaviour (Burns, 1979).

Self-concept is essentially a more flexible and culturally transportable explanation of individual differences. The theory of self-concept takes account of cultural factors, while not being prescriptive about categories in which we can place people. It does not hold the attraction of some personality theories which can be readily put to use by employing personality questionnaires which then produce a description of the individual as perhaps an 'introvert' or 'extrovert'. By thus categorizing people, personnel specialists in organizations can recruit individuals which match a certain 'profile'. This is not so easy with self-concept theories! Self-concept is also directly related to the central notion of communication.

In a summary of the differences between self-concept theories and personality theories we can say that 'personality' (in the way we have described it above) is a manifestation. Although theories differ as to whether this is derived from deep psyche (for example Freud) or from more 'surface' qualities (in the extreme, Skinner, 1953), it comprises the qualities which are determinable by observation or measurement via questionnaires. Self-concept on the other hand is focused on the internal world of the individual, which may mean that some aspects of the self-concept are not discernible by observation or questionnaire techniques. However, although the focus is on self (from the self point of view), the nature of self is a product of interaction: is a social or cultural product. The self-concept, although not necessarily being publicly determinable in its entirety, is thought of as conscious in most theories of self. That is, an individual is aware of his or her self-concept, either immediately, or perhaps through therapy (for example, Rogers, 1951).

Deep structure

There is, though, an aspect which is not directly covered in these two approaches: the unconscious or (as Harre *et al.* 1985, describe it) 'deep structure'. Those aspects which are not directly discernible (for example the 'id' of Freud) may be derived from the individual psyche or may be socially generated. Harre *et al.* (1985) represent this as a hierarchical structure of control of human actions as illustrated by Figure 3.2. Much work in psychology has been undertaken at levels 1 and 2, but very little at Level 3 which is largely hidden from consciousness. Harre *et al.* (1985) suggest that structure of mind and the social order have developed hand in hand, mostly through the facility of language, and that the implied rules by which Level 3 controls the two lower levels are discoverable.

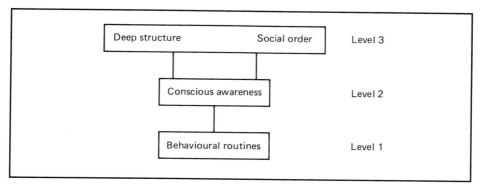

Figure 3.2 *Hierarchical Structure of Control (Adapted from Harre, Clarke and De Carlo, 1985)*

There is nothing mystical in this. It could be claimed that this derives from a sociological approach which is rooted in the work of Durkheim (1915). Durkheim studied the 'totemism' of aboriginal tribes of Australia and Indian tribes of North America (perhaps the latter provides the popular image of Red Indians dancing round a totem pole). The members of each clan (a subdivision of a tribe) are seen to worship a particular animal (for example, crow) which is also the name of the clan.

Durkheim maintained that the origins of the religious beliefs by which their lives were governed, were derived from the identification with the society (clan) in which they lived. This was seen to be greater and more powerful than the individual clansman. The rituals (associated with dancing round the totem pole) reinforced and drove these beliefs home.

Thus the deep-seated beliefs which were acted upon unconsciously were no more than a set of implicit rules derived from the society in which the individuals lived.

Much personality theory could be seen to be investigated at Level 1, and self-theory at Level 2. Freud and Durkheim, for example, provide explanations at Level 3.

We will now look at some example of personality theory, and other indicators of individual differences. It is difficult in such a short space to be comprehensive in coverage, and the interested reader is advised to take up some of the references at the end. We will then look at some of the problems of the use of personality theories across cultures. Finally, we shall look in more detail at the notion of self-concept to see both how it is related to communication and how it might help us to overcome some of the cross-cultural problems inherent in personality theories.

Personality and individual differences

Ribeaux and Poppleton offer the following definition.

> Personality consists of the individual characteristics, in particular the modes of thinking, feeling and behaving which in their organization and patterning determine the individual's manner of interaction with his environment (Ribeaux and Poppleton, 1978, p. 163).

This definition shows the breadth of such a concept subsuming other areas of study such as social perception, motivation, learning, and management styles which we consider in other chapters. Personality can be understood as a complex network of interrelated aspects and tendency which combine sometimes in harmony and sometimes in conflict to give each individual a different pattern or profile.

Despite considerable controversy, and its lack of what some would regard as scientific rigour, Freud's (for example, 1940) theory of personality remains original, comprehensive and influential throughout Europe and North America. It deals with both the structure of personality and the development of personality. In both of these aspects, it is the 'libido' or instinctive energy which provides the dynamic for development and the interrelationships between the different parts of the personality.

Freud's theory of personality

The structure of personality consists of the 'id', the 'ego' and the 'superego'. The id is unconscious and provides a power-house and reservoir of instinctive energy which drives the system. The libido energy is sexual in nature, but perhaps not in the modern day usage of the term, and we will look at this later when considering the developmental process. The ego is the interface between id and the outside world. It is concerned with obtaining satisfaction for the demands of the id. This goes beyond the 'primary process' of simply pleasure seeking to the 'secondary process' where the demands of the id can be postponed through the faculties of learning, thinking and perceiving which are all part of the ego and are mostly conscious. Through these faculties the ego also defends the organism from an overwhelming flow of energy often in the form of anxieties caused by dangers in the outside world – such as physical and personal threats – and from inside – such as excesses of sexuality or aggression. Defence mechanisms are brought into play for this purpose. Such mechanisms are 'repression' (energy is blocked off or made unconscious), and 'displacement' where, for example frustrations are taken out on a different object or person to the one causing it (your partner when you get home rather than your boss at work, perhaps). Defence mechanisms may be useful but can cause distortions of personality if frequently used. 'Sublimation' is a more positive defence mechanism where excess sexual energy is channelled into creative work.

The 'super ego' represents the demands of society which are internalized and act as a person's conscience. The two parts of the super ego consist of the 'ego-ideal' which represent desirable and socially acceptable ways of thinking, feeling and acting and the 'conscience' which makes negative judgements when the individual does not live up to these standards. For example, guilt feelings may ensue.

While the id is unconscious and the ego and super ego mainly conscious, the two latter may contain aspects which are 'preconscious' or available for recall but not immediately conscious. There is also much material which has been repressed, not being entirely lost, but has been consigned to the unconscious. This repressed material can affect behaviour in irrational ways and is the basis of mental ill-health. We can represent Freud's personality structure as in Figure 3.3. The ego and super ego therefore act as filters for the unconscious energy flow of the id.

Many criticisms can be made against Freud's theories in terms of their not being scientific and lacking in predictive power. However he did pioneer the study of mental

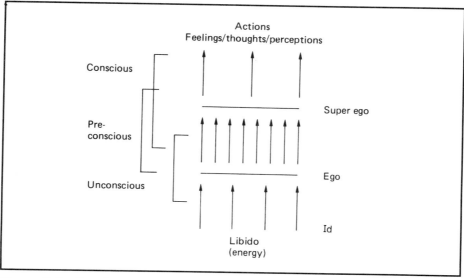

Figure 3.3 *Freud's structure of personality*

life which is not open to the scrutiny of observable behaviour. In this area traditional scientific methods may not be appropriate. Indeed, the techniques that he pioneered are still unsurpassed. Newer techniques being mainly a refinement of the old. Freud also provided a complete system of personality which, again, is still used extensively today in Western society, and is still argued against!

Jung's personality theory

Jung (1921) helped to develop in far more detail the idea of personality types, moving on from Freud's description of personality structure and development. In his description of personality types, Jung worked with two broad dimensions. One of these dimensions which consisted of two 'attitudes' – extroversion and introversion – focused on a person's orientation to the world. The other dimension consisted of four 'functions' and focused on the apprehension of stimuli, as follows.

Sensation – establishing the fact of what is there through perception;
Thinking – understanding and interpreting the meaning of what is perceived;
Feeling – evaluating its desirability or pleasantness;
Intuition – forming hunches or drawing conclusions without using the other functions.

Jung juxtaposed these functions as follows.

Rational functions: Thinking ⟷ Feeling
Irrational functions: Sensation ⟷ Intuition

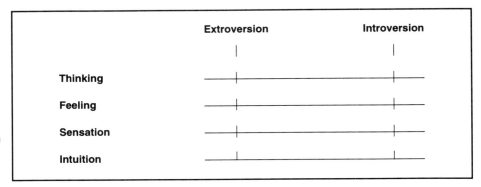

Figure 3.4 *Combination of Jung's two dimensions*

Thinking and Feeling are opposites, but both involve deliberate acts of cognition. Sensation and Intuition are also opposites and are reflexive functions (non-rational, not pathological in Jung's term 'irrational'). All individuals possess the characteristics of all four functions, but one becomes dominant over the other as a mode of experience and a particular organization of personality.

By combining these two dimensions (apprehension of stimuli – functions, and direction of libido movement – attitudes) Jung developed eight 'personality types' by combining functions and attitudes as illustrated in Figure 3.4.

Derivatives of Jung's theory

This provides an interesting, although certainly not a conclusive, view of personality which has been taken on board by latter-day psychologists, most notably Myers–Briggs (Myers–Briggs Type Indicator, I B Myers, Consulting Psychologists Press). The Myers–Briggs schema represents a development of the Jung model, and perhaps a clarification of the juxtaposition of types as shown in Figure 3.5.

The last category is an addition to Jung's model. Judgers are quick to make decisions as they close off their perceptions or collections of data and move to an early decision, whereas Perceivers would defer a judgement until all data have been explored. An

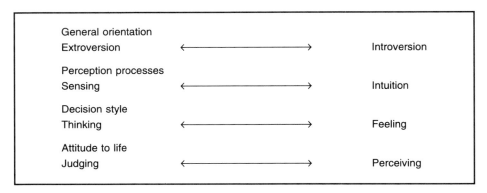

Figure 3.5 *Myers–Briggs development of the Jung Model*

interesting aspect of this is that Judgers are more likely to be closed in their acceptability of new ideas and like to have a well defined environment, whereas the Perceiver is more open and willing to accept data which conflicts with accepted ideas (see Hogan and Champagne, 1987). As a more subjective orientation Judging is seen as less change-oriented than the objective or rational function of Perceiving.

One interesting development from this theory is the idea of 'intuitive' management of Agor (for example 1986), which focuses on the way managers make decisions, based on a distinction between 'intuitive' and 'thinking' types.

Activity 3.1 Thinking versus intuition

The following questionnaire is adapted from Agor's (1985) Intuitive Management Survey, which in its turn is adapted from two of the scales of the Myers–Briggs Type Indicator. You should tick (✓) either (a) or (b) response as you feel appropriate.

1 I usually relate better to
   (a) imaginative people
   (b) realistic people

2 When I do something in my job I like to do it in
   (a) the accepted way
   (b) in a way of my own design

3 I would rather be considered as someone who has
   (a) vision
   (b) common sense

4 The higher praise would be to say someone is
   (a) practical
   (b) ingenious

5 I would prefer to have a friend who
   (a) has many ideas
   (b) is solid and dependable

6 I prefer
   (a) theory
   (b) certainty

7 I prefer to
   (a) build
   (b) invent

8 I can handle better
   (a) statements
   (b) concepts

9 I prefer to deal in
   (a) facts
   (b) ideas

10 I prefer to work with
   (a) concrete reality
   (b) abstract constructs

11 I learn best from
   (a) theory
   (b) experience

12 I can better handle
   (a) literal meanings
   (b) figurative meanings

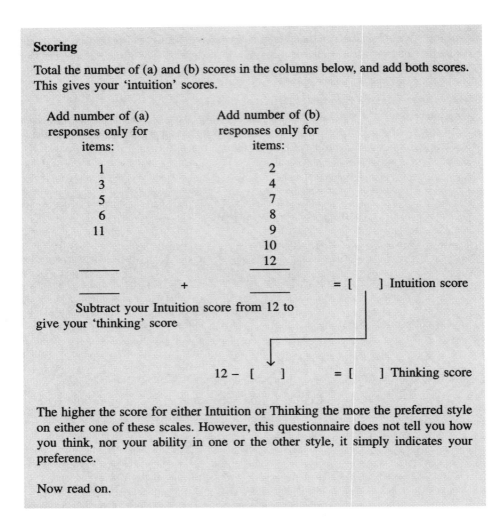

Scoring

Total the number of (a) and (b) scores in the columns below, and add both scores. This gives your 'intuition' scores.

Add number of (a)
responses only for
items:

Add number of (b)
responses only for
items:

1	2
3	4
5	7
6	8
11	9
	10
	12

_____   +   _____   = [   ] Intuition score

Subtract your Intuition score from 12 to give your 'thinking' score

12 – [   ]   = [   ] Thinking score

The higher the score for either Intuition or Thinking the more the preferred style on either one of these scales. However, this questionnaire does not tell you how you think, nor your ability in one or the other style, it simply indicates your preference.

Now read on.

While drawing heavily on Myers–Briggs, Agor (for example, 1986 and 1987) sees 'intuition' as something which can be developed and an attribute or decision-making style which should be worked towards. He therefore sees it as an adaptive quality and one which is more capable of managing change than is the more rational mode of 'thinking'.

Agor describes 'intuition' and 'thinking' in terms of the same Myers–Briggs types, and in terms of right and left brain functioning respectively. He describes these two styles as in Table 3.1.

Agor uses the Myers–Briggs scales for 'thinking' and 'intuition' in his 'Agor Intuitive Management Survey' (1985). There are references to right brain and left brain functioning within Agor's fairly extensive publications. Hemispherical brain function-ing research has grown over the last few years, and developments look interesting, although perhaps not conclusive.

We have therefore followed through from Jungian theory of personality to some latter-day uses of such 'type' psychology. There are dangers in using such categories, the main one being that everybody must fit into a 'type' or combination of types. While

Table 3.1 *Agor's typification of thinking and intuitive types*

Thinking	Intuition
Deductive	Inductive
Objective	Subjective
Emphasizes facts	Emphasizes feelings
Solves problems by breaking down in parts and approaching the problem logically step by step	Solves problems by looking at the whole and using hunches to solve the problem

this has its appeal, and is relatively easy to explain, it may be an over-simplification of personality. Types may also be derived more from the imagination of the theory originator, rather than the subjects themselves.

Factor analytical theories of personality

Factor analytical methods have been used to try to overcome some of the problems of psychologists imposing a framework of psychological types on their subjects, by drawing factors from the data they collect from their subjects, using the statistical methods of 'factor analysis'. Variables are grouped together to provide broader 'factors'. Cattell (for example 1965) used this method to identify sixteen different personality factors outlined in Table 3.2 (his 16PF questionnaire is well known in the UK and USA, for example, as an aid to personnel selection).

Table 3.2 *Descriptive outline of Cattell's sixteen personality factors*

Factor	Low score description	High score description
A	Reserved	Outgoing
B	Less intelligent	More intelligent
C	Affected by feelings	Emotionally stable
E	Humble	Assertive
F	Sober (serious)	Happy go lucky
G	Expedient	Conscientious
H	Shy	Socially bold
I	Tough-minded	Tender-minded
L	Trusting	Suspicious
M	Practical	Imaginative
N	Forthright	Shrewd
O	Placid	Apprehensive
Q1	Conservative	Experimenting
Q2	Group dependent	Self-sufficient
Q3	Casual	Controlled
Q4	Relaxed	Tense

Eysenck (see for example, 1953), using similar methods, reduces the number of personality factors to two dimensions: introverted–extroverted and stable–unstable as in Figure 3.6 which shows the relative positions of some of the 32 traits identified, against these two dimensions.

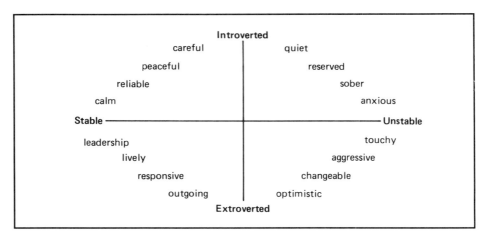

Figure 3.6 *Eysenck's two dimensions of personality (adapted from Aiken, 1988)*

The area of personality and personality measurement can be a controversial one, even within the culture which gives rise to such typifications and measurement techniques (see for example Kline, 1988). The problems are compounded when trying to use such conceptualizations and measures across cultures.

Personality theories and different cultures

There are two main problems in looking at personality differences across cultures:

1 personality typographies are 'analogous' constructs (they are analogies or representations of reality rather than the reality itself) which are developed in a particular socio-cultural context: they are culturally bound in both conception and representation;

2 personality constructs in the West are most often represented in some quantifiable way, and connected very closely to ways of measuring a person's personality along particular dimensions or scales (as we have seen above); measurement may be appropriate in some (Western) cultures but not in others.

Although much has been written in the West on the problems of cultural bias in intelligence and ability testing (see Cronbach, 1990 for example), far less has been written on the transferability of personality schema to different (perhaps Eastern) cultures. Kim (1990) discusses the shortfalls of 'modern psychology' and argues for an 'indigenous psychology' which begins within the specific cultural context and describes the culture within which psychological constructs are to be developed. This type of psychology recognizes that psychological phenomena are both meaning- and context-dependent. It is only through starting from an indigenous approach that cross-cultural comparisons can be made in order to investigate and develop 'universals' across cultures.

Mini Case 3.2 Indigenous personality constructs

Berry *et al.* (1992) describe examples of personality theories which are derived from other than Western cultures (the interested reader is referred to this publication). One example is an Indian description of personality (Paranjpe, 1984) which in outline can be represented as follows.

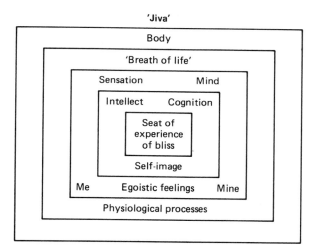

Jiva represents everything concerning the individual through the various stages of life, represented by the above five concentric layers. Contained within the body is 'the breath of life' which represents all the physiological processes. Within this is the 'mind' which controls the sensory functions, and has egoistic feelings of 'me' and 'mine'. Within this is the intelligent and cognitive aspects of the individual. This includes the self-image and self-representation. Within this is the seat of experience of 'bliss'. This represents an inner self which can be achieved through attaining a higher state of consciousness. This is achievable through restraint and control of the mind through such practices as yoga, and involves an inner quietness and 'detachment' from the stimuli of life. Achieving this detachment has been linked to a lack of stress, when one gives up control, in direct contradiction to Western psychology which accentuates the importance of gaining control over the outcome of one's actions.

The other problem of personality typification across cultures which we mentioned above is that of measuring personality dimensions in different cultures. Lonner (1990), for example, points to five major problems in measuring psychological attributes across cultures.

1 The familiarity of psychological testing to the cultural group concerned. The United States and much of Western Europe are familiar with tests and questionnaires of various sorts. This may not be true for other cultures. With self-report questionnaires, some cultures are more conducive to accurate self-report and self-assessment than other cultures.

2 The psychological constructs used may not be universally valid. As mentioned above, much research has been done on different concepts of intelligence between cultures, with the Western norm of quickness of thought being regarded as intelligent, and in other cultures (the Baganda of Uganda for example) intelligence is associated with wisdom and slow thoughtfulness. To what extent is the distinction between extroversion and introversion relevant in other cultures, for example, and is a concept of stable–unstable easily transferable to different cultures (see the reference to Eysenck above)?

3 The bases of comparison may not be equivalent across cultures. Comparisons may be difficult at the level of social norms. For example the difference between 'politeness' by asking as many questions as possible of the other person's family, as opposed to the 'politeness' of being non-intrusive in a social encounter. Comparison may also be difficult at the level of linguistic translation. For example, it would be necessary to find not just a linguistic equivalent but also a conceptual equivalent when translating 'Republican' preferences (USA) or 'Conservative' preferences (UK) when investigating political attitudes across cultures, to state one obvious example. There are also many examples of such linguistic difficulties in the management field such as the English 'leader' and 'skills' which are difficult to directly translate even into other European languages.

4 Verbal test stimuli may not be appropriate, and non-verbal stimuli may be more appropriate in other cultures. From the comments made in (3) above, we can see that translations may be difficult verbally. One assumption is that if you purge tests of verbal stimuli they may travel better between cultures. Even this is fraught with difficulty as prior experience is known to strongly influence perception. This may colour what is actually 'seen' by the person taking the test and may not be equivalent across cultures.

5 There is a tendency to use 'deficit' language when interpreting test scores between cultures. This has been quite common in intelligence testing where the Western norm is used to judge cultural sub-groups or immigrant groups. This may also happen when using personality questions where extroverts/stable types are often seen as the norm in the West. This may not be true for other cultures, and what is regarded as 'stable' may differ between cultures.

Self-concept, communication and cross-cultural comparison

From self-concept theory, the concept and measurement of self-esteem as an evaluative construct may be problematic when looking between cultures. However, the self-image as a descriptive construct may be extremely useful in comparisons across culture, in order to gain knowledge of how individuals from different cultures see themselves, without imposing any ethnocentrically devised psychological categories on another culture (although the research methods themselves may be problematical).

Let us first look at the structure of self to illustrate this point, then see how the two aspects of self-image and self-esteem can be measured. We will then look at self-concept and communication.

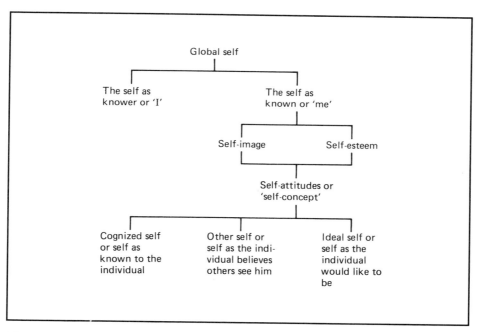

Figure 3.7 *Burns' (1979) structure of self*

Burns (1979) provides the structure of self shown in Figure 3.7. The global self is the total person comprising the 'I' or the process of experience, and the person as known or 'me'. The latter is person specific as it takes the form of self-image or percept that a person has of himself or herself, on which an evaluation is put: the self-esteem. It is these two aspects of the self-as-known which form the self-concept which comprises that self which is known to the individual, that which the individual believes others see (compare the Johari Window concept in Chapter 1), and the ideal self which the individual strives towards.

Activity 3.2 Self image

In order to provide a representation of the image you have of yourself:

1 Design a personal 'coat of arms' with descriptions of yourself in each of the quadrants below as follows.

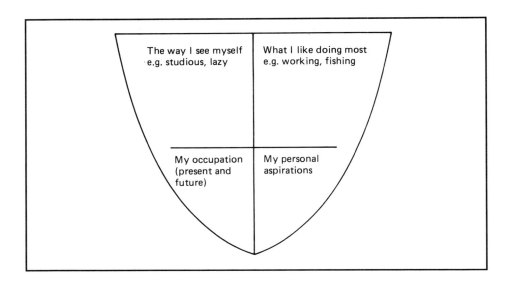

The way I see myself
e.g. studious, lazy

What I like doing most
e.g. working, fishing

My occupation
(present and
future)

My personal
aspirations

2 Write down five words, phrases or sentences to describe yourself.

1. . . . .

2. . . . .

3. . . . .

4. . . . .

5. . . . .

3 Now write a short description of yourself.

These three activities should make you think about the way you see yourself, largely in a non-evaluative way. However, there are bound to be some value judgements attached to the description you make of yourself. Try to see where these occur.

Ziller and associates (see, for example, Ziller et al., 1968 and Ziller, 1973) distinguish the following aspects of self-concept, the measures for which they derive non-verbally. The methods used may well be appropriate for cross-cultural use.

1 *Self esteem*: the value or importance attributed to the self in comparison with others. Subjects are shown a row of eight circles and asked to select one to represent themselves. The more to the left the subject selects the circle the more importance he or she attributes to self, the more to the right the least important.

2 *Power*: the degree to which a person feels he or she is inferior or superior to other significant persons. A column of circles is shown this time, with the subject asking to select the one which represents him or her. The higher the position of the selected circle on the vertical plain the higher the assumed power of the individual.

3 *Individuation*: the degree to which a person differentiates him or herself from his/her peers. This ranged from being 'like' others to being 'different' from others. This measure was derived from a selection of a circle which was different or the same as those circles representing peers.

4 *Identification*: the identification of self with other persons, that is the extent to which a person would put him or herself in a 'we' category. The measure is derived here from locating a circle representing self close to or away from a circle representing a significant person such as a parent or friend.

5 *Social dependency*: the degree to which a person perceives him or herself as a part of a group of others, rather than seeing the self as a separate entity. The subject is given a paper with circles representing parents, teachers and friends arranged in a triangle. He or she is then asked to locate a circle representing self anywhere on the paper but not on one of the other circles. Dependency is assumed if the self circle is placed within the 'triangle'.

6 *Centrality*: the degree to which the person adopts an inward or outward orientation. The person is asked to draw within a large circle one circle representing self and one representing a friend. If the person places the self circle in the middle of the large circle this is taken as a measure of self centrality (the circle drawn first is usually the one which is placed closer to the centre, thus being another indicator of self centrality).

7 *Complexity*: the degree of differentiation of the self-concept. This is measured by asking the person to choose from a series of figures, from less to more complex, that figure which represents their self.

This technique of Ziller and associates known as the 'self–social symbols task' is not without methodological problems. For example Burns (1979) criticizes it for its rag-bag of theoretical concepts. However these measures have been validated by reference to indicators which represent similar self attitudes. Although the current author does not know of any cross cultural application of this type of measure of self-concept, it would seem a fruitful method to use in different cultures because of the low dependency on verbal stimuli. It could also be seen from looking at the above aspects of self-concept defined by Ziller and associates, that some have cultural correlates in the categories used by Hofstede (see Chapter 2). For example, we could expect 'power' to measure higher in a high power distance culture. We could also expect that measures of individualization might measure lower, and identification and social dependency might measure higher for individuals in high collectivist cultures. In this way we can see self-concept as a cultural construct.

Self-concept is fundamentally tied up with the process of interpersonal communication. Argyle (1967) describes the self-concept as a social construct having its origins in social behaviour. He identifies three ways in which self-image originates:

1 through the reactions of other people, so that feedback from our interactions with others gives rise to our image of ourselves;
2 by comparing ourselves with significant people such as siblings, friends and those continually present;
3 through playing roles: roles give individuals identity.

Argyle (1967) also points to the behavioural consequences of self-image. These are principally the presentation of 'face'. People present themselves in a certain way and try to get others to accept this particular image. If others do not there may be embarrassment and a breakdown of interpersonal communication. This involves:

1 projecting a self-image: an identity is projected in communication depending on your own and other's roles (for example manager–subordinates) so that self-images presented may be different depending on your role (for example manager, mother, son);
2 seeking esteem: feedback from those which the individual feels are significant should be positive in order to maintain self-esteem. This therefore involves projecting a positive image, and some concealment of self may take place in order to achieve this. It may be noted that there is some (American) evidence that people with lower self-esteem prefer to travel and live abroad than those with higher self-esteem (Perlmutter, 1954);
3 disconfirmation of self-image and self-esteem: when this occurs there is often embarrassment and disruption of interpersonal communication. There needs to be a degree of acceptance of the self-definitions offered. It may be difficult to obtain a high degree of common acceptance when communicating cross-culturally, particularly when projecting yourself in a foreign language. Cross-cultural transactions may be awkward or uncomfortable because of this. A similar effect occurs when roles are not reciprocated. For example, a manager acts like he feels a manager ought to act, but the corresponding role of 'subordinate' is not reciprocated, therefore the transaction breaks down. Again, the possibility of this occurring is compounded when communicating across cultures (for example, a Danish manager who manages in a French subsidiary may find difficulty with the different perceptions of the power distance the manager should maintain: see the discussion on Hofstede in Chapter 2). We would also note that the concept of 'face' and face saving tends to be strong in collectivist societies such as Japan and China, where every effort is made to maintain the face of the other person as well as your own (see this in connection with negotiating behaviour, for example, in Chapter 13).

Conclusions

We have argued throughout that the 'self-concept' is a more useful idea than 'personality' in understanding interpersonal communication, and therefore cross-cultural transaction. In so doing we have tried to give examples of theories and recent research in the area of personality and self concept.

We began by looking at the various aspects of individual differences with the 3Cs model of context–content–conduct, stating that it was important to consider these three aspects in a cross-cultural situation, and then went on to consider both self concept and different theories of personality. We warned, however, that personality theories in general are derived from Western minds, and that imposing these cognitive frameworks on other cultures may be problematic. We therefore provided an example of an indigenous 'personality' in the Indian concept of 'Jiva'. We also pointed out the main problems of using psychological testing in other cultures, where the methods themselves, as well as the theories may be inappropriate.

For the practising manager, these theories may well seem rather remote. However, the fact that many human resource management practices, such as selection, rely heavily on such theories and measurement method may have serious implications when used uncritically across multinational companies.

For the manager generally, doing business internationally is not a case of interacting with national cultures so much as interacting with individuals, who have their own individual character and attributes. These characters are often summed up by some sort of reference to 'personality'. For both cases (selection practices and inter-cultural interpersonal interaction generally) we must ask if these conceptualizations are relevant. There are no easy answers to this question. We can even question the validity of the (Western) idea of an individual self, and therefore the whole basis of personality theory. We can quote Berry *et al.*

> The claim is made generally that the Western conception of self is of an individual who is separate, autonomous, and atomized (made up of a set of discrete traits, abilities, values, and motives), seeking separateness and independence from others ... In contrast, in Eastern cultures relatedness, connectedness, and interdependence are sought, rooted in a concept of self not as a discrete entity, but as inherently linked to others. The person is only made "whole" when situated in one's place in a social unit (Berry *et al.*, 1992, p. 94).

In some cultures, therefore, it may not be a relevant question to ask about individual differences! This is an important factor for international managers to take into account.

References

Agor, W. H. (1985), *Agor Intuitive Management Survey*, Bryn Mawr, Penn.: Organization Design and Development Inc.

Agor, W. H. (1986) 'The logic of intuition: How top executives make important decisions', *Organizational Dynamics*, 14, 4, pp. 5–18.

Agor, W. H. (1987) *How To Use and Develop Your Intuitive Powers For Increased Productivity*, Bryn Mawr, Penn.: Organizational Design and Development Inc.

Aiken, L. R. (1988) *Psychological Testing and Assessment*, (6th edn.), Boston: Allyn and Bacon.

Argyle, M. (1967) *The Psychology of Interpersonal Behaviour*, Harmondsworth: Penguin.

Berry, J. W., Poortinga, Y. H., Segall, M. H., and Dasen, P. R. (1992) *Cross-cultural Psychology: Research and Application*, Cambridge: Cambridge University Press.

Burns, R. B. (1979) *The Self Concept*, London: Longman.

Cattell, R. B. (1965) *The Scientific Analysis of Personality*, Harmondsworth: Penguin.

Cooley, C. H. (1902) *Human Nature and the Social Order*, New York: Charles Scribner's Sons.

Cronbach, L. J. (1990) *Essentials of Psychological Testing*, (5th edn.), New York: Harper Collins.

Durkheim, E. (1915) *The Elementary Forms of the Religious Life* (Translator: Swain, J. W.) London: Allen and Unwin.

Ewen, R. B. (1988) *An Introduction To Theories of Personality*, (3rd edn.), Hillsdale, New Jersey: Lawrence Erlbaum Associates.

Eysenck, H. J. (1953) *The Scientific Study of Personality*, London: Methuen.

Eysenck, H. J. (1971) *Race, Intelligence and Education*, London: Temple Smith.

Freud, S. (1940) *Outline of Psychoanalysis*, (standard edn. 1969 vol 23), London: Hogarth Press.

Goffman, E. (1959) *The Presentation of Self in Everyday Life*, Harmondsworth: Penguin.

Guy, V. and Mattock, J. (1991) *The New International Manager*, London: Kogan Page.

Harre R., Clarke, D. and DeCarlo, N. (1985) *Motives and Mechanism*, London: Methuen.

Hogan, R. C. and Champagne, D. W. (1987) *Personal Styles Inventory*, Organizational Design and Development Inc, USA.

Jackson, T. (1984) 'Interpersonal Communication', Unpublished Master's Thesis, Keele University.

Jung, C. G. (1921) *Psychological Types*, (Collected Works, Vol 6, 1976) New Jersey: Princeton University Press.

Kim, U. (1990) 'Indigenous psychology: science and application' in Brislin, R. W. (ed) *Applied Cross-cultural Psychology*, Newbury Park, Calif.: Sage.

Kline, P. (1988) *Psychology Exposed: Or the Emperor's New Clothes,* London: Routledge.

Lonner, W. J. (1990) 'An overview of cross-cultural testing and assessment' in Brislin R. W. (ed), *Applied Cross-cultural Psychology*, Newbury Park, Calif.: Sage.

Malinowski, B. (1927) *Sex and Repression in Savage Society*, New York: Harcourt Brace.

Mead, G. H. (1934) *Mind, Self and Society*, Chicago: University of Chicago Press.

Paranjpe, A. C. (1984) *Theoretical Psychology: The Meeting of East and West*, New York: Plenum.

Perlmutter (1954) 'Relations between self-image, image of the foreigner and the desire to live abroad', *Journal of Psychology*, 38, pp. 131–7.

Ribeaux, P. and Poppleton, S. E. (1978) *Psychology at Work*, Basingstoke: MacMillan.

Rogers, C. R. (1951), *Client-centred Therapy*, Boston: Houghton Mifflin.

Skinner, B. F. (1953) *Science and Human Behaviour*, New York: Macmillan.

Ziller, R. C. (1973) *The Social Self*, New York: Pergamon.

Ziller, R. C., Long, B. H., Remana, K. and Reddy, V. (1968) 'Self esteem: a self-social construct', *Journal of Consulting and Clinical Psychology*, 33, pp. 84–95.

Section 2
Theory and process of leadership and motivation

This section looks at those aspects which are important for effective leadership, namely, motivation, power and influence, and the theory and process of leadership.

The fact that there are cultural differences in these aspects means that what works in one culture may not work in another culture. Hence, a leader in one country may not have the same attributes as a leader in another country.

A consideration of these cross-cultural issues is important for the manager operating in the international arena.

4

Motivation and cultural factors

Objectives

Following this chapter you should be able to:

1 Explain the importance of managers' self-motivation and motivation of others.
2 Explain and critique current (American) theories of motivation in their international applications.
3 Develop a cross-cultural awareness of motivational factors.
4 Document own motivational influences.

Key concepts

- Motivation
- Attribution theory
- Expectancy theory
- Static-content theories of motivation
- Achievement motive
- Affiliation motive
- Power motive
- Job satisfaction
- Cultural portability (of motivation theories)

Introduction

Theories of motivation which have gained currency in management thinking are predominantly North American in origin. If we are to understand why motivation is important in the self-motivation of managers and in the management of others, we must first turn to these prevailing theories, before looking at the cross-cultural implications to international management.

Mini Case 4.1 Man in a boat

Heider (1958) describes a concept of motivation by using an analogy of a man rowing a boat across a lake where the outcome (getting to the other side) may be determined partly by the wind and currents and partly by the individual rowing. If the man did nothing and was blown to the other side we could not draw any conclusion about his motivation nor his ability to get to the other side. If, on a calm day, he rowed vigorously to get to the other side, then we could say that he was intent on getting there, having both the motivation and the apparent ability to do so. McClelland (1987) tells us that to understand an outcome of someone's behaviour we have to determine that it was the person's intention to achieve the outcome, and that he or she had the necessary skills or abilities to arrive at that outcome.

Discussion. You might put yourself in the position of that man rowing the boat, but instead of a boat it is your career. How well is it going? Firstly, do you have a clear direction in which you are going? How motivated are you to get there? What skills and knowledge do you have to reach your target? Do you need to acquire these? How much help are you receiving from your organization (your professional body or institution)? Is this helping or hindering you? What about environmental factors generally? Are you rowing against the tide, or with the tide?

We have already outlined a descriptive framework (3Cs model introduced in Chapter 1) for understanding organizational behaviour. This refers to the context in which actions take place, to the content or intent and perceptions of the actors, and the conduct or actual behaviour of the individuals concerned. We can now apply this framework to an understanding of motivation by referring to Heider's analogy above.

- *Context.* To what extent are environmental factors determining the outcome? That is (in Heider's analogy) how strong are the currents in the lake?

- *Content.* What is the intent of the individual in pursuing an outcome? That is, is the individual intent on rowing to the other side of the lake?

- *Conduct.* Does the individual have the necessary skills and ability to achieve the outcome? That is, can the man row with sufficient strength and in the right direction?

- *Outcome.* Has the outcome been achieved? That is, has he got to the other side of the lake?

The question which we are asking, by using this analogy is why has a particular outcome been achieved (the man getting to the other side of the lake) and involves the consideration of motivation or intent in the light of both environmental factors and factors of ability (a consideration of content, against both context factors and conduct factors). In an organization this involves the interaction between organizational pressures and objectives, and the intentions, perceptions, and objectives of the individuals who work within an organization.

This also involves the 'attribution' of causation by individuals within organizations. That is, how do managers themselves see outcomes?

Attribution theory

Managers may attribute success or failure in their jobs to either their own behaviour, what they did or did not do (internal control) or to 'luck' or problems within the organization which is beyond their control (external control), or a combination of the two (for example, the facilities or opportunities were not available to them to receive the necessary training to properly perform the job, although they could have taken more advantage of the opportunities that were available).

Rotter (1966) has developed an I–E (internal–external) scale to measure an individual's position on this 'locus of control' dimension in general terms. That is, individuals can be divided into those who tend to give 'internal' explanations and those who tend to give 'external' ones. However, I–E explanations given by individuals depend on their own self regard and circumstance. For example, when student teachers were asked to explain the performance of their pupils, they attributed failure to the child and success to their own teaching methods (studies made by Johnson *et al.*, 1964). These, Miller and Ross (1975) describe as 'self-protection' and 'self-enhancement' effects. Other studies have tended to minimize these 'motivational' effects.

Cross-cultural studies have revealed differences in locus control. For example, Jaeger and Kanungo (1990) state that an external locus of control is characteristic of basic assumptions of human nature in developing countries, in contrast to the prevalent belief in an internal locus of control in the developed world. Berry *et al.*, (1992) point out that studies have indicated that persons from the Far East are more external than those in Western countries. However, they also point out that generally men are more internal than are women, and that an internal locus of control is also connected with achievement orientation. Also, low socioeconomic status tends to go with external locus of control, and this may explain why black Americans have consistently been found to be generally more external than white Americans. There are no significant differences between European countries and between Europe and the United States. Japanese score relatively high on external locus of control.

Kelley (1967, 1973) suggests that people use 'covariation' information, referring to variables of persons (consensus), entities (distinctiveness) and time (consistency). An example will help to clarify this.

A manager may judge that a job is difficult to perform if most people who do that job find it difficult (consensus).

If Jill finds the job difficult, does she also find other jobs difficult? If not it may be that that particular job is more difficult than the others she has done (distinctiveness), particularly if other people find this job difficult (consensus).

Does Jill always find this job difficult, or just sometimes (consistency)? Where most people find the job difficult (high consensus), where Jill finds other jobs easy (high distinctiveness) and always finds the job difficult (high consistency) the outcome will be attributed to the entity (that particular job) rather than to the particular attributes of Jill.

We can locate motivation within a scheme of causal attribution. In the story of a man rowing a boat across a lake, was he motivated to reach the other side, or was he simply blown to the other side? Can we attribute internal causes to his success, or external causes such as the speed of the current? In organizations it is often the case that the difference between external causes and those causes internal to the individual are not clear, and different individuals might have different perceptions of whether good performance is due to external or internal factors.

Table 4.1 *Internal and external causes of poor performance*

Internal	External
Low confidence level	Distressing news
Poor attitude	Insufficient opportunity
Stress	Unclear instructions
Fear of failure	Lack of support
Procrastination	Difficult environment
Different set of goals	Lack of authority
Performance anxiety	Inadequate resources
Lack of knowledge	Low strategic direction
Low needs arousal	Too much work
Needs arousal inappropriate to job	No recognition for job well done

Source: Stewart, 1986.

A useful method adapted from attribution theory is suggested by Stewart (1986) to analyse performance by reference to perceived internal and external causes.

Using self-rating and superior's ratings, a manager's current poor performance is assessed to determine the perceived source of the problem, that is, whether it is related to *internal* or *external* causes: an internal cause may be something of which the manager can gain control, or is it something external to the manager where structural changes may be made in order to improve performance, or is it beyond organizational control. Examples of internal/external causes are listed in Table 4.1. Stewart (1986) goes on to provide a method for determining the source of poor performance.

Activity 4.1 Internal and external causes of performance problems

You will only be able to complete this activity if you currently work in an organization, or if you have recent experience of doing so. However, you may still follow the procedure through in order to gain an understanding of the method.

Focus on a performance problem concerning a person with whom you are familiar. This person may even be yourself. Place a cross on each of the three scales as you think appropriate.

1 Does the person perform other tasks poorly?

INTERNAL   EXTERNAL

Always   Usually   Occasionally   Seldom   Never

|_____|_____|_____|_____|

2 Is the task performed poorly at other times?

Always   Never before

|_____|_____|_____|_____|

3 Do other managers perform this task poorly?

None   Everyone

|_____|_____|_____|_____|

If the person usually performs poorly in most tasks that he or she does, then the cause is very likely to be internal, but if the particular job is the only one which has been a problem at the same level, then the cause is likely to be external. If the poor performance is really an exception, and the person usually does a good job, then the cause of poor performance this time is likely to be external. Conversely if the person always performs poorly in this job then it is probably attributable to internal causes. If all persons perform this particular task poorly, then it is likely to be an external cause of the problem. If the current job holder is the only one that performs poorly, then it is probably an internal cause.

By combining scores on the three scales for each case investigated, we can interpret them as follows.

1

This pattern is a clear indication that it is an external problem of the job itself, and needs to be restructured.

2

As the current job is being performed poorly, and others do not have a problem with it, then this pattern shows an internal cause of poor performance.

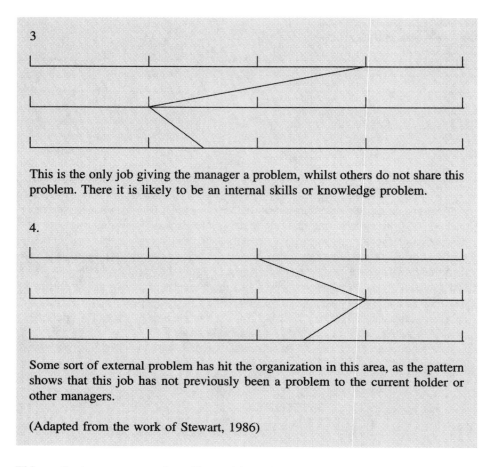

3

This is the only job giving the manager a problem, whilst others do not share this problem. There it is likely to be an internal skills or knowledge problem.

4.

Some sort of external problem has hit the organization in this area, as the pattern shows that this job has not previously been a problem to the current holder or other managers.

(Adapted from the work of Stewart, 1986)

This method, as an example, will provide an indication of where the problems are coming from, and it can be adapted to analyse good or poor performance. It therefore develops from an individual attribution of causality and systematizes and makes apparent where problems of performance may occur.

If attribution theory attempts to explain the individual's own explanation of outcome of his or her performance, expectancy theory looks at how individuals make choices about which courses of action they take in respect of outcomes they are likely to achieve.

Expectancy theory

The answer which expectancy theory (also called instrumentality or process theory) gives is that individuals will choose a course of action (make a decision) by considering the rewards which they perceive, which satisfy their own motives, according to their ability to successfully perform an act which will result in the reward. There are a number of models based on this theory, stemming mainly from the work of Vroom (1964), and being developed by such as Porter and Lawler (1968) and Campbell and Pritchard's (1976) VIE (valence, instrumentality, expectancy) model.

This theory assumes that individuals are rational decision makers who will choose between alternatives on the basis of which course of action is more advantageous.

The 'valence' is the anticipation of attractiveness of an outcome to the individual, or a person's desire to achieve a particular end. When the end is achieved it may not be as attractive as thought. For example, on achieving promotion, which seemed an attractive goal to pursue, the reality was quite different for a manager who did not enjoy the new responsibility at all. Valence is quite a difficult concept to measure as there is a need to distinguish between, for example, the attractiveness of extra pay or a reduction in working hours.

Instrumentality is the next element in the model. This is the perceived likelihood that performance is followed by a desired outcome. It usually refers to the likelihood of a first level outcome or the immediate effect of a person's action. This may be, for example, an improvement in job performance leading to a second level outcome such as a promotion or something else of benefit to the individual: the object of the individual's action or the reason for acting in a certain way.

Finally, expectancy is a subjective link which the individual makes between his or her effort in a specific action and its result. If he or she expends a certain amount of effort in a particular direction, will the desired result be obtained?

The following model combining the three elements discussed above, is adapted from Porter and Lawler (1968).

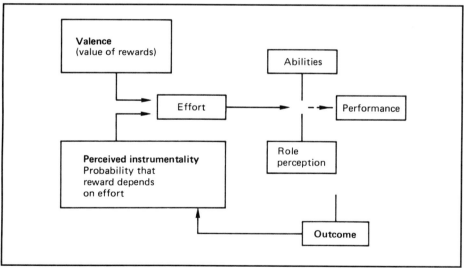

Figure 4.1 *Valence, instrumentality and expectancy model (adapted from Lawler and Porter, 1968)*

Instrumentality is combined with expectancy as 'perceived instrumentality'. Ability and Role perception modifies the effort taken to perform adequately. Role perception is an attitude, and refers to the kind of activities the individual feels are necessary to carry out according to the way they see their role in relation to the desired outcomes. A feedback loop shows the connection between outcome and expectancy.

> ## Mini Case 4.2 Expectancy theory in practice
>
> Although valence, instrumentality and expectancy are difficult to measure, it is worth taking account of these factors when trying to motivate people at work.
>
> Managers should try to identify valent outcomes, or outcomes which are important to employees, rather than assuming they know what their employees want.
>
> Employees must also see that differences in their actual performance will result in different outcomes or rewards. In other words, if they work harder than their colleagues, this will pay off. At the same time, simply expending energy will not lead to good performance if the employee does not have the necessary competence to do the job. There will be an increasing loss of self-confidence if this is the case.
>
> George Thomas has been an employee of a large company for some years. Despite continual efforts he has not been promoted. It always seems that the people who have been in the company the longest get the promotion, and this is usually after the person they replace leaves the company after long service.
>
> What does this tell you about the 'perceived instrumentality' of the reward system in this company? What do you think will happen to George?
>
> Tom Smith has been a salesman in his company for about four years. He works on a base salary plus commission. He earns what he needs and has no incentive to increase his earnings by increasing his sales. He is content, but his manager wants him to increase his sales figures.
>
> What does this tell you about the 'valence' of the outcome of his efforts for Tom? Is the manager doing the right thing, as he is obviously not motivating Tom? Is Tom in the right job?

Both attribution theory and expectancy theory focus on the process of motivation: attribution theory on people's perceptions of how an outcome was achieved, which will influence future performance and motivation towards particular actions; and expectancy theory on how desirable an outcome is in terms of its attractiveness, the perceived effort needed to achieve the outcome, and the perceived likelihood that the outcome will follow the action taken.

These theories are fairly 'transportable' across cultures, as they do not provide the 'content' of motivation. We next examine what Bowditch and Buono (1990) call 'static-content need theory' as this is the aspect within motivational theory which may not be portable from one culture to another.

Static-content theories

These theories try to answer the question, 'What outcomes are attractive to an individual and why?'

Motivation has an effect both on managerial performance *per se* and employee performance (via the ability of managers to motivate) and therefore by implication on management performance. To perform well managers need to be both motivated and

Table 4.2 *Management control of motivating influences*

Factors	*Examples*	*Degree of management control*
Organizational	Nature of jobs	
	Physical/technical environment	
	Reward system	
	Supervision	
	Available information	
	Organizational goals	
	Organizational structure	High
Social	Reference groups	
	Peer groups	
	Work groups	
	Role set	Moderate
Psycho-social	Needs	
	Perceived abilities	
	Aspirations	
	Personal objectives	
	Perceptual set	Moderate to low
Psycho-biological	Genetics	
	Nurture	Nil

motivators. Of course, it is not within the power and influence of most managers within an organization to influence the motivation of employees in all aspects. Myers and Myers (1982) describe those factors which motivate both managers and those which the manager manages, and the relative control which managers have over these influences. This is represented in Table 4.2.

Clearly, organizational management can control those influences within the organizational structure and environment, can be aware and make allowances to modify or moderate those influences which arise entirely or partly outside the workplace, such as peer influence and personal goals, but can do nothing to directly affect genetic influences other than through appropriate selection of employees, and possibly through training and communication to change aspirations and reassess personal goals.

The literature on employee motivation has an abundance of comparisons between different theoretical models: particularly Maslow's and Hertzberg's models. These provide an idea of what motivates people in different situations. For example, both Maslow and Hertzberg had an idea of the need to satisfy more basic needs (physiological, safety and social factors in Maslow's scheme and Hygiene factors in Hertzberg's) before the higher order motivators could be addressed (Maslow's esteem and self actualization and Hertzberg's 'Motivators').

Maccoby (1976) developed an idea of management motivation based on the different types of managers he identified, as follows.

Craftsmen: Traditional, motivated by work ethic and thrift. Likes process and likes to build. Helps others do a good job. May go along with other's goals they do not 100 per cent agree with. Seeks interesting work.

Jungle Fighter: Motivated by the achievement of power. Peers are seen as potential enemies or accomplices, and subordinates are used to accomplish their ends. Jungle fighters build empires.

Company man: Functionaries deriving motivation from belonging to a powerful and protective organization. Are concerned for people and are committed to the organization.

Gamesman: Are motivated by challenging ideas and taking risks where the game is to win. They are team players and identify with the aims of the company. Other people are not used through personal ambition but to accomplish organizational goals.

Maccoby's (1976) schema is an interesting one as it points to individuals being different and being motivated by different factors. It is well recognized that managers need to be highly motivated in order to perform well. This may mean different things for different people in different situations. Apart from being motivated by financial rewards, the Craftsman is motivated by a problem to be solved, by the intrinsic nature of the work itself, by producing something of quality, working alone or in small groups with well defined and structured projects. The positive aspect of the Jungle fighter is the motivation to succeed in a crisis situation, largely through not building social interdependencies as they are not motivated by working with people for a common end. Company men are not motivated by risk taking. They are company-dependent and make good middle managers, as they are sensitive to and motivated by social interdependencies within the work group. They are good negotiators, motivated to mediate between conflicting interests. Gamesmen are motivated to win, and have the energy, and usually the youth, to achieve objectives through motivating the team. They like to be autonomous and are likely to go to the top in organizations.

Kakabadse *et al.*, (1987) tell us that an individual's motivation is a result of an interaction of needs, incentives and perceptions. The extent to which incentives at work meet the perceived needs of individuals is important. There is both an objective element and a subjective element here. The assumption is that the individual must earn enough money to satisfy basic needs (Maslow, for example), but what happens after this? How does the individual see his or her 'higher' needs, and to what extent are the incentives offered and the incentives inherent within the job actually satisfying the needs of the individual according to that individual's perceptions of the situation.

Both Maslow (1954) and Herzberg (*et al.*, 1959), as we have mentioned above, address the issue of individual needs, stating that the more basic needs have to be satisfied first before individuals can pursue and satisfy the higher needs of self-actualization for example. However, the hierarchical arrangement which Maslow suggests cannot be rigidly applied. Kakabadse *et al.* (1987) offer an example of a university academic who, because of the changes in higher education may not enjoy the job security of automatic tenure, and may be struggling to satisfy the lower order need of job security at the same time as addressing the higher order need of self-actualization through pursuing research and publication. This may be similar to a management position where job security is dependent on job performance and risk taking to achieve results. A bad decision may result in job loss, a good decision may result in praise, job success and self-satisfaction.

McClelland's achievement motive

McClelland (1987) argues that needs are not necessarily universal as Maslow suggests, and through forty years of research on human motivation identifies four major motivational needs systems:

- *Achievement motive:* the need to achieve task goals.
- *Power motive:* the need to influence and control.
- *Affiliative motives:* the need to develop interpersonal relationships.
- *Avoidance motives:* an anxiety which motivates individuals to avoid certain experiences (fear of failure, of rejection, even fear of power and success, for example).

Murray (1938) preceding McClelland's work, measures the strengths of the first three of these 'need' systems by self-report questionnaire.

Activity 4.2 Achievement, affiliation, and power motivation

Before you proceed complete the following questionnaire which is adapted from questionnaire items used by Murray and adapted from McClelland (1987).

From each set of items (1–4 below) choose response (a–c) which is most like you.

1
a I set myself difficult goals which I attempt to reach.
b I am happiest when I am with a group of people who enjoy life.
c I like to organize the activities of a group or team.

2
a I only completely enjoy relaxation after successful completion of exacting pieces of work.
b I become attached to my friends.
c I argue zealously against others for my point of view.

3
a I work hard until I am completely satisfied with the result I achieve.
b I like to mix with a group of congenial people, talking about any subject which comes up.
c I tend to influence others more than they influence me.

4

a I enjoy working as much as I enjoy my leisure.
b I go out of my way to be with my friends.
c I am able to dominate a social situation.

Now add your responses as follows.

- The number of (*a*) responses [   ] Achievement
- The number of (*b*) responses [   ] Affiliation
- The number of (*c*) responses [   ] Power

This simple questionnaire will give you an idea of the differences between McClelland's three different types of motives, as well as an idea of your own preferences. The larger the score for each the more likely your preference lies in the particular area (or areas).

McClelland (1987) himself develops the approach to measuring the strengths of each motivational needs system, derived from the Thematic Apperception Test approach of Murray (1938). He uses pictures which contain a neutral content (for example, a picture of a person studying) but which may suggest achievement to the subjects (for example, achievement in an examination) who are asked to write a 'story' about the stimulus. The content of the story is then coded to give a score on Achievement Motivation (*n Ach*). Stories may be coded as in Table 4.3.

Table 4.3   *A coding system for achievement motivation*

For each of the following characteristics found in the story give +1 , give −1 for non-appearance in the story as follows:

Characteristic	Example
Achievement imagery	'He is trying to do well in the exam'
Need	'He wants to get high marks'
Positive anticipatory goal state	'He will feel great if he does well'
Negative anticipatory goal state	'He will feel bad if he fails'
Positive goal state	'He is happy because he has done well'
Negative goal state	'He is unhappy because he failed'
Actions	'He has been revising every night this week'
Obstacles in the environment	'His friends think he is a swot for revising so much'
Help	'He has been given a lot of help from his teacher'

Source: adapted from McClelland, 1987.

McClelland (1987, p. 196) also provides coding schemes for Affiliation and Power arousal in stories, and provides an analysis of the same story on Achievement, Affiliation and Power, where the stimulus is a picture of a man at a drawing board. Where 'George is an engineer who wants to win a competition' + 1 will be given for Achievement. 'George is an engineer, working late and worried that his wife will be annoyed', will receive + 1 for Affiliation. 'George, a famous engineer, wanting to win a competition to establish himself as the best engineer in the world' will be given + 1 for Power.

There are doubts about the validity of such 'projective' techniques generally in psychological measurement, and many of these questions are raised by Kline (1986). A major criticism, apart from the difficulty in establishing validity for these tests, is that they try to measure too much (which may not be the case for the Thematic Apperception Test), frequently the whole personality sphere. Another criticism is that it is difficult to develop 'reliability' for these tests: usually this means consistency from one test to another using the same subject.

Incentives

We have so far looked at some of the theory associated with different psychological 'needs' of individuals. We previously looked at an idea of motivation comprising needs, incentives and expectations (after Kakabadse *et al.*, 1987). We will now focus on incentives.

Incentives focus on the external factors of motivation (*context*), rather than the internal needs or drives of individuals (*content*). This is the area over which the manager has more influence in motivating subordinates: making sure the incentives match the needs. To a large extent, recent work on this has focused on the satisfaction of needs within the framework of Maslow and Herzberg (for example Alderfer, 1972). It is not the intention to dwell too much here on incentives at work, other than to mention those external factors which may be affected by managers, namely:

- *Job design*: the way a job is designed influences the amount of intrinsic motivation, that is, the satisfaction of doing a job well or the enjoyment derived from the job, as well as the amount of autonomy within that job.

- *Participation in decision making*: closely connected to the way jobs are designed and the management style of the manager and the structural communication arrangements within an organization, this may also influence the amount of intrinsic reward derived from a job.

- *Promotion opportunities*: providing extrinsic rewards, and satisfying a range of needs within Maslow's hierarchy including increases in pay, and self-fulfilment.

- *Working conditions*: satisfying more basic needs of comfort and well being. A prerequisite to higher order needs satisfaction.

- *Pay*: usually regarded as high in the list of extrinsic incentives of a job, and probably more complicated than merely satisfying Maslow's lower order needs. Money is also part of a symbolic system within Western Society representing a person's 'worth' within society. Money may therefore be bound up with higher order needs such as self-actualization.

Incentives are therefore bound up with needs (desires). If individuals do not have a need to participate in decision making within an organization, this cannot very well be used as an incentive. Consideration should also be given to such motivational models as Maccoby's (1976) and McClelland (1987) in deciding which incentives to offer which managers.

The portability of motivational theories

We have considered both process theories of motivation and static-content theories, and have said that whilst process theories may explain motivation 'universally', content theories may not.

Certainly, McClelland (1987) has devoted considerable time in India, developing achievement motivation in entrepreneurs through training programmes. It could also be argued that managers from the former Soviet bloc could benefit from such training to become more attuned with Western capitalist business. But, is it appropriate? Also, why have certain motivational theories found currency in countries such as the United States (for example, Achievement Motivation) but not in others?

This is a question which Hofstede (1980 and 1991) addresses. He compares the work undertaken by McClelland between 1925 and 1950 over a large number of countries with his own, and finds that there is a correlation between the level of the achievement motive (as defined by McClellend) and a combination of 'uncertainty avoidance' and 'masculinity'. Children investigated by McClelland (1961) were found to have a high achievement motivation in countries which also showed a weak uncertainty avoidance and a strong masculinity. This correlation can be approximately illustrated as in Figure 4.2.

We have shown the approximate positions of some countries on this chart (see Hofstede, 1991, p. 123 for the exact positions of fifty different countries), with Portugal

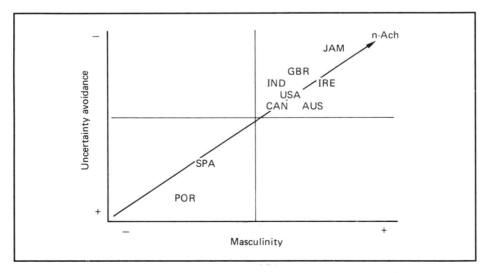

Figure 4.2 *McClelland's achievement motivation compared with Hofstede's masculinity and uncertainty avoidance.*

Table 4.4 *Cultural differences indicating motivational factors*

	Motivators
East Asian	*Western*
Equity	Wealth
Group	Individual
Saving	Consumption
Extended family relations	Nuclear and mobile family
Highly disciplined/motivated workforce	Decline in work ethic and hierarchy
Protocol, rank and status	Informality and personal competence
Avoid conflict	Conflict to be managed

Source: adapted from Harris and Moran, 1987.

and Spain in the left hand bottom quadrant, and the 'Anglo-Saxon' countries and ex-territories (Jamaica, Australia, New Zealand, Canada and India, as well as Great Britain and Ireland) in the top right hand quadrant, some of which were identified by McClelland as showing 'a need for achievement'. This perhaps indicates that the concept itself might be applicable to other cultures, but that the motive attributed to the need to achieve is not universally distributed throughout the world. It could be argued that this motive could be developed in other cultures, or that it would be inappropriate to do so. We can perhaps see why McClelland's methods were acceptable in India, as a former British Commonwealth country!

From Harris and Moran (1987) we can also see that different factors are more likely to influence what Kelly *et al.*, (1991) call life goals (generalized measures of work motivation) depending on the national and regional culture. Harris and Moran distinguish broadly between East Asian and Western culture as shown in Table 4.4.

They believe this classification holds, despite differences in national culture within these two broad regions. It may be that factors such as those described here result in different motivational influences in job satisfaction.

To illustrate the influence of cultural factors on motivation, we can focus for a minute on job satisfaction. Hui (1990) describes a discrepancy model of job satisfaction. This is illustrated in Figure 4.3. Here the degree of dissatisfaction with

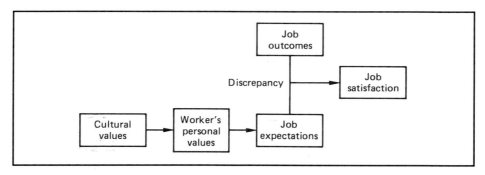

Figure 4.3 *Hui's (1990) discrepancy model of job satisfaction*

work derives from perceived discrepancy between actual outcomes of the job and the job holder's expectations. Where there are insufficient resources to get the job done well, such as in technologically backward or impoverished countries, there may be low job satisfaction. Conversely, where workers' expectations are very high and the outcomes are not the desired and expected high results, job satisfaction may be low. De Boer (1978) gives India and the Philippines as examples of the former, with Japan and France as examples of the latter.

A person's expectations of a job are also influenced by personal goals and the cultural values in which he or she has been socialized. This is where cultural factors make a difference to motivation at work, and several studies have shown that individuals from different cultural backgrounds have different attitudes towards their work. Hui (1990) reports studies which found that French Canadians are more satisfied in their work than English Canadians; in a study of over ten countries (de Boer, 1978) Sweden had the highest population who were satisfied with their job (63 per cent), then the United Kingdom (54 per cent), Brazil (53 per cent) and Switzerland (50 per cent), with Japan having the smallest proportion of satisfied workers (20 per cent). Other researchers have drawn the same conclusions about Japanese workers, with a possible explanation that they are strongly committed and motivated, but job outcomes do not conform to expectations and thus do not lead to job satisfaction.

Job satisfaction is really a subset of overall motivation. A person can undertake a job which draws little intrinsic motivation, but may be motivated to do well in that job to gain promotion. In a way, 'satisfaction' depicts a state of equilibrium in the sense that it is neither a pulling nor pushing force for moving a person to do something: it merely means that they are happy with what they are doing, and that they may not want to alter or change the job or themselves. The consequences of this may be high performance.

Mini Case 4.3 Motivation in a bank department

In the International Operations Department of a large UK bank, staff were generally bored with their jobs. They were trained specifically on their current tasks, and had little idea of the 'whole picture' or what was going on around them. They could not, for example, provide 'cover' for the person sitting next to them if they were on holiday or sick.

It was also well recognized that if a member of staff, supervisor or junior manager had consistently good annual appraisals they would be transferred to another department: a 'high flying' department such as International Marketing. In this way high performing staff would be lost to the department. This worried the management. As a consequence it was very difficult to get an excellent appraisal report, in case the high performer would be lost to the department. This caused problems amongst those 'high flying' members of staff and junior management who wanted to get on in the bank.

Despite these problems, most staff were happy, although their jobs were generally boring and the high fliers found it difficult to 'escape' from this department. The main reason for this contentment was the good social atmosphere. Mostly, people were very good friends, they socialized at lunch time and in the evenings. They enjoyed going to work because they enjoyed the companionship. Productivity was generally good.

Discussion. What does this tell you about motivation, or more specifically work satisfaction in this case?

Perhaps more important as an indication of general motivation to take a course of action, to improve job performance, or to make a career move, is the concept of life goals. There seems to be some consistency of certain life goals across cultures. A study by Kelly *et al.,* (1991) looked at the relative importance of six life goals relating to: community, family, leisure, religion, wealth and work. They compared six different national cultures: Japan, United States, Korea, Taiwan, Mexico and Philippines. Managers in these countries were asked to indicate (on a 100 point scale) how important in their lives were the following areas:

- their leisure, such as hobbies, sports, recreations and contacts with friends;
- their community, such as volunteer organizations, union and political organizations;
- their work;
- their religion, such as religious activities and beliefs;
- their wealth: the things they own;
- their family.

They found work or family rated as highest importance across all six countries, with work receiving the highest weighting in Japan, Taiwan, and Mexico, and family receiving the highest weight in the United States and Philippines. In Korea these two areas were rated more or less equal highest. The most variable area across the six national cultures was found to be religion. This was rated third highest in the Philippines (predominantly catholic), and last in Japan and Taiwan. Leisure was rated from third to fifth across the six countries, leisure being weighted slightly higher in the United States and Taiwan, and wealth slightly higher in Japan, Mexico and Korea. Community was rated the lowest in all but Japan and Taiwan.

A possible conclusion is that work and family are highly valued irrespective of national culture, whilst other life goals are mainly culturally dependent (Kelly *et al.,* 1991).

Activity 4.3 Motivation inventory

The following personal inventory comprises items relating to those areas in your job and life which motivate you, and are satisfied in your job and life. The discrepancy between these is usually problematic, and constitute what Hui (1990) calls 'job satisfaction'. The inventory will help you to understand those areas which motivate you, and to understand how static-content theories of motivation are related to the concept of job satisfaction.

When you have finished, look back on those items which you have scored highly to see which areas motivate you. Compare these particularly with low scores in the 'satisfied' category. This may indicate to you the possible choices you may have to make in your life and your career.

Instructions

For each of the following items, indicate how important the factor is to you (5 = very important, 3 = moderately important, and 1 = not important) in the first box. In the second box indicate how satisfied this factor currently is in your current situation (5 = completely satisfied, 3 = moderately satisfied, 1 = not satisfied)

	Important 5–1	Satisfied 5–1
YOUR JOB		
1 Excellent working conditions	[ ]	[ ]
2 Living/working in area of choice	[ ]	[ ]
3 Lots of leisure time	[ ]	[ ]
4 Job security	[ ]	[ ]
5 Opportunity for high earnings	[ ]	[ ]
6 Working in co-operative group	[ ]	[ ]
7 Getting recognition for good job	[ ]	[ ]
8 Opportunity to advance	[ ]	[ ]
9 Having development opportunities	[ ]	[ ]
10 Using your abilities fully in your job	[ ]	[ ]
11 Sense of accomplishment from a challenging job	[ ]	[ ]
12 Freedom in your job to adopt own approach	[ ]	[ ]
GENERALLY		
13 To acquire possessions: property money, goods	[ ]	[ ]
14 To conserve: collect, repair, save possessions	[ ]	[ ]
15 To order: arrange, organize, be neat and tidy	[ ]	[ ]
16 To construct: organize, build	[ ]	[ ]
17 To achieve: recognition, ambition, power, do difficult things well	[ ]	[ ]
18 To exhibit: excite, amuse, thrill others, attract attention	[ ]	[ ]
19 To defend: against shame, belittlement, criticism	[ ]	[ ].
20 To preserve: self respect, good name, pride	[ ]	[ ]
21 To dominate: influence, control, lead, direct	[ ]	[ ]
22 To cooperate: follow, serve	[ ]	[ ]
23 To empathise: imitate, emulate others	[ ]	[ ]
24 To obey: be well behaved, avoid blame	[ ]	[ ]
25 To be unconventional: be unique, different, contrary	[ ]	[ ]

26 To be autonomous: have freedom and
    independence   [ ]   [ ]

27 To affiliate: form friendships, join, cooperate   [ ]   [ ]

28 To enquire: explore, learn   [ ]   [ ]

29 To teach: explain, interpret   [ ]   [ ]

30 To have fun: relax, amuse   [ ]   [ ]

(Adapted from categories listed in Carr, 1979)

Summary

We have said that static-content theories do not travel well between cultures, and that process theories are perhaps more portable, because they focus on certain 'universals' in the way motivation works, rather than focusing on what motivates people. However, it may be that the most fruitful research on cross-cultural comparisons of motivation have been based on static-content models, as it is only by looking at the content of motivation that we can gain any comparisons.

The research of Kelly *et al.*, (1991) comparing Eastern with Western countries indicates that there may be important similarities between cultures on those 'life goals' which are important generally to job motivation. In particular they point to work and family as being universally important (within the confines of their six countries study).

The main conclusion from this discussion is that managers, particularly those managing across cultures, should look very closely at what motivates people working under them and with them, and not to attribute their own motivators to other people. Both expectancy theory, and static-content theory indicate this. Motivation is an important aspect of job performance. Without motivated individuals, despite high levels of competence and the opportunity within the organization to perform, nothing will move in an organization. We can modify this statement to say that either a whip (compulsion) behind staff, or a carrot (inducements) may cause otherwise unmotivated individuals to move in the direction required. Again, short of inflicting physical pain, we still have to discover what inducements to use and what form of coercion! Better if individuals are self-motivated because their own life goals, expectancies and career objectives coincide with the objectives and goal of the organization for which they work.

References

Alderfer, C. P. (1972) *Existence, Relatedness and Growth: Human Needs in Organizational Settings*, New York: Free Press.

Berry, J. W., Poortinga, Y. H., Segall, M. H. and Dasen, P. R. (1992) *Cross-cultural Psychology: Research and Application*, Cambridge: Cambridge University Press.

Bowditch, J. L. and Buono, A. F. (1990) *A Primer On Organizational Behaviour*, New York: John Wiley.

Campbell J. P. and Pritchard, R. D. (1976) ' Motivational theory in industrial and organizational psychology', in Dunnette, M. D. (ed.) *Handbook of Industrial and Organizational Psychology*, Chicago: Rand McNally.

Carr, J. B. (1979) *Communicating and Relating*, Menlo Park, California: Benjamin/Cummings Publishing.

de Boer, C. (1978) 'The polls: attitudes towards work', *Public Opinion Quarterly*, 42, pp. 414–23.

Dunnette, M. D. (ed.) (1976) *Handbook of Industrial and Organizational Psychology*, Chicago: Rand McNally.

Harris, P. R. and Moran, R. T. (1987) *Managing Cultural Differences*, Houston: Gulf Publishing.

Heider, F. (1958) *The Psychology of Interpersonal Relations*, New York: Wiley.

Herzberg F., Mausner, B. and Snyderman, B. (1959) *The Motivation to Work*, New York: Wiley.

Hofstede, G. (1980) 'Motivation, Leadership and Organization: Do American Theories Apply Abroad?', *Organizational Dynamics*, Summer, 1980, pp. 42–63.

Hofstede, G. (1991) *Culture and Organizations: Software of the Mind*, London: McGraw-Hill.

Hui, C. H. (1990) 'Work Attitudes, Leadership and Managerial Behaviour in Different Cultures' in Brislin, R. W. *Applied Cross-Cultural Psychology*, Newbury Park: Sage.

Jaeger, A. M. and Kanungo, R. N. (1990) *Management in Developing Countries*, London: Routledge.

Johnson, T., Feigenbaum, R. and Welby, M. (1964) 'Some determinants and consequences of teacher's perceptions of causation', in *Journal of Educational Psychology*, 55, pp. 237–46.

Kakabadse, A., Ludlow, R. and Vinnicombe, S. (1987) *Working in Organizations*, Harmondsworth: Penguin.

Kelley, H. H. (1967) 'Attribution theory in social psychology', *Nebraska Symposium on Motivation*, 15, pp. 192–238.

Kelley H. H. (1973) 'The processes of causal attribution', *American Psychologist*, 28, pp. 107–28.

Kelly, L. and Worthy, R. (1981) 'The Role of Culture in Comparative Management: A cross Cultural Perspective', *Academy of Management Journal*, 24, 1, pp. 164–73.

Kelly, L., Whatley, A. and Worthy, R., (1991) 'Self-appraisal, life goals, and national culture: an Asian-Western Comparison', *Asia Pacific Journal of Management*, 7, 2, pp. 41–58.

Kline, P. (1986), *A Handbook of Test Construction*, London: Methuen.

McClelland, D. C. (1961) *The Achieving Society*, Princeton, NJ: Van Nostrand.

McClelland, D. C. (1987), *Human Motivation*, Cambridge: CUP.

Maccoby, M. (1976) *The Gamesman*, New York: Simon and Schuster.

Maslow, A. H. (1954) *Motivation of Personality*, New York: Harper and Row.

Miller, D. T. and Ross M. (1975) 'Self-serving biases in the attribution of causality: fact or fiction?' *Psychological Bulletin*, 82, pp. 213–25.

Murray, H. A. (1938) *Explorations in Personality*, New York: Oxford University Press.

Myers, M. T. and Myers G. E. (1982) *Managing By Communication: An Organizational Approach*, New York: McGraw-Hill.

Porter, L. W. and Lawler, E. E. (1968) *Managerial Attitudes and Performance*, Illinois: Dorssey Press.

Rotter, J. B. (1966) 'Generalized expectancies for internal versus external control of reinforcement', *Psychological Monographs*, 80, 1 whole No. 609.

Stewart, D. (1986) *The Power of People Skills*, New York: John Wiley.

Vroom, V. H. (1964) *Work and Motivation*, New York: Wiley.

5

Power and influence in organizations

Objectives

Following this chapter you should be able to:

1 Explain the bases of power and influence in organizations.
2 Explain the cultural differences in the basis of power in different organizations.
3 Analyse and document the use of power in an organization in the context of its culture.

Key concepts

- Power prerequisites: resources, dependencies and alternatives
- Power levers
- Organizational culture and power
- Communication and power
- Influence and organizational currencies
- Exchange theory
- In-group and out-group distinctions in collectivist cultures

Introduction

Anyone who has ever worked in an organization will know that effectiveness in your career is not simply a matter of being good at your job and being highly motivated. Purely on a pragmatic level, or 'common sense' level, it would seem that those people who have the 'loudest voices', who get themselves heard, or who are in 'the right place at the right time' get recognized and get promotion.

There are many determinants of who 'gets on' or who is influential in an organization. These determinants or factors may be different in different organizations, and indeed, may be different from one culture to another, whether between organizational or national cultures. We can again refer to the 3Cs model of context–content–conduct to explain the range of these factors of power in organizations. Factors in power relations include:

Context
- Organizational structure
- Distribution of work tasks and professional competences within an organization and wider environment
- Organizational reward systems
- Organizational and environmental resources
- Distribution of information in an organization
- Available alternatives or opportunities within an organizational environment
- The culture within an organization and wider society
- The individual's formal authority and control position within the organization
- The individual's informal alliances within the organization.

Content
- Individuals' goals and objectives within an organization, and the interactions, synergies and conflicts between different individuals' objectives
- Individuals' motivation towards the pursuit of objectives, and determination in the face of opposition and conflict
- Individuals' perceptions of the organization and the power relationships within it.
- Individuals' 'personality', personal preferences and orientations.

Conduct
- The individual's competences (both job competences and those relating directly to the use of power) *vis à vis* those of others in the organization and the pool of competences in the organization's environment
- The actions of individuals within the context of others' actions and organizational relationships and structures.

Many of these factors are overlapping, and the majority are context-related, that is power can only be wielded within the setting of an organization or society. However the cross-cultural implications of this are substantial as power is context-specific. Particularly if we make a distinction between objective power and subjective power the difficulties are compounded.

Objective (or formal) power is based on the objective position of a person in the organization who can wield power, for example the chief executive of an organization can wield power because of his position. This is based on control and authority.

Subjective (or informal) power is based on a person's ability to influence other people in such a way as to change their actions in some way. It is independent of objective power, although it can be used to gain a formal position of power. It is based on influence.

When a company acquires another company, objective power may be used to coerce or control the new subsidiary, to change its culture and to modify the actions of individuals within it (we have seen an example of this in Chapter 1). Subjective power is more difficult to use across organizational cultures in this way as it assumes a good understanding of the other culture, as well as the use of its informal and formal networks and structures.

We are here going to assume the 'content' of power, which is mainly concerned with the motivation of individuals to wield power and influence, as this was dealt with in Chapter 4. We are going to concentrate on the context factors, and the way that individual actions of conduct are related to the context factors of organizational and national culture.

In this chapter we divide an analysis of power relations into three broad headings (after Kakabadse *et al.*, 1987), namely:

- prerequisites,
- power levers,
- organizational culture.

We first look at the prerequisites of power, especially from the point of view of organizational resources. We then look at power levers and organizational culture in juxtaposition. This provides an analysis of an organizational situation whereby the reader may focus on his or her own organization to look at the way power is used. Finally, we look at the problems of using a concept of power in other cultures and use the example of Chinese family businesses to illustrate some of these difficulties.

Prerequisites of power

Katz and Kahn (1978) describe three dimensions of power, or what we can consider to be prerequisites to wielding power in an organization:

- Resources;
- Dependencies;
- Alternatives.

The ability to hold and to use resources in an organization is fundamental to the use of power. These resources may be tangible or intangible. They may be money, physical strength, skills, information, or, even, good looks. With resources a person has the potential to control part of his or her environment, particularly when those resources are scarce, and in demand. This brings us on to the second point.

Dependencies refers to other people's dependence, need or desire for the resource which you command. It is no good simply having a resource if nobody wants this. You only have power if you have got something which others require. This may be information, intelligence or personal charm. It may be access to promotion which only your boss can supply. If demand is high for that resource and if it is scarce (see below) and, if you can supply it, you may wield power in an organization

Alternatives stem from the question of availability of the resource. If there are a number of alternative sources of the required resource, and if others do not necessarily have to go to you, then you will not wield as much power as if you were the only source to which people could go. If good looks were at a premium, but everybody in the organization was good looking, you would not be in a particularly good position to get the promotion offered as if you were the only good looking person in the organization.

Myers and Myers (1982) add another dimension to these three prerequisites for wielding power: the dimension of communication. Power is based on consent between, say, a leader and followers. Unless this consent is engineered satisfactorily by the leader, then the power cannot be wielded. The leader, therefore, has to communicate the messages of power clearly and unambiguously to the followers.

Mini Case 5.1 In search of the universal management panacea

A resource which still seems to be in great demand, certainly in the United States, and to a lesser extent in the United Kingdom, is the key to successful management: the 'quick fix' solution to all questions of management success. In an article in *Business* magazine Clutterbuck and Crainer (1988) explore the qualities of management gurus: the ability to supply ideas to managers in an easily packaged form for which the management population is happy to spend millions of dollars.

'Management gurus' are able to wield great power in terms of their command of huge speaker's fees, royalties and their influences generally on management thinking. They are able to supply a scarce resource, which is in great demand.

The search for the universal panacea has been big business since 1945: with the realization that a single idea can be sold successfully and profitably given time and energy. Not only is the idea itself important, but the marketing and self promotion of the idea is crucial.

Buck Rogers, formally of IBM found that a career as a guru was more profitable. He charges $12,000 per appearance which he rations to ninety a year. Others, including academics can command up to $20,000 a day. Much is fashion related, but it is also the role of gurus to create the fashion. Over the decades the following trends in panaceas were observed:

1950s	Management by objectives
1960s	Decentralization
1970s	Corporate strategy
1980s	Corporate culture
1990s	Responsiveness to change (provisional prediction)

John Humble (who himself may be regarded as a guru) in the same article identifies the following characteristics of a guru:

- *Integrative power*. The guru must be able to place his topic in the context of broader economic developments and business trends.
- *Intuitive thinking*. He or she must be alert to trends long before others.
- *Longevity*. The guru is usually present and in the public eye for some time. One good idea is not enough. They must continually generate good ideas.
- *International influence*. The ideas must be global in scope and be taken up around the globe by enthusiasts with global perspectives.
- *Missionary zeal for what they believe in*. There must be a genuine concern to spread the word. The extensive speaking tours taken by gurus cannot simply be motivated by money.
- *Ability to listen*. Not only must the guru believe in the rightness of what they are propounding, but must have an ability to continually listen, to keep learning, and never close their minds to other ideas.

We might, therefore, view the success of a management guru as an example of wielding power, by utilizing scarce resources, as follows.

Exercise of power ⎯⎯⎯⎯⎯⎯⎯⎯⎯⎯⎯⎯⎯⟶

Prerequisites	*Mediated by*	*Outcome*
Resources An idea which meets the requirements of practising managers to solve problems or be successful Dependencies A need on the part of practising managers to gain information in the particular area Alternatives A lack of good alternatives which are easily available and well 'packaged'	An ability to communicate ⟶ the idea, to persevere and to put the message in a form which is readily available and acceptable	Acceptance of ideas Influence on management decision-making Acquisition of money

We can see from the above that 'influence' is shown as an outcome of power, a utilization of power in a particular area. Miller (1986) speaks of 'zones of influence' outside of which a personal power will be ineffective. Whilst management gurus may have considerable influence generally over what managers do, they have no direct influence over day to day policy within a specific organization: unless they hold an organizational position in that company or perhaps consult to a particular company. Similarly, managers may have quite a small zone of influence. An accounts managers will have influence in his own department as a result of his organization position, and his knowledge and skills. He may also have influence generally over the organization because of his knowledge of the company's accounts. The day to day running of the sales department will go on unaffected by his influence, and the influence of the sales manager may only be confined to her immediate department.

Cohen and Bradford (1989) speak of influence without authority in organizations, and focus on informal rather than formal power relations. What is most important to our current discussion on power perquisites being a function of resources, is that these writers take this a stage further by using an exchange model to look at how influence is managed in organizations, by utilizing resources. This approach is well known in sociology and social psychology, and probably originated by Homans (1958) and Blau (1964).

Cohen and Bradford (1989) tell us that the way influence is acquired without formal authority is through 'the law of reciprocity': that is, the belief that people should be paid back for what they do or provide. If people believe that their actions will be paid back, influence is possible. Put in another way, if I have something which you want, I may be able to get you to do something for me. This is exactly the same as the resource model we have discussed above. However, looking further at this through the concept of reciprocity, organizational transactions are seen as a series of exchanges. You give your time to an organization because you get paid for it. You do what your boss asks because he can fire you or give you promotion. Exchange relations may also be based on intangibles such as the giving of praise, gratitude or admiration.

If people are not getting an equitable exchange, then they may become impatient or disgruntled and finally disillusioned. If employees are putting their best effort into their

Table 5.1 *Organizational currencies*

Category	Currency	Example
Inspiration-related	Vision	Involvement in task which has a wider significance
	Excellence	Having a chance to do things well
	Moral/ethical correctness	Doing what you think is 'right'
Task-related	Resources	Proving money, personnel, space, budget increase, etc.
	Assistance	Helping with projects
	Co-operation	Providing task support, quicker response times, approving a project, etc.
	Information	Proving organizational or technical knowledge
Position-related	Advancement	Proving opportunity which can lead to promotion
	Recognition	Acknowledging accomplishments
	Visibility	Providing chance to be known by higher ups in the organization
	Reputation	Providing enhancement to the way a person is seen
	Importance/insiderness	Offering a sense of belonging to the right in-group
	Network/contacts	Proving chance to link in with others of significance
Relationship-related	Acceptance/inclusion	Proving friendship
	Personal suport	Providing emotional backing
	Understanding	Listening to others' concerns
Personal-related	Self-concept	Affirming own values and self-esteem
	Challenge/learning	Sharing tasks which increase own skills and abilities
	Ownership/ involvement	Letting others have ownership and influence
	Gratitude	Expressing appreciation or indebtedness

Source: adapted from Cohen and Bradford, 1989.

work, but never getting praised for it, never getting recognition, and finally not getting the promotion they feel they deserve, then they will loose faith in the job, the manager and perhaps the organization. The manager, may then have little influence in this situation, other than that provided by his or her formal position in the organization.

Cohen and Bradford (1989) use the metaphor of 'currency' in order to conceptualize the resources one person has to offer and what the other person needs or desires in order for one to influence the other (for A to influence B in such a way that B does something that he would not otherwise have done, that is to wield power as in one definition in Chapter One). We can therefore think of a trading of resources or currencies.

Cohen and Bradford (1989) draw up a list of commonly traded organizational currencies as shown in Table 5.1.

Using organizational currencies

Currencies are partly subjective, as one manager may value 'praise' more highly as a currency than another manager who might see praise as patronizing or as a cheap way to repay a favour. Payment may not necessarily come directly from the other person, but may be self-generating through satisfaction of a job well done, or to fit a person's beliefs about being benevolent or virtuous or committed to the organization. However, in these circumstances the exchange is still interpersonal because the person with influence has set up the conditions which generate these 'self-payments', particularly if this relates to the accomplishing of organizational goals: that is, the manager of the organizational unit has created an atmosphere and ethos whereby people want to serve the organization. Where self-generated payments are made as a result of personal virtues or values, for example, 'doing the right thing', then this may be predominantly intrapersonal (that is, within the person rather than between persons) in nature rather than as a result of preconditions set up by the manager.

The question of creating mutually satisfactory exchanges (establishing 'exchange rates') is problematic and dependent on an understanding of what is important to the person to be influenced. It is therefore important to understand the perceptions and objectives of the person over whom you wish to gain influence.

Cohen and Bradford (1989) describe the following process for influencing others.

1 Think of the person to be influenced as an ally, and not as an adversary. It is necessary to find areas of mutual benefit and to develop a trusting relationship.

2 Know the world of the potential ally, including pressures as well as personal needs and objectives. It is necessary to know which currencies are valued. This may be different depending on the culture from which the person is drawn, and his or her own personal values and objectives. It is not possible to be self-oriented, or to be ethnocentric if you are going to influence, nor to revert to stereotyping the individual which may prevent seeing his or her needs and perceptions. A clue to understanding driving forces of this nature within an organizational culture is to look at how performance is measured and rewarded. Through this it may be possible to see why a person acts in a particular way, in order to be seen as a good performer.

3 Be aware of key goals and resources available, which the potential ally values. This involves also the influencer being aware of what he or she has to offer the potential ally. Even an employee low in the formal organization, may have currency which the boss requires. It is a question of knowing what is wanted, where it is available, and how it can be offered by the influencer.

4 Understand the exchange transaction itself, to enable win-win outcomes to be achieved. Problems may occur as follows.
   - Not knowing how to use reciprocity. This involves being aware of the ally, his or her needs, and how to present this in such a way that you are not being manipulative.
   - Preferring to be right rather than effective. Sometimes sticking to principles may get in the way of acting pragmatically in order to meet the needs of your ally, as well as your own. Some compromise might be needed.
   - Overusing what has been successful. It may be necessary to modify your approach in the light of what is appropriate in a situation, and not sticking with what has been successful in the past, as this may be inappropriate. A good repertoire of influencing strategies is necessary in any organization, and this is particularly true of one with international dimensions.

We have so far looked at the prerequisites of wielding power in an organization by focusing on a resource based approach. It could be argued that when looking at influence as a separate phenomenon to power, we can regard power as just another resource to use for bargaining or currency (for example, Handy, 1985). Alternatively, we could see influence as an outcome of wielding power (see Mini case 5.1 above): that is, if you are in a powerful position you are better able to influence others (although this may be just another way of saying that you have something that others want, that is access to a powerful person, and therefore can use this as currency in influencing others).

Let us now turn to the next aspect of power described by Kakabadse *et al.*, (1987), power levers.

Power levers

Power levers, or what Hodge and Anthony (1988) call the 'foundations of power' can be described as strategies which individuals can employ. A number of texts describe five or six power bases or 'levers', which can be traced back to an original article by French and Raven (1959) where five such power bases are described. No doubt the most developed of such categorizations is that of Kakabadse (for example, Kakabadse *et al.*, 1987) which are viewed as operational strategies (hence the term 'lever'). We have further categorized these into objective and subjective bases of power (see Table 5.2).

These levers can be used either separately or in combination in order to wield power in an organization. Quite often, for example, a manager will have power in an organization because of his or her position (legitimate power), and therefore will be able to operate a reward system whereby employees are given praise and ultimately promotion as a result of their good performance and possibly loyalty to the manager

Table 5.2 *Power levers*

Power lever	Description	Example
Objective		
Legitimate	Wielding authority and control through virtue of one's organizational position	Being in a position to issue commands or directives which are acted upon, as one's authority is regarded as legitimate by those carrying out the instructions.
Reward	Granting of rewards to others	Bestowing of money or status on employees
Coercive	Being able to punish or compel through physical characteristics or organizational position	Sacking someone for doing a poor job
Subjective		
Personal	Applying personal charm or charisma to gain sympathy and support, usually through interpersonal interaction	Being able to enthuse someone to want to get the job done, to gain the favour of a charismatic leader, such as a 'guru' or religious leader
Expert	Having skills or knowledge which are needed in particular situations, or being seen to have such knowledge or skills	The knowledge of a computer specialist who can solve problems through use of particular applications
Information	Having information which is needed by others in particular circumstances	Being privy to strategic information in the organization as a result of one's organizational position, or having personal knowledge about someone, whose reputation could be damaged if it were disclosed.
Connection	Having access to a large network of people inside and outside the organization who may be able to provide resources or connect with those who can	As a result of networking at conferences, having access to alternative employment, or information.

Source: adapted from Kakabadse *et al.*, 1987.

(reward power). The manager may have the authority to start disciplinary procedures and if necessary to dismiss an employee who brings the company into disrepute or perhaps is a poor performer (coercive power). The same manager may also have a highly regarded technical expertise in his or her field, and may be invaluable to the company, and be a major source of professional knowledge for his staff (expert power). As a result of his or her position in the company, the manager may have access to strategic information which is not available to the manager's peers, who look to him or her for such information (information power). He or she may have a personality which attracts others and instils in others a sense of loyalty to the manager (personal power). With such a charismatic personality, the manager finds it easy to network inside the organization and outside at conferences, and has built up a good contact base (connection power).

An alternative picture is of a manager who has a position in an organization and therefore has legitimate power, but has few interpersonal skills, cannot network, does not gain the respect of peers and staff, and therefore is only effective as an administrator and not as a personal leader. He or she may have 'objective power', but not 'subjective power'. The opposite may be true, in that an individual in an organization may hold no formal power, but may be a good networker, may have a strong personality and have acquired relevant knowledge and skills. This person may have considerable subjective power in the organization.

A complication is that of the situational aspect of power levers. What may be appropriate in one organizational or national culture may not be appropriate in another.

Organizational culture and power

There are a number of classifications of organizational and national culture and we have, for example, looked at that of Hofstede (see Chapter 2). 'Power distance' describes the national cultural dimension of Hofstede (for example, 1991) which is based on the degree to which:

- employees are afraid to express disagreement with their boss;
- the boss is autocratic or paternalistic, and
- the employees agree with their boss's decision-making style (that is, the employees express a preference for an autocratic or paternalistic style and the positive end of the dimension).

The use of power levers in the context of a high power distance culture will be quite different to that in a lower power distance culture. It is unlikely that a manager with a consultative style in a high power distance organization will have an appropriate style to wield considerable power in that organization.

Taking a framework provided by Harrison (1972) to describe organizational cultures, Kakabadse *et al.*, (1987) outline the use of power levers in each type of culture, as follows.

Power culture. This type of organizational culture is typified by a strong central source of power, perhaps by one entrepreneur in a young company, or by a small group controlling and manipulating activity in the organization. They may be advised directly by technical specialists who enable the entrepreneur to retain his or her control. Subordinates anticipate the needs and wishes of those at the top. This type of organization can be highly competitive, as well as very stimulating for those that are seen as strong, and able to take on the burden of responsibility. There may be much political in-fighting, and the wielding of power depends very much on the personal charisma of leaders as well as risk-taking, intuition and change. Administration and technical expertise are likely to be seen as constraining rather than facilitating. Other levers used may be connection and information power levers, with skilful use of reward and coercion.

Role culture. This is an organizational culture where the definition of roles and rules predominate. The boundaries of what people can do according to their job descriptions and areas of responsibilities are important, as are the rules governing their conduct within these roles. Formal communication systems and patterns are defined, as are procedures for reporting up and down the organization. Little is left to individual intuition or innovation, and such organizations operate in a stable environment, such as in the banking environment of a decade ago in Western Europe. Senior managers are responsible chiefly for co-ordination, guided by rules and procedures. Individuals are secondary to formal task and role definitions. Individuals are selected for particular roles because they are seen to fit into these roles. Performance is dependent on whether a person is able to carry out the duties of the particular role. Power comes from the organizational role, not from the person. The main power lever in these circumstances is the 'legitimate' power lever.

Task culture. These types of organizations are based on the need to solve new problems and to innovate, usually in a fast changing market or when dealing with a changing technology, such as the consumer electrics industry over the last twenty years. Work is often carried out in teams, where the continuation and functioning of the team is more important than the individual. Teams may be established on an *ad hoc* basis to solve particular problems, or may be established for longer projects as in product innovation. Formal roles are not important as work proceeds on the basis of expertise, controlling one's own work, flexible working relationships and mutual respect of others' competences. This is quite the opposite of a role culture, as formal working relationships and tight structures would stifle innovation and flexibility. However, in periods where resources are scarce in periods of no growth, the different work teams may be put into a competitive situation regarding the negotiation of resources. Formal procedures may need to be established to impose an element of control, to reduce risk, and therefore begin to change the organization to a role culture. General Electric Company was an example of a company which experienced rapid growth due to mergers and acquisitions, and in order to impose some control on the internal competition for resources, had to move towards a role culture. The converse is that the clearing banks in the UK of a decade ago, have had to undergo substantial changes in the face of competition in the last few years, having to change from a tightly structured role emphasis, to a more innovative and market-led approach to solving problems. These two cultures seem not to be particularly stable, when markets and economies experience substantial change as follows.

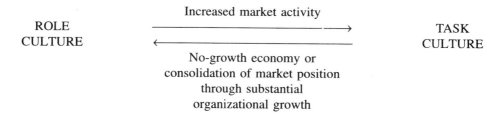

Table 5.3 *Power levers and organizational cultures*

Power lever	Culture types			
	Power	*Role*	*Task*	*Person-oriented*
Reward	Rewards to key figures in supporting roles	Rewards for successfully adopting appropriate behaviour for role	Rewards given for high task performance	Reward inherent in being accepted by peers
Coercive	Actions are punished if they threaten key power figures	Coercion necessary for those working outside accepted roles and rules	Coercion and sanction needed against poor task performance	Coercion by threat of expulsion from group
Legitimate	Rules not likely to be adhered to by key power figures	Behaviour acceptable which is confined to defined authority areas	The interests of fulfilling the task legitimizes challenging senior management and disbanding team when task is completed	Behaviour according to loyalty to the people you work with, not directly to the organization
Personal	Strong charismatic figures, and manipulative behaviour	Personal power comes from being seen to fairly administer rules and allocation of work	Charisma is gained by exhibited problem-solving skills	Personal power by sharing and developing personal growth, and generating atmosphere within which this can take place
Expert	Not based on professional excellence but being able to mantain influence over others	Working within own remit and role, so as not to threaten existing role structure	Skills and knowledge must constantly be updated to solve new problems	Work standards determined by members of the group. Individuals are expected to work to these standards
Information	Information useful only for achieving personal ends	Information flow with role structure and within existing patterns and procedures	New information constantly needed, to be shared amongst professional group, to solve new problems	Relevant information to be shared in group
Connection	Vital for generating a closed-shop culture which is available to exclusive few	Only contacts required to fulfil role	Needs a wide network of like-minded experts within and outside organization. Loyalty to network not organization	A personal and emotional link with people you like is appropriate.

In order to wield power within a task culture, the 'expert' power lever is most useful, together with 'connection' and 'information' levers, with an emphasis on the effective use of small group working.

Person-oriented culture. Person-centred organizations are unusual, where the objective is for the organization to serve the needs of individual. Small consulting and professional firms, computer departments, and academic institutions are such examples which may be partly person-oriented. Here the organization is not particular important, as individuals operate within a professional environment in which they can easily go to another organization to get employment. University departments may provide a role structure for teaching and research, but academics may also be involved in such other activities as personal research, publication and consultancy which enhances their own reputation and career, but only indirectly the reputation of the institution.

Mini Case 5.2   Mixing cultures and power levers

The current author has witnessed the problems of a mix of cultures, where in a major UK bank, a training and development consultancy unit was established to meet the needs of developing new solutions to performance problems throughout the bank (task culture).

Consultants were recruited from outside the bank for full-time internal positions; specialists in their own field who were concerned with their own reputations and careers within the profession (person-oriented). The culture of the bank was at that time predominantly oriented towards formal procedures and organizational structures, and away from innovative approaches (role culture). Some of the consultants were training specialists directly recruited from the Army where they were used to working within a role culture. The senior manager in charge of the operation had come directly from main stream banking and was used to working in a highly structured role culture.

The problem was (which was not directly articulated by top management) how to manage such a unit in order to take account of these diverse organizational factors.

Discussion. Perhaps before reading further, you may like to think how you would address this problem!

It was likely that the senior manager could use his position by using the *legitimate* power lever. He could also use his network in the bank which he had cultivated over the years (something which the hired consultants would not have). Therefore the lever of *connection* could be used to wield some power within this situation. He would also be in a position to obtain information from higher management which may be important for both the successful operation of consultancy projects and for the personal careers of consultants in the bank, if that were desirable. He could therefore use the *information* power lever. *Reward* and *coercion* power levers could also successfully be used by the distribution of projects to consultants by the senior manager. This, in fact, was a lever that was increasingly used in order to reward what was seen as good performance. The ability to give reward by the issuing of 'good' projects to chosen consultants, and uninteresting projects to those consultants who were not in favour. The latter was used as a 'coercive' lever.

The senior manager was not seen as an expert in the field by the consultants, and this caused a general feeling of disrespect towards him, and a criticizing of his ability to judge good or poor performance, and therefore to use his power levers of reward and coercion. He was therefore unable to use the *expert* power lever, and this had implications for his use of the other power levers which were available to him. He was also seen as generally a weak leader, mainly because of his lack of expert knowledge, and his 'personal' power lever was not used skilfully in this circumstance.

Let us now summarize the seven power levers in the context of these four organizational cultural types (see Table 5.3).

The matrix of power levers and their use in different organizational cultures gives a good guide to practising managers who may need to transfer their skills quickly and effectively from one organization to another. By using such a framework, cross-culturally operating managers may gain a good knowledge of the cultural environment within which they are currently working. In addition, the simple questionnaire in Activity 5.1 may also help.

Activity 5.1 Understanding an organization's culture and power levers

Focus on an organization with which you are familiar. Against each item place a tick [✓] if this is more like the organization, and a cross [✗] if this is less like the organization. Be sure to place either a tick or a cross. Do not leave any blanks.

In the organization:

[ ] 1 Rules are not necessarily adhered to by key players.

[ ] 2 Information is desired by key players to achieve personal ends.

[ ] 3 Sanctions are taken against people who do not conform to what is expected of them within their immediate job descriptions.

[ ] 4 There is no 'personality cult', managers gain personal respect because they discharge their duties well.

[ ] 5 Individuals are not expected to make extensive contacts outside what is required to do their current job.

[ ] 6 Sanctions are taken against those who do not perform well against objectives, and who are seen not to be competent in their area of specialism.

[ ] 7 Personal status is gained in this organization through exercise of specialist skills and knowledge.

[ ] 8 Task specialists in this organization tend to network with like-minded specialists inside and outside the organization.

[ ]   9   Those managers who are most respected place emphasis on creating an atmosphere where individuals can develop in a situation of mutual trust.

[ ] 10 People develop links with others in the organization not because of a need to network for professional or career gain, but because they like them.

[ ] 11 Work standards are set by the group and members are expected to adhere to them.

[ ] 12 People show loyalty to the people they most interact with in the organization, rather than to the organization itself.

[ ] 13 The greatest sanction against individuals is to be rejected by the group.

[ ] 14 There is a constant drive to obtain new information so that teams of people can strive towards new ways of solving problems and to innovate.

[ ] 15 Rewards are given for high performance, and achievement of specific objectives.

[ ] 16 Usually information flows within formally accepted chains of command, people are not expected to seek organizational information outside these bounds.

[ ] 17 Managers are respected who keep within the bounds of their authority.

[ ] 18 Rewards are given for performing well within the confines of your immediate job description.

[ ] 19 Attaining numerous contacts throughout the organization and outside is vital to key players, to keep others out of the game.

[ ] 20 Management competency can best be described as an ability to influence others.

[ ] 21 Mistakes are punished if they are seen to threaten power holders in the organization.

[ ] 22 Leaders in this organization seem to manipulate others to meet their ends.

[ ] 23 People are expected to gain and use expertise only within the bounds of their job, and not outside this.

[ ] 24 Achievement of specific task objectives is important, and it would be appropriate to challenge senior management if meeting these objectives so demanded it.

[ ] 25 The continued development of personal skills and knowledge to undertake specialist tasks is valued.

[ ] 26 The greatest reward is to be accepted by your peers.

[ ] 27 There are few secrets within the work group, and all information is expected to be shared.

[ ] 28 People in this organization are rewarded for being loyal to key individuals.

To analyse your responses, where you put a tick [✓] against the item place a tick across the relevant item number on the grid below. If you put a cross against an item there is no need to do anything. When you have ticked off all the items in the grid below, add all the ticks across (do not add the numbers in each cell), and add all the ticks down.

	Reward	Coercive	Legit	Personal	Expert	Inform	Connect	TOTAL
Power	28	21	1	22	20	2	19	
Role	18	3	17	4	23	16	5	
Task	15	6	24	7	25	14	8	
Person	26	13	12	9	11	27	10	
TOTAL								

It may be obvious to you by the high score against one organizational culture type that your organization belongs in that category. However, it may be that the organization is poised between different cultural types. Look through the power levers to see where you have placed the ticks, to gain a view of which types of power levers are likely to be successful in your organization.

National cultural characteristics

We have provided the basis for the study of contextual factors, particularly organizational culture on what constitutes the successful wielding of power and appropriate behaviour for those seeking power. We have already mentioned the difficulties this may entail when functioning in different national cultures, and specifically mentioned power distance differences in different countries (for example Hofstede, 1991). Similarly, we should consider the cultural issue of collectivism versus individualism, as the type of culture which has spawned much of the power theory we have been discussing is drawn from highly individualistic societies, where much power can be accessed through an individual's own competences. We can perhaps mention even the differences between countries such as the United States and France, which are both fairly individualistic (see Chapter 2 for a comparison), but where, in France, there is more of an emphasis on formal qualifications, rather than on 'self-made men', as a prerequisite to get to the top of an organization. There is also more emphasis on being male, as women in France as a rule have tended not to reach the top (Barsoux and Lawrence, 1990). Inheritance may also be more important in France than in the United States as a way to power. It may well be that individuals in the United States and perhaps the United Kingdom, can consciously choose or adapt a style such that power levers are employed as appropriate, but this may not be the case in other cultures, where power is determined in an organization purely by birthright.

Chinese family businesses

As an example of a strongly collectivist culture, and the way power is handled in organizations, we can look at the example of a Chinese family business (see Hui, 1990). Collective cultures are typified by their distinction between in-group and out-group and the differences associated in the behaviour of, and towards those who are members of the in-group and those who are not. Chinese family businesses (outside of the People's Republic of China) are perhaps typical of such collectivist behaviour, where businesses tend to be run by a close circle of family members, with key positions being filled by family members and close friends. The following features can be seen which are associated with a definite in-group/out-group distinction.

- *Identity and impact.* Unlike in most Western countries where people's identity and impact in an organization are determined by what they have achieved, in the Chinese firm this is determined by the person's relationship to the owner. Status is thus related to belonging to the boss's in-group, rather than to whether one is hard-working or not. Views and opinions will be heard if expressed by a member of the in-group, but are not likely to be heard if expressed by others.

- *Theory* X *and theory* Y. McGregor's (1960) distinction between the assumption – theory X – which sees employees to be lazy and not motivated by anything but money and inducements, who need to be cajoled and coerced into performing, and theory Y which sees employees as responsible and self-motivating, is typical of the distinction made between the attitudes of the boss to out-group employees (theory X), and attitudes towards in-group employees (theory Y). Subordinates are therefore treated accordingly.

- *Differential treatment.* In-group members will be seen as having more commitment to the organization and are the ones who are more likely to receive favours and get promotion. Out-group employees are controlled by formal contracts of employment, and are not likely to be seen as having long-term commitment to the company.

- *Mistrust.* Interpersonal trust is difficult to generate towards those who are not regarded as close friends and family members. This type of trust is difficult to engender between two people in an organization who consider each other not to be a member of the same in-group.

- *Autocratic management.* Without trust, problems within the organization are likely to be kept to the in-group circle, and a great deal of secrecy will prevail. Out-group members will be expected to carry out specific tasks without being concerned with the business as a whole. Upward influence will be discouraged, and the management are unlikely to solicit information from employees in their decision making.

- *Power distance.* Chinese bosses are seen as 'stern father figures'. They command respect and fear. Delegation is seen to be giving away control and influence in the affairs of the company to outsiders, which is unacceptable. In order to strengthen their position, Chinese bosses are often boastful of their achievements and disparaging towards their subordinates' contributions, attributing outstanding performance to external factors. This is in contrast to Japanese bosses who recognize their employees' achievements and develop within employees a strong belonging-ness to the company.

- *Interdepartmental rivalry.* Loyalty in larger Chinese companies is often to the smaller unit of the department rather than to the organization itself. Often there is little knowledge of and interest in the wider organization, with characteristics of in-group and out-group behaviour. This may lead to interdepartmental rivalry.

It is often the case that large numbers of employees of a Chinese firm are regarded as out-group members, and will not be able to obtain a position of power, or even to gain interpersonal influence within such an organization! It may therefore be difficult to conceive of the wielding of power and the use of power levers in quite the same way in these circumstances.

Summary

We have concentrated very heavily on context factors and the way in which we must understand the culture of an organization in order to effectively use 'power levers' in any organization in which we are working. The concept of power and personal influence is integral to an understanding of leadership, and we will deal more specifically with personal influencing styles in Chapter 6. Certainly a distinction can be made between subjective power which is based more on personal influencing tactics, and more objective positional power. In large power distance, collectivist and possible uncertainty avoidance cultures we may find that objective sources of power may be more appropriate than subjective sources.

By using the example of Chinese family business, we can see that concepts of in-group and out-group in a highly collectivist society, influence the way we can conceptualize power and its uses.

We will consider personal influencing styles in the light of contextual leadership factors in the next chapter.

References

Barsoux, J.-L. and Lawrence, P. (1990) *Management In France*, London: Cassell.

Blau, P. (1964) *Exchange and Power in Social Life*, New York: John Wiley.

Clutterbuck, D. and Crainer, S. (1988) 'The Corporate Sages', *Business*, September.

Cohen, A. R. and Bradford, D. L. (1989) 'Influence without authority: the use of alliances, reciprocity and exchange to accomplish work', *Organizational Dynamics*, 17, 3, pp. 4–17.

French, J. R. P. and Raven, B. (1959), 'The bases of social power', in Cartwright, D. (ed) *Studies in Social Power*, Ann Arbor: Institute for Social Research.

Handy, C. (1984) *The Future of Work*, Oxford: Blackwell.

Harrison, R. (1972) 'How to describe your organization', *Harvard Business Review*, Sept/Oct.

Hodge, B. J. and Anthony, W. P., (1988) *Organizational Theory*, (3rd edn.) Boston: Allyn and Bacon.

Hofstede, G. (1991) *Culture and Organizations: Software of the Mind*, London: McGraw-Hill.

Homans, G. (1958) 'Social behaviour as exchange', *American Journal of Sociology*, 63, pp. 597–606.

Hui, C. H., (1990) 'Work attitudes, leadership and Managerial Behaviour in Different Cultures', in Brislin, R. W. *Applied Cross-Cultural Psychology*, Newbury Park: Sage.

Kakabadse, A., Ludlow, R. and Vinnicombe, S. (1987), *Working in Organizations*, Harmondsworth: Penguin.

Katz, D. and Kahn, R. (1978) *The Social Psychology of Organizations*, New York: John Wiley.

McGregor, D. (1960) *The Human Side of Enterprise*, New York: McGraw-Hill.

Miller, D. (1986) 'Configurations of strategy and structure', *Strategic Management Journal*, pp. 55–76.

Myers, M. T. and Myers, G. E. (1982) *Managing By Communication: An Organizational Approach*, New York: McGraw-Hill.

6

Leadership

Objectives

Following this chapter you should be able to:

1 Explain the basis of leadership in terms of personal and situational factors.
2 Explain the problems of applying leadership theories in different national cultures.
3 Document your own leadership styles.

Key concepts

- Leadership versus management
- Transformational and transactional leadership
- Positional, personal, and processional leadership
- Likert's management systems
- Trait, behaviour, and situational theories
- Kotter's agenda setting, network building, and agenda implementation

Introduction

We begin this chapter with a look at the meaning of leadership, followed closely by a consideration of the main abilities of leaders. A contrast is made between 'managers' and 'leaders' and the reasons why these are different are explored. One of the problems with conceptualizing leadership is that this may well be a cultural product. Certainly there are differences between organizations, and it is likely that there are major differences between national cultures.

With this background we look at the predominantly Western theories of leadership, including trait, behaviour and situational theories. Particularly of relevance to the last of these theories is the idea of leadership 'styles' the relevance of which differs from situation to situation, although it is possible to modify and adapt styles at a personal level. By again employing the 3Cs model of context–content–conduct, we look at some of the cultural implications of leadership and some of the variations. Finally, we look briefly at leadership of international teams, where it is often necessary to lead across a number of different cultures, taking into consideration the various assumptions of leadership.

What is leadership?

The concept of 'leadership' is a nebulous one, and the fact that it is often separated from the role specific concept of 'management' in Anglo-Saxon texts is an interesting point of departure. Leadership is thought of as belonging to the individual rather than given by virtue of his or her position in the organizational. It is seen as an ability to motivate others and to influence them.

So, for example, Cadbury-Schweppes in the UK, in their appraisal documentation define leadership as:

> Getting the best out of subordinates individually and collectively, achieving objectives in the most effective way;

and W H Smith Ltd see the attribute of leadership as follows:

> Leadership: Shows skill in directing group activity, has natural authority and gains respect of others. Capable of building an effective team. Involves all team members and gives advice and help where required (Jacobs, 1989).

This ability may be a result of specific 'traits' or personality factors of the individuals, or could be a result of the developing of skills (group skills, influencing skills, and so on). However, by the fact that individuals can only lead others in a particular environment, leadership behaviour must account for and be adaptable towards the specific context. This has led to a situational or contingency approach to leadership, and this has been the approach most applied in cross-cultural studies of leadership. However, the converse of this is that a leader can affect the culture of an organization by the style he or she uses. This is particularly the case of a chief executive officer of a smaller company, or one just starting business.

Kakabadse *et al.*, (1987) identify three common features in definitions and descriptions of leadership as follows:

- leadership is an influencing process;
- it requires at least two people, namely a leader and a follower or followers;
- it occurs in situations of attempting to achieve specific objectives, either explicit or implied goals.

Leadership abilities

Perhaps another clue to what leadership is, can be deduced from a survey conducted by Management Centre Europe in 1987, of over 1,000 managers all over Europe of leadership qualities they expect of their CEOs. The list is as follows (see Mainguy, 1988):

- the ability to build effective teams
- the ability to listen
- the capability to make decisions on their own

- the ability to retain good people
- the ability to surround themselves with good people.

Bennis tells us that:

> Leaders are people who do the right thing; managers are people who do things right. Both are crucial, and differ profoundly. I often observe people in top positions doing the wrong thing well (Bennis, 1991, p. 398).

He lists four leadership competences after surveying 60 American corporate leaders who were identified as true leaders, rather than managers, who affect the culture of their organizations and who are the social architects of their organizations, creating and maintaining values. These competences are:

- *Management of attention*. An ability to draw others to them because they have a vision or a dream, a set of intentions, and an agenda; and an ability to communicate a focus of commitment by the people they attract. Leaders are at their most effective when they have a clear sense of outcome and precisely what they want to achieve.

- *Management of meaning*. An ability to communicate that vision and expected outcome in a tangible way, cutting across organizational layers and across geographic divides in an organization. The message must make sense to those that need to act on it. Metaphors or models are useful in order to communicate, even through the jamming signals of opponents and interest groups.

- *Management of trust*. Principally this means reliability and consistency, letting people know from which direction you are coming.

- *Management of self*. An ability to know one's own skills and employing them effectively. A positive attitude also seems to go with this aspect of leadership.

The other way in which Bennis (1991) describes leadership is through the effects it has on those who follow. He describes this effect as 'empowerment'. Organizations with effective leaders manifest the following four aspects.

- People feel significant. They feel that there is a meaning to what they do, and that they make a difference to the organization.
- The valuing of learning and competence. Mistakes are seen as feedback to enable employees to do better.
- The feeling that people are part of the community. If there is effective leadership, so there is a good team spirit, and a feeling of belongingness.
- A feeling that work is exciting. People are motivated and excited about the work they do.

Leaders and managers

Another theory which may help us to understand the difference between a manager in a supervisory function and 'leadership' is that of 'transformational' leadership which is contrasted to 'transactional' leadership (see for example Burns, 1978, and Tichy and

Devanna, 1986). Transactional leadership sees the leader–follower relationship solely as a process of exchange: that is an employee will work for a reward, return, favour or other organizational currency (see Chapter 5). Transformational leaders are more visionary and inspirational, able to go after goals and motivate their followers with strong emotional appeal. Qualities of transformational leaders are as follows (see Bowditch and Buono, 1990).

- They are change agents. They make a difference, innovating and creating an organization which is adaptable.
- They have courage and are outspoken. They take risks and stand against the *status quo*.
- They have a belief in people. They have an empathy with people even though they themselves are powerful. They seek to empower others.
- They are value driven. They are consistent in their articulation of core values, and act according to these values.
- They are life-long learners, learning from their mistakes as well as their successes, capable of self-reflection and adaptation.
- They can deal with complexity, ambiguity and uncertainty, able to cope with socio-cultural and political aspects of the organization as well as the technical domain.
- They are visionary. They can create a dream and translate this into images which others can follow.

Kotter (1982, 1990) undertook a study of general managers and concluded that those who are effective leaders tend to follow this process:

- Agenda setting: figuring out what to do in the face of uncertainty, ambiguity and information overload.
- Network building. Developing a wide network of people, which is far wider than the manager's immediate subordinates, including peers, outsiders, their bosses' bosses, their subordinates' subordinates, and so on.
- Agenda implementation. Using the network within which norms and values have been engendered by the successful leader, to implement the agenda. This is based on the leader's interpersonal skills, use of resources and information base, and the use of symbolic communication to influence and motivate.

He contrasts 'leadership' with 'management' as demonstrated in Figure 6.1. We can say in this respect that managers produce predictable results, in a consistent way in

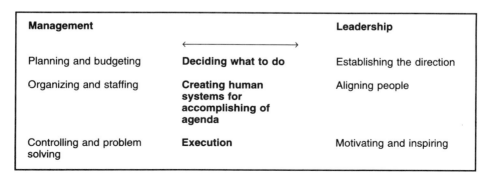

Management	Deciding what to do ←————————→	Leadership
Planning and budgeting	Deciding what to do	Establishing the direction
Organizing and staffing	Creating human systems for accomplishing of agenda	Aligning people
Controlling and problem solving	Execution	Motivating and inspiring

Figure 6.1 *Kotter's (1990) distinction between Management and Leadership*

conformance with stakeholders' (for example, shareholders, customers, employees) expectations, whereas leaders produce change. Kotter (1990) found that in the twelve United States companies he studied, there were strong managers but few strong leaders. He argues that the consequences of this could be a rigid company with little innovation, not capable of dealing with change.

Leadership: a product of culture?

Although, these aspects of leadership may provide us with a better understanding of what is meant by this term, it may be argued that one of the reasons why Bennis's work, for example, has been so acceptable within the American culture is that he reads the culture well and provides managers with what they want within the context of that culture! Whether these types of concepts would be as readily acceptable in other cultures (for example in a collectivist, high power distance, high uncertainty avoidance, and feminine culture in Hofstede's sense) remains to be seen.

The way we explore leadership here, therefore, is to look at the various theories of leadership (bearing in mind that this approach in itself might be quite ethnocentric), and then to look at the application of leadership principles across cultures.

Mini Case 6.1 Follow the leader*

Single interviews with the person responsible for Human Resources were conducted in three UK high technology companies, in order to determine the view of leadership as regards recruiting and developing leaders. The ideas of what leadership is differed, as did the perceived role of leaders within each organization.

Company *A*

There is a clear distinction made between 'management' and 'leadership', with the former representing the basic skills of organizing, delegating and controlling, and the latter the ability to motivate and encourage people and make them do what they want to do. A leader cannot therefore rely on his or her authority, but will try to persuade and influence people. These qualities are not sought directly in graduate recruits, but such individuals are expected to develop leadership abilities whilst working for the company. Leadership training exists, and leadership qualities are looked for in the promotion of managers.

Company *A* has many competent managers but only a small number of leaders. With 55,000 employees world-wide there is a need for tight controls, and the formal authority of managers is important. The corporate culture does not develop leaders as it is not entrepreneurial enough, with the possible exception of the sales department. People tend to sit and wait for things to happen, they need

---

*I am indebted to Sophie Wegener, second year Berlin Stream at EAP, 1990–91, for this information.

108

encouragement. The changing environment may necessitate more risk and a development of more leaders. It is a core development need for managers as the skills employed can motivate employees to stay in the good times as well as making it through the bad times.

Company *B*

In this interview leadership was defined as the ability to sell ideas to people, having a vision and making people share this vision. As the management style is participative, managers have to be leaders to be successful in working in teams, to persuade people, to know the right things to do.

Recruitment in the past has been very much on a 'gut feeling' basis, although now the more extensive use of psychometric testing is providing a more scientific approach. Training courses exist to develop leadership skills. Here managers learn to coach, persuade, and negotiate. Following a study of how the top 5 per cent of management manage a new development programme was introduced, giving a four step guide-line to managers to:

1 define a purpose and direction to be agreed on
2 build a vision for the future
3 make a step by step action plan
4 review and measure the process.

Promotion arises out of networking in the organization, and as a result of where you are 'known'. Appraisal looks for leadership qualities and focuses on team work and customer satisfaction.

In general there are more leaders than managers in the company.

Company *C*

Every employee who comes into the company has an introductory presentation which includes two contrasting images of a rocket with a driver and passengers. In the first instance the rocket is simply being driven, people sitting there with blank faces. In the second image the rocket is being pushed by the passengers. The message is that managers lead people who share the same objectives. This is seen as a useful device for employees coming from more bureaucratic organizations into Company *C*'s open and fast moving, flexible organizational style. People are expected to give more than was expected by their job description in their former companies.

Leadership is something which is sought in everyone. Outside everyone's core job there are a number of changing projects requiring innovative and proactive people. Anyone could manage a project, and could lead a small team of people with no formal reporting line. Managers, as leaders, are expected to communicate well, be interactive with employees, get people to participate, delegate, share ideas and objectives. The leader counsels rather than gives direct advice, and passes down credit to employees when it is due.

Leadership is identified through methods which include psychometric testing and interviews in the recruitment process.

Discussion. Look at these three different companies and identify what is meant by 'leadership'. Why are there differences? Is there any relationship between 'leadership' and entrepreneurship as you understand it, in any of these examples?

Theories of leadership

McCormack and Ilgen (1985) outline three different points of view of leadership as:

- *Positional*: related to the job and position that a person is in, to exercise the power and authority which comes with the job. Little or no credit is given to the individual in his or her own right. This aspect of leadership is hardly distinguishable from that of 'management', and in organizations which exhibit a strong 'role' culture (see Chapter 5) there may be little scope for the following view of leadership.

- *Personal*: where it is the personal attribute of the individual which enables him or her to be a leader. This has given rise to research on abilities and other personal variables to distinguish between effective and ineffective leaders. This view of leadership may be prevalent in all organizations which do not impose strong bureaucratic constraints, such as in a 'power' or 'task' culture (see Chapter 5).

- *Processional*: this focuses on the process of leadership and about what people have to do in order to influence others and achieve group goals. This process is obviously influenced by both person and the job he or she has (e.g. Katz and Kahn, 1978). The position of Katz and Kahn in this work is that the degree of influence of a 'leader' exceeds that of simply applying standard operating procedures, and therefore may be applicable in all types of organizational cultures.

Related to these three basic concepts of leadership are three major theories of leadership outlined by McCormick and Ilgen (1985): trait theory (relating to the person); behaviour theory (relating to processional approaches) and situational–moderation theories (looking at contextual influences on leadership styles and effectiveness). We can view these theories in terms of a continuum from aspects of leadership which are essentially inherited and cannot be changed, to those aspects which can most easily be changed, going from trait theories to situational theories as illustrated in Table 6.1.

Trait theory was popular before the mid-1950s, but much research led to dead-ends! It was found difficult to correlate particular attributes and characteristics directly with leadership success. For example, although leaders tended to be strong on intelligence, social skills and task skills, the number of non-leaders possessing these traits was large (e.g. Gibb, 1954). Interest has been rekindled of late with such studies as Ghisselli (1971) and Campbell *et al.* (1970) showing that through a consideration of specific management positions, traits can be identified which relate to leadership success in the particular position. This is currently the basis of psychometric testing procedures for selection purposes.

Table 6.1 *Continuum of leadership theories*

Cannot be changed		*Most easily changed*
Trait	*Behaviour*	*Situational*
Natural leaders are born with the required personality traits	Leadership behaviour not easily modified.	Leadership styles may be the easiest aspect to adapt to specific situation
	Needs changes of attitudes as well as development of appropriate skills	May be necessary to have a good understanding of the organizational culture
	Behaviour may be cultural dependent	

Kotter (1990) for example, argues that the following four attributes are found singularly in many managers, but only all four are found in leaders:

• intelligence/intellectual skills; needed for the agenda setting process (see above);
• drive/energy: needed to push self and others forward;
• mental health/emotional stability: for effective interactions with others;
• integrity: to forge alignment with followers who are looking for honesty and can believe in the leader.

Much interest shifted towards behaviour theories and away from trait theories in an attempt to see how leaders are able to influence the group. Much of the research led to the identification of two major groupings of leadership behaviour, one of which is staff-centred, the other production-centred. Research undertaken initially at the University of Michigan has led to studies which show that one group of behaviours are better than the other (for example the Human Relations School which favours a staff-centred approach: see Morse and Reimer, 1956) and developed into complete leadership 'systems'. The latter, in particular is the 'managerial grid' of Blake and Mouton (1985 for the third version). Variations of this have been developed over the years (for example Tannenbaum and Schmitt, 1973). We later look at this as 'orientations' of leadership representing objectives and intentions.

The contingency model (Fiedler, 1967) was developed, perhaps, as a response to the need to incorporate the contextual arrangements of an organization in a relationship with individual styles of behaviour. From behavioural studies it became apparent that no specific behaviours were best for all situations: leadership is situationally dependent!

Fiedler's (1967) schematic of leadership behaviour incorporates the task-oriented/person-oriented dichotomy of past work, but concludes that behaviour pertaining to these two styles is appropriate depending on the situation. The situation is defined in terms of favourableness to the leader where:

- the leader has greatest influence over the workgroup (leader–member relationship);
- a more structured task favours the leader situation (degree of task structure);
- The more reward/punishment the leader has command of the more influence he or she will have (formal power position).

The degree of likely success of leaders employing one of the two leadership styles can be analysed using these situational factors above. For example, where there is a high degree of formal power (high power distance cultures in Hofstede's (1991) view), a task-oriented or authoritarian style will be more successful. In situations which are neither favourable nor unfavourable to the leader, a more democratic or people-oriented style will be more successful. Where the leader is presented with a situation which is unfavourable on all of the above three counts, then a more authoritarian style will be more successful. The approach of Hersey and Blanchard (1977), which has been commonly applied in practical management training situations, is one of the best known 'situational' approaches.

Personal style and leadership

There is no doubt that the concept of 'leadership' refers to the qualities or attributes of a person, although we can say that leadership is situationally dependent, that is, that one style of leadership may be applicable in one culture and not in another. However, not everyone will become a recognized leader, and provide leadership for an organization. A leader can make use of situational factors (can even create situational factors) in order to influence, to wield power, to change behaviour and the organization in pursuit of particular goals. There is also no doubt that we are talking about something different to 'management'. A manager simply looks after something!

The definition of 'manage' in the Collins English Dictionary, for example, is 'to be in charge, administer', whereas to 'lead' means to 'show the way, to by going with or ahead'. A 'manager' is defined as 'a person who directs or manages an organization', and a 'leader' as 'a person who rules, guides, or inspires others' (The Collins English Dictionary, 1986). The immediate translations of these terms to French, for example, are a bit confusing. Barsoux and Lawrence (1990) talk about 'cadre' for manager: a term drawn from the military, and reflecting a view of management not too far removed from the term's origins. This, however, is applied to the class of industrial and commercial leaders who have led France into the level of prosperity it enjoys today (Barsoux and Lawrence, 1990). However, leader and manager can both be directly translated to 'chef', to mean in charge of (see the Collins Robert French Dictionary, 1987). The current usage of the terms 'decideur' and 'gestionnaire' (corresponding to leader and manager) may be a result of the American/UK debate being taken up in France.

This withstanding, it is self-apparent that in any society leaders emerge. Their personal strategies in each case might be quite different, and their bases of power might be different from one culture to another to reflect the type of cultural variation described by Hofstede (1991) for example. A useful guide to different leadership styles in different organizational 'systems' is provided by Likert (1967).

Activity 6.1 What are your leadership styles?

The following questionnaire is adapted from the work of Likert (1967). You will need to focus on a specific organization with which you are familiar. Against each item, place a tick [✓] on the scale which seems the most appropriate for the organization. Place a zero [0] on the scale which most represents the situation you would prefer to work under.

1 To what extent do superiors have confidence and trust in subordinates?

No confidence or trust	Have a condescending trust, like master–servant relation	Substantial but not a complete trust	Complete confidence and trust

2 To what extent do subordinates have trust and confidence in their superiors?

No confidence or trust	Have a subservient confidence and trust	Substantial but not a complete trust	Complete confidence and trust

3 To what extent do superiors show supportive behaviour to others?

Little or no supportive behaviour	A supportive yet condescending manner	Shows supportive behaviour quite generally	A complete supportive manner in all situations

4 Do subordinates feel free to discuss important things about their jobs with their immediate superior?

Do not feel free at all to discuss things with superior	Do not feel very free to discuss things with superior	They feel rather free to discuss things with superior	They feel completely free to discuss with superior

5 Do superiors try to get subordinates' ideas and opinions in problem solving and decision making, making constructive use of them?

Seldom get subordinates' ideas	Sometimes get ideas from subordinates	Usually, and try to make constructive use of them	Always, and always, try to make constructive use of the ideas

To analyse your responses you should use the following template.

Likert's management systems

Exploitive authoritative	Benevolent authoritative	Consultative	Participative group

Under what 'management system' does your organization lie? Where would you prefer it to lie?

The questions asked above provide a good description of each of these 'management systems'. They correspond to the items in Likert's (1967) questionnaire which refer only to the organizational variable he labels 'leadership process used'. There are other items which refer to other variables such as motivational forces, communications processes and decision making.

It is likely that we would find 'exploitative authoritarian' organizations in high power distance cultures, and 'participative group' organizations in low power distance cultures (see Hofstede, 1991). Likert (1967) seems to make both a value judgement that participative group is better, and produces some (American) evidence to support the effectiveness of such organizations against more authoritarian organizations.

The point we are making here, is that these 'systems' support and nurture particular leadership styles. A leader who brings in subordinates, tries to influence them rather than coerce them is more likely to be more effective in a 'participative group' organization, but ineffective in an 'exploitative authoritarian' organization where a leader would be expected to coerce and punish, and possibly would not gain respect if he or she used a more participative approach.

We should perhaps be careful in favouring any particular personal style of 'leadership' above others as this might not be appropriate in every situation. The ability to influence, for example may imply different things depending on the type of management system in operation. Let us now try to summarize the interconnection between personal attributes and context factors, before we proceed to look specifically at personal factors in leadership, by using the 3Cs model (first introduced in Chapter 1).

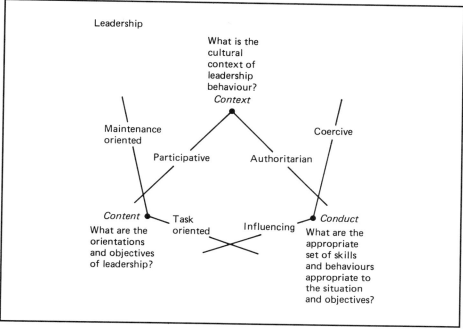

Figure 6.2 *The 3Cs of Leadership*

There is much overlap between these various aspects of leadership which we can describe as follows. Context can be defined on a continuum ranging from authoritarian to participative. Content can be defined on a continuum between maintenance oriented and task oriented. Conduct can be defined on a continuum between influencing behaviour and coercive behaviour.

We may deduce that there may be some overlapping as follows: authoritarian with coercive, maintenance with participative, task with influencing. This is clearly seen in Figure 6.2. However, this may not be guaranteed. There may also be overlapping of influencing with maintenance orientation, and coercive with task orientation (perhaps this is a function of the limitations of the diagram in Figure 6.2 rather than in the model itself). When we look at leadership in any organization, in any culture, we can gain an impression of leadership by focusing on these three dimensions.

Cross-cultural problems in applying concepts of leadership

We can now look more specifically at some of the cross-cultural problems of applying concepts of leadership by focusing in turn on each of the 3cs: context, content and conduct.

Context

We have already said that the authoritarian–participative dimension corresponds closely with Hofstede's concept of power distance, where authoritarian styles of

Power distance		
Small	**Medium**	**Large**
e.g. Denmark Norway Sweden	e.g. USA Netherlands	e.g. France Belgium Portugal
Subordinates Have weak dependency needs Expect to be consulted	Medium dependency need Expect to be consulted but will accept autocratic behaviour	Strong dependency need Expect superiors to act autocratically
Superior is: A loyal democrat	Mostly a resourceful democrat	Mostly a benevolent autocrat
Privileges for superiors: Are not acceptable	Accepted to a degree	Are expected

Figure 6.3 *Characteristics of subordinateship according to power distance (adapted from Hofstede, 1980)*

leadership are more applicable in large power distance cultures. Likert (1967) favours a participative style of leadership, as does McGregor (Theory Y as opposed to Theory X). Both write from the United States, a medium power distance culture. Hofstede (1980) tells us that participation in this sense is assumed to be a management initiative rather than a subordinate initiative. While we could expect a more 'Machiavellian' theory of leadership to arise in a larger power distance culture (for example France where there is little concern for participative management) in countries which have a smaller power distance to the United States (principally the Scandinavian countries, Israel and Germany) there is a great deal of sympathy for participative models where the subordinates take the initiative. These are models which do not gain a great deal of currency in the United States.

Hofstede (1980) further reminds us that leaders cannot choose their leadership style at will, and this is greatly dependent on the nature of subordinates or followers upon which leaders depend. We can illustrate this by Figure 6.3.

We are told by Hofstede (1980) that managers have little difficulty adapting from a smaller to a larger power distance culture where they simply take a more autocratic position. The difficulty is in adapting from a large to a small power distance culture. He reports cases of US managers having difficulty adapting to the 'industrial democracy' of Sweden, Germany and even the Netherlands (with only a slightly smaller power distance on Hofstede's scale), still maintaining the 'managers prerogative' which simply may not be accepted in low power distance countries.

Content

We identified earlier a common theme running through much leadership theory which represents a distinction between staff or maintenance orientations and task or performance orientations. Although there is a great deal of overlap with the context dimension just explored, we argue that this aspect is theoretically independent of the participative–authoritarian dimensions. That is, it is purely logical to assume that we can have a participative organizational system with a task orientation or a maintenance orientation. The same would apply for an authoritarian organizational system.

We therefore view 'orientation' as containing intentions and objectives. That is, it is the objective of a leader to get tasks done, to focus on performance of staff. Or, it is the intention of the leader to ensure that social relations are built up in an organization to allow for the effectiveness of the organization. This may be a conscious or unconscious choice, may be determined by the nature of the organizational system (participative–authoritarian) and/or the propensities of the leader. That is, it may be a matter of the leader interpreting the culture of the organization. This is interpreted through the specific actions of the leader, and the success of such a strategy will depend on the leader's skills. Smith *et al.*, (1989) looked to see if leadership 'styles' of this nature could be generalized across cultures. They compared data from four countries:

	Maintenance	Performance
UK	Seen as more task-centred than the other countries. More consultative. Use equipment. Explain new tasks. Consult widely about change. Hope for suggestions about work improvements and respond positively to them	Show disapproval of late-comers and evaluate the work of the group as a whole
USA	Showing consultative and participative behaviour, but not task-centred behaviour as in UK. Do not show disapproval of late-comers, do not send written memos, do not meet socially outside work, and not likely to talk about immediate work problems	Show core task behaviour, dress like subordinates. Are addressed formally by subordinates and do not meet them socially.
Hong Kong	Discuss subordinates' personal problems with others in their absence. Spend time socially with subordinates at work and after hours. Talk about work problems.	Exhibits all the behaviour aside, and discuss career and plans, have more frequent meetings with subordinates, and encourages communication with work groups.
Japan	Speaking to others about a subordinate's problems in their absence rather than face to face. Teach new job skills. Talk about work problems, sending written notes	Meeting socially after hours. Arranging help with workload of employee with difficulty, check work quality. Also, teach new job skills and discussing difficulties in subordinates absence (as aside).

Figure 6.4 *Different national characteristics of Maintenance and Performance leadership orientations (See Smith et al, 1989)*

United Kingdom, Hong Kong, USA and Japan. They found that what was seen as 'maintenance' behaviour and 'performance' behaviour actually differed from one country to another. We can summarize their findings as in Figure 6.4.

It is therefore the Americans who make a more clear distinction between maintenance and performance leadership behaviour than the British, Japanese or the Chinese. In the British data, consideration for maintenance can be expressed by talking about the task. In the Chinese data, maintenance behaviour is shown by tactfully resolving personal difficulties in an indirect manner, and performance behaviour is shown by encouraging co-operation.

The distinctions between western and eastern influences are also apparent. In the USA and UK, behaviour which exerts pressure on subordinates is more closely linked with performance orientation than in the Japanese and Hong Kong data. Also planning and goal facilitation are linked with a performance orientation in the eastern countries. Smith *et al.* (1989) align this with Hofstede's dimension of collectivism versus individualism, where in individualist cultures leaders are expected to exert direct pressure towards a goal, and in collectivist cultures leadership may emphasize reciprocal influence processes.

What this study shows, is a distinction between these two orientations on leadership style in the four countries, but the type of behaviour exhibited is different from culture to culture, and the degree of distinction varies from East to West.

Conduct

The behaviours we have distinguished in the model in Figure 6.2 are influencing versus coercive. It could be assumed that the latter would be more prevalent in a large power distance culture, and the former in a small power distance culture. We might also conclude that what constitutes coercive behaviour or influencing behaviour may be different in different cultures. The organizational 'currencies' of influencing behaviour discussed in Chapter 5 are a case in point, where those things which are seen as desirable 'resources' in one culture may be different from that in another. At this point in time we do not have access to specific research data which can verify these assumptions.

Conclusion: becoming an international leader

We have discussed the ethnocentrism of American theories of leadership, and we have discussed the appropriateness of different styles and orientations of leaderships in different cultures. We have said that there may be a difference between a 'manager' and a 'leader', but the positional versus the personal nature of leadership may vary from culture to culture. We have looked at the various cultural differences by referring again to our descriptive model of context–content–conduct, contrasting the context dimension of participative–authoritarian, the content dimension of maintenance–task oriented styles of leadership, and the conduct dimension of coercive–influencing behaviour.

But, what about leading an international team, with many cultures? How do we lead trans-culturally, in order to take account of a combination of needs and assumptions of different nationalities and different cultures? We look at some of these aspects in other parts of this text. For now, a few basic points may suffice.

1 Know yourself and your culture well. You should have a good idea of your strengths and development needs, your preconceptions. It is also helpful if you know how other people see you, particularly the team within which you are working, and how other people see your culture.

2 Know your personal goals. You should have a clear idea of what your personal goals are in the team situation and what you want to get out of it. You can share these thoughts with others as a way of gaining insight into their personal goals. If you can do this successfully this will engender trust and open relations, but go easy on this. Not everyone will react the same, and there will certainly be cultural differences.

3 Make the team objectives specific and clear. Your biggest problem may be that team members from high uncertainty avoidance cultures may require a great deal of certainty in what to expect. Provide this certainty. It does not matter that other team members can cope with higher levers of ambiguity. Being more certain will not harm relations in this respect.

4 Gain consensus on group roles. Members from high power distance cultures may require strong leadership from you, whilst others may find this offensive, and may be looking for a looser more participative approach. Discuss the difficulties at the beginning and ask what team members think. This may give rise to a certain ambiguity which may give problems with high uncertainty avoidance members. Be firm in stating objectives for the group and specifying a timetable for deliberation of group process. The group process is important. You must address this before going on to the task.

5 Use all the resources of the team. There may be big differences between group members, between nationalities, between professions, between men and women. Use the intuitive approaches, the rational approaches, the diverse cultural experiences, the different expectations in achieving the group objectives. Discuss the process itself from time to time, and be aware of any problems which individuals are experiencing. Talk to them privately, or raise points in open session. Use your judgement on this.

References

Barsoux, J.-P. and Lawrence, P. (1990) *Management in France*, London: Cassell.

Bennis, W. (1991) 'The four competences of leadership', in Kolb D. A., Rubin, I. M., and Osland, J. S. (eds), *The Organizational Behaviour Reader* (5th edn.) Englewood Cliffs, New Jersey: Prentice-Hall.

Blake R. R. and Mouton, J. S. (1985) *The Managerial Grid III*, Houston: Gulf.

Bowditch, J. L. and Buono, A. F. (1990) *A Primer On Organizational Behaviour*, New York: John Wiley.

Burns, J. M. (1978) *Leadership*, New York: Harper and Row.

Campbell, J. P. (1970) *Managerial Behaviour, Performance and Effectiveness*, New York: McGraw-Hill.

Fiedler, F. (1967) *A Theory of Leadership Effectiveness*, New York: McGraw-Hill.

Ghiselli, E. E. (1971) *Explorations in Managerial Talent*, California: Goodyear.

Gibb, C. A. (1954) 'Leadership' in Lindzey, G. (ed.) *Handbook of Social Psychology*, Reading, Massachusets: Addison-Wesley.

Hersey, P. and Blanchard, K. (1977) *Organizational Behaviour: Utilizing Human Resources*, Englewood Cliffs, New Jersey: Prentice-Hall.

Hofstede, G. (1980) 'Motivation, leadership and organization: Do American Theories Apply Abroad?' *Organizational Dynamics*, Summer, pp. 42–63.

Hofstede, G. (1991) *Cultures and Organizations: Software of the Mind*, London: McGraw-Hill.

Jacobs, R. (1989) 'Getting the measure of management competence', *Personnel Management*, June.

Kakabadse, A., Ludlow, R. and Vinnicombe, S. (1987) *Working in Organizations*, Harmondsworth: Penguin.

Katz, D. and Kahn, R. L. (1978) *The Social Psychology of Organizations*, New York: John Wiley.

Kotter, J. (1982) 'What effective general managers really do', *Harvard Business Review*, 60, 6, pp. 156–67.

Kotter, J. (1990) *A Force For Change*, New York: Macmillan.

Likert, R., (1967) *The Human Organization*, Tokyo: McGraw-Hill Kogakusha.

McCormick, E. J. and Ilgen, D. (1985) *Industrial and Organizational Psychology*, London: Allen and Unwin.

Mainguy, W. (1988) 'Leadership qualities: Europe's CEOs are surveyed by Management Centre Europe', *European Management Journal*, 6, 3.

Morse, N. C. and Reimer, E. (1956) 'The experimental change of a major organizational variable', *Journal of Abnormal and Social Psychology*, 52, pp. 120–9.

Smith, P. B., Misumi, J., Tayeb, M., Peterson, M. and Bond, M. (1989) 'On the generality of leadership style measures across cultures', *Journal of Occupational Psychology*, 62, pp. 97–109.

Tannenbaum, R. and Schmitt, W. H. (1973) 'How to choose a leadership pattern', *Harvard Business Review*, May/June 1973.

Tichy, N. M. and Devanna, M. A., (1986) *The Transformational Leader*, New York: Wiley.

Section 3
Organizational Theory and Process

This section focuses on organizational issues. Firstly we look at structural aspects and how we might understand and analyse the organization within which we work. Secondly, we look at organizational culture.

International organizations are often complex, and cannot be understood in simple structural terms. Although we look specifically at international structures, we also look at different perceptions of organizational issues from a cultural point of view.

For the international manager working in different organizations in Europe and across the globe, an understanding of how to analyse complex structures and organizational processes is essential.

7

Organizational structure and the international environment: systems and actions

---

Objectives

Following this chapter you should be able to:

1. Distinguish the main theories of organizations.
2. Analyse an organization as a system, and as social action.
3. Explain the main international pressures on organizations to change and become more adaptive, and what their implications are.
4. Describe the major structural approaches to organizing internationally.

Key concepts

- Multinational, Global, International, and Transnational Organizations.
- Systems Theory, and structuralism.
- Action Theory, and phenomenology.
- 7-Ss approach to organizational analysis.

Introduction

The purpose of this chapter is to explore concepts of organizations within an international business environment. In order to do this we refer firstly to the three factor model of context–content–conduct which we introduced in Chapter 1 to distinguish two concepts of organizations: a 'system's approach and an 'action' approach. These two approaches can be seen in terms of two 'schools of thought':

- structural functionalism (context)
- phenomenology (content).

Both seek to explain behaviour within organizations (our third factor of conduct: see Figure 7.1).

Following this theoretical approach to the way organizations may be conceptualized, we turn our attention to the more traditional focus of organizational analysis by looking at the structures or forms of organizations. In so doing we introduce a framework for classifying organizations operating across nations. Bartlett and Ghoshal (1989) use this framework to cut across most of the confusion in describing cross-border organizations. They distinguish:

- multinational organizations;
- global organizations;
- international organizations;
- transnational organizations.

By reference to this model of cross-border organizing we can also gain considerable insight into the environmental influences pressing hard on organizations, and how their consequent structures may influence behaviour within them.

Organizational theory

If we use the 3Cs descriptive model introduced in Chapter 1, we can think about what goes on within organizations as in Figure 7.1 with their associated theoretical origins.

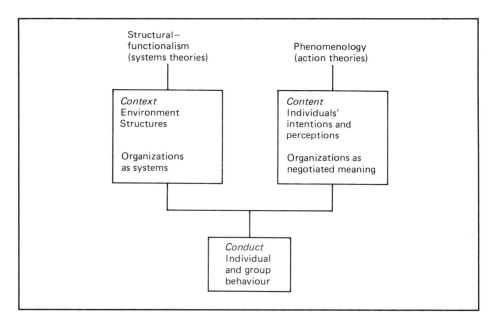

Figure 7.1 *The 3Cs of organizations*

These theories on the whole approach their subject matter from different perspectives, but there is some overlap. The two schools of thought which this framework brings together are structuralism (context) and phenomenology (content). Within the context of these two schools of thought other, connected, theories are discussed. By using this basic descriptive framework, we try to provide an overall synthesis. We can regard organizations above all else as a 'process' of communication, and that organizations function well or badly depending on the effectiveness of communication within them, and with others outside them. First, let us look at these two broad theories and then we can discuss how they may be drawn together in a common methodology.

Organizations as systems

'Structuralism' is used very broadly to represent the various, mainly sociological, theories which emphasize the pre-eminent influence of social structure on human actions. They assume that human beings are not free agents but act according to the norms and rules laid down within the society and within the social organizations in which people live and work. Structural Functionalism within early British and American sociology and social anthropology (for example, Parsons, 1949 and Radcliffe-Brown, 1952), and Systems and Open Systems approaches in social psychology (for example, Katz and Kahn, 1978) represent a major theme within the structuralist framework.

Here goals, and the means of obtaining these goals are socially defined by a society, or social organization, which operates 'functionally' to maintain itself and to achieve certain goals. Just like a human organism, its component parts (organs) function to maintain the whole and achieve its ends. Open systems theory recognizes the problem of regarding a social structure as a discrete entity like a human organism. A commercial organization, for example, contains many influences from the external environment by the involvement of its members in other, outside, organizations and social groups, from relations with clients, customers, and suppliers.

The point of this theory is that people's objectives and actions are structurally driven, rather than structure being people driven. People's actions are defined by the roles they are given within the social structure, despite there being some room to interpret these roles by the individuals occupying them.

This approach is well described by Rogers and Agarwala-Rogers. An organization is seen as

> An open system in continuous interaction with its environment; the system and its environment co-determine each other. The system must be analysed as a whole in order to be understood properly. The organization is composed of sub-systems which are interdependent; individuals are the carriers of the organization (Rogers and Agarwala-Rogers, 1976, p. 30).

Functionalism

Modern Systems Theory is derived from such 'functionalist' theories as Merton (1949) which stresses a theory of actions which may be 'functional' and thus support the system, or 'dysfunctional' and therefore are destructive towards the system. Functions can also be 'manifest' or obvious functional actions, or 'latent': actions which have unintentional or unobvious functional tendencies. In other words, individuals' actions are defined in terms of the needs (or goals) of the social system, rather than the other way around. Parsons (1949, 1951) is also a leading figure in functionalist theory and attempts a synthesis of the major elements within this general area. He explores the functioning of interlocking systems and subsystems which are bound by a 'central value system', or a shared orientation towards action. By developing stable expectations about individuals and role behaviour, the system can persist despite changes in its individual membership.

Parsons therefore defines an organization as 'a social system organized for the attainment of a particular type of goal' (Parsons, 1964, p. 56). This goal is at the heart of the 'central value system' which the organizational analyst has to discover before ascribing functions to particular parts of the organization. However, the value system of a society is reflected in the goals of the organizations which operate within it.

Open systems

This wider social aspect, which emphasizes an open system approach is developed by Katz and Kahn (1978). The main basis of this theory is that organizations rely on input from outside the organization. This is then translated into through-puts, and lastly outputs back into the wider environment. Organizations therefore survive on feedback from the external environment. They are very much a product of the national or international society within which they function. Inputs or feedback in the organization can be from consumer behaviour. For example the strong environmental lobby of the 'green' movement has influenced the business goals (at least the publicly proclaimed ones) of many organizations. The UK company Body Shop, for example, is very much a product of the environmental lobby of the 1980s. But the way national cultural values influence corporate goals can be more fundamental and ongoing than the example of the green issue, and we will look at some of these influences later in this chapter.

The emphasis of open systems theory on the limit of the system not being bound within the confines of the organization itself, raises the problem of how we draw boundary lines round the system. Where does the external environment start and end, if it ends at all? Even a national company which, say, does not trade outside its national boundaries may be affected by world events generally. Is there any bound to the system of an international organization? The organization's internal boundary is also difficult to determine. Can a business organization include its customers within its boundary or not? Perhaps this would be relevant for some business organizations and not for others.

Components of the open systems model

Kolb *et al.* (1991) describe the open systems model as shown in Figure 7.2. They describe the separate components of the system by points 1 to 8.

1. *System*: a set of units or components which are actively interrelated and operate in a uniform way as a total entity. This focuses on the processes of interdependences of components rather than on constant attributes. Open systems theory suggests that

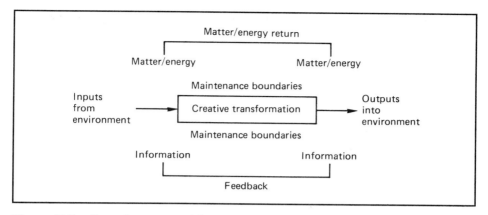

Figure 7.2 *Open Systems model: process (adapted from Kolb et al. 1991)*

there is no such thing as a completely closed system with rigid boundaries that are not penetrated by energy and information from the outside. Some systems, however, are more open than others, interacting more freely with their environment.

2. *Inputs*: matter/energy into the system from the environment comprising raw materials, human resources, power; and information into the system in the form of data and knowledge about the environment or about production techniques and product development. All organizations have input subsystems such as marketing information, personnel, and research and development departments.

3. *Creative transformations*: the transformation of energy through processes in the system to transform inputs into outputs. Thus, people are trained, products are manufactured, information is analysed. This often leads to a high degree of differentiation and specialization of services within the system requiring co-ordination and integration within the system to hold everything together.

4. *Outputs*: products, knowledge, or services which are put into the environment and are useful for the survival of the system or comprises its waste. Organizations often have specialized subsystems to deal with such outputs, for example a sales department or environmental pollution inspectorate.

5. *Maintenance boundaries*: defined (physically or psychologically) to control the input/output process and to delineate the system's identity. Boundaries might comprise a fence or wall around a factory or a prison. They might comprise a bookkeeping system for controlling inputs and outputs of money into and out of the system. They may constitute norms for behaviour of members, or membership cards to denote identity of members within a system.

6. *Matter/energy returns*: essential for the survival of a system which must take in energy and matter from the environment in a higher state of complexity or entropy than it outputs back into the environment. It requires energy for the transformation process, to repair and maintain itself, and to ensure its ongoing survival through its outputs. So, organizations take in raw data, and transform it into a less complex state of useful information. It takes in untrained people, and trains them to perform a particular set of tasks. It takes in raw materials, and transforms this into a recognizable and saleable product.

7. *Feedback*: required to keep a system on course. This is particularly through negative feedback which can alert an organization taking a wrong course, for example, in its marketing strategy. Systems cannot survive without negative feedback, and the means to deal with and react to it.

8. *The environment*: the suprasystem of which the system (in this case an organization) is a part. Thus an organization is part of the wider national society, and even the European or World community. Other systems within the suprasystem interrelate with it.

Properties of open systems

In addition to these aspects of an 'open system' there are certain properties of such systems, pointed out by Katz and Kahn (1978), of which we should be aware.

1. *Systems functions are cyclical.* Events occur in a repetitive cycle of inputs, throughputs, and outputs, occurring in sequence time and again. Systems are therefore dynamic, and function over time.

2. *Equilibrium seeking.* Systems move towards a situation where all components are in equilibrium. Where changes result in an imbalance, so different parts of the system move to restore the balance.

3. *Increasing differentiation.* As systems grow, so their level of complexity and differentiation of functions increases. More components, more feedback loops and more transformation processes are added.

4. *Equifinality.* Different configurations of the system and different combinations of processes may lead to the same end state.

5. *Systems survival requirements.* Systems have a tendency to dissipate their energy and to run down over time. In order to prevent this, certain functions can be performed. In an organization this may include goal setting and adaptation to the environment.

The interdependence of parts

The model described above focuses on the characteristic of a system of interdependence of the parts, and how this relates to the functioning of the system as a whole. Nadler and Tushman (1991) for example describe this as 'fit' between the various organizational components. If the different parts of an organization fit well together the system will function effectively. If there is poor fit, there will be problems.

Simplistically, these components of an organization could be thought of as people, tasks, technology and structure (Leavitt, 1965). Nadler and Tushman (1991) see these components as factors within the input–transformation–output process as Figure 7.3 illustrates.

Inputs	Examples:
Environment of the system	Markets, Competitors
Resources available to the system	Capital, Raw material
Organizational strategies developed over time	Organization mission, Long-term plans

↓

Transformational processes	
The organization's tasks	Task dimensions: e.g. complexity, predictability
The individuals in the organization	Intelligence, skills, training, attitudes
The organizational arrangements	Grouping of tasks, goals, plans, reward sys-
The informal organization	tems, hierarchy

↓

Outputs	
Individual behaviour	Absenteeism, turnover, task performance
Group behaviour	Intergroup conflict and collaboration
Systems functioning,	achieve its goals
	utilize its resources
	successfully adapt over time

Figure 7.3 *Open systems model: components (adapted from Nadler and Tushman, 1991)*

The question of fit between the components shown in Figure 7.3 is most pertinently asked in connection with the transformational processes variables as follows.

What is the 'fit' between:

1. *Individual–organization.* Are individuals' needs met by the organizational arrangements? Do members hold clear perceptions of organizational structure? Do individuals' and organizational goals converge?

2. *Individual–task.* Are individuals' needs met by the nature of the tasks they undertake? Do the skills and abilities of individuals meet the requirements of the tasks?

3. *Individual–informal organization.* Are individuals' needs met by the informal organization, and does the informal organization make best use of individual resources in compliance with informal goals?

4. *Task–organization.* Are the organizational arrangements adequate to meet the demands of the tasks? Do the organizational arrangements motivate behaviour sufficiently to accomplish tasks?

5. *Task-informal organization.* Does the informal organization facilitate task performance? Are the demands of the task met by the informal organization?

6. *Organization-informal organization.* Are the goals, rewards, and structures of the informal organization consistent with the goals and needs of the formal organization?

The 'informal organization' is described by Hodge and Anthony (1988) as:

informal or de facto relationships that are not necessarily sanctioned by the organization, although they might be perceived to actually exist and are thus considered by some to be the real structure. These include informal work groupings of employees, informal leaders, informal channels of communication and informal power and status differentials.

In the following Activity we pick up on some of the points made so far.

Activity 7.1 Diagnosing organizations as systems

You should focus on an organization with which you are familiar, or research an organization which is new to you.

1. You should first identify the system:

   - What is the unit of analysis?
   - What are its boundaries? How are these defined?
   - What is its membership?
   - What other systems does it interact within the suprasystem?

2. What are key variables in the Input–Transformation–Output process? You should refer to Figure 7.3. You do not have to undertake a detailed description of each, but to identify those aspects of the process which are most important to the system itself and to the outcomes of the system.

3. What are the states of 'fit' between the key variables within the transformational process, and what are their relationships with outputs? You should look for problems, and areas in which poor fit is affecting outputs.

4. What are the critical systems problems? This stems from your analysis of 'fits'. You must determine which behaviours are adversely affecting outputs in terms of goal achievement, resource utilization and adaptation to the environment. You can then make a judgement on what requires attention.

The 7-Ss approach

Another approach to looking at the interconnectedness of organizational or systems components is the 7-Ss framework originally developed by Anthony G. Athos (see Pascale and Athos, 1981; Waterman *et al.* 1980). This model is now well known through the analysis of the Japanese consumer electric giant, Matsushita by Pascale and Athos (1981). The argument (and perhaps the point of departure from established systems models) is that western organizations tend only to pay attention to some of the components of the system (typically the so-called 'hard' aspects) ignoring others which Japanese organizations have tended to concentrate on (the 'soft' aspects of organizations). By using the 7-S framework, we can explore the interconnectedness of all relevant organizational components. These are represented in Figure 7.4.

> **'Hard' aspects of the organization**
> *Strategy*
> Plan of action which uses company's resources to achieve particular goals
>
> *Structure*
> The division of tasks and how they are coordinated, usually revealed in the organization chart.
>
> *Systems*
> Procedures which make the organization work
>
> **'Soft' aspects of the organization**
> *Staff*
> The different personnel categories: their reward, career and development systems; their motivations, attitudes and behaviour
>
> *Style*
> The cultural style of the organization and how key managers behave in order to achieve the goals of the organization
>
> *Skills*
> What the organization and individuals do best: their capabilities
>
> *Superordinate goals*
> The organization's guiding concepts, values and aspirations, going beyond formally stated objectives, which an organization tries to imbue in its members.

Figure 7.4   *The 7-S framework*

While it is true that many western organizations are beginning to concentrate on these softer aspects of management, and much has been written on them in recent years, a consideration of 'superordinate goals' is one aspect which Western organizations have tended to largely ignore. Look at the following case.

Mini Case 7.1 The Matsushita of Pascale and Athos

Pascale and Athos tell us that Konosuke Matsushita started off as an apprentice in a cycle shop in 1918, then founding his business in the consumer electrics business to become one of the fifty largest corporations in the world. He based his initial strategy on developing his own distribution system, dealing directly with retailers. This was in direct contrast with Japanese practices. Matsushita has been built on developing market share and passing on the cost savings from high volume production to consumers in lower prices. The company does not introduce new products but improves on the quality and price structure of imitations of original products. Extensive R&D is invested in to this purpose. Its assumptions are that profits are tied to growth, and that long-term investment in growth will eventually pay off in profits.

Matsushita introduced decentralization into his domestic organization to retain its entrepreneurial characteristic. With each product, independent progress could be clearly measured, managers would be self-sufficient and close to consumers, small divisions would be flexible, and divisional management would gain the required training for general management positions. Together with this decentralization, the founder sought to alleviate the problems which this brought: decreasing control, low interdivisional co-operation, and reduced strength to cope with threats to a whole product group. He did this by centralizing accounting, by introducing a central 'bank' for divisional profits, and by centralizing the personnel and training functions.

The entrepreneurial spirit which was nurtured within the organization was also tempered by a rigorous planning system which comprised five-year, two-year, and six-months plans. The latter were very detailed operating plans and reviewed on a monthly basis. Performance was measured on the basis of attaining objectives set out in the six-months plans, and rewards given accordingly. Aberrations and failures to achieve objectives had to be explained.

The publicly expressed management style was in 'developing extraordinary qualities in ordinary men'. Top management took a 'hands on' approach with Matsushita talking with his divisional heads every day, and spending time on the shop floor. Local managers were expected to take initiatives and solve problems where they occurred. The prevailing management style was tough-minded and pragmatic, encouraging competition and conflict. Disagreements were solved on an impersonal basis with facts provided and 'acceptance time' built into the process of conflict resolution, to allow time to think about the problem in a different way.

As with many Japanese companies, emphasis was placed on training. Professional staff started in the company by six months of selling, and also spent time on the production line. Promotion was accompanied by training for the new job. Five per cent of employees were rotated to different divisions to encourage integration. There were lifelong employment policies to maintain shared values which were encouraged also through the training process. The company encouraged employee suggestions, with monetary rewards. The number of suggestions were also used as a measure of divisional morale.

The skills of Matsushita himself were revealed in terms of innovation, efficiency and managing people, and in his ability to put together and manage an organization which balanced and reinforced all aspects and components working together. His policy was to step back and to let others develop in this mould in order to continue with a dynamic and strong organization which would be capable of adaption to the environment and growth.

The main integrating force in all this is what has been termed superordinate goals or the shared values which are instilled largely through training, and which are stated as follows.

Business principles

1 Recognize responsibilities as industrialists
2 Foster progress
3 Promote the general welfare of society
4 Promote further development of world culture.

Employee creed

Progress and development can only be achieved by the combined effort and co-operation of everyone in the company. This should be kept continuously in mind in devoting efforts to the ongoing improvement of the company.

The seven spiritual values

1 National service through industry
2 Fairness
3 Harmony and co-operation
4 Struggle for betterment
5 Courtesy and humility
6 Adjustment and assimilation
7 Gratitude.

Discussion. Can you now analyse this mini case using the 7-S framework? What are the seven components, and how do they all fit together?

It is only the hard components of this model which have been emphasized in organizations in the west, whereas the soft components of this system are developed in harmony with the hard aspects in Japanese companies and this is reflected in the example in Mini case 7.1 above. The central component in this system are the 'superordinate goals' which give meaning to and pull everything together.

The message of systems theory

The message of systems theory is therefore an important one. It is that the various components of an organization should fit together into a cohesive whole. Each part should combine with other parts in an interrelationship which contributes to the maintenance of the whole. Each part is interdependent with other parts such that if one part suffers a breakdown, this would have a major effect on the other parts and to the whole. Not only do the interdependent parts contribute to the maintenance of the system, they also contribute to the attainment of the goals of the organizations. The more clearly communicated and understood are these goals, then the more responsive can be the organizational parts.

Open systems theory sees the organization as part of a suprasystem from which it takes energy and information and outputs energy and information according to the goals of the organization. Again, the parts of the whole contribute to the attainment of these goals by working together in a transformational process which converts inputs into outputs.

This view sees the system as primary, the society or the organization as influencing or directing effort. This is not the only way of looking at organizations, and we will now proceed to another view.

Organizations as meaning systems

Phenomenology is a term mainly drawn from social philosophy (for example Schutz, 1972), and has been developed as a sociological theory (for example Berger and Luckmann, 1966 and Cicourel, 1964). It also has its origins in psychological theory

(Goffman, 1959) and has developed as an approach to psychotherapy and psychology in client-centred approaches to therapy (Rogers, 1951), in 'attribution' theories (Kelley, 1967, 1973) and 'personal construct' theory (Kelly, 1955). A sociological consolidation of these theories is given by Silverman (1970) in his book *The Theory of Organizations* in what he calls the 'action' frame of reference. This perspective makes the following assumptions.

• Action is the subject of interest rather than behaviour.

• Action arises from meanings ('behaviour' in contrast can be meaningless).

• Meanings are our definitions of social reality.

• These arise from our interactions with society, become formalized and are handed down as social facts to succeeding generations.

• These social facts are also interpreted by the individual, but are reinforced by continual reaffirmation in everyday actions.

• Individuals in interaction modify, change, and transform these social meanings.

• Explanations of human action (for example management performance) must take account of these meanings which individuals assign to their actions.

The meaning of actions

A phenomenological approach is therefore concerned with the meanings of our actions (actions are behaviours which have meaning) or the interpretation of a social situation by the individuals concerned. It sees the social environment as a product of meaning negotiated between interacting individuals, and is therefore viewing organizations from the opposite direction to structuralism, or a systems approach.

The systems approach to analysing organizations is by far the most prominent in the literature. This, of course, sees the goals of the organization, and the wider society, as the main motivating and determining force of individual attitudes and behaviour within organizations. This view particularly stresses the effects which the organization and its environment have on the individual. Silverman (1970) criticizes systems theory because it 'reifies' organizations, that is, it makes them into objects in their own right, whereas an organization is no more than a conceptual construct. So, what about individuals and their perceptions of themselves, their goals, and their perceptions of the organizational roles they occupy?

Systems approaches have focused on motivation derived from organizational goals. 'Scientific management' approaches (for example, Taylor, 1911) on the other hand have emphasized the view of man as an economic creature pursuing economic gains, giving rise to a management emphasis on financial incentives and time and motion studies. Whilst this approach focused on the individual and his or her motivations, the naive concept of human motivation being derived purely from economic needs was clearly not adequate, and other psychological approaches have largely superseded this concept. The Human Relations School (see Brown, 1954), on the other hand, put forward a view of individual motivation being derived from membership of primary groups. The logical outcome of this theory was that management should work through the small groups in an organization, rather than through the individual in developing views of the situation related to goals of the organization.

The conflict of goals

Like the systems approach, this view focuses on the 'executive' goals rather than those of the individuals within the organization, and has stressed that these goals of management are those prevalent within the organization. It is not necessarily the case that goals and motivations of individuals within organizations coincide with the goals of the organization. Indeed, these may conflict. In systems theory this problem is considered only from the position of 'fit' between organizational goals and individual goals: that is, organizational goals are greater than the individual, whose goals are in some way subordinated to those of the 'organization' (an object seen as quite distinct from its members).

Individual motivation and organizations

It is the approach of many organizational psychologists (as Silverman, 1970, points out) to concentrate on the motivations of the individuals as distinct from organizational goals. Individuals are seen as having 'personality needs'. Maslow (1954) for example, sees these as physiological, safety and social needs, in that order, and finally the need to strive towards your full potential. These needs are seen as exerting direct influence upon behaviour. Thus by demonstrating the need or motive upon which it is based we explain behaviour. From this view, if there is a conflict between the needs of individuals and the goals of the organization, this can be resolved by changing the organizational structure, or to use the structure of the organization to encourage the development of stable work groups which can participate in the development of the organization.

So, the 'organizational psychologists' school (Silverman, 1970) represents a view which stresses motives and needs of individuals who work within organizations. However, different psychologists stress different motivating forces. These include seeing individuals as needing to interact with others in small groups (Brown, 1954), seeing individuals as working towards 'self-actualization' or the development of higher needs for personal achievement (Maslow, 1954), and seeing man as a complex animal with a variety of motivations varying according to the situation. Organizational psychology (according to Silverman, 1970) falls short of a comprehensive analysis of interaction between individuals in an organization because it does not seem to consider the effects of such factors as technology on behaviour and relationships in the organization.

Technology and organizations

The way technology is organized, the physical arrangement of plant, machinery and office equipment, and the nature of technology used, all affect behaviour and relationships between people in an organization. For example, the extensive use of computer technology can greatly hamper interpersonal communication within an organization, as can the use of more traditional manufacturing equipment which both creates noise and confines individuals to a particular process in a particular space. Much has been written, for example, about the dissatisfaction which production line working creates, leading to a workforce 'alienated' from the organization in which they work (for example, Blauner, 1964).

Marx's original idea of alienation went further than this, attributing its causes to the prevailing economic system (see for example, Bottomore and Rubel, 1961). The concept of alienation rather goes against systems theory, and also provides a theory which shows a relationship between economic and technological factors and attitudes and behaviour in organizations.

Action analysis

We can therefore see that individuals do not necessarily perceive the organization and its goals from the authorized, executive view. While a systems theorist may regard this simply as dysfunction within the system, Silverman (1970) uses this as the basis of an 'action analysis' which looks at organizational behaviour from the standpoint that action arises out of the meaning given to social reality by the interactors themselves. These meanings are given to individuals by the society in which they interact, but it is by interacting that social reality is created, and therefore 'while society defines man, man in turn defines society' (Silverman, 1970, p. 127). Organizations are therefore viewed as negotiated action. By interacting in the organization, meaning is negotiated and created. In its naïve form, this phenomonological approach largely ignores power relations in an organization, and the fact that individuals may be dismissed from the organization if they are not able to conclude satisfactory negotiation on the reality of the situation (in other words, if they do not fit in, they can be dismissed!).

From these assumptions discussed above, Silverman (1970) goes on to provide a procedure for analysing organizations by examining the following six interrelated areas in the following order.

1. The nature of the role system and patterns of interaction in the organization. This should be considered from a historical perspective in the way that this has been developed, and the extent to which it represents the shared values of the role holders.

2. The nature of the involvement of typical role holders. Whether they are alienated, morally involved, or simply are involved in their roles through instrumental reasons (for example, it pays the bills!). Also look at the main motivators involved such as work satisfaction, money rewards, security, and the ways these are derived from their backgrounds outside the organization, such as job history, family commitments, social background, and from their experience of the organization itself.

3. The role holders' definitions of their situation within the organization and their expectations about others' likely behaviour. This should be with reference to the way they see resources at their disposal, and at the disposal of others, such as power, moral authority and belief in individual opportunity.

4. The typical action of different actors and the meaning they attribute to their actions.

5. The nature of the consequences of their actions, both intended and unintended. This should be looked at with reference to the involvement of the actors, and the degree to which these expectations have become institutionalized within the role system.

6. Changes in the involvement and ends of the various actors within the organization, and in the role system of which they are a part. This should be with reference to why there are changes. These may be due to changes outside the organization such as political or legal changes, and the different experiences of successive generations.

It is probably more difficult, conceptually, to undertake a study of this sort. This is probably why systems theory is so predominant in organizational analysis: it is easier to understand, and easier to operationalize!

The application of different organizational theories

Ribeaux and Poppleton (1978) take the view that different organizational theories have their place in different aspects of organizational life, depending on their use. These also relate to particular motivational theories as shown in Figure 7.5.

				→
Organizational theory	Classical hierrarchical	Systems theory	Action theory	?
Motivational model	Rational economical man	Social man	Self-actualizing man	Complex man
Management approach	Scientific management	Human relations	Job enrichment	Diagnostic

Figure 7.5 *Organizational theories, management approaches, and motivational models (adapted from Ribeaux and Poppleton, 1978)*

Figure 7.5 not only charts the progress of organizational theory since the beginning of the century, it also shows the interconnection between motivational models and organizational theories, and with management 'fashions'. Ribeaux and Poppleton (1978) take the view that man is complex, responding to all these different motivational models in different situations. Any theory of organizations should take account of this multidimensional view and any associated management approach must be diagnostic in approach as suggested by Schein (1965).

Considering context–content–conduct

Perhaps, a fruitful way forward is to consider all aspects of what we have termed the 3Cs within an organizational setting. Rather than regarding organizations as just a setting for group and individual behaviour, we should consider it as:

- a structure (a framework of both physical operating boundaries and a network of rules both implicit and explicit which regulate the way individuals and groups relate to each other, including power relations);

- as a meaning system comprising negotiated and agreed upon meaning as well as a system of meaning ambiguity where there are different perceptions and objectives operating;

- and, as a forum within which meaningful action takes place according to agreed upon rules and objectives, or where there is a lack of agreement, but action takes place according to implicit or explicit objectives of individuals, groups and systems and patterns of work.

The latter presupposes a need for competences to successfully achieve objectives or to take necessary action (these competences may be present or not). We can represent this as follows (see Figure 7.6).

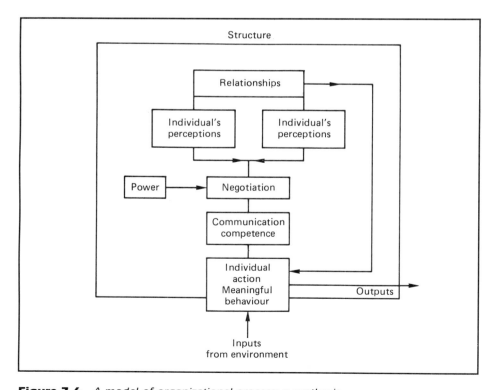

Figure 7.6 *A model of organizational process: a synthesis*

Here, the structure is defined by its boundaries and the systems which operate within it. Action is conduct by way of establishing relationships within the structure, and negotiating objectives within these relations. Power relations may come into play, with one person or group being able to dominate another. Relationships are thus created and maintained, and give rise to co-operative action, which in turn produces outputs into the environment. Inputs from the environment include cultural and value aspects from the wider society, but only really affect the organization through the internal process of communicative actions.

We can at this stage perhaps regard Figure 7.6 as an incomplete picture of organizational process which must be refined and adapted. It is offered at this stage as an attempt at synthesis, and not as a model which can be fully operationalized.

Both the structural and perceptual/meaningful actions aspects are equally important when looking at cross-border organizational operations. In the remaining part of this chapter we concentrate on the structural aspects of organizations by focusing on international organizational structures, and look more specifically at cultural input and implications in Chapter 8.

International organizational structures

A great deal has been written lately on the need to develop new and more adaptive forms of organization, as a result of increased internationalization. Particularly the changes in Europe, and the needs of cross-border operations have prompted discussion on these issues. Van Dijck (1990) of Tilburg University in the Netherlands has pointed to the tendency towards transnationalization as evidenced by:

- increase in cross border operations, investment and strategies in Europe;
- increased international mobility of young graduates, professional and managers;
- more inter-company competition in Europe than between countries;
- within multinational companies, a need to balance international strategy with local conditions and needs;
- a move towards new organizational structures, away from development and direction from the headquarters, towards 'managing diversity' by networking structures which take account of the efforts and initiatives from all operating countries;
- changing employment structures in Europe in terms of worker mobility, workers' rights and legal and social aspects of business – towards a 'Social Europe'.

There is an indication that old structures will not be sufficient to deal with these changes.

Smiley (1989) suggests that there is a shift from 'multi-domestic' organizations to global organizations which operate across borders to meet converging consumer tastes. This signifies a need for more flexible, temporary organizational forms which can be adapted quickly to a changing marketplace. He even suggests that the word 'structure' will have to be conceived in its scientific form as meaning a 'union of parts'. So rather than talking about structure we will be talking about the 'form' of an organization.

Autonomous work groups: adapting international organizations

McCalman (1989) also points to the development in organizations of autonomous work groups, devolving decision making and innovation down the organization, in order to offer a more flexible response to shorter product life cycles, increased levels of global competition and more sophisticated customer demand. Let us look at the following case.

Mini Case 7.2 Autonomous work groups in DEC

The case of Digital Equipment Corporation's manufacturing plant in Ayr, Scotland, which responds to the need to adapt the American organization to the commercial requirements of the European market in computer technology, is examined by McCalman (1989). The problem of organizational adaptation is clearly highlighted by a quote from Konosuke Matsushita, on western style management.

> We will win and you will lose. You cannot do anything about it because your failure is an internal disease. Your companies are based on Taylor's principles. Worse, your heads are Taylorized too. You firmly believe that sound management means executives on one side and workers on the other, on one side men who think and on the other men who can only work. For you, management is the art of smoothly transferring the executives' ideas into the workers' hands.

DEC's Ayr plant was opened in 1976, and by 1989 employed over 1200 people. Its initial production concept was based on the traditional role of American branch plants in Europe, to configure, assemble and test systems for the European customers, adding little value to products which were made in American plants.

However, this role did not meet the needs of a highly competitive market which was extremely important to the American company in terms of dollar revenue. A need to be adaptable, and flexible to meet customers' needs, and a political pressure to increase its local sourcing of components meant that the company had to rethink the way production was organized.

DEC adopted the approach of 'high-performance work design' in order to meet the requirements for new product development from the Ayr plant, the pressures of typically a three-year product cycle, and a volatility of the market during the early 1980s which made forecasting from one quarter to the next very precarious.

As well as securing extra funding to evolve from final assembly to test, to complete manufacture, they had to find a production process which was flexible enough to handle variation in demand as well as attaining an objective of meeting unit costs which were competitive with other DEC plants, particularly with those in the Far East.

Employees were retrained and autonomous work groups were set up to respond to the need for flexibility and skills acquisition, to meet product and market changes. Management styles were rethought, as the situation demanded a

---

supportive rather than a directive style. There was a turning away from the concept of mass production (and perhaps Taylorism) towards a belief that change was a natural process which could be managed through a flexible workforce and production organization.

McCalman (1989) describes six dimensions of this change process.

1. *Focus*. A clear management view of future products and the organization design required to manufacture them, with a shared vision which helped to sell the changes both upwards and to the workforce.

2. *Support policies*. Employees were encouraged to develop their skills through a skills-related reward system. Job demarcation was rare. As such employees were encouraged to develop in areas in which they were not immediately engaged and to contribute to the business.

3. *Work organization*. Autonomous work groups were established each with around twelve members, with full responsibility for product assembly, test, fault finding and problem solving and maintenance, using flexitime without clocking in and out, and being responsible for their own discipline. Each member was encouraged to develop skills and pass them on to others in the team.

4. *Management style*. The new style involved supportive back-up for the teams rather than directive co-ordination. Those managers who found this difficult could move to other parts of the company. Team leaders had the job of encouraging group autonomy and then to withdraw from the group. Decision making in the groups was slow at first, but after a while they learnt to resolve problems and call on management experience where required.

5. *Project management*. Project managers were designated responsible for obtaining the new product line, to liaise with colleagues to persuade them that the approach to organizing was appropriate, and to gain a competitive edge.

6. *Involvement*. The process of engendering ownership of the process was started long before the changes were implemented. A project team was established to do this some twelve months prior to the new production system. Regular meetings were held to promote and develop enthusiasm and commitment, and the new language of 'flexible working', 'product-ownership' and 'front-to-back responsibility' was frequently employed.

Through this new organization of autonomous work groups, management in Digital identified key characteristics which facilitated high performance, namely:

- willingness to change
- speed of communication
- employee 'ownership' of product and process
- multifunction career patterns
- better business awareness and priority-setting
- multi-skilling which enhanced flexibility.

It is perhaps through organizational design such as in DEC that western companies operating in Europe can operate more competitively and meet some of the criticisms of Konosuke Matsushita.

Discussion. It is obvious from this case that organizational structure cannot be changed in isolation from other factors such as management style, economic factors, training, and employee attitudes. Explore some of the interrelated factors in the DEC case. What were the main prerequisite factors of success in this case?

International organizational forms

In the case of organizations operating across borders, such as with DEC, the way international structures and the interrelatedness of parent company and subsidiaries are organized is significant in the way action takes place, and ultimately in the commercial success of a company.

Bartlett and Ghoshal (1989) distinguish four organizational forms.

Multinational

This type of organization responds to the need to exploit national diversity. Recognizing that, for example, consumer tastes and needs of technology may be based on local conditions and national culture. This type of organization will therefore have a strong national presence which is able to respond to national diversity. It will be decentralized and nationally self-sufficient, sensing and exploiting local opportunities, and developing and retaining knowledge within each national unit. Its organizational model may be depicted by Figure 7.7.

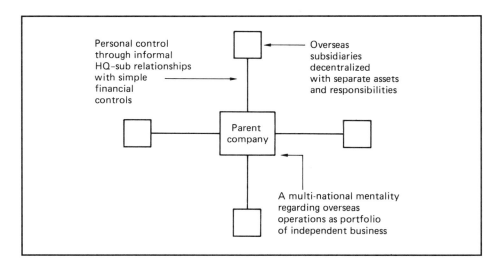

Figure 7.7 *Multi-national organization (adapted from Bartlett and Ghoshal, 1989)*

There is therefore very little direct influence from the parent company, and interpersonal communication between the different cultures may be quite limited. An example of this type of organization is the American ITT with a need to respond on a local basis to specific regulations, requirements and formats in the telecommunications switching industry.

Global

Here the organization exploits the cost advantages of centralized global-scale operations based on centralized knowledge development which is retained at the centre, and the implementation of the parent company's strategies. It responds to the trends of growing globalization of tastes, fashions and consumer demand generally. This type of organization is centralized and globally scaled. An organizational model of a global organization is shown in Figure 7.8.

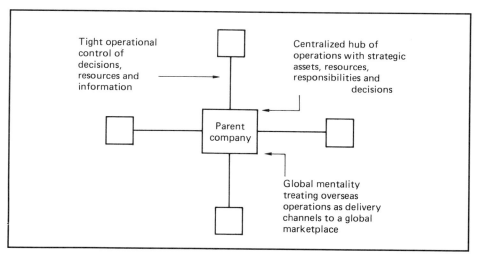

Figure 7.8 *Global organization (adapted from Bartlett and Ghoshal, 1989)*

An example of a global enterprise is the Japanese Matsushita, which exploits and promotes the globalization of taste in consumer electrics, being exports based with research and development, manufacturing and branding being concentrated at the centre.

International

Here, the organization exploits the parent company's knowledge and adapts it world-wide. Sources of core competences are centralized, but other competences may be decentralized. The role of overseas operations is to adapt parent company's

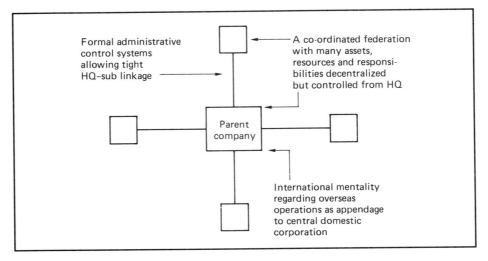

Figure 7.9 *International organization*

competences to the local environment. Knowledge is developed at the centre and then transferred to the overseas subsidiaries. Such an organization can be depicted by the model illustrated in Figure 7.9.

Procter and Gamble is a good example of an international organization. Many of its research and development functions are centralized, but branding and packaging of products is undertaken at local level to meet the needs of national tastes and legislation.

Transnational

This type of organization is an ideal type in the eyes of Bartlett and Ghoshal (1989) and is something towards which many cross-border companies ought to be striving. It seeks to integrate the separate forces operating in the international marketplace, which each of the three organizational forms described above addresses only partially. These three forces are:

- *Global integration*: the trend towards greater integration of global tastes. Product trends such as Coca Cola and Macdonalds are examples, as is the demand for the same consumer electric goods around the developed world. Global organizations address this particular market force.

- *Local differentiation*: the demand of local and national tastes, and of protectionism from national governments tend towards multinational organizational structures, and to an extent international organizational structures.

- *World-wide innovation*: the cost of innovation is great and more cost-effective, usually, if research and development are centralized, and such products emanating from the centre are marketed globally, or are adapted internationally in local centres around the world. The corollary of this is that centralized research and development functions may not take account of the expertise and resources available in local centres, and may in fact be missing opportunities to maximize efficiencies in new product development.

Transnational organizations address these issues by deploying dispersed, interdependent and specialized capabilities and assets, by facilitating differentiated contributions from national units in order to integrate world-wide operations, and by developing knowledge jointly and sharing it world-wide. In order to achieve these organizational characteristics management has a role in legitimizing and encouraging diverse perspectives and capabilities, developing multiple and flexible co-ordinating processes, and building shared vision and individual commitment. A model of a transnational organizational can be illustrated by Figure 7.10.

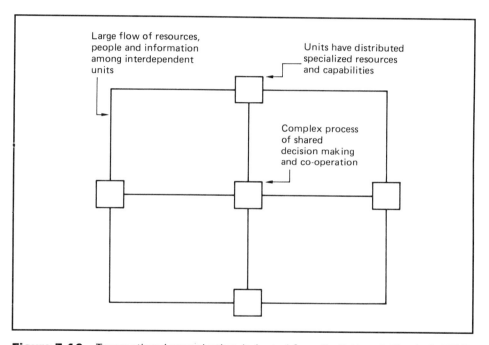

Figure 7.10   *Transnational organization (adapted from Bartlett and Ghoshal, 1989)*

The organizational models of the previous three structures are described as:

- Global: centralized hub;
- Multinational: decentralized federation;
- International: co-ordinated federation.

Bartlett and Ghoshal (1989, p. 61) describe the transnational model as an 'integrated network' which 'emphasises the very significant flow of components, products, resources, people, and information that must be managed in the transnational. Beyond the rationalization of physical facilities, the company must integrate tasks and perspectives; rich and complex communication linkages, work interdependencies, and formal and informal systems are the true hallmark of the transnational.'

Summary and conclusions

In this chapter we have examined organizational structures and how these may be regarded. While the most prominent theory of organizations in the management literature is Systems Theory, we have also introduced an approach based on the meaning systems within organizations, and have thus discussed an 'action' approach which looks at organizations as a negotiated meaning between different perspective, perceptions and objectives. Within this type of approach we should not forget the influence of power relations and manipulation of meaning systems through influence and coercion. This particular aspect was developed in Chapter 5, and we have not gone into this in any detail here.

Partly within the Systems tradition, and partly as a bridge with Action theory, we discussed the 7-Ss approach, and how this conceptual framework was applied to the Japanese giant Matsushita by Pascale and Athos (1981).

An attempt at a synthesis of the different organizational theories was attempted, pointing out that different aspects of each theory may be important when we analyse how organizations actually work.

We then turned to look at international organizational structures, discussing first the imperative to change and adapt organizations within the international arena, and then discussing the work of Bartlett and Ghoshal (1989), and the 'ideal type' of international organization which they term the 'transnational'.

It is perhaps within this context of international change and adaption that we need to adopt a flexible approach towards analysing organizations and how they work. Despite its difficulty in both conception and application, the phenomenological approach of Action Theory is useful for taking into consideration the diversity of perceptions and perspectives in an international organization, while systems theory is useful in understanding environmental and structural influences on individuals working within a complex, cross-border organization. We consider the issue of change by organizational structural analysis later in the text in Chapter 15.

References

Bartlett, C. A. and Ghoshal, S. (1989) *Managing Across Borders: The Transnational Solution*, London: Hutchinson.

Berger P. L. and Luckmann T. (1966) *The Social Construction of Reality*, New York: Doubleday.

Blauner, R. (1964) *Alienation and Freedom: The Factory Worker and his Industry*, Chicago: University of Chicago Press.

Bottomore, T. B. and Rubel, M. (eds.) (1961) *Karl Marx: Selected Writings in Sociology and Social Philosophy*, Harmondsworth: Penguin.

Brown, J. A. C., (1954) *The Social Psychology of Industry*, Harmondsworth: Penguin.

Cicourel, A. V. (1964) *Methods and Measurement in Sociology*, New York: The Free Press.

Goffman, E. (1959) *The Presentation of Self in Everyday Life* (1971 edn.), Harmondsworth: Penguin.

Hodge, B. J. and Anthony, W. P., (1988) *Organizational Theory*, (3rd edn.), Needham Heights, Massachusetts: Allyn and Bacon.

Katz, D. and Kahn, R. L. (1978) *The Social Psychology of Organizations*, (2nd edn.) New York: John Wiley.

Kelley, H. H. (1967) 'Attribution theory in social psychology', *Nebraska Symposium on Motivation*, 15 pp. 192–238.

Kelley, H. H. (1973) 'The processes of causal attribution', *American Psychologist*, 28, pp. 107–28.

Kelly, G. A. (1955) *The Psychology of Personal Constructs Vols 1 and 2*, New York: Norton.

Kolb, D. A., Rubin, I. M. and Osland, J. S., (1991) *Organizational Behavior: An Experiential Approach* (5th edn.), Englewood Cliffs, NJ: Prentice-Hall.

Leavitt, H. J. (1965) 'Applied organizational change in industry', in March J. G. (ed.) *Handbook of Organizations*, Chicago: Rand McNally, 1965.

McCalman, J. (1989) 'Performance organizations in the 1990s: flexibility for manufacturing management', *European Management Journal*, 7, 3.

Maslow, A. H. (1954) *Motivation of Personality*, New York: Harper and Row.

Merton, R. K. (1949) *Social Theory and Social Structure*, Glencoe, Illinois: The Free Press.

Nadler, D. A. and Tushman, M. (1991) 'A congruence model for diagnosing organizational behavior', in Kolb, D. A., Rubin, I. M. and Osland, J. S., (eds.) *The Organizational Behaviour Reader*, Englewood Cliffs, NJ: Prentice-Hall.

Parsons, T. (1949) *The Structure of Social Action*, Glencoe, Illinois: The Free Press.

Parsons, T. (1951) *The Social System*, Glencoe, Illinois: The Free Press.

Parsons, T. (1964), *Structure and Process in Modern Societies*, Glencoe, Illinois: The Free Press.

Pascale, R. T. and Athos, A. G. (1981) *The Art of Japanese Management*, New York: Simon & Schuster.

Radcliffe-Brown, A. R. (1952) *Structure and Function in Primitive Society*, London: Cohen and West.

Ribeaux, P. and Poppleton, S. E. (1978) *Psychology at Work*, Basingstoke: Macmillan.

Rogers, C. R. (1951) *Client Centred Therapy*, Boston, US: Houghton Mifflin.

Rogers E. M. and Agarwala-Rogers, R. (1976) *Communication in Organizations*, New York: The Free Press.

Schein, E. H. (1965) *Organizational Psychology*, Englewood Cliffs, NJ: Prentice-Hall.

Schutz, A. (1972) *Phenomenology of The Social World*, London: Heinemann.

Silverman, D. (1970) *The Theory Of Organizations*, Aldershot: Gower.

Smiley, T. (1989) 'A challenge to the human resource and organizational function in international firms', *European Management Journal*, 7, 2.

Taylor F. W. (1911) *Scientific Management*, New York: Harper Row.

van Dijck, J. (1990) 'Transnational management in an evolving European context', *European Management Journal*, 8, 4.

Waterman, R. H., Peters, T. J. and Philips, J. R. (1980) 'Structure is not organization' reproduced in Kolb, D. A., Rubin, I. M. and Osland, J. S., (eds.) *The Organizational Behaviour Reader* (5th edn.), Englewood Cliffs, NJ: Prentice-Hall.

8

Organizational cultures and management styles

Objectives

Following this chapter you should be able to:

1 Explain the meaning of organization culture and describe the different theories which seek to explain this.
2 Describe the nature of the interaction between different national and organizational cultures.
3 Explain the meaning of the term management styles, and how this relates to organizational cultures.
4 Analyse an organization in terms of its culture and management styles.

Key concepts

- Organizational culture
- Management styles
- Organizational explicit and implicit 'rules'
- Thick and thin culture
- Primal, rational, developmental, and metaphysical management domains of Lessem.

Introduction

Culture is a concept which is implicit throughout this text, and we described this as a theme in Chapter 1, providing specific definitions. The fact that the concentration of this text is a cross-cultural one, means that is is difficult to escape from discussions of the implications of culture in any of the subject areas discussed in this text. Here we look more specifically at the idea of organizational culture as part of our investigations into the nature of organizations so far. It is that part of organizational life we have considered mainly under the heading of Content in the 3Cs model of context–content–conduct, as it involves the perceptions, beliefs and objectives of individuals, albeit in interaction and negotiation with one another. However, the concept of cultures is far from being a purely phenomenological one (see Chapter 7). In fact culture can be explained as an interaction between structural and phenomenological aspects. Harre *et al.* (1985), for example, illustrate social action by reference to three levels of investigation (see also Chapter 3) as follows:

- Level 1: behavioural routines
- Level 2: conscious awareness
- Level 3: deep structure and social order.

They suggest that structure of mind and the social order have developed hand in hand, mostly through the facility of language, and that the implied rules by which level 3 controls the two lower levels are discoverable.

The way culture has developed as both social order and 'mind set' can be illustrated by reference to the 'founder' of structural functionalist sociology, Emile Durkheim.

Mini Case 8.1 Totemism in the context of organizational culture

Durkheim (1915) examined the nature and origins of religious beliefs from a sociological point of view by studying the 'totemism' of aboriginal tribes of Australia and Indian tribes of North America (perhaps the latter provides the popular image of Red Indians dancing round a totem pole). The members of each clan (a subdivision of a tribe) are seen to worship a particular animal (for example, crow) which is also the name of the clan.

Durkheim maintained that the origins of the religious beliefs by which their lives were governed, were derived from the identification with the society (clan) in which they lived. This was seen to be greater and more powerful than the individual clansman. The rituals (associated with dancing round the totem pole) reinforced and drove these beliefs home. Rituals enacted through, for example, dancing round the totem as a symbol of both the society and the religious belief system, forged a strong connection between the society which collectively was stronger and greater than the individual, and the beliefs which kept the society together.

Thus the deep-seated beliefs which were acted upon unconsciously were no more than a set of implicit rules derived from the society in which the individuals lived. Thus Durkheim provided an explanation for one aspect of culture which forged a deep link between the social systems and the beliefs of individuals.

Discussion. To what extent can we apply this to modern organizations, where rituals (from gift presentation ceremonies, to morning meetings, and even the singing of the company song) are performed in order to forge an identification link between the individual and the company?

Definitions of organizational culture and management styles

Do we not act, for the most part unconsciously, to a set of rules which are derived from our own experiences within society, which we adopt and through which we view our world? This is perhaps how we can view culture both in the societies within which we live and in those in which we work (in many European languages, French, Spanish, Italian, for example, the word for society and company is the same). In this chapter we look at organizational culture as a set of implicit and explicit rules, and we also look at the way in which individuals interpret these rules through their own 'styles' of acting. We can therefore provide the following definitions.

- *Organizational culture*: those explicit and implicit rules within an organization which influence the way individuals act, and which are derived from the interaction between the social order (social arrangements in the organization) and the 'mind sets' (beliefs, perceptions and attitudes derived from the wider society) of significant individuals in the organizations.
- *Management styles*: the ways in which key individuals within the organization interpret these explicit and implicit rules.

Durkheim is concerned mainly with the way religious (and cultural) beliefs are formed. Hodge and Anthony (1988) tell us that because culture is a group phenomenon, to understand culture we must understand how groups are formed and how they produce culture. 'Sharing' is an essential concept to understand in culture as there would be no culture without shared values, goals, and norms. Therefore commonality is the lifeblood of cultural formation. The reason why individuals form groups in the first place is because they seek need satisfaction. We could equally apply this to the early formation of primitive groups to satisfy the need for safety and comfort within a group as we could to the formation of a modern company to satisfy the needs of the individual founders for a livelihood, wealth, independence, or self-fulfilment. Individuals bring their own goals, values, beliefs, and hopes to the group process, often from a wider society, in order to find a situation within which they can achieve what they want. From this beginning they must strive towards commonality of shared values and norms, as the 'glue' which holds the group together.

Group formation and organizational culture

Schein (1985) describes four stages of group formation as in Table 8.1.

Firstly, the question of who will lead the group is crucial. In selecting someone to give the group direction, societal cultural beliefs are brought into play, as what individuals think and value will influence the selection. So, selection may be on the basis of age, sex, perceived style of behaving (for example, a 'strong' leader). Initial leaders, of, for example, a business enterprise, may have a strong influence on the future culture of the organization, in terms of attitudes towards employees (authoritarian or participative practices) or customers (for example a regard for quality) or perhaps towards the society as a whole (for example, social responsibility and ethical business practices).

The second stage concerns the issues of role differentiation, peer relationships and group membership. Successful first efforts to settle the initial authority question and gain an element of commercial success for example, are likely to engender a positive attitude towards membership of the group.

150

Table 8.1 *The formation of group culture*

Stage	*Assumption*	*Focus*
1 Dependency/authority confrontation	A leader is needed to guide and direct the group	Selection of leader
2 Confrontation intimacy, role differentiation, peer relations	The group is a success and membership is rewarding	Consensus and group harmony
3 Creativity/stability conflict	There is a need for innovation but stability is also required	Continuity and accomplishment of the team
4 Survival and growth issues	Because the group has survived it must be right	The *status quo* and resistance to chance

Source: adapted from Schein, 1985.

The third stage involves confronting the ongoing need for innovation (the impetus for group formation in the first place) and the need for stability to curb the disruptive force of creativity which could risk the future of the group.

Finally, the group matures to be confronted by survival and growth issues. It learns whether the founding values and norms are appropriate for its continued survival and expansion within its environment. It may continue as a group, or may disband with the members combining with and forming other groups.

The underlying question throughout these stages, which may be to varying degrees regarded as ongoing, is whether the group can forge a culture which it requires to survive. Let us look, therefore at the nature of cultures and the forms they take. In so doing we make a distinction between the 'rules' which bind organizational cultures, and their interpretation by individuals within the organization.

Organizational culture: understanding the rules

There is not an easy distinction between 'organizational culture' and 'management style' as they often seem to overlap. Perhaps the main distinction can be thought of in terms of organizational culture providing a set of beliefs or values (we have called these 'rules') and manager's style being embodied in actions. Let us look first at organizational culture.

The concept of culture is largely drawn from social anthropology. We saw in Chapter 1 the classic definition of Tyler (1871): 'that complex whole which includes knowledge, belief, art, morals, law, custom and any other capabilities and habits acquired by man as a member of society' and the more modern definition which is applied to organizations is that of Williams *et al.* (1989) who state that 'culture is the commonly held and relatively stable beliefs, attitudes and values that exist within the organization'.

An often used concept is that of a strong or weak culture (for example, Deal and Kennedy, 1982). The degree to which the values and beliefs in an organization are defined and commonly accepted, and adhered to may differ widely between a new and an older organization, the type of business the organization is in, from where the members of that organization are drawn (for example in a multinational company this may be across many countries and national cultures) the top management styles and actions, and the perceptions and actions of the organizational members. Also part of the value system of a corporation may be its looseness, the extent to which people can interpret and even break commonly accepted rules. The degree to which values and beliefs are shared denotes the strength or weakness of a culture.

Another useful concept about organizational culture is whether it is a healthy or unhealthy one. A strong culture may support top management or denigrate it; may be healthy and positive towards organizational goals, or may be cynical towards top management and therefore negate management objectives.

Hodge and Anthony (1988) use the concept of thick and thin cultures. An organizational culture is said to be thick if it is accepted throughout an organization and adopted and internalized by the vast majority of organizational members. Thin cultures are not central to the group and therefore do not provide cohesion. The differing attitudes towards dress from one department to another might indicate a lack of a formal code of dress such as the norm that men in UK banks wear dark suits.

Mini Case 8.2 Thick culture in Goldman Sachs

Goldman Sachs and Company in New York, an investment bank, recruit talent from the cream of leading business schools. They look for individuals who are intelligent, motivated, confident, team players who have both maturity but with characters which are still pliable enough to be moulded. Once hired, the young recruit will usually prepare for a lifetime career in the same department, developing a high level of expertise and commonality with the departmental members. Outsiders are not usually brought into the organization, nor is the Company interested in how its competitors do things. It is therefore quite insular but takes pride in this aloofness. This has become a company asset rather than a liability.

It is also very choosy about its clients, adhering to a strict policy about whom it will do business with. Clients must therefore have sound management practices, produce only products and services of high quality, show profits for all their businesses, and benefit the public in some way. They also maintain other standards such as not underwriting any deal involving non-voting stock as they have a strong belief that shareholders should have voting rights, and not being involved in any hostile tender offers. In addition to this the Company believe service to its clients is of primary importance, over and above any obligations they might have to the Wall Street banking community. It is extremely cautious about moving into new areas, and opportunities have to be studied and studied, the decision-making process being very lengthy. This leads to few mistakes but occasional lost opportunities.

The organization is very tightly controlled at the top through operating procedures and its overheads, but departments are allowed a great deal of autonomy in entrepreneurial activity and innovation. The *status quo* is maintained in its structure and operations by its inbreeding of long-term employees.

The wealth of partners is substantial (each of its seventy-five partners in 1984 earning $5 million per year), this is mostly on paper, as actual salaries are modest and ostentation is frowned upon.

The main lubricants for smooth operations are the attitude towards doing the job well and working as a member of the team.

With the central idea that as an investment bank, the company is in business to make money, the central hub of the wheel of its culture is greed. This is the energy that drives the wheel. But this greed is channelled in such a way that it works for and benefits the entire company. There is little 'backstabbing' and politics, as the team working attitudes encourage people to work together for the common good. For example, those senior members who do not make it to a partnership are kept happy with a high level of perks and symbolic benefits such as the use of the vice presidents' dining room.

The culture of Goldman Sachs is mainly a long-term result of the joint leadership of its co-chairmen, John Weinberg and John Whitehead, who both joined the Company in the 1940s, planning together how they would run the firm, and having the chance in 1976 to achieve this when the former chairman Gus Levy died.

In the words of John Whitehead:

> There are things about Goldman as an institution that make it unique: its team spirit, the pride in what we do, the high standard of professionalism, the service orientation . . . That's the essence of Goldman Sachs' culture, the things that have made us what we are, and I would say that culture has been the key to our success'

Despite its success, there is a downside to this culture. Often people work until two o'clock in the morning, there are marriage breakups, psychological problems with individuals' subordination of their egos and personal life to the business. These great demands are perhaps addressed and overcome by recruiting individuals who are suited to the culture, while continually reinforcing the culture for those in the organization.

(*Source*: adapted from McGoldrich, 1984)

Discussion. How has Goldman Sachs managed to generate and maintain this 'thick' culture and what are the risks inherent within it? How can it continue to inculcate this culture into newcomers, and gain this high level of commitment from its employees?

Hofstede (1989) describes culture as a mix between values and practice while Williams *et al.* (1989) refer to beliefs being at the unconscious level, attitudes and values at the reportable level and behaviours being at the observable level.

Hofstede (1989), in addition to the national cultural dimensions he has identified (see Chapter 2), of power distance (degree of inequality accepted), uncertainty avoidance (preference for structured or unstructured situations), individualism (acting as individualists or collectivists) and masculinity (hard versus soft values) describes organizational cultures along the following dimensions:

- process-oriented versus results-oriented;
- job-oriented versus employee-oriented;
- professionally-oriented versus parochially-oriented (the extent to which members identify with their profession or with the organization);
- open versus closed systems (style of internal and external communication, for example the ease with which newcomers are admitted);
- tight versus loose internal control (formality and punctuality);
- pragmatic versus normative ways of dealing with the environment (flexible or rigid).

Perhaps the most useful way of regarding culture is as a set of implicit and explicit rules. We have discussed this at an early stage in this text (see Chapter 1). We can illustrate this as in Table 8.2.

There may be no clear distinction between implicit and explicit rules, and explicit rules are not necessarily legislated for in the organization. There may also be no clear distinction between rules and behaviour (adherence to rules), although observing behaviour is one method of extracting the rules of an organization. Within this concept

Table 8.2 *Organizational culture as explicit and implicit rules*

Explicit rules	*Rules about artefacts*
	Ties and dark suits to be worn
	Managers only to use managers' toilets
	Parking places allocated by seniority
	Rules about how people should behave
	Should deal with customers promptly
	Should attend early morning meetings
Implicit rules	Should not be involved with a union
	Should put in extra hours at home
	Should be punctual in the morning no matter how late you were working the previous night
	Work through informal network where possible
	Rules about the attitudes people have
	Be cynical about top management
	Regard company as a good employer
	Rules about values people should have
	Can deviate from these rules only if not officially caught doing so.
	'Stabbing other people in the back' is frowned upon but justifiable if helps promotion.

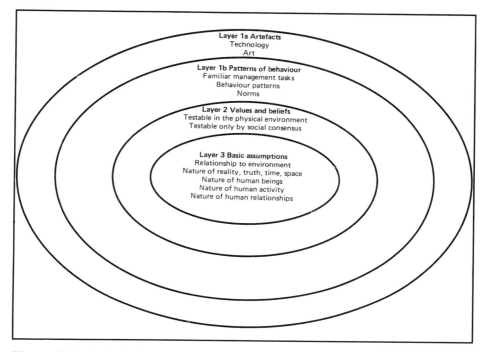

Figure 8.1 *Peeled-onion conception of organizational culture (from Hunt, 1991)*

of 'rules' we should also accept that analysis should take place at various levels. If we look at Hunt's (1991) 'peeled-onion' analogy we can see that 'rules' are difficult to tap at the 'basic assumptions' inner-most layer (Figure 8.1), as these are both implicit and possibly unconscious in the way they influence actual behaviour.

Management styles: interpreting the rules

Generally speaking the actions of individuals arise from a combination of culturally guided behaviour and interpretations of role within that culture: in other words, styles of behaviour which individuals adopt. Styles are a combination of what the individual brings with him or her into the organization (for example, national culture, family or peer influence), the way the organizational culture (rules) is recognized, interpreted and adhered to, and the way the individual actually enacts his or her role.

We can subdivide concepts of management styles into overriding organizational management styles, learning styles (considered later in Chapter 10), and doing styles.

Likert (1967) has referred to the management styles of organizations as management 'systems'. He identifies four management systems: exploitive–authoritative, benevolent-authoritative, consultative, and participative–group (see Chapter 6). He has published a comprehensive questionnaire to elicit the required information from employees working under the respective management systems, using variables of motivation, communication, interaction, decision-making, goal setting, control and performance.

Likert's concept of 'system' is of an all-pervasive style within which the management of an organization is conducted. It is not a personal style but a prevailing approach to management which sets the scene. Likert (1967) therefore describes situational styles rather than personal styles.

'Learning' and 'doing' management styles, on the other hand are a characteristic of the individual within a particular environment. Although two distinct characteristics, they have some overlap, and encompass:

- the way managers learn;
- the way they work (e.g. plan, implement decisions);
- the way they relate to others;
- the way they relate to the future (e.g. manage change)
- how they regard performance (e.g. process versus results)

'Classical' management theory provides frameworks for viewing the way managers relate to work and to people through McGregor's (1960) Theory X (economic orientation) versus Theory Y (people orientation), and Blake and Mouton's (1985) 'concern for production' versus 'concern for people', as we have seen in Chapter 5.

Contingency theory (Fiedler, 1967), as we discussed in Chapter 6 suggests that there is no good or bad style of management, merely appropriate styles to match the group–task situation. Reddin (1970) develops this theory, providing a model of the effective manager as having both 'flexibility' and 'resilience', and the ineffective manager as exhibiting 'drift' and 'rigidity'. It is the effective manager who can adapt to the situation by recognizing what is required without being swayed by circumstance, and slipping and sliding from one approach to another. Reddin combines this concept of effective management (flexibity/resilience versus drift/rigidity) with a situational dimension of Task Orientation versus Relationship Orientation. In this way he develops a model (Three Dimensional Management) which looks at these orientations (situational dimensions) and how they relate to ineffective, neutral and effective management.

An effective manager in Reddin's terms would therefore be able to adapt from the exploitative–authoritarian to the participative–group situational styles (management systems) of Likert (1967). Although it would seem unlikely that management selection processes were working very well if a manager found him or herself in this position to have to adjust so radically, there is increasing pressure on managers working across borders to be adaptable in the way Reddin suggests.

Other classifications of management styles include Brianas's (1986) statistical probability model using broad classifications along a continuum from 'traditional' or authoritarian styles to 'developmental' or consultative styles. He relates this to management effectiveness and to levels of stress, stating that 'innovative' management is less stressful and more effective. We have already seen in Chapter 6 that Smith *et al.* (1989) take a cross-cultural approach using the two broad classifications of leadership styles of:

- Performance
- Maintenance

This follows similar classifications such as House's (1971) path–goal approach, and focuses on the orientation of leadership behaviour. Smith *et al.* (1989) conclude (across four national cultures: UK, USA, Hong Kong and Japan) that these two focuses can be identified across cultures but specific behaviours associated with them are different between cultures (see Chapter 6 for details).

The relationship between the organizational context, (its underlying structure, rules, and assumptions), the way individual managers interpret these underlying rules through their individual styles of action and what is regarded in any organization as good performance is fundamental. We now look at the way different cultures view management performance.

Organizational cultures and national cultures

We have said that management and organizational action are essentially rule-bound. Systems of beliefs and values are manifested in corporate cultures and interpreted by individuals which are manifested in styles of action. These interpretations in style are themselves culture-bound and determined by the cultural influences (both organizational and national cultures) on an individual. The stronger (or 'thicker') the culture the less it is open to individual interpretation of the rules.

One exposition of the way culture is reflected in what is seen as the results of management activity, and which is particularly useful in understanding organizational cultures across borders, is that of Lessem (1989). Lessem looks at the evolution of business and management over time and across the globe, characterizing approaches to management in the West (United States), East (Japan), North (Britain and Europe), and South (Africa). He looks at *Entrepreneurial* management (the early stage of a company's development and typified in the West); Executive or *Rational* management as a second, bureaucratic stage typified in the North, but also borrowing heavily from literature and business schools in the West; *Developmental* management, often a third stage to break down bureaucracy and develop quality, and typified in the East; and finally Transformational or *Metaphysical* management aimed at higher ideals, and being a final, but continuing stage, which is typified in a few international companies and possibly in the South.

These different cultural approaches to management may determine both the competences which managers should have, and the nature of their results. Let us adapt from Lessem (1989) what he calls 'attributes' of managers in the four 'domains' of management. We have combined and summarized his approach in Table 8.3.

To be an effective entrepreneural manager you need certain 'primal' (Lessem, 1989) attributes of hard work, enthusiasm, shrewdness, will power, an ability to improvise, an instinct for the marketplace, and imagination. It is only at a more mature stage in the development of an organization when a manager needs to rationally plan for optimum performance of the organization, and turn attention inwards towards greater operational efficiency. Team work, control, strategy, analysis are all attributes which are required in this situation. Only when organizations are unable to compete on a purely production basis, when attention turns to quality of product and quality of life, that managers need to be developmental in approach. Quality circles are a typical feature of this type of organization, and self-development is an attribute which can lead to corporate self-renewal.

Table 8.3 *Cultural attributes of managers*

Function	Entrepreneurial	Executive	Developmental	Transformational
Physical	Hard work	High productivity	Intense interactivity	Energy flow
Social	Raw enthusiasm	Effective teamwork	Quality circles	Corporate culture
Mental	Native shrewdness	Management control	Manager self-development	Process & change
Emotional	Sheer will-power	Competitive strategy	Co-operative strategy	Business interfusion
Analytical	Improvisation	Formal organization	Corporate architecture	Natural management
Intuitive	Market instinct	Analytical marketing	Planned evolution	Unlimited possibilities
Imaginative	Imagination	Systematized innovation	Corporate renewal	Spiritually based vision

Source: adapted from Lessem, 1989.

Metaphysical management, a more difficult concept to grasp, needs higher ideals such as transformations (through, for example, world peace, conservation of natural resources, *glasnost*) at a global level or a 'higher order' concept of corporate culture.

What about the implications of these different organizational cultural characteristics for management styles, that is, the way managers are expected to perform in an organization? For the entrepreneur, starting and developing a business, profits are most important and reflect directly the entrepreneur's ability to achieve results. With rational management, and the exercising of 'executive' abilities, the efficiency of the operational unit is of primary importance. Making the most out of both physical and human resources, to use them for optimum processing or production is all important where volume is paramount and the organization of resources is key.

For developmental management it is the design and quality of the service or product which is central to management results. It is only by producing well designed and quality products that business can remain competitive in a highly discriminative, selective, and educated marketplace. We can also suggest that the 'product' of a

West	North	East	South
Time			→
Profit	**Efficiency**	**Quality**	**Higher ideals**
Entrepreneural	Executive	Developmental	Transfomational

Figure 8.2 *Management results and organizational culture*

metaphysical manager is to achieve certain specified higher ideas. Schematically we can therefore represent management results, evolving over time, and geographically, by Figure 8.2.

It is therefore essential that managers understand the culture of their organization and for internationally, or even nationally, mobile managers who may work in different contexts to quickly understand the 'rules of the game'. Even if they are to work at slight variance to prevailing organizational norms, they must understand what those norms are and how much they can deviate from them without, ultimately, losing their job!

Methods of 'auditing' organizational culture are numerous and we look now at certain qualitative approaches to this.

Auditing organizational culture

Hodge and Anthony (1988) describe a way of looking at organizational culture through 'rites' and 'ceremonies' in the anthropological tradition, and describe particular manifestations of these indicators for which the observer can look (see Table 8.4).

Table 8.4 *Manifestations of corporate culture*

Manifestation	Description
Rite	An elaborate dramatic event, through social interaction, usually before an an audience.
Ceremony	A system of several rites on one occasion
Ritual	A standardized set of management techniques which do not usually give rise to particular results
Myth	A dramatic narrative of imagined events used to explain origins or organizational transformations
Saga	A historical story describing accomplishments of groups or individuals
Legend	A handed-down narrative of a significant event, usually embellished
Story	A combination of truth and fiction about a true event
Folktale	A completely fictitious narrative
Symbol	Any object, act or event which conveys specific organizational meaning
Language	A manner in which group members speak or write to convey meaning to each other
Gesture	Movement of part of body to convey meaning
Physical setting	The physical surrounds which convey meaning
Artefact	Manufactured material objects used to facilitate culture expression

Source: adapted from Hodge and Anthony, 1988.

Activity 8.1 Understanding organizational culture

We can simplify those categories in Table 8.4 by using the following indicators of culture in an organization which can be described and interpreted in terms of their meaning and implications. Apply these to an organization with which you are familiar.

Describe:

- those *Ceremonies* that are conducted publicly;

- those *Stories and myths* about the origins and episodes in the history of the organization;

- the particular *Language and mannerisms* used by organizational members that identify them as members of this organization;

- the *Physical surrounds* in which people work, which are somewhat different from other organizations;

- those *Artefacts* or physical objects which denote identity or rank in this organization.

As an example of the latter, to denote rank in an organization in which the present author recently worked, the size of chair and the height of its back were used to denote transition from one rank to the next, where actual authority and pay were not necessarily an obvious indicator.

Another qualitative approach which you can use follows on from the discussion on 'rules', where the *rules* of the organization can be documented as follows.

In the organization, with which you are familiar:

- Explicit Rules
  - What are the rules about artefacts (things)?
  - What are the rules about how people should behave?

- Implicit Rules
  - Are there any implicit rules about the way people should behave? What are these?
  - What are the rules about the attitudes people should have?
  - What are the rules about the values people should have?

- Deviation from rules
  - How far can people deviate from these rules? What happens if they do?

An approach to auditing an organization's culture is described by Schein (1985).

Step 1. *Entry and focus on surprises.*
An outsider enters the group to observe and get a feel for the culture, and watches for surprises that are not expected.

Step 2. *Systematic observation and checking.*
The outsider makes sure that the surprises really are surprises.

Step 3. *Locating a motivated insider.*
An informant is used to give his or her assessment of the culture.

Step 4. *Revealing the surprises and hunches.*
The outsider reveals his or her assessment to the insider to get their reactions.

Step 5. *Joint exploration to find explanations.*
Accuracy of outsider's assumptions are checked by the insider and together use observations to explain behaviour.

Step 6. *Formalizing hypotheses.*
Collaboration between insider and outsider to formulate statements about the culture based on the data gathered. Hypotheses are used as a model of the culture.

Step 7. *Systematic checking and consolidation.*
The outsider can now formulate specific questions based on the information so far obtained, and can gather more systematic evidence based on questionnaire, interviews and stories or critical incidents.

Step 8. *Pushing to the level of assumptions.*
The hypotheses are validated and the model is tested by seeing how the cultural assumptions actually affect behaviour by a programme that seeks to drive or modify this behaviour.

Step 9. *Perpetual recalibration.*
The model is fine-tuned, is tested on other insiders to see if it really does reveal cultural assumptions, but being mindful that for those who are unaware of cultural implications within the organization, this may come as a shock!

Step 10. *Formal written description.*
The formal description is written down, checked, and kept current.

Activity 8.2 A profile of organizational culture

A quantitative method, discussed by Turnipseed (1988), and generating a profile of an organization culture, uses the following categories. Apply this to an organization with which you are familiar, place a number in the box from 1 to 5 using the following guide.

[5] To a great extent,
[3] To a limited extent,
[1] Not at all.

Relationship Dimension

Involvement
[ ]

To what extent are staff committed to their jobs

Peer cohesion
[ ]

To what extent are staff friendly and supportive of each other

Supervisory support
[ ]

To what extent is management supportive and encouraging to staff

Personal Growth Dimension

Autonomy

[ ]

To what extent are staff encouraged to be self-sufficient and make own decisions

Task orientation
[ ]

What emphasis is placed on good planning and getting the job done

Work pressure
[ ]

To what extent does time pressure dominate the work situation

Systems Maintenance and Change Dimension

Clarity

[ ]

To what extent do staff know what to expect in their daily work

Control

[ ]

To what extent does management use rules and pressures to maintain control

Innovation

[ ]

What emphasis is placed on variety, change, and new approaches

Physical

[ ]

To what extent does the physical setting contribute to a good working environment.

Look at the relative scores which you have given. These will indicate to you whether this is a positive or a negative culture, and where the problems arise. Write a description of the culture and what needs to be done to overcome some of the problems where these exist.

Using the profile derived from these categories, Turnipseed (1988) compares a more effective and a less effective organization where higher scores for the more effective organization are shown for involvement, peer cohesion, autonomy, task orientation, work pressure, innovation, and physical comfort, and lower scores on clarity. Scores are more or less equal for the two organizations on supervisory support and control. While not offering this small scale research as evidence of a clear link between organizational culture and climate, and organizational effectiveness, it does offer a potential method which could be used on a larger scale to explore this link.

Culture and management styles: some problems

We have therefore looked at the realm of how managers perform, according to what we have called cultural 'rules' and depending on how these rules are interpreted by individual actors. One of the main problems of many approaches taken in the literature to organizational culture is that it is seen as monolithic: that there is one culture for any given organization. This is particularly true of the concept of 'strong' cultures (for example Deal and Kennedy, 1982). Ouchi and Wilkins (1985) for example, argue that we should be thinking in terms of sub-cultures. Hunt (1991) points to dangers in taking the monolithic approach. Firstly, that making assumptions of a single culture may lead to overlooking diversities in sub-cultures; and secondly, aspects detected in an organizational sub-culture may be generalized by the researcher and applied to the whole organization. There may also exist 'counter-cultures' where there are 'non-basic' assumptions across an organization and these are counter to each other (Hunt, 1991). Hunt therefore speaks of 'sites of culture'. Examples could be at the executive top of an organization, or through a 'vertical slice' such as a department, or a 'horizontal slice' across a particular job type at a particular hierarchical level. We could also add a 'stakeholders' culture, which has implications for the way performance in organizations may be seen quite differently between 'sub-cultures'.

Perhaps a side-effect of trying to conceive of broad categories of cultures across whole organizations is the problem of stereotyping. Typologies such as Hofstede's (1991) may lead to trying to categorize organizations into one or the other category, or at best, applying a mix of categories across a whole organization. Whichever way, there is a tendency for the researcher to impose categorizations on to organizations, leading to gross stereotyping.

The structural approach described in this chapter, which tries to analyse cultures in terms of separate components (for example, Hodge and Anthony, 1988, and to an extent Turnipseed, 1988), may suffer from the problem of reductionism or taking the phenomenon apart. In doing this we may be missing its central essence. Schein (1985) offers a process approach which tries not to impose a structural nor a categorizing analysis on the culture. It may be that by trying to approach a culture from the point of view of the participants within it, may be the most fruitful way of trying to analyse an organizational culture, rather than imposing categories or reducing it down to component parts which miss the broader and most important (for the participants) aspects.

We can perhaps follow Van Maanen and Barley (1985) in thinking of organizational culture in terms of Venn diagrams, each small circle representing a sub-culture, clustered and overlapping to represent a collective understanding where one group's values and 'rules' approximate those of others. However, we can perhaps develop this concept by thinking in terms of interpersonal units. Each member of that unit will interact with members of other units. Therefore no one unit will be discrete or isolated from other interpersonal units, but will network through individual members with other units on a molecular basis (that is, a series of linked atoms in molecular structure).

It may be that 'culture' can only be ascertainable through the way it is (or in terms of inter-connecting sub-cultures, the way that they are) interpreted by individuals, and manifested in their management 'style'. In order to really begin to understand the nature of an organizational 'sub-culture', and its implications for how managers perform, and the way the individual interprets the culture through his or her personal style, we should therefore focus on the individual and the interpersonal unit(s) within which he or she interacts.

Conclusion

In conclusion, we have looked at the issue of organizational culture and style as *context* in the sense of being the structural rules within an organizational situation (culture) and the interpretation of these rules (style), the latter overlapping on the analytical factor of *content*, discussed in previous units of this text.

We have discussed ideas of how culture is formed, first through a look at the sociological study of totemism, as an illustration of how social order in connected with 'mind set'. We then looked at ways culture is formed through successive stages of group development. We proposed that organizational culture constituted a system of explicit and implicit rules, and that the way these rules are interpreted by key individuals in the organization constitute what are termed management 'styles'.

We then turned to a particular view (that of Lessem, 1989) of how organizational cultures and management styles are tied in with both national cultures and with the transition of organizations over time. Thus we discussed the idea of primal, rational, developmental and metaphysical management.

It is possible to discover a great deal about organizations by studying their 'rules' and following some of the approaches to auditing organizational culture in this chapter.

Although we have not provided a comprehensive survey of the very large field of culture and management style, we have tried to give a flavour of some of the approaches and methods used. This field also opens up into the area of learning styles (see Chapter 10) and leadership styles (see Chapter 6).

References

Blake, R. R. and Mouton, J. S. (1985) *The Managerial Grid III*, Houston: Gulf.

Brianas, J. (1986) 'Management styles: a matter of statistical probability' *Training and Development*, October.

Deal, T. E. and Kennedy, A. A. (1982) *Corporate Culture: The Rites and Rituals of Corporate Life*, Reading, MA: Addison-Wesley.

Durkheim, E. (1915) *The Elementary Forms of the Religious Life* (trans. Swain, J. W.), London: Allen and Unwin.

Fiedler, F. (1967) *A Theory of Leadership Effectiveness*, New York: McGraw-Hill.

Harre, R., Clarke, D. and De Carlo, N. (1985) *Motives and Mechanism*, London: Methuen.

Hodge, B. J. and Anthony, W. P. (1988) *Organizational Theory*, Boston: Allyn and Bacon.

Hofstede, G. (1989) 'Organizing for cultural diversity' in *European Management Journal* 7, 4.

Hofstede, G. (1991) *Culture and Organizations: Software of the Mind*, London: McGraw-Hill.

House, R. J. (1971) 'A path-goal theory of leadership effectiveness', *Administrative Science Quarterly*, 16, pp. 321–38.

Hunt, J. G. (1991) *Leadership: A New Synthesis*, Newbury Park, California: Sage.

Lessem, R. (1989) *Global Management Principles*, London: Prentice-Hall.

Likert, R. (1967) *The Human Organization*, Tokyo: McGraw-Hill Kogakusha.

McGoldrich, B. (1984) 'Inside the Goldman Sach Culture' *Institutional Investor*, January pp. 53–67 and cited in Hodge and Anthony (1988) *Organizational Theory*.

McGregor, D. (1960) *The Human Side of Enterprise*, New York: McGraw-Hill.

Ouchi, W. G. and Wilkins, A. L. (1985) 'Organizational Culture', *Annual Review of Sociology*, 11, pp. 457–83.

Reddin, W. J. (1970) *Managerial Effectiveness*, London: McGraw-Hill.

Ribeaux, P. and Poppleton, S. E. (1978) *Psychology at Work*, Basingstoke, Macmillan.

Schein, E. H. (1985) *Organizational Culture and Leadership*, San Francisco: Jossey-Bass.

Smith, P. B., Misumi, J., Tayeb, M., Peterson, M. and Bond, M. (1989) 'On the generality of leadership styles measured across cultures', *Journal of Occupational Psychology*, 62, pp. 97–109.

Turnipseed, D. L. (1988) 'An integrated, interactive model of organizatinal climate, culture and effectiveness', *Leadership and Organizational Development Journal*, 9, 5, pp. 17–21

Tyler, E. B. (1871) *Primitive Culture*, cited in Levi-Strauss, C. (1963) *Structural Anthropology* (trans. Jacobson, C. and Schoel, B. G.), Harmondsworth: Penguin.

van Maanen, J. and Barley, S. R. (1985) 'Cultural organization: fragments of a theory' in Frost, P. J., Moore, L. K., Louis, M. R., Lendberg, C. C. and Martin, J. (eds.), *Organizational Culture*, Newbury Park, CA: Sage, pp. 31–53.

Williams, A., Dobson, P. and Walters, M. (1989) *Changing Culture*, London: Institute of Personnel Management.

Part Two
The Effective Global Manager

Introduction to part two

This part of the book is very focused and reflects a view of the qualities required by managers managing globally. internationally, or cross-culturally. By definition a 'European manager' is necessarily an international one, by virtue of the fact that Europe contains many nations, with different cultures. The European manager, therefore, should possess a number of qualities, competences, attributes or capabilities which will enable him or her to be effective within this environment. Building from Part One, we use organizational behaviour as a vehicle to encourage potential and actual managers to critically look at these requirements, and to develop those which are important.

Following a discussion of what a European manager might be (which in many ways is not that conclusive) we take a view on what attributes are required, as follows.

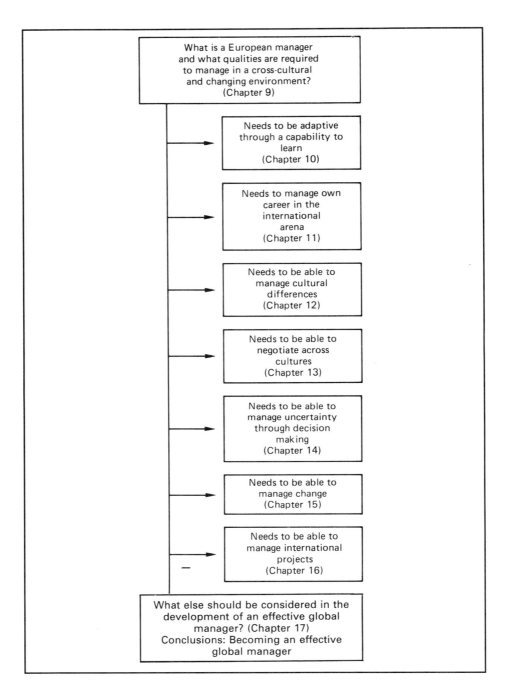

The reader is therefore invited to take a developmental view as he or she goes through Part Two. By entering into the debate about the requirements for European management, the reader can take a look at their own capabilities, compare these with what they believe the effective global manager requires, and commence a development programme based on the chapters of Part Two.

Finally, we provide some conclusions about becoming an effective global manager looking at this within the context of international organizations and their requirements.

Section 4
The European Manager in the Global Marketplace

This section is fundamentally about the development of international managers from a European perspective. Firstly, we look at what a European manager is and what competences should he or she have. We then look at two important aspects of developing towards the required competences: the ability to be adaptive through a process of learning, and the wherewithal to develop an international career.

9

The role of the European manager in the global marketplace

Objectives

Following this chapter you should be able to:

1 Explain critically the nature of a 'European' manager within the international context.
2 Compare and contrast the requirements for European management with those for American and Japanese management.
3 Discuss those competences required of managers working in an international environment.

Key concepts

- European, Anerican and Japanese management
- Global management
- Management competences
- Structuralism, phenomonology and behaviourism

Introduction

The first question we must address is 'Why is the role of the European manager relevant to the study of organizational behaviour?' This question can best be answered by reference to the framework (first introduced in Chapter 1) for understanding organizational behaviour: the 3Cs descriptive model of context–content–conduct. Here, we further elaborate this descriptive model, and show how it may be used to understand the nature of European management. In so doing, we are able to contrast the requirements for American and Japanese management: looking at some of the similarities and some of the differences. We then focus more on the concept of 'management', how we can understand what managers do and how they do it, particularly with reference to the idea of management 'competences'. We then explain how this can help us identify the requirements for effective European management.

The main focus of Section 2 of this text is to help readers think about their own development, and to pursue this in line with their own thinking about the specifications for international management. The discussion on the requirements for an effective global manager in this chapter leads naturally on to the following chapters in this section where the themes and preconditions for managers working in an international environment are discussed in more detail.

A conceptual framework for understanding European management

Before we look at European management we must first develop the conceptual tools in order that we know what we are looking at. To do this we can use the framework of context–content–conduct. Each of these three aspects refer not only to a set of conceptual tools, but also to a body of theory out of which these tools have developed.

We can represent these three aspects of management and their theoretical origins as illustrated in Figure 9.1. Thus (as we have seen in previous chapters) 'context' is the environment within which managers operate, including both 'hard' structure and technology, as well as 'soft' rules or conduct which we associate with the culture and operating environment of an organization. 'Content' refers to those perceptions, objectives, and motives of participants within the organization which actually drive the organization and provide it with a purpose (or purposes). 'Conduct' is the way people behave and the requirements for that behaviour such as the competences and skills necessary to perform.

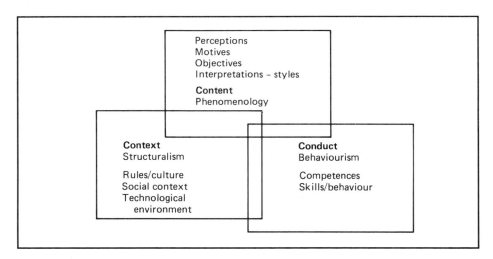

Figure 9.1 *Aspects of management and three schools of thought*

The three schools of thought which this brings together are structuralism (context), phenomenology (content), and behaviourism (conduct). Structuralism and phenomenology are explained in some detail in Chapter 7, and a brief summary of all three theories follows.

Structuralism

- a broad term covering mainly sociological and social psychological theories;
- emphasizes the pre-eminence of the social structure;
- norms and rules are laid down by the social structure;
- goals are socially defined;
- 'structural functionalism' looks at organizations as living organisms, with an interdependence of parts and each contributing to the maintenance of the whole;
- 'open systems' theory looks at the wider influences outside the immediate organization, which it sees as an input–throughput–output system;
- objectives and actions are structurally driven rather than structure being people driven.

Another approach is to try to explain the underlying structure of 'rules' of an organization (Harre *et al.*, 1985), and we have seen this in Chapter 8.

In order to operate effectively within an organization (whether it be national or international in scope) a manager should be able to:

- understand the social structure operating within an organization;
- understand the underlying rules operating within these systems, how they apply to management roles, and how they determine individual managers' understanding of these rules;
- be able to operate within this social structure, conforming where necessary, changing it where necessary and where possible.

A structuralist approach, therefore, concentrates on the context of performance, and its prevailing influence on what people actually do: the goals for which they aim, and how they achieve them.

Phenomenology

- drawn mainly from social philosophy and psychological theory;
- focuses on the individual as controller of his or her own destiny;
- the individual shapes the social structure, rather than being shaped by it (although we should not forget about the power and influence within organizations, see Chapter 5);
- the social structure is a collection of individuals with their own perceptions, objectives, and motives, rather than the social structure being an 'entity', enjoying a life of its own; social meaning is negotiated;
- speaks of 'action' which is meaningful to the actors, rather than 'behaviour', which somehow can be divorced from the meaning systems of individuals and of organizations (see behaviourism);
- action is influenced by:
  - the self-concept (the way individuals see themselves and the values they place on these perceptions;
  - interpersonal perceptions (the way individuals see others around them, for example, self-fulfilling prophecy or prejudice);

- attribution (how individuals explain cause and effect through internal or external factors, and self-fulfilling prophecy through belief in 'fate' for example) (see Chapter 1).

A phenomenological approach is therefore concerned with the meanings of our actions (actions are behaviours which have meaning) or the interpretation of a social situation to the individuals concerned. It sees the social environment as a product of meaning negotiated between interacting individuals, and is therefore approaching human performance from the opposite direction to structuralism.

For managers to be effective they need to be able to:

- understand how they see and judge themselves, and develop a positive self-image;
- understand their own social perceptions of others (whether they are of the same or different nationalities and cultural backgrounds);
- understand how they (and others, perhaps from different cultural backgrounds) explain events such as their own and others' career progression, or the progress of negotiations, or business and economic events;
- understand how this all influences their own, their colleagues' and their staffs' performance.

A phenomenological approach therefore concentrates on the meanings that individuals negotiate with others through interacting with them. Before proceeding to consider behaviourism, let us briefly examine a case which illustrates the attribution of events through different meaning systems.

Mini Case 9.1 The Chinese calendar

Putti and Chia (1990) describe a case of a Dutch firm, Vermeer Electronics, operating in Singapore. The predominantly Singaporean work force, consists mainly of machine operators working in teams.

The action begins with Seng Meng, the young Chinese team leader and his team visiting one another at their homes on Chinese New Year, reminding each other that the new Year of the Tiger is not a good year (the Tiger is destructive, strong and merciless). Some Chinese avoid having babies in this year, and fifty years or so ago, some parents would even abandon baby girls born in this year through fear that they might inherit some of the characteristics of the Tiger.

Back at work, things started to go wrong. Accidents started to happen. A huge pane of ceiling glass had crashed down badly hurting two members of the team; an operator had his hand jammed in a machine, two operators were scalded with steam, another's foot was fractured by a compressor; operators were struck with strange illnesses. Some of his men reported to Seng Meng that they had felt themselves being pushed by something. To this he retorted that they should not be so clumsy. He spoke to them of 'self-fulfilling prophecies', but he himself felt uneasy.

Then things started to happen to him. He tripped and caught his shirt in a moving machine, which was stopped in time to prevent injury.

In the meantime, their Dutch manager Clemens was becoming concerned, but did not believe the operators' initial explanations of bad luck. He believed in hard work, in relying on himself, and on logical and scientific explanation. When Clemens received Seng Meng's explanation of *chare* or a spell of bad luck or evil, with a letter signed by 205 operators requesting that a *lamoloh* be brought in to remove the *chare*, he was amused but dismayed. He had been trying to dismiss the accidents as coincidences or freaks, but this was becoming more difficult.

A *lamoloh* is a professional who removes *chare* by incantations and prayers, and who is paid hundreds and sometimes thousands of dollars for this service. Not all the operators had signed the letter as some did not believe in this. Some were Muslims, Hindus, Christians or Buddhists. Clemens was tempted to try this solution. The problem was, who would pay for this service? How would this affect the image of this modern company if the newspapers found out? Would it offend those workers who did not believe in this solution? What would happen if the *lamoloh* were employed but was unsuccessful? or if he were successful?

Discussion. What are the implications? How should the manager deal with these different meaning systems and explanations of cause and effect?

Behaviourism

We will here go into more detail on behaviourism, as we have not already done this in previous chapters. Also it leads on to a common approach to management performance: competences. We will be taking this up later in this chapter.

The term 'behaviourism' is used here to denote those psychological theories which centre around the importance of observable behaviour. In the extreme, behaviourism sees overt behaviour as the only means of explaining the psychology of a person, and sees behaviour as a response to stimuli in the environment and not a result of an inner cause. Although 'inner states' are accepted, they are not deemed relevant to a scientific explanation of behaviour in Skinnerian terms (for example, Skinner, 1953).

We are not here concerned with 'pure' behaviourism, albeit to note the origins of this approach. The emphasis on 'skills' of more contemporary psychologists is a descendant of behaviourism, and is relevant to an understanding of management.

Particularly relevant is the work of Argyle (for example 1967) and colleagues (for example Argyle *et al.*, 1981), on social skills. The approach of Morgan (1979) and Rackham *et al.* (1971) also represent the behaviourist/skills tradition in the more practical setting of management training. Rather than the 'behaviour' being the start and finish of behaviourist interest, in social skills theory the 'skilled performance' is the end product of both internal and external processes. Argyle's (1967) skills model shows the skilled performance as emanating from both the objectives of the work being undertaken and the internal motivations of the 'performer', and we will look at this later.

Our area of interest is therefore in skilled performances which comprise acts which have meaning for the individual managers concerned and the organization. To be a 'skilled' performer the manager requires certain competences, inner resources or knowledge to be able to perform successfully. Success is measured against recognized standards of achievement which can be either referenced to laid down criteria or norms of the wider management group. Often these can be related to actual results.

Prien (1981), for example, describes categories of knowledge, skills, and ability as constituting a capability to perform. There are numerous examples of categorizing performance which are listed in Fleishman and Quaintance (1984). Among these are Berliner's Classification Scheme which broadly classifies performance in 'processes' such as perceptual processes, and communication process; divided into 'activities' such as problem solving and decision making; and, 'specific behaviours' such as compares, computes or estimates (compare this to the definitions of behaviour, actions and acts above).

In summary, we can say that behaviourism:

- emphasizes overt behaviour, largely ignoring feelings and attitudes;
- concentrates on skills;
- concentrates on the means (behaviour) towards the ends (results);
- but, may miss much of the subtleties of human life.

An effective manager should:

- understand the goals or end results to which the performance is addressed;
- be aware of those competences and skills required to do the job;
- understand the process of management performance.

Table 9.1 *Implications of three theories of organizational behaviour*

Context Structuralism	*Content Phenomenology*	*Conduct Behaviourism*
Systems theory	Process/Action theory	Social skills theory
Socio-technical approaches	Organization Development (OD) approaches	Training
Redesign system to improve Quality of Work Life (QWL)	Change culture, match individual/organizational objectives	Develop skills of managers

These theories, and the three approaches to understanding management and organizations which they represent, have implications for the way change is seen and implemented in organizations. Typically, they represent contemporary theories of organizational change and consultancy practices, as shown in Table 9.1.

Applying the framework to an understanding of European management

Let us now apply the descriptive model of *context–content–conduct* to an understanding of European management by focusing in turn on these three aspects. We will first summarize the main characteristics of European management within this framework, and then discuss them.

Context of European management

- increased technological change;
- integration of a variety of cultures;
- a need for different types of management structures such as international project teams and networking organizations;
- the decline of a young work-force due to demographic changes and the need for organizations to be more flexible and people-oriented;
- a changing of organizational and cultural 'rules' and an interfusion of such rules and cultures requiring both organizations and individuals to adapt.

Whilst this description of the strategic and operating environment is not unique to Europe, it does characterize some of the important aspects of the context of European management. Tijmstra and Casler note, for example the increasing merger and acquisition activity on an international basis in Europe. 'Since 1985 mergers and acquisitions in the European Community have increased eight-fold. Where in 1985 less than 15% of this activity involved a foreign partner, in 1989 nearly 50% of all M&A activity included an international partner' (Tijmstra and Casler, 1992, p. 31). Similarly joint ventures and alliances have greatly increased over the same time period.

The nature and scope of such activity are likely to be more concentrated and complex than that of other economic regions such as the United States home market, and possibly the Japanese. In order to effect such change across countries with widely different cultural traditions and language, the wholesale deployment of new technology is necessary to aid communication, as is the use of different types of organizational structures as Bartlett and Ghoshal (1989) note (see also Chapter 7 of the current text).

Content of European management

- a variety of perceptions, objectives and motives of individuals;
- often a resistance to change which needs to be overcome;
- a need to consider individuals' objectives, which may be quite varied, in the context of the organization's objectives;
- a need to consider and marry up the individual styles of managers with the culture and styles of the organization;
- different organizational 'policies' of management performance (a need for this to be adequately defined, and agreed, but to remain flexible enough for the changing context).

With the geographical scope of organizational change it is likely that it will be more complex than when simply undertaken on a national basis, and more fraught with problems of differing perceptions, attitudes, objectives and motives to take into consideration, as well as the added problems of resistance to change. The problems of different styles of management (see Chapter 8) may compound difficulties of integration.

The different 'policies' on management performance also will have to be understood. For example, Management by Objectives (MBO) has been a current method used for management appraisal for a couple of decades in Anglo-Saxon countries, but may not be so appropriate, for example, in a French company environment. Methods and criteria for performance evaluation should be clearly defined whilst keeping a degree of flexibility. Flexibility may also apply to the differing styles which managers may need to adopt.

Conduct of European management:

- a need to develop the appropriate management skills to meet the needs of the individual (in relation to management styles and the 'performance policies' of organizations);
- a need to develop not just the 'how' of management skills, but also the 'why' of management action (that is, understanding the context, content as well as the skills or conduct of management performance).

While it is useful to identify and isolate specific competences and skills required to perform the job of management, this may not be sufficient for understanding the requirements for a European manager to perform adequately. Perhaps more important are the attitudes and flexibility towards managing change, and managing across-cultures. For this, skills are not sufficient. A sound educational foundation is necessary in order to enable managers to 'think around corners' and to work side by side with members of other national cultures.

The American and Japanese models of management

We can identify (following Thurley and Wirdenius, 1989) contrasts between the American and the Japanese models of management (see Table 9.2).

Hence, American management theory is firmly built on the tenets of scientific management (Thurley and Widenius, 1989), using a systematic approach to improving task performance. An individualist approach allows classical management theory to define roles in terms of specific jobs and responsibilities, where managers are individuals with their own interests and personalities. In order to serve organizational goals group norms are fostered through a human relations approach. Change

Table 9.2 *American and Japanese models of management*

American	Japanese
Task performance	Job rotation
Job definition	Generalist roles
Individualism	Collectivism
Human relations	Employee protection
Rational management	Rationalism
Strategic management	Pragmatism
Specialist know-how	Work-group innovation

management requires a planned approach to changing structures and cultures. Organizations should define business strategies required to achieve market position and design structures to fit these needs.

Japanese management emphasizes equality as the basis for competition and co-operation (Thurley and Widenius, 1989), basing its practice on collective responsibility where all members feel responsible for the organization. Individuals do not own their jobs as they may have to do anything, needing training to perform a variety of jobs. In this spirit, employees should be trusted to get on with their jobs and should have their potential stimulated. Employees should be protected by the organization as they are vulnerable, while life careers should be planned. There is a recognition that everything changes and management should be adaptive and pragmatic, and flexible enough to change to the new circumstances. Finally, the work ethic is connected with the individual's interaction with the work group. It is through the work group that employees gain their identity and associate their activity with the *michi* or 'the way'.

These *contextual* 'rules' and cultures have implications for individuals' motives and objectives, and their management behaviours. It also influences the way we see that behaviour. For example, it is difficult to speak of individual management competences in the Japanese collectivist context.

Thurley and Wirdenius (1989) therefore characterize these differences between Japanese and American management theory and practice as: work security versus individual freedom; organizational loyalty versus job competence; consultation and involvement versus management authority; and, work group innovation versus specialist knowhow. However Reading (1992) is not so complimentary towards the Japanese way. In his book *Japan – The Coming Collapse*. He states:

> The quality of life in Japan remains depressingly poor. Most Japanese are overworked, overcrowded and ill-housed, coerced to conform to group norms by employers, bureaucrats and yakusa gangsters. . . . Most workers are paid serfs, chained to their employers. When young Japanese leave school or university and choose a job, they do so for life. The brightest may even be kidnapped by potential second-rate employers, and held captive until all better jobs have been filled. . . . Although the danger of losing one's job is slight, companies have absolute power to decide where their employees work and what they do. . . . Individual prosperity depends on collective success, to which all must contribute. The suicide rate is high and death from overwork, *karoshi*, is commonplace (Reading, 1992).

This represents a slightly different angle on Japanese collectivism.

The importance, in economic terms, of the European Community, and perhaps the imperative for developing a management approach which is typically European, is stated by Tijmstra and Casler (1992, page 31):

> the European Community's share of world trade between 1960 and 1987 increased from 41% to 44% of the total. In contrast the US share declined from 20% to 15% in the same period while the share of Japan and New Industrial Countries increased from 3% to 17%. And in 1989 Europe's direct investment abroad was by far the highest in the Triad:
>
> Europe 85.1 billion $
> USA   31.7 billion $
> Japan   44.2 billion $

Let us now look at the characteristics of the European context of management.

The European context of management

We can summarize this context by expressing the following opinions about the growing complexity of the European Community, as follows:

- there is no national identity across the European Community as there is in Japan and the USA, for example there is no equivalent of the 'American Dream';
- there is no common language or culture;
- change is more complex than in America or Japan, particularly with events in Eastern Europe and the former Soviet Bloc, and this is in some ways artificial in creation: manufactured by the architects and politicians of the Single European Market, signifying a higher level of creativity needed to manage in this environment;
- there will be increasing cross-border activity through mergers and acquisitions, joint ventures and 'greenfield' situations requiring approaches to management such as project management and networking;
- there will be a greater emphasis on new technology as a means of competing and communicating;
- there will be an increasing demand for linguistic skills, perhaps at the expense of more traditional management skills;
- in sum, there is a need to manage increasing diversity (between cultures rather than trying to create a uniformed culture), ambiguity and complexity.

There is therefore no doubt that the 'European' manager will need to be 'international', at least in perspective if not in actual location. We could therefore think of managers in Europe acting locally, European-wide or internationally. Despite the term 'global' having certain connotations of uniformity and homogenization of markets across the world (see Bartlett and Ghoshal, 1989), we have chosen this term to express the required perceptions of European managers on the world stage (the *Collins English Dictionary* defines this term as 'covering, influencing, or relating to the whole world').

Before we look more closely at the European manager and the competences required to perform as an effective global manager, we must first discuss the concept of 'competences'. We mentioned above that this way of identifying characteristics of individual management performance may not be appropriate to Japanese collectivism, and indeed, it is typically an Anglo-Saxon invention. None the less, it is a useful way to conceptualize the requirements of management, which we employ despite some of its shortcomings.

Management competences

The idea of management 'competences' is drawn from the basic assumptions of the skills approach in social psychology which suggests we can understand social action by looking at its component parts. One of the best illustrations of this is the skills model of the Oxford psychologist Michael Argyle (1967), shown in Figure 9.2.

This is seen as a conscious process directed towards making changes in the environment. It requires some sort of motivation in order to drive the process, and

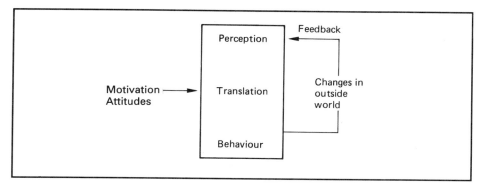

Figure 9.2 *Argyle's skills model (adapted from Argyle, 1967)*

specific attitudes (particularly towards intended goals) may influence the process and its outcome. It requires an ability to perceive the changes to be made, to understand how they can be achieved, and the ability to apply this understanding to the perceived situation and to formulate whatever action is required. We can monitor the actual changes made and compare them with our intentions. Through our ability to perceive what we are doing, we can then make suitable adjustments to our behaviour to try to ensure that the desired result is achieved. The factors involved in such a 'skilled performance' (in Argyle's, 1967, terms) are therefore:

- the motivation to perform (as well as the attitudes towards the performance and subject of the performance);
- knowledge and understanding of what is required;
- the ability (capability) to translate knowledge into specific behaviour;
- the performance itself which provides evidence that the above three factors are present.

The concept of 'skills' has a long pedigree. The latter day equivalent of such an approach (which is largely based in behavioural and reductionist psychology) is the concept of 'management competences'. Thus Boyatzis (1982) sees competences as an effective mix of motives, traits, skills, aspects of one's self-image or social role, or body of knowledge used by individuals. Constable more specifically sees competences as 'the ability to use knowledge and skills effectively in the performance of a managerial role. All management skills must, therefore, be competences when performed effectively' (Constable, 1988, p. 19). He therefore points to a more tangible list of attributes such as an ability to make sound judgements, creativity, willingness to take risks, and high energy levels. He defines competences (Constable, 1988, following Boyatzis', 1982, definition of 'skills') as: 'the ability to demonstrate a system or sequence of behaviour as a function related to attaining a performance goal'. This is in fact very close to the concept of skills (or skilled performance) posited by Argyle (1967) above.

Boyatzis (1982) further focuses on different types of competences by conceptualizing them in terms of 'types' and 'levels'. The former are associated with various aspects of behaviour and an individual's ability to demonstrate such behaviour. So, 'planning' competency is associated with 'setting goals', 'assessing risk' and developing a sequence of goal-related activities. 'Levels' of abstraction are seen by Boyatzis (1982) in terms of:

- the motive and trait level;
- the self image and social role level;
- the skills level.

At the motive and trait level 'planning' might be reflected in a desire to achieve certain goals; at the self image and social level this might entail having a self image of thinking ahead and being positive, and this would be projected in the manager's social role; and at the skills level the manager would perhaps develop a plan of action, assess risk and implement the plan through a series of behaviours. By using the 'type' and 'level' concept Boyatzis (1982) was able to empirically derive a number of competency clusters. A summary of this is shown in Table 9.3.

Table 9.3 *Boyatzis's competences clusters*

Cluster	Competence	Level
Goal and action management cluster	Concern with impact	Skill, Motive
	Diagnostic use of concepts	Skills, social role
	Efficiency orientation	Skill, motive, social role
	Proactivity	
Leadership cluster	Conceptialization	Skill
	Self-confidence	Skill, social role
	Use of oral presentation	Skill, social role
Human resource management cluster	Managing group process	Skill
	Use of socialized power	Skill, social role
Directing subordinates cluster	Developing others	Skill, social role
	Spontaneity	Skill
	Use of unilateral power	Skill, social role
Focus on others cluster	Perceptual objectivity	Skill
	Self-control	Trait
	Stamina and adaptability	Trait
Specialized knowledge	Specialized knowledge	Social role

Source: adapted from Boyatzis, 1982

Contemporary examples of the application of competences to identify what is required of managers can be seen in the following examples.

Cadbury-Schweppes' categorization of managers' competences is related by Glaze (1989) as follows.

Strategy
- vision
- critical thinking
- innovation
- environmental awareness
- business sense

Drive
- self
- motivation
- initiative
- tenacity
- energy
- independence
- risk taking
- resilience

Relationships
- sociability
- impact
- acceptability
- awareness

Persuasion
- oral communication
- written communication
- flexibility
- negotiation

Leadership
- delegation
- subordinate development

Followership
- followership
- team-work

Analysis
- problem analysis
- numerical analysis
- listening
- creativity
- judgement
- intuition

Implementation
- planning and organizing
- decisiveness
- organizing sensitivity

- management control
- work standards
- detail handling
- compliance
- stress tolerance
- adaptability
- commitment

Personal factors
- integrity
- management identification
- career ambition
- learning ability
- technical/professional

National Westminster Bank (Cockerill, 1989)
- Information search (to make decision)
- Concept formation (on basis of information)
- Concept flexibility (consideration of alternatives)
- Interpersonal search (understanding others ideas and feelings)
- Managing interaction (team building)
- Developmental orientation (creating a developmental climate)
- Impact (to gain support for ideas and initiatives)
- Self-confidence (confidence for implementing own ideas)
- Presentation (communicating ideas)
- Proactive orientation (implementation)
- Achievement orientation (ambitious yet attainable goals)

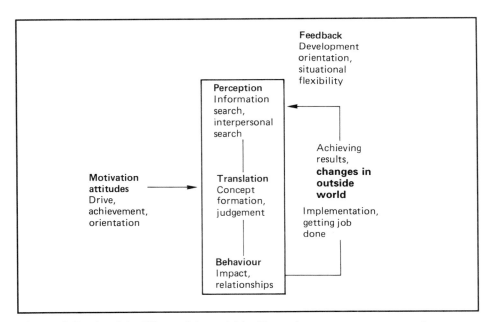

Figure 9.3 *Argyle's skills model overlaid with contemporary management competences*

We can overlay Argyle's (1967) skills model with the most commonly prescribed competences from contemporary lists in the UK as demonstrated in Figure 9.3. Thus, we can think of the requirements for effective management within this conceptual framework and apply this to the requirements of European (global) managers.

European (global) competences

Firstly, we must try to answer the question of what is a European manager before we can discuss what competences that person may require.

A survey of more than forty large European companies by Bournois and Chauchat (1990) revealed the answer that a 'Euromanager' could be any one of the following:

- any manager from a member country of the EC (defined, often, by the man in the street);
- a manager working in his home country for a company based in another European country (defined by the employing company);
- a manager working outside of his home country for a company from his own country (defined by the country the manager is working in);
- a manager undertaking a career spanning several EC countries and working for a large company that operates beyond the borders of its home country (defined by the managers themselves).

We can perhaps add that a European manager can expect to work as an international manager within a homebase (Europe) and therefore function interculturally.

Ashridge Management College undertook a survey of nearly fifty American, British and Japanese international companies to determine which characteristics of international management they most valued (Barnham and Oates, 1991). The results were the following list of broad competences in order of perceived importance:

- strategic awareness
- adaptability in new situations
- sensitivity to different cultures
- ability to work in international teams
- language skills
- understanding international marketing
- relationship skills
- international negotiating skills
- self-reliance
- high task-orientation
- open, non-judgemental personality
- understanding international finance
- awareness of own culture

Sue Davison (in an unpublished paper) argues that the idea of competences of international managers may not be sufficient in an understanding of the requirements for managing across cultures. She suggests an ability to: deal with frustrations, isolation, failure; and learning how to network, gain support and anticipate differences.

She adds that such qualities as 'helicopter view', intuition and cultural sensitivity may be difficult to directly teach and acquire. So, are qualities needed of international managers untrainable 'traits'? However, she adds, interpersonal skills can be learned at the level of managing intercultural teams no matter what personality traits one might possess. This, together with an understanding of one self as well as the other person's culture is something which can be developed.

We will shortly go on to look at two particular company cases of views of European managers. First, however, it may be instructive to list your own views of what constitutes a European (global) manager.

Activity 9.1

Look at the model of management performance shown in Figure 9.2. Can you superimpose your ideas of the competences required for European management on this model as we have done in Figure 9.3 for UK management competences?

In order to clarify ideas on the nature of European management the following case is presented.

Mini Case 9.2 European managers in two international companies

In January 1990 the *Financial Times* held a conference in London on 'Creating a Euro-workforce in the '90s'. Two of the contributors to a debate on the internationalization of managers were John B. Stewart, Director of Human Resources, Ford of Europe, and Craig Dinsell, Vice-President, Human Resources, American Express in Europe.

Ford operates in fifteen different European countries. It has, over the last twenty years, developed a policy of managers who have a national responsibility also having a European responsibility as well, so that the Director of Engineering in Germany is also the executive responsible for co-ordinating the engineering of engine and transmission systems in the European R&D locations. This principle is established down to middle management level. Thus managers have learnt to work in a European environment, taking account of different legal requirements, customs and practice, as well as working with cross-cultural teams. There is also the practice of assigning managers to work in different foreign locations. So it is normal to find a senior British manager working in Cologne or a German working in Valencia. Business is conducted in the local language, but English is the language of the company.

With a growing globalism and the need to see its European managers as part of the 'global village', these practices within Europe are likely to be extended to the world arena. This all means that the job of the international manager in Ford will be characterized by:

- accelerating change;
- increasing technical complexity of decision-making;
- a need to exert influence and leadership in a participative manner rather than through the traditional command structure;
- learning from experience, implementing continuous improvement, and taking a systems view of the business rather than a narrow specialist or functional view.

Successful international managers will therefore be measured on their ability to anticipate change and master complexity and paradox.

American Express see that they have globally oriented products which should be capable of delivery locally, and therefore must be locally relevant. In order to meet the challenges of a new Europe, they do not want to create a bureaucratic structure which ossifies their management talent. Instead they have set the following goals for organizational development:

- create a refreshed and common vision and values across Europe;
- optimize the organization and its resources both locally and internationally;
- ensure continued excellence in its people management;
- consistently develop management talent;
- enhance its international team by recruiting the best people
- provide the best employee relations environment.

Of their international managers they are looking for the following competences:

- leadership skills: an ability to create business vision, direction and values which motivate others;
- the intellect, flexibility, courage and imagination to recognize and respond to the rapid pace of change;
- the cultivation of a broad knowledge of the history, culture, law and languages of Europe, and the ability to set aside nationalism and its prejudices and stereotypes;
- a willing team member who can work in multinational project groups and be willing to move to different countries and cultures.

Discussion. Do you share the same ideas about European management? Are any other attributes missing from this list? When looking at the concept of competences, Polanyi (1967) uses an analogy of a police identikit, where we can choose from thousands of pieces of physiognomy to build up a picture of 'a face', but it is still not quite right, some inexplicable quality is missing. Is this the same for the competences outlined here. Is something missing overall from the description of the international manager? What could it be?

Conclusions

We can now answer the original question of this chapter: what is the relevance of the nature of European management to a study of organizational behaviour? The answer is that it provides us with the main subject of study for the remainder of this text. Namely, those competences which we have discussed above, and possibly others as well, are those we should be developing in European and international managers. The following aspects of effective global management are the ones we are going to look at in the following chapters. These are:

- an awareness of own competences and attributes in line with the needs for global management;
- the need to learn to learn in order to be adaptive;
- the need to manage your own career in order to be effective throughout your professional life;
- the ability to manage uncertainty through a capability to make decisions in a complex and rapidly changing environment;
- the ability to manage difference through an understanding of intercultural communication, and to negotiate across cultures;
- the ability to manage change and an understanding of the problems encountered;
- a knowledge and ability to effect structural change and redesign organizations;
- the ability to manage international projects;
- an awareness of your own development needs in the international context, and an understanding of how to develop towards becoming an effective global manager.

References

Argyle M., (1967) *The Psychology of Interpersonal Behaviour*, Harmondsworth: Penguin.

Argyle, M., Furnham, A. and Graham, J. A. (1981) *Social Situations*, Cambridge: CUP.

Barnham, K. and Oates, D. (1991) *The International Manager*, London: Business Books/The Economist Books.

Bartlett, C. A. and Ghoshal, S., (1989), *Managing Across Borders*, London Hutchinson.

Bournois, F. and Chauchat, J.-H., (1990) 'Managing Managers in Europe', *European Management Journal*, 8, 1.

Boyatzis, R. E. (1982) *The Competent Manager*, New York: John Wiley.

Cockerill, T. (1989) 'The kind of competences for rapid change', *Personnel Management*, September.

Constable C. J. (1988) *Developing The Competent Manager in a UK Context*, Report for the Manpower Services Commission, Sheffield: Manpower Services Commission.

Davison, S. 'International competencies – are they useful as models?' (unpublished).

Fleishman, E. A. and Quaintance, M. K. (1984), *Taxonomy of Human Performance*, New York: Academic Press.

Glaze, T. (1989) 'Cadbury's dictionary of competence', *Personnel Management*, July.

Harre, R., Clark, D. and De Carlo, N. (1985) *Motives and Mechanisms*, London: Methuen.

Morgan, R. G. T. (1979) 'Analysis of social skills: the behaviour analysis approach' in Singleton, W. T., Spurgeon, P. and Stammers, R. B. (eds.) (1980) *The Analysis of Social Skills*, New York: Plenum Press.

Polanyi, M. (1967) *The Tacit Dimension*, New York: Doubleday.

Prien, E. (1981) 'The function of job analysis in content validation', *Personnel Psychology*, 30, pp. 167–74.

Putti, J. M. and Chia, A., (1990), *Culture and Management: A Casebook*, Singapore: McGraw-Hill.

Rackham, N., Honey, P. and Colbert M. *et al.* (1971) *Developing Interactive Skills*, Northampton: Wellens Publishing.

Reading, B. (1992) *Japan – The Coming Collapse*, London: Weidenfeld and Nicolson (abstracted in *Sunday Times*, 3 May 1992).

Skinner, B. F. (1953) *Science and Human Behaviour*, New York: Macmillan.

Thurley, K. and Wirdenius, H. (1989) *Towards European Management*, London: Pitman.

Tijmstra, S. and Casler, K. (1992) 'Management learning for Europe', *European Management Journal*, 10, 1.

The adaptive manager: learning

Objectives

Following this chapter you should be able to:

1 Explain the importance of individual learning to the need for a high degree of adaptability in the Global arena.
2 Explain critically the different theories of the learning process.
3 Explain the concept of learning styles, describe the different approaches, and identify differences between cultures.
4 Identify your own learning styles and explain the implications for your own learning.

Key concepts

- Behavioural learning theories
- Cognitive learning theories
- Experiential learning
- Learning styles
- Action learning

Introduction: learning and the adaptable manager

Perhaps one of the most important capacities of a manager working across different cultures, is the ability to learn quickly and effectively in order to adapt from one situation to the next, in order to cope with high degrees of change and ambiguity. For this reason we now look at the learning of individuals.

We first look at the main theories of the learning process, taking a more traditional approach in contrasting behavioural with cognitive approaches. However, the main body of this chapter is concerned with the different ways people, as individuals, learn. This involves an examination of the styles of learning. Theorists and management teachers in the United States, and more recently in the United Kingdom have largely taken a lead in this area, developing a number of different theories or classifications of learning styles. Thus we look at the work of de Bono (for example 1970), Honey and Mumford (1982), and Revans (for example 1965). The latter takes us on to a discussion of the concept of Action Learning, a major contribution to recent management development practice. This part of the chapter, therefore tries to answer the question, how do we learn? More specifically it asks the question, how do different people learn differently? In this connection we look at some of the cultural differences in how people learn.

In this section we encourage readers to examine their own learning styles in order that they can better understand how best they can learn and adapt to and take a lead in different situations and circumstances.

Theories of learning

Traditional approaches to learning opposes two fundamental theories: the behaviourist or stimulus–response approach; and the cognitive or information processing approach. In brief, behaviourist approaches study only behaviour which can be observed. We learn habitual behaviour as a result of our responses to stimuli in the environment. We are conditioned by the responses we give and their subsequent outcomes. Thus, if we always receive rewards for performing a certain behaviour, we are likely to carry on with that behaviour. Problem solving is initially by a sequence of trial and error.

Cognitive approaches are more complex, as the process of learning is seen as more complex. As well as being concerned with observable behaviour, cognitive approaches also focus on mental process, assuming that behaviour is determined by memory, cognitive processes and expectations. Thus we learn cognitive structures and thus alternative ways to achieve goals. Problem solving involves understanding and insight.

Behavioural approaches (see also Chapter 9 for an explanation of the basic theory) achieved a high degree of currency because they were amenable to laboratory research, but were seen as being devoid of any deeper psychological explanation because of the purist position of not accepting as relevant any cognitive or subconscious aspects. Thus cognitive theories grew largely out of this criticism of behaviourism. However, behaviourism is important simply because so many approaches to management learning are descended from the concepts originally developed by Skinner (for example 1953): behaviour modification in such techniques as assertiveness training; programmed learning or its modern day equivalents in computer based training; and skills based training.

From the traditional stimulus–response behaviourism of Watson and Pavlov, Skinner developed a more sophisticated notion of 'operant conditioning'. Pavlov's experiments showed that an animal could be conditioned to react to a conditioned stimulus such as a light flashing on when this is continually followed by the reward of food. The animal will therefore salivate (the conditioned response) when the light flashes. Whereas, in Pavlovian conditioning the conditioned stimulus (the light) precedes and elicits the response (salivation), Skinner argues that the vast majority of learning is due to what happens after the behaviour has occurred. Thus behaviour is shaped and maintained by its consequences. So, those behaviours which are 'reinforced' by producing effects in the environment which strengthen them, are more likely to occur in the future. Such behaviours Skinner refers to as 'operants', and to the process, 'operant conditioning' (Skinner, 1953). A stimulus that increases the likelihood of that behaviour occurring again when it is present is called a 'positive reinforcer', and when that stimulus is removed is called a 'negative reinforcer'.

Thus the concept of reinforcement by reward is important in behavioural psychology, and the absence of such a reward is regarded as a negative reinforcer. So, if you constantly get praised by a supervisor at work you are likely to carry on with the behaviour which led to the praise. If such feedback is absent, then you will not learn what the required behaviour is. Thus the importance of feedback is also stressed in latter day derivatives of behaviourism. Punishment is not necessarily the opposite of reward. Punishing a behaviour because it is wrong may lead to hostility and resentment. This may be particularly damaging in the work place.

In the field of instruction, 'programmed learning' was developed on the principles that correct responses could be reinforced and the trainee went through the programme at his or her pace. This concept has been taken up in many applications of computer based training (this is perhaps a case where the technology is dictating the method, as programmed learning had all but died out before the advent of computer based training). Also 'behaviour modification' techniques have been used in both training and employment practices where the required behaviour is encouraged by positive reinforcement, and wrong behaviour is discouraged by negative reinforcement. Thus time keeping may be improved by giving cash incentives to those who start work early. Managers can be trained in the use of positive reinforcers.

Cognitive theories grew largely as a reaction to behaviourism (often being called stimulus–stimulus theory as opposed to the stimulus–response theory of behaviourism). Thus Tolman (1932) sees behaviour as purposeful and that learning is an expectation based on a meaningful connection between two stimuli. Reinforcement is replaced in his theory by confirmation, and behaviour is generated by expectancy and need. Thus learning is based on a need system, on beliefs and values, and on what happens when behaviour actually takes place. So, a person may have a particular goal, say to reach a certain destination, as the person needs to get home. The person takes a certain road as he or she believes that this may be the correct option. If this behaviour is confirmed, the person is likely to take the same road in the future in order to achieve the goal of getting home. Thus this type of learning involves the particular value or belief system in the choice of goal. It also involves insight by picking up whatever clues could be gleaned about the correct road home, perhaps even taking a guess. It also involves the development of a 'cognitive map' which in the future would guide the person's behaviour in finding his or her way home. Hilgard and Bower (1967) list the following features of the cognitive approach to learning.

• The perceptual features of the situation are important to learners in order that they can see what leads to what, and relations between the different elements. Any learning problem should be structured so all features are open to inspection.
• How the required knowledge is organized is important for the instructor. Thus a progress from simple to complex should not be from unrelated parts to the whole, but from smaller wholes to more complex wholes.
• Learning with understanding is more permanent than rote learning.
• A process of building assumptions and testing them through confirmation or cognitive feedback is a basis of learning as a type of hypothesis testing process rather than as reinforcement process.
• Goal setting is important as motivation for learning. Successes or failures in achieving goals will largely determine future setting of goals.
• Divergent thinking which leads to inventive solutions is to be encouraged, along with convergent thinking which leads to logically correct answers.

Cognitive theories therefore lead to a conception of different styles of thinking. We now turn to the related field of learning styles. The main concentration in the literature

(Kolb 1976; Kolb *et al.*, 1991; Honey and Mumford, 1982, the latter being largely derived from Kolb) has been in establishing the processional or sequential aspects of learning, together with the preferences of individuals to adopt particular learning styles.

Learning as an experiential process

Kolb (for example see Kolb *et al.*, 1991) sees learning as an experiential process or cycle comprising four stages as follows:

1 concrete experiences, followed by;
2 observation and reflection, leading to;
3 formation of abstract concepts and generalizations, leading to;
4 testing of the implications of concepts for future action, which then lead to new concrete experiences.

Kolb sees this as the way learning happens, as it is governed largely by the pursuit of goals which are appropriate to our own needs. Thus we seek experiences which are related to these goals, we interpret the experiences in the light of these goals, and form concepts which are relevant to our needs and goals. When goals are not clear, learning tends to be erratic (Kolb *et al.*, 1991). As a result of personal preferences and inclinations, individuals tend to emphasize a particular aspect of the learning cycle. Kolb uses the examples of the mathematician who emphasizes abstract conceptualization, the poet who values concrete experience, the manager who is concerned with application of concepts, and the lover of nature who develops observational skills. The development of such preferences may provide both strengths and weaknesses.

Cross-cultural differences in the learning process

In the cross-cultural context, Hughes-Weiner (1986) qualifies this learning process described by Kolb.

• *Concrete experience*: people from different cultures are likely to have different backgrounds and different experiences. For example readiness for classroom learning may therefore be quite different between different cultural backgrounds.

• *Reflective observation*: as a result of different behaviour patterns, socialization and institutional and work experiences, individuals from different cultures may make different assumptions about what they see and understand through their experiences. People from different societies are likely to acquire different bodies of knowledge.

• *Abstract conceptualization*: because people from different cultures may have different cognitive frameworks, this may lead to focusing on irrelevant information or misinterpretations in a particular situation, thus drawing wrong conclusions and theories in a different cultural situation to their own.

• *Active experimentation*: behaviour differences between cultures may lead to misinterpretations and misattributions to the meanings of such behaviour outside their own cultures, leading to confusion and frustration.

Learning styles

Kolb (1976) uses the 'Learning Styles Inventory' to quantify individual preferences for learning styles based on the four stages of the learning cycle. Honey and Mumford (1982) take a similar approach, and we can compare their classifications as we go through those of Kolb.

Activity 10.1 Learning styles

The following questionnaire is adapted from that of Kolb (see Kolb *et al.*, 1991. The interested reader is referred to the original questionnaire in this text).

In the following sets of four descriptions, mark the one most like you with a 4, the one least like you with a 1, the one second most like you with a 3, and the one third most like you with a 2.

1 [ ] responsive	[ ] tentative	[ ] logical	[ ] realistic
2 [ ] feeling	[ ] watching	[ ] thinking	[ ] doing
3 [ ] accepting	[ ] observing	[ ] evaluating	[ ] experimenting
4 [ ] intuitive	[ ] detached	[ ] analytical	[ ] active
5 [ ] present-oriented	[ ] reflecting	[ ] rational	[ ] pragmatic
6 [ ] experience	[ ] observation	[ ] conceptualization	[ ] responsibility

CE = _____	RO = _____	AC = _____	AE = _____
Concrete Experimentation	Reflective Observation	Abstract Conceptualization	Active Experimentation

Scoring

For each column add up the scores. This score will indicate that style (or phase in the learning process) which you favour most.

Interpretation

Now read below the descriptions of these styles.

Concrete experimentation is Kolb's first mode of the experiential learning cycle and starts with involvement in new experiences. As a learning style, there is a preference for intuition rather than logical thinking skills, dealing with immediate human problems and concerned with present reality. There is a value on relating to people and having an open-minded approach to life.

This compares with Honey and Mumford's (1982) *Activist*. They use the 'Learning Styles Inventory' (1982) to measure learning styles preferences, and refer to the Activist style as preferring the here and now of immediate experiences, and being open-minded and enthusiastic. Short-term problem solving is favoured, with brainstorming as a technique. Individuals with this learning style are easily bored.

Reflective observation is Kolb's second mode in the learning cycle stressing reflecting on and observing experience from difference perspectives. The style is concerned more with understanding rather than practice, reflection rather than action, and looking for new perspectives on an issue or problem. Relying on own thoughts and feelings, there is a value on patience, impartiality and thoughtful judgement.

Honey and Mumford call individuals with this learning style *Reflectors*, who prefer to stand back and ponder, to collect data and reflect on them, postponing reaching definite conclusions for as long as possible. They tend to be somewhat distant and observe rather than being involved directly in the action.

Abstract conceptualization is the third mode which concentrates on creating concepts which integrate observations into logical theories. A preference is given to logic, ideas and concepts, thinking rather than feeling. Science is of more interest than art, with a value placed on precision, rigour, and systematic planning.

This compares with Honey and Mumford's *Theorists* who like to adapt and integrate observations into complex but logical theories. Thinking is vertical and logical. The maximization of certainty is valued, which may lead to the rejection of anything which does not fit into the theory.

Active experimentation is the final mode (although the process is ongoing and cyclical) in the learning cycle. It emphasizes using theories to make decisions and solve problems. Individuals who favour this mode work actively to influence people and situations, and prefer practical applications and solutions rather than the pursuit of truth and rigour for its own sake. An emphasis is placed on doing rather than observing, achieving and getting things done. A value is placed on results.

Honey and Mumford describe such individuals as *Pragmatists* who like to try ideas and techniques in practice to see if they work. They search out new ideas and look for opportunities to put them into practice. They are practical and respond to a challenge with the attitude that there must be a better way of doing this!

These four modes (Kolb, 1976) or styles (Honey and Mumford, 1982) are conceived as dimensions of learning as shown in Figure 10.1. As a result of using either

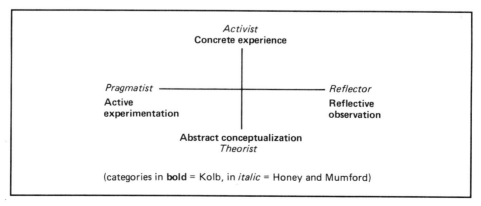

Figure 10.1 *Kolb's, and Honey and Mumford's learning styles categories*

instrument (Kolb, 1976 or Honey and Mumford, 1982), an individual can gain a score along each dimension. The highest score shows the preference.

Kolb (1976) goes further in analysing the scores by combining them for each learning mode. The learning styles types thus derived are as follows.

Convergent (combining *active experimentation* with *abstract conceptualization*). The strengths of this style are problem solving, decision making and practical application of ideas. These individuals tend to do well in intelligence tests where there is a single correct answer (convergent). The weaknesses are in dealing with human situations, social and interpersonal issues which do not have a single solution.

Divergent (combining *concrete experience* with *reflective observation*). Strengths here are in imaginative ability and awareness of meaning and values, viewing concrete situations from many perspectives, organizing relationships into a meaningful whole, and dealing with alternative ideas (divergent). The weaknesses are in convergent, logical thinking and scientific method.

Assimilation (combining *reflective observation* with *abstract conceptualization*). The strengths here are in the ability to create theoretical models, assimilating disparate observations into integrated explanations, favouring pure science rather than applied science. The weaknesses are in the application of logical methods and dealing with human issues.

Accommodative (combining *active experimentation* with *concrete experience*). The strengths are in doing things, carrying out plans and tasks and getting involved, being adaptive, opportunistic and risk taking. The weaknesses are that accommodators are often seen as impatient or 'pushy', they are liable to reject theory if it does not quite fit with reality, rather than trying to adapt it or rethink it.

Learning styles and thinking styles

Certainly these style types are very akin to thinking styles. Much work has been undertaken in the UK by de Bono (for example, 1970) on thinking styles, referred to as 'lateral' thinking and 'vertical' thinking. These are similar respective to Kolb's divergent and convergent learning styles types. While both styles are required, de Bono has spent much time on the development of lateral thinking. While lateral thinking is concerned with generating alternatives, vertical thinking is concerned with selecting one of these alternatives and using it.

Activity 10.2 Lateral thinking

There are many examples of problems and puzzles which set out to illustrate and test the use of lateral thinking. The following is such an example.

Every morning a man goes to the office block where he works. He gets into the lift, and presses the button for the fifth floor. He then gets out and walks to the twelfth floor where he works. In the evening he gets into the lift on the twelfth floor and presses the button for the ground floor. On reaching the ground floor he gets out of the lift and goes on his way home.

> What is happening?
> The lateral thinker may not just go for the logical or obvious answer, but would generate different alternative answers. He or she might then go for the explanation which explained the behaviour. In this case there is one answer, and you will find this at the end of the chapter.

We can summarise the differences between vertical and lateral thinking as follows.

Vertical thinking:

- chooses
- is selective
- is judgemental
- is analytical
- is interested in where an idea came from
- seeks continuity of ideas
- is relevant
- looks for the obvious
- is closed promising a minimum result

Lateral thinking:

- changes
- is generative
- suspends judgement
- is provocative
- is interested in where an idea is going to
- seeks to introduce discontinuity
- is exploratory, nothing is irrelevant
- seeks to avoid the obvious
- is open, and increases chance of a maximum result, but may end up with nothing.

Cross-cultural differences in learning styles

Some work has been undertaken on the differences in styles of learning between different cultures. For example, Jalali (1989) compared the learning characteristics of school fourth, fifth and sixth grade students of Afro-, Chinese-, Greek- and Mexican-Americans in the United States. She obtained the following preferences.

- *Afro*: quiet, warm atmosphere with bright light, mobility, routine, and patterns; frequent feedback from the instructor; action-oriented experiences; and, afternoon and evening sessions rather than morning.

- *Chinese*: sound, bright lighting, morning study, variety rather than routine learning, and peer learning.

- *Greek*: learning alone, mobility, variety and auditory instruction.

- *Mexican*: low lighting, structured learning, learning alone, tactile and visual instruction, and feedback from the instructor.

Hayes and Allinson (1988) undertook a study of 127 British middle managers, 40 Indian mid-career managers, and 28 East African mid-career managers, using a questionnaire with two learning styles dimensions:

- *analysis*: a theory building and test approach rather than an intuitive approach;
- *action*: a trial and error approach as opposed to a reflective or contemplative approach.

They found that there were significant differences between the three nationalities such that the British managers scored high on action, East African managers scored lowest on both analysis and action, and Indian managers scored much higher on analysis than the other two nationalities.

The thinking styles of de Bono described above have been equated with right (lateral) brain activity and left (vertical) brain activity. This has been the subject of much research over the past decade (see for example, Springer and Deutch, 1981). While this research is not uncontentious, it is worth mentioning a piece of cross-cultural research undertaken by Talbot and Geyer (1991). They used a questionnaire called the Hermann Brain Dominance Instrument which distinguishes four thinking styles, corresponding to four quadrants of the brain, as follows.

A   cerebral left: logical, quantitative, fact based
B   limbic left: planned, organized, sequential
C   limbic right: emotional, kinaesthetic, feeling-based
D   cerebral right: holistic, intuitive, integrative

They found the following differences for males and females from the United States, Germany, Mexico, and Japan, including Americans in Japan and Japanese in America. Although the comparisons show that there are probably more differences between males and females, with males more dominant on quadrant A and women more dominant on quadrant C across each of these nationalities, from the published figures there seem to be differences between female Japanese, female Americans in Japan and female American homemakers, who have considerably lower scores for quadrant A, than female Americans resident in USA and Germans and Mexican females. The only explanation given for this is that most of the females with a low A quadrant score were homemakers! Unfortunately, this paper does not publish statistically significant test figures for the comparison of means between groups, and it would seem that there is actually little difference between nationalities. However, this is interesting research which perhaps needs to be followed up with larger samples in the non-American and non-German groups in order to arrive at statistically significant results.

Action learning

The stress on the work of Kolb in the United States and Honey and Mumford in the UK has been on the experiential nature of learning: that is, we learn from experience (see the learning cycle discussion above). An approach to both individual and organizational learning, based on this concept of learning by doing, which has been widely adopted in British and international companies is that of 'action learning'. This was originally developed in the 1960 by Reg Revans (for example Revans, 1965) when he began to set up educational programmes in Belgium, India and Egypt, based on these principles.

He sees learning as inextricably bound up with the process of management. He argues that everyone in the organization should be engaged in learning, and this presupposes the availability of information in the organization sufficient to enable learning to take place throughout the organization. He also sees the scientific method as providing the model for effective learning. Revans (1965) suggests that there are four forces bearing on management decision making:

- the need for economy of time and management effort;
- the analytical approach of the scientist, available to the manager, while not forgetting intuition which is the first weapon of management;
- the ability to understand and contain variability and risk through the use of statistical methods;
- a greater understanding through the social sciences of human beings as a determinant of success in the enterprise.

He goes on to develop this into a specific methodology of management learning which he calls 'system beta' with five phases:

- *survey*: the first phase of observation;
- *hypothesis*: theory development and conjecture;
- *experiment*: testing in practice;
- *audit*: the comparing of actual and desired results;
- *review*: relating the specific result with the overall context.

Apart from the final stage of review, the first four phases match Kolb's stages of the experiential learning cycle.

Revans also describes a 'system gamma' which is the personal predisposition of the individual manager, his or her mental set, or subjective consciousness. This has an influence on the way problems are approached and tackled. A further system 'system alpha' describes the relationship between the impersonal situation and the personal value system of he individual manager, illustrated in such questions as 'what values are guiding my actions?', 'what is preventing the fulfilment of those values?', and 'how can I unblock these barriers?'

It was on these basic principles that action learning was established: on the premiss that knowledge can only be the outcome of action. But the understanding of 'self' goes hand in hand with external impact, so that you cannot change the external world without your own internal development. This internal development, and understanding of the relationship between self and external, work-related issues, is facilitated by a small group (a 'set' of four or five learners), coming together regularly to support and help one another, and mediated by a facilitator. Activity is directed through individual projects within the participants' organizations.

This learning process combines the methodology of the scientific and analytical, with the commitment of the self, and the need to examine motives and beliefs under the scrutiny of the group process.

Conclusions

We have concentrated in this chapter on looking at individual differences of learning styles, looking first at the traditional distinction in the literature between behaviourist and cognitive approaches to learning. Stemming from the cognitive approach, we have followed the work of Kolb in describing the nature of the experiential learning cycle, and have developed this into a discussion of learning styles which also encompassed the work of Honey and Mumford, and de Bono. A development from this in the construction of a learning methodology was then described when we briefly looked at the work of Revans on action learning which has been widely used in various countries of the world.

While there are some indications that there are cross-cultural differences in the ways people learn, there is no conclusive evidence to suggest that there are significant differences in learning styles between national groups. There is evidence that there are learning style differences between occupational groups, and even between subject specialists. This will be looked at more specifically in the next chapter on managing careers.

In conclusion, we can add that learning is important to managers in an international environment where there is a need to adapt to change and to differing and often ambiguous circumstances. If we understand how we learn, then we can adapt learning opportunities to meet both our strengths and our weaknesses.

Answer to Activity 10.2 The man is a dwarf, he can only reach as high as the fifth floor button! A usual answer which people give is that he wanted the exercise, but this does not really explain why he does not walk down as well as up. Unless you conclude that he is tired at the end of the day!

References

de Bono, E. (1970) *Lateral Thinking*, Harmondsworth: Penguin.

Hayes, J. and Allinson, C. W. (1988), 'Cultural differences in the learning styles of managers', *Management International Review*, 28, 3.

Hilgard, E. R. and Bower G. H. (1967) *Theories of Learning*, New York: Appleton.

Honey, P. and Mumford, A. (1982) *The Manual of Learning Styles*, Maidenhead: Peter Honey.

Hughes-Weiner, G. (1986) 'The "learn-how-to-learn" approach to cross-cultural orientation', *International Journal of Intercultural Relations*, 10, pp. 485–505.

Jalali F. A. (1989) 'A cross-cultural comparative analysis of the learning styles and field dependence/independence characteristics of selected fourth-, fifth-, and sixth-grade students of Afro, Chinese, Greek and Mexican-American heritage', unpublished doctoral thesis, St John's University, New York, quoted in Cushner, K. (1990) 'Cross-cultural psychology and the formal classroom' in Brislin, R. W. (ed.) (1990) *Applied Cross-Cultural Psychology*, Newbury Park, Calif: Sage.

Kolb, D. A. (1976) *The learning styles Inventory*, Boston, Mass: McBer and Co.

Kolb, D. A., Rubin, I. M. and Osland, J. (1991) *Organizational Behaviour: An Experiential Approach*, Englewood Cliffs, NJ: Prentice-Hall.

Revans, R. (1965) *Science and the Manager*, London: MacDonald.

Skinner, B. F. (1953) *Science and Human Behaviour*, New York: Macmillan.

Springer, S. P. and Deutch, (1981) *Left Brain, Right Brain*, New York: Freeman.

Talbot, R. P. and Geyer, R. L. (1991) 'Comparing cross-cultural thinking preferences', in *National Productivity Review*, Spring, 1991, pages 181–93.

Tolman, E. C. (1932) *Purposive Behaviour in Animals and Men*, California: University of California Press.

11

Managing careers

Objectives

Following this chapter you should be able to:

1 Explain the relative importance of personal career management across cultures.
2 Document your own career needs and objectives.
3 Develop a personal strategy appropriate for a career in international management.

Key concepts

- Career planning and objectives
- Career strategies and choice
- Life stages
- Career anchors

Introduction

In this chapter we focus on personal career management. The major focus is firmly on the individual as manager of his or her own development. In many ways, this chapter represents a culmination of the work already done in the two preceding chapters on the need for and nature of European management, and on learning styles.

We therefore first look at the importance of personal career planning in a cross-cultural context, and then view it in the light of personal styles and preferences, particularly of learning styles. We then invite the reader to carefully document his or her objectives and look at the consequences of this for a career in international management.

The importance of personal career planning

Career planning is important to both manager and to the organization* for which he or she works, for the following reasons.

- *Employee loyalty*: if an organization has a good career programme, then good and ambitious employees can be retained.

---

* As a result of the fact that this book is written by an English author, we inevitably assume the position of a career of an international manager from a western culture. This is problematic if we change the focus to a western Human Resources manager responsible for international career development (including subsidiaries) in a multinational company, when the different attitudes towards careers must be taken into account. Finally, at the end of the chapter we adopt the stance of the (western) international manager with a career and the importance of taking personal responsibility for that career.

- *Avoiding future shock*: an organization should be prepared for the future; there is a need for both individuals and the organization as a whole to 'learn to learn'. This is all part of a good career programme.

- *Performance motivator*: knowing the context of your job is a good motivator. Even though the current job may be uninteresting to you in its own right, a planned career puts it into perspective. Thus, management trainees in the bank where the current author worked were first put into the 'machine room' of a branch. This was in common with all first-comers to branch banking. The job involved keying-in data and was very routine and boring. However, it was all part of learning about banking. In the context of rapid career progression on the bank's management development programme, it was a useful learning experience rather than a boring job which caused some lesser privileged trainees to quit!

- *Integrating objectives*: a good career programme should integrate the needs and objectives of the organization in its future development, with the needs and aspirations of individuals. It is often the case that if the two sets of objectives do not meet, then either the individual may leave for another organization which better matches his or her aspirations, or if the organization retains large numbers of individuals working at variance to the organization's objectives, then this will spell trouble for the organization.

Not only do managers as individuals have a responsibility to themselves for career development, they also have a key role to play in the organization in respect of other people's careers. Managers (undoubtable in an individualist, but not necessarily in a collectivist culture: see discussion below) therefore should:

- include career development within the performance appraisal and review process: to develop people a manager needs to unify the person's career path, their current job, performance appraisal and the feedback they provide;

- facilitate job experience and training to fulfil an individual's career plan: this encourages motivation as well as developing the individual and the organization for the future.

Career planning is therefore important to both the individual and the organization for which they work. The main emphasis, however, in this chapter is on the individual as manager of his or her own career.

Career strategies and choices

Stewart (1986) describes career planning strategies as akin to drawing a road map, as follows:

- career goals: the starting point is deciding where you want to go;
- career path planning: secondly, you have to decide how you want to get there, as there are alternative routes;
- training and job experience: you need to acquire the skills and knowledge to get where you want to go, and for when you get there;

- ongoing assessment: at any one time you need to know how far you have come, how far to go, and what else you will need to get there.

Of course, people adopt different strategies and career patterns based on a number of assumptions, some of which are derived from their cultural background. We can outline three different possibilities.

- Chance: you may rely on pure chance to provide the right job at the right time. This may work if you keep moving, giving yourself the chance to be in the right place at the right time. This seems to be a well used strategy. Of course, the degree to which events are left to chance or fate, may vary from one culture to another (for example between Moslem and Christian societies) as well as from one individual to another.

- The company will take care of your career. In this type of strategy you rely on the organization to provide the right opportunities. This can work in a paternalistic company. For example, a belief that the company will provide may be implicit in a Japanese company. To use this strategy in a western paternalistic company, perhaps you need to be able to 'sell yourself' within the company, to make sure that you are noticed!

- Self-designed. This is looked at as the ideal in the more individualistic cultures of North America and Western European. Following this type of strategy, you are more likely to be motivated and a high performer. You will have a clear idea of your personal goals, skills and motivation. You will also know how to prepare for the next step in your career and will be able to balance the personal costs and benefits involved.

There are a number of factors which we can point to which both influence the type of career strategy we adopt, and the type of career we pursue, on which we will focus over the next few pages. These are:

- culture: we can use Hofstede's (1991) cultural dimensions to illustrate this;

- motivation: such as the relative prominence of motivators such as McClelland's (1987) achievement motive, power motive and affiliation motive;

- life stages: the stages of life which you are going through, as illustrated by such authors as Levinson (1986) and Gould (1979). The significance and importance of life stages may differ according to any of the other factors mentioned here, and in particular with cultural differences;

- thinking and learning styles: we can use Kolb's (1991) and Honey and Mumford's (1982) learning styles to illustrate this. We could also include other personal factors such as those relating to personality and to intelligence.

Culture and career strategies

We have previously examined Hofstede's (for example, 1991) dimensions of national cultural values: power distance, individualism/collectivism, masculinity/femininity and uncertainty avoidance. Hofstede (1991) addresses specifically the implications of masculinity/femininity and of uncertainty avoidance on career choice, and we can make assumptions about the possible implications of the other dimensions.

Uncertainty avoidance

The main correlated factors of the uncertainty avoidance in Hofstede's research in IBM in over fifty different countries were as follows:

- job stress
- adherence to organizational rules
- a preference for a long-term career in the organization.

It would seem that the higher a national culture is on the uncertainty avoidance index, the more people wish to reduce uncertainty in their life by maintaining a long-term career in the same company. It is more likely that employees would wish to stay with one company throughout their careers in such high uncertainty avoidance countries as Greece, Portugal, Belgium, Japan and France than they would if they were from low uncertainty avoidance countries such as Canada, USA, India, Great Britain, Ireland, or Denmark.

Certainly for France, this coincides with what Barsoux and Lawrence find with respect to management careers:

> The notion of career strategy seems fairly weak in France. The managers (we) interviewed tended to be vague about what they hoped to achieve by what age. No doubt this has something to do with a certain reticence to 'count one's chickens' or to appear overtly ambitious. . . . The few who did reveal specific goals and timescales had to be prompted to do so. It could be posited that this toned-down view of careerism is related to the rather predictable nature of career progression – and the fact that one's education holds sway over all other possible variabilities (Barsoux and Lawrence, 1990, p. 61).

It would seem that once on the company career ladder (which is largely determined by your higher education qualification: perhaps a function of power distance which we will discuss later), the strategy of letting your company take care of your career (see the three different strategies discussed above) is a fairly typical one.

Collectivism/individualism

The concept of performance appraisal and career planning as outlined above may be anathema in a highly collectivist society. Hofstede comments:

> In a collectivist society discussing a person's performance openly with him or her is likely to clash head-on with the society's harmony norms and may be felt by the subordinate as an unacceptable loss of face (Hofstede, 1991, p. 66).

It is not likely, therefore, that career planning can be discussed openly in terms of the employee's strengths and weaknesses. Certainly, bad news such as an employee's poor performance would be communicated via an intermediary or through the indirect method of withdrawing a usual favour in such collectivist societies as China, Malaysia, Thailand, or Japan.

The following 'work goals' were identified in Hofstede's analysis of collectivism/individual as follows (Table 11.1)

Table 11.1 *Work goals in collectivist and individualistic societies*

Individual	Collectivism
Having personal time to spend on personal life	Having training opportunities
Having the freedom to develop your own approach to your job	Having good physical working conditions
Having challenging work to do, to obtain personal sense of achievement	Fully using skills and abilities in the job

Source: Hofstede, 1991.

On the individualism side are inherently individual values of personal life and freedom, and on the collectivism side are things which the organization does for employees such as providing suitable conditions and opportunities.

This must not only influence the types of career 'choice' available to individuals from opposites sides of this dimension, but also influence the attitudes towards career planning and career mobility.

Another aspect of a collectivist culture which has a bearing on career choice, is the fact that employers do not employ individuals, but members of an 'in-group'. It may be that employees who are not members of the in-group will not have a career in a company. People are expected to act according to the interests of their in-group, and this logically assumes that out-groups exist which do not show allegiance to your in-group, and therefore are not to be trusted as loyal employees.

While in an individualistic society such as the USA or UK, the employment contract is seen in commercial terms where it is possible in the interests of the individual's career or finances to break off a relationship with one employer and go to another, in a collectivist society such as Japan an employment relationship often involves family connections, and is characterized by mutual obligation of protection by the employer and loyalty by the employee. A 'career' is not then regarded in the same way in these two types of cultures.

Power distance

We have already mentioned, in connection with high uncertainty avoidance, that in France your career is often taken care of if you have the necessary academic qualification. We may assume that education distinguishes rank in many French companies as an indicator of power distance. France is a high power distance society according to Hofstede's (1991) research. However, education is only one factor in the way in which power is distributed in high power distance cultures. According to

Barsoux and Lawrence (1990) this factor is important in France. The money your family has, your family background, class and caste may all be factors which distinguish different hierarchical levels in both organizations and the society as a whole.

Not having access to the career ladder may be a hindrance (and indeed a factor in not having a concept of career in the first place) to anyone's career in any society. In a high power distance society we are more likely to find, on the one hand, those with easy access to a career because they have the necessary prerequisites, and those on the other hand who have no hope of pursuing a career as they do not have the prerequisites and they do not have access to the prerequisites themselves.

Masculinity/femininity

As a cultural value there are four main ways in which this dimension influences careers and career planning:

- the regard for females as part of the workforce;
- the attitudes to different jobs as being either masculine or feminine;
- the centrality of work to a person's life;
- the attitudes to achievement and competition.

Essentially, in a society high on Hofstede's (1991) masculinity index, men are supposed to be tough and women tender. Another aspect is the difference between a masculine society and a feminine society: the difference between assertiveness and modesty. Also, as Hofstede points out, what is considered 'feminine' and what is considered 'masculine' differs considerably between cultures:

> Women dominate as doctors in the (former) Soviet Union, as dentists in Belgium, as shopkeepers in parts of west Africa. Men dominate as typists in Pakistan and form a sizeable share of nurses in the Netherlands. Female managers are virtually nonexistent in Japan but frequent in the Philippines and Thailand (Hofstede, 1991, p. 80).

These implications for careers are, firstly, that in some societies women may not be seen as part of the workforce, or if they are they may occupy the lowest level jobs, or some jobs which are usually ascribed to women such as nursing. This will also vary in industries. For example heavy engineering is not usually seen as an industry for females in the UK. Banks, despite employing a majority of females in the UK, have a small minority in middle to senior management positions. Women tend to prosper more in the UK in such occupations as local government employees and some branches of the civil service, but still tend not to reach the senior management positions in large proportions.

Secondly, and following on from the above point, certain jobs may be viewed as 'feminine' and some as 'masculine'. In IBM, Hofstede (1991) identified six occupational groups from most 'masculine' to most 'feminine'. These were: salesmen, professionals such as engineers and scientists, skilled technicians, managers, unskilled and semi-skilled workers, and office workers (the latter being the most feminine). This generally goes from the more competitive and achievement oriented occupations, to the less competitive and less achievement oriented jobs. This brings us to the next point.

Hofstede (1991) distinguishes masculine and feminine societies by the degree to which work is central to people's lives and the degree to which assertiveness and competition is stressed (usually for men). These are broad generalizations across a national culture, and we would also expect to see considerable differences between occupational groups and sub-cultures in the same country. However, this may have implications for the centrality of career planning to one's life.

To the cultural dimensions of Hofstede, we can add two further dimensions examined by Jaeger (see Jaeger and Kanungo, 1990; and, Jaeger, 1990) in connection with differences between developed and developing countries.

Long-term/short-term focus

Management in developing countries tends to have a short-term time and activity orientation which is less conducive to planning. Thus career planning in many developing countries (for both the organization in planning its resources, and for the individual in planning his or her future) would be inhibited by this short-term time orientation. It would also be limited by a lack of belief in the change ability and creative potential of individuals. Also, connected (western) management techniques which would also be limited would be strategic planning and Management By Objectives (MBO) which have implications for career planning in the West but may be inappropriate in developing countries.

External/internal explanations of causality and control of outcomes

Research has been undertaken on individual differences in 'locus of control' by such writers as Rotter (1966), whereby some individuals are more likely to attribute external causes to outcome which are beyond their control, and others are more likely to attribute internal causes which they control (see also Chapter 4). Hence you may attribute your lack of career progression to your inabilities (internal causes) or to the patronage and unfair promotion practices in the company (external causes). Jaeger and Kanungo (1990) notice a tendency in developing countries to attribute external causes to events in people's lives. As the above example will show, this 'locus of control' is not particularly conducive to personal career planning.

We may expect to see an emphasis on career planning where competition and assertiveness are stressed, and where work is central to a person's life (masculinity); where there is a stress on individual attainment (individualism); where there is access to prerequisites of attaining promotion and position (a function of power distance); and, where there is a degree of tolerance for uncertainty (low uncertainty avoidance). Career planning is also more likely to be used where there is a longer term time orientation, and where events are more likely to be attributed to internal rather than external causes.

Needless to say, we find these factors more prominently in the Anglo-Saxon countries where personal career planning is seen as part of the development of managers!

Motivation, career strategies and choices

McClelland (1987) has accumulated research findings over the years which indicate a connection between achievement motivation and national economic development, whereby the more highly motivated a population is to achieve (through content analysis of mainly children's literature in the country) the more likely it is that the specific country is economically prosperous (see also Chapter 4). There may also be a connection between the need to achieve and the motivation to plan a career. The reader will remember that McClelland discusses three main types of motivation:

- the achievement motive
- the power motive
- the affiliation.

While it may be possible to argue that power motivation may imply the need to plan a career, it is unlikely that an individual with a more dominant affiliation motive is likely to feel the need to plan a career! However, it is particularly in the lack of the achievement motive (we could intuitively posit) where we might find a lack of a need to plan a career. We also pointed (in Chapter 4) to an apparent correlation between countries which McClelland found high on achievement motivation with those which were both high on masculinity and low on uncertainty avoidance (Hofstede, 1991, and Figure 4.2 of the current text). From the discussion of Hofstede's cultural dimensions above we can see that low uncertainty avoidance and high masculinity were also good indicators of the relevance of career planning.

Other cross-cultural work undertaken on motivation is that of the Meaning of Working International Research Team (MOW, 1987) who looked at the centrality of work to people's lives in eight different countries. Subjects were asked how important working was for them in relation to other life roles (leisure, community life, religion and family). Work centrality would seem to be a concomitant of the importance of career planning. However, when this is taken with different national cultural dimensions (Hofstede, 1991) discussed above, this does not seem to be the case, as the eight countries, from high to low work centrality are as follows: Japan, Yugoslavia, Israel, US, Belgium, Netherlands, West Germany and Britain.

So, in the previous discussion on cultural dimensions we would assume that in Japan personal career planning would be largely unimportant and in Britain largely important. However, the results from the MOW (1987) team would indicate otherwise!

It may be that on an individual basis personal career planning may be more or less appropriate depending on those factors which motivate the individual. At the same time, we should be mindful of more general national cultural factors, which may mean that career planning is more or less appropriate generally. This has tremendous implications for human resource specialists working across cultures in multinational organizations.

Career anchors

Schein (1978) believes that after a few years experience in the world of work people develop specific aspects of their working 'self-concept' (see Chapter 3 for a discussion of self-concept) comprising a self-perception and self-evaluation of their:

- talents and abilities
- motives and needs
- attitudes and values.

These three self-concept components make up what Schein calls an individual's 'career anchor'. This acts as both a driving force and a constraining force whereby if the work situation does not live up to the individual's expectations and needs, the career anchor will pull him or her back to something which is more in line with the self-concept. He identifies six such career anchors as follows.

- *technical/functional*: feeling competent in their specialist technical field;

- *managerial*: seeing their competence lies in management *per se*, and having abilities in analytical, interpersonal, and emotional areas and involving a capacity to deal with risk and uncertainty;

- *security/stability*: relying on the organization to look after them, and conforming to the requirements of their job to maintain job security;

- *creativity*: wanting to create and build projects of their own, normally being quite visible, and often overlapping with other anchors such as the need for autonomy or managerial abilities;

- *autonomy/independence*: the need to be free from organizational constraint, usually so they can pursue their own technical or professional competence, needing to set their own standards and pace;

- *social/moral*: the need to do something which is valued by society and is recognized by other people.

Some of these anchors may well be culturally influenced if we compare them with our previous discussion on cultural dimensions. For example, the need for security and stability may be most prominent in a high uncertainty avoidance culture.

If we identify those anchors which are appropriate to us, we may better understand those pushing and pulling forces within our jobs and careers. However, another aspect of career choice is the various life stages we go through as we grow older. We will now explore this.

Life stages and career choices

A career which seems appropriate to a young MBA graduate may not seem appropriate in mid-life. For example, when unattached with few emotional and family ties, a job which involves a great deal of travel may seem appealing. However, the appeal may fade if, in later life, you have a family and children's education to consider, where you are constantly 'uprooting' to take the family to yet another country, or if you are spending many nights in hotels on business trips abroad when your family is at home!

A number of authors have described the transition of 'life stages' and the implications for careers. Thus Levinson (1986) describes the developmental tasks of each life period as follows (based on approximate ages):

209

Approximately

16–25 years:	Leaving the family
25–35 years:	Getting into the adult world
35–38 years:	Period of transition
38–50 years:	Settling down and becoming your own person
50–57 years:	Mid-life transition period
57– years:	Restabilization and settling into middle age.

Gould, on the other hand focuses on subjective inner experiences of individuals through a sequence of different life periods, as follows:

Approximately

16–19 years:	Getting away from parental domination
19–24 years:	Exchanging friends for own family
24–29 years:	Aspiring to build for the future
29–35 years:	Asking what you are doing and why
35–43 years:	Having a sense of urgency to achieve goals
43–49 years:	Coming to terms with yourself as a stable personality
49– years:	The valuing of emotions and the mellowing of friendships.

While individuals can be seen to progress through different life stages, Berry *et al.* (1992) describe such 'ontogenetic' development as an interaction between a biological organism and environmental influences. Different emphases are placed on the relative importance of nature and nurture, and this is reflected in different schools of thought on life stages. They identify: maturation theory; stage theory; differentiation theory; life span developmental theory; and context-specificity theory. While it is not important to detail these various theories, it is important to note that the latter three theories stress environmental factors, and if we accept the primacy of such factors, we cannot conclude that all people of all cultures go through the same stages.

Perhaps all we can conclude at this juncture is that people do go through life stages and these have implications for the way they see their careers. Both organizations and individuals should take account of these life stages, and human resources specialists in multinational companies should take account of different life stages in different cultures.

Learning styles and career preferences

Wolfe and Kolb (1991) show how learning styles might relate to career preferences. From limited studies they report, firstly, preferences of different learning styles types (see Chapter 10) for undergraduate study, and secondly, occupational groups and learning styles types as follows (strengths of each group are shown in brackets as a reminder of the description of each):

Convergers (problem solving when there is one answer)
• engineering
• nursing.

Divergers (dealing with alternative ideas)
- psychology
- English
- political science
- history.

Assimilators (creating theoretical models)
- mathematics
- economics
- sociology
- chemistry.

Accommodators (carrying out plans, getting involved)
- business.

This is consistent with the theory and with other studies undertaken in the United States. This is also consistent with findings on learning styles of five occupational groups (Wolfe and Kolb, 1991) as follows.

Personnel: divergers
Marketing: assimilators
Engineering: convergers
Research: assimilators
Finance: assimilator/converger borderline.

Honey and Mumford (1982) have also published scores for their Learning Styles Questionnaire for different occupations groups in the UK, whereby:

- salesmen seem to be more activitist and pragmatist;
- trainers seem to be marginally more reflector and pragmatist;
- marketing managers seem to be low on activist but higher on reflector, pragmatist, and theorist;
- engineering graduates seem to be very low on activist and high on reflector;
- research and development managers seem to be very low on activist and high on reflector;
- production managers seem very low on activist but high on theorist and pragmatist;
- finance manager seem very low on activist, but high on reflector, theorist and pragmatist.*

There is some reason to suppose that there may be differences between occupational groups in terms of learning styles. Learning styles may lead to individuals making a broad choice about their future occupation, or the way certain occupations are trained (starting at the selection of specific school subjects) may encourage particular learning styles.

* Note that Honey and Mumford (1982) do not publish figures for statistical significance of differences between means of occupational groups in this case. It is therefore difficult to conclude that there are significant differences between all these groups.

Documenting your personal career objectives

The following (Activity 11.1) is adapted from the Life Goal Inventory of Kolb *et al.* (1991). It is specifically relevant to the preceding discussion, as it does not assume the centrality of any particular factor, such as work, in your life. It will help you to balance those sometimes conflicting factors. These are: status and respect; personal relationships; satisfaction from your leisure; spiritual growth and religion; material possessions and rewards; learning and education; career satisfaction. Some of these factors may receive more prominence in some cultures and not in others. The only assumption that the activity makes is the desirability of having goals. We will discuss this again in the light of your conclusions and in connection with choices in international careers.

Activity 11.1 Life goals

In each of the following categories you should list your specific goals giving as much detail as you can. If the category is not relevant to you, you may ignore it. If any other category is important to you, you should add this. When you have listed each goal you should then list them in order of importance. You may at this stage feel that some are not important and can leave them off your list. Try not to have more than ten prioritized goals on the final list. You should then note any conflicts in these goals and state how you may overcome these conflicts. You should also review your list of goals in terms of how these goal are going to be achieved. Some may seem easy to achieve, others may be difficult. Try to identify such difficulties and state how they might be overcome.

Status and respect

You should consider to what group(s) you wish to belong and what your goals are within these groups. What sort of respect are you looking for and from whom?

Status and respect goals:

1

2

3

Personal relationships

You should state what your goals are in respect of friends, family, colleagues, etc.

Personal relationship goals:

1

2

3

Satisfaction from your leisure

What are your goals for leisure activities: those things you enjoy doing and interests you wish to cultivate?

Satisfaction from leisure goals:

1

2

3

Spiritual growth and religion

What are your goals for your spiritual life and religious life?

Spiritual growth and religion goals:

1

2

3

Material possessions and rewards

You should state your goals for the possessions you want and the level of financial prosperity which is important to you.

Material possessions and rewards goals:

1

2

3

Learning and education

You should state the level of education you want, and specific skills and knowledge you wish to develop

Learning and education goals:

1

2

3

Career satisfaction

You should now state your career goals as specifically as you can, including any specific positions you wish to hold

Career satisfaction goals:

1

2

3

Other goals

State whatever other goals you may have.

1

2

3

Now list your goals in priority order, noting what you have to do to achieve each one, stating where they might conflict with other goals.

Goals in priority order	What you need to do to achieve them	Conflicts with other goals
1. . . . .
2. . . . .
3. . . . .

4. . . . .

5. . . . .

6. . . . .

7. . . . .

8. . . . .

9. . . . .

10. . . . .

Choices in an international career

We now look at the management of careers from the point of view of somebody (perhaps the reader) choosing and managing an international career. We first look at the criteria which companies use for selecting managers for international assignments (see also Chapter 9), we then look at the choices which international managers themselves have for making decisions about international assignments. Finally we look, through a case study (Mini Case 11.1), at the issue of women in international careers and the type of choices they and their companies must make.

Criteria for choosing international managers

Phatak (1992) lists nine areas which companies look for in selecting their international managers.

- *technical ability*: the ability to do the job is of course a prerequisite;

- *managerial skills*: those skills which are associated with being an effective manager are important;

- *cultural empathy*: sensitivity to other cultures and a non-judgemental understanding of other cultures is probably essential;

- *adaptability and flexibility*: this includes the ability to integrate with other people and other cultures and different types of business operations, being adaptable to change, having the ability to solve problems within different frameworks, sensitivity to differences in different cultural situations, and flexibility to manage a continuous operation despite gaps in information and assistance;

- *diplomatic skills*: an ability to deal with others, negotiate and to represent the parent company on foreign assignment; this may even involve interaction with politicians and government officials in some developing countries;

- *language aptitude*: the ability to learn a language quickly is a useful attribute;

- *personal motives*: a positive reason for wanting to take on foreign assignments;

- *emotional stability and maturity*: this involves having the staying power and emotional maturity to maintain equilibrium in a foreign environment as well as being non-judgemental in relationships with others;

- *adaptability of family*: this factor is most important to the success of a foreign assignment, because if the family get homesick or they simply are unhappy in the foreign environment, this may lead to low performance and other problems of the international manager.

Similar factors are outlined in Dowling and Schuler (1990) as follows:

Job factors:
- technical ability
- managerial skills
- administrative abilities
- knowledge of host country and headquarters operations.

Relational dimensions:
- tolerance of ambiguity
- behaviour flexibility
- being non-judgemental
- cultural empathy and low ethnocentrism
- interpersonal skills.

Motivation:
- belief in the mission
- congruence with career plan
- interest in overseas experience
- interest in the specific host country
- willingness to learn new attitudes and behaviour patterns.

Family situation:
- spouse willing to live abroad
- adaptive and supportive spouse
- stable marriage.

Language skills:
- knowledge of host country language
- understanding of non-verbal communication.

The above lists are helpful to the potential international manager who wishes to develop a career plan, as a guide to those abilities and skills which need to be cultivated. They are also useful to human resources specialists who wish to select and train managers for an international career.

Also of importance is understanding why individuals accept assignments as international managers and why they reject them.

Reasons for choosing, or for not choosing international assignments

Adler (1991) surveyed 1,129 MBA students in business schools in the United States, Canada and Europe in order to determine reasons why they would accept international assignments, and why they would not. Table 11.2 is a summary of the results listed in order, with the most popular responses at the top.

Table 11.2 *Reactions to international assignments*

International assignments	
Reasons for accepting	*Reasons for not accepting*
The cross-cultural experiences, seeing other cultures, learning new languages (52.2%)	Location unsuitable, 'uncivilized', dangerous or hostile, politically unstable (58.5%)
A more interesting job with more responsibilities, more status or autonomy (40.2%)	Unsatisfactory job, boring, high risk of failure, isolation from home company (34.6%)
Higher salary (27.7%)	Problems with family or spouse such as dual career, spouse unwilling to move (33.4%)
Career advancement (20.7%)	
Good location, climate, politically stable, good social life (15.9%)	Inadequate salary package (22.9%)
	Unwilling to make new life abroad, and to learn new languages or adapt to culture (19.4%)
A more satisfying life, with more freedom, fun, excitement, more variety and higher quality life (10.9%)	
Good situation for spouse or family (3.5%)	Unwilling to disrupt home country life (13.8%)
Short-term assignment (2.6%)	Contract too long (5.8%)

Source: adapted from Adler, 1991.

We can therefore gain an idea of some of the attractions of an international career and some of the problems through this snapshot of reactions to international assignments.

We finish this chapter with a reference to one of the cultural problems of careers for women in international management by looking at an illustrative case study.

Mini Case 11.1 An assignment in Egypt

A large British international hotel chain has a policy of developing its managers through international assignments. Promotion prospects can usually be increased by taking on one or two international assignments early in your career. It is often the case that if you take on a foreign assignment at assistant manager level, and make a good job of it, you often end up becoming manager in that location or are promoted to another position in another location.

The head of international operations, Paul Smith received a request for Mary Jones, an assistant manager in the company's Manchester hotel to fill an forthcoming vacancy of assistant manager in their Cairo hotel.

Paul Smith called Mary for an interview. He explained to her that he did not think this was a suitable assignment for her. The Arab environment does not usually encourage female managers. None of the company's hotels in Arab countries have female managers. Paul added that to appoint Mary to this position would be a mistake for her and for the company. Saying that the Arab view of women is somewhat different to that in Britain, he offered to look at other international assignments which may be more suitable for her.

Mary was adamant. She had carefully looked into this position and thought it was suitable for her. She had relevant experience to do the job well and to make a success of the position. She really wanted this position. Paul Smith promised he would think about it and let her know.

Discussion: What should Paul Smith do and why?

(*Source*: adapted from Hodgetts and Luthans, 1991.)

Summary

We have looked at career development from two main standpoints. The first is that of the individual manager or potential manager, probably from a Western country, who wishes to pursue and develop his or her own career within an international context. The other standpoint has been from the point of view of all those responsible for managing other people's careers in different cultures (this does not just imply an international human resources director working in a multinational company). We have therefore tried to couple sound advice with a discussion on the cultural differences in career choices and strategies.

We first looked at the importance of career development, and then explored the different choices available in terms of career strategies. We then turned to the factors which influence the type of career choice. These were culture, motivation, life stages and career anchors, and learning styles. This led to the documentation of personal career goals, followed by a discussion of choices in international careers. This should provide the basis on which individuals can make choices about their career objectives and strategies, and help those who have to manage cultural differences in career development.

References

Adler, N. J. (1991) *International Dimensions of Organizational Behaviour* (2nd edn.), Boston: PWS-Kent.

Barsoux, J.-L. and Lawrence, P. (1990) *Management In France*, London: Cassell.

Berry, J. W., Poortinga, Y. H., Segall, M. H. and Dasen, P.R. (1992) *Cross-cultural Psychology: Research and Application*, Cambridge: Cambridge University Press.

Dowling, P. J. and Schuler, R. S. (1990) *International Dimensions of Human Resource Management*, Boston: PWS-Kent.

Gould, R. L. (1979) *Transformation*, New York: Simon and Schuster.

Hodgetts, R. M. and Luthans, F. (1991) *International Management*, New York: McGraw-Hill.

Hofstede, G. (1991) *Cultures and Organizations: Software of the Mind*, London: McGraw-Hill.

Honey, P. and Mumford, A. (1982) *The Manual of Learning Styles*, Maidenhead: Peter Honey.

Jaeger, A. M. (1990) 'The applicability of Western management techniques in developing countries: a cultural perspective', in Jaeger and Kanungo (1990).

Jaeger, A. M. and Kanungo, R. N. (1990) *Management in Developing Countries*, London: Routledge.

Kolb, D. A., Rubin, I. M. and Osland J. (1991) *Organizational Behaviour: An Experiential Approach*, Englewood Cliffs, NJ: Prentice-Hall.

Levinson, D. J. (1986) 'A concept of adult development', *American Psychologist*, 41, 1, pp. 3–13.

McClelland D. C. (1987) *Human Motivation*, Cambridge: CUP.

MOW (Meaning of Working) International Research Team (1987) *The Meaning of Working*, London: Academic Press.

Phatak, A. V. (1992) *International Dimensions of Management* (3rd edn.), Boston: PWS-Kent.

Rotter, J. B. (1966) 'Generalized expectancies for internal versus external control of reinforcement', *Psychological Monographs*, 80, 1 (whole no. 609).

Schein, E. H. (1978) *Career Dynamics: Matching Individual and Organizational Needs*, Reading Massachusetts: Addison-Wesley.

Stewart, D. (1986) *The Power of People Skills*, New York: John Wiley.

Wolfe, D. M. and Kolb, D. A. (1991) 'Career development, personal growth, and experiential learning', in Kolb, D. A., Rubin, I. M. and Osland J. S. (1991) *The Organizational Behaviour Reader* (5th edn.), Englewood Cliffs, NJ: Prentice-Hall.

Section 5
Managing in a Multi-national Context

We now focus more specifically on areas of development for the global manager. We consider the necessary understanding and analysis required for managing cultural differences. While we draw on many of the issues so far discussed in this text, we take a more pragmatic approach to understanding and managing difference. We then look at the skills and knowledge required for negotiating with international partners. Then we turn to the management of uncertainty, by focusing on risk and decision making in the organizational and international contexts.

12
Managing cultural differences

Objectives

Following this chapter you should be able to:

1 Explain the basis upon which cultural differences may be understood.
2 Examine another culture by employing a framework for analysis.
3 Develop an understanding of individuals from other cultures with whom you do business.

Key concepts

* Barriers to cross-cultural understanding:
  * misperceptions,
  * misinterpretations,
  * misevaluations
* Pragmatic understanding of culture:
  * culture,
  * company,
  * character.

Introduction

In a book called *The New International Manager*, Guy and Mattock (1991) present an approach to cross cultural management based on the development work of Canning International Management Development. The book begins with a preface by the Director of Canning, Bill Reed, who ends his introduction by saying 'when setting about the task of managing across cultures, the truly wise know only too well that they know nothing'.

Thus, in this chapter we take our lead from this excellent book in looking at an approach to cross-cultural management which assumes that we do not know a great deal about the culture with which we are about to deal, and that we need to find out as much as we can in order to effectively manage the differences with which we are confronted. Certain approaches are well documented (and have already been described in the first half of this text). The approach of Hofstede (for example 1991) provides a broad framework from which we can conceptualize national cultures within dimensions of 'power distance', 'uncertainty avoidance', 'individualism' and 'masculinity'. This may provide some clues about the nature of the culture concerned, but may not answer specific questions about how we should interact with individuals from specific functions within specific organizations in certain industries.

Guy and Mattock (1991) provide the following framework for managing, and doing business internationally, which goes beyond a simplistic or stereotyped view of national culture.

Firstly, there are three 'constants' in the framework, on which information needs to be gathered. These are:

- *Culture*: the cultural background and upbringing of the foreign colleagues will affect the way they make decisions.

- *Company*: a consideration of the company, divisional and departmental culture is essential for understanding how this may be different from yours, and how you might bridge the gap.

- *Character*: above all, the foreign colleague is an individual with individual characteristics of values, motives and moods.

These are the three aspects we will be looking at in this chapter.

Also there are three 'transient' aspects which need to be affected, but need as their decisional base the information gathered on the three constants. These are:

- *Tactics*: any negotiation or cross-cultural interaction requires the use of tactics which should take the cue from what you have found out about the three constant aspects.

- *Timing*: the attitude to time and the pace of events is one of the marked differences between cultures which should be taken into consideration.

- *Talk*: This is the point of contact. It raises certain questions of language, as well as the skills needed to be acquired to be convincing in the international arena.

We will be looking generally at the latter aspects in the next chapter when we discuss specific approaches to international negotiation.

In the current chapter we take this framework as the basis for considering the management of cultural differences. As such, this chapter represents a prelude to considering, and acting on, more specific aspects of managing in the multi-national context, such as cross-cultural negotiation, managing uncertainty and managing change.

Barriers to cross-cultural understanding

There are dangers in having preconceived ideas of a national culture and imposing these assumptions on an actual situation. Similarly, there are dangers in going in blindly, and not having any idea about the cultural background of your foreign colleague, business associate or client. Some of these dangers are described by Adler (1991) as cross-cultural misperceptions, cross-cultural misinterpretations and cross-cultural misevaluations, as follows.

Misperceptions

People from different cultural backgrounds do not see things the same. Because of differences in home background, education, interests and values, the same things can be viewed quite differently by different individuals (see also Chapter 1). This is because perception is:

- *selective*: we have to screen out stimuli from our environment or we would suffer from overload. We do this according to the perceptual patterns we have learnt, our cultural background as well as specific tasks and interests. For example the driver of a car will see different things (as he is concentrating on the road) to the passenger (who may be more interested in the scenery);

- *learned*: we are not born with a ready view of the world and an understanding of the meaning and relative importance of things around us. We learn these things through our experiences;

- *culturally determined*: we learn to see the world and the things around us in certain ways as a result of growing up in a particular culture with its world view, religious beliefs and value structures;

- *constant*: our perceptual patterns remain more or less constant, and this is the way we make continuing sense of our world without getting too many surprises;

- *inaccurate*: while this filtering system helps us to keep our sanity, we inevitably see things which are not there and do not see things which are there. Essentially, we see things we expect to see.

If we assume that others see things the same way that we do, misunderstandings will occur. Similarly we cannot force others to have the same perceptions as ourselves.

Mini Case 12.1 Thai road markings

A Canadian expatriate was driving in Thailand when his car was hit by a Thai motorist who had crossed over the double white lines in the middle of the road to pass another car.

The Thai driver would not admit that he was at fault, and the Canadian flagged down a passing policeman. After a great deal of seemingly futile discussion with the policeman, the Canadian asked him 'What do the double lines in the middle of the road signify?' To this the policeman answered that 'They indicate the centre of the road and are there so that I can determine how far the accident is from that point'. It had not occurred to the Canadian driver that they indicated anything other than 'no overtaking'! (from Adler, 1991).

Discussion. Can you relate other examples of different perceptions of roadcraft in other countries? For example pedestrian crossings seem to have different significance in different European countries.

Misinterpretations

Adler (1991) defines 'interpretation' as giving meaning to observations and their relationships, or the process of making sense of perceptions. Thus, interpreting our perceptions guides our actions. We base these interpretations on assumptions we make. This is drawn from our experience. Thus we know what a chair is for example (by the way, it is a cultural object in western society), we do not have to relearn that it is an object for sitting on each time we see one. When driving we selectively perceive the traffic lights and their colour. We interpret the red light as meaning stop, and we act accordingly.

In order to interpret our world we place things into categories so that we can cope with the masses of stimuli which impose on our senses. Thus we simplify our environment.

We can miscategorize by using inappropriately the categories we employ in our own culture to that of a foreign culture. Thus, in some cultures (and some organizations in Western Europe) women are not employed as managers, but often as secretaries. There might be a tendency for a Japanese businessman (from a high masculinity country from Hofstede's, 1992, research) to mistake a female executive's voice at the end of a telephone in Sweden (a low masculinity country according to Hofstede) as the secretary not the boss!

A negative side of categorization is stereotyping which normally refers to the prior categorization of ethnic or cultural groups. However, Adler (1991) claims that stereotypes can be both helpful or harmful depending on how they are used. They can be helpful in guiding understanding and action in a new situation when stereotypes are:

- consciously held and understood to be a group norm not a specific individual's characteristic;
- descriptive and not evaluative;
- accurate, and based on facts not assumptions or myth;
- a broad first guess which can be refined after first-hand experience, and modified also to allow for individual differences.

Everybody stereotypes, but subconsciously held stereotypes or prejudices are hard to discard, and may do damage if inaccurate.

Sources of misinterpretation are:

- subconscious cultural assumptions, which are misapplied in other cultures. The present author, for example has experienced the difficulties of Spanish management students in adjusting to the interactive educational methods and group discussion of management education in the UK, while he himself has difficulties sometimes with the Spanish practice of talking whilst the teacher is talking. Both of these difficulties are a result of cultural assumptions which work fine when the respective nationals work within their own cultures, but do not make perfect sense when applied to the other culture. On the one hand, the teacher is firmly in control and knows his subject, and on the other hand, the students are not at all disrespectful to the teacher;
- lack of cultural self-awareness. Before we can be fully understanding of another culture we must have a firm understanding of our own.

Activity 12.1 Cross-cultural awareness

If you are able, ask people you know from other countries to describe people in general (if possible business people) and the national characteristics of your own country. You can also do the same for them.

Are you surprised at the description, or not? If you have asked persons from more than one nationality, have you received different descriptions?

If we are culturally self-aware, we can also perhaps anticipate the effects of our behaviour on other people from other cultures;

• projected similarities. Seeing people from other cultures merely as a reflection of yourself is common and usually mistaken. It is a form of parochialism which assumes that your cultural values and perceptions are universal.

Activity 12.2 Role reversal

If you can put yourself in the shoes of your foreign colleague or client, and imagine what it would be like to be him or her, this will reduce the effects of projected similarity. It will help you to see both the differences and similarities.

You are that foreign business person.

• What type of family do you come from?
• What economic and social conditions did you grow up with?
• What type of education did you receive?
• How did you choose your profession and how did you get your position?
• How did you get to meet your spouse?
• What are your main goals in working for your organization?
• What are your life goals?

Misevaluation

The last aspect of cultural misunderstandings outlined by Adler (1991) is cultural misevaluation. This involves a value judgement of whether something is good or bad. With our own culture as a 'self-reference criterion', and since no other culture is like our own, we therefore judge other cultures as inferior. Here is an example.

Mini Case 12.2 Gifts and bribery

In some African countries it is normal to offer 'gifts' of money to policemen, customs and minor government officials in order to ease your journey. These personnel are often very lowly paid and rely on such gifts for their, and their family's, livelihood. It is accepted for companies to give large donations to all political parties on the basis that any one of them could be in power in the future, and that they may have long memories of who did not contribute to party funds. It may also be appropriate to offer financial incentives to executives of the customer company in order to affect business between your own and your client's company.

What are your reactions to such practices? What would you do if you were confronted with one of these situations? Would you encourage your company to engage in such practices in order to do business in one of these countries? (See also Chapter 14 which may provide some of the answers in a discusion on ethical decision making.)

A pragmatic understanding of culture

How can we try to overcome these problems, and how best can we find out about the other person's culture? We have already suggested some of the ways we can try to overcome the barriers to intercultural understanding, for example, by first understanding our own culture. Guy and Mattock (1991) suggest a more pragmatic 'model building' of a foreign culture than is often seen in the academic literature on culture.

The current author often uses with his management students the analogy of 'landing on an alien planet'. Rather than have preconceived ideas of the planet and the society which we might find there, we need to have some basis for understanding the new culture we might find. Social anthropologists have been quite expert in doing this, where they have gone into a 'primitive' society (often having a colonial presence in the particular country), and have set about learning as much as they can about the culture: their only preconceived ideas being those they had transposed from their own culture! While it is often impossible for the business executive to adopt the approach of ethnography (see for example, Fettermen, 1989) in undertaking lengthy and detailed field research in a foreign culture, Guy and Mattock (1991) offer a solution, by suggesting that we focus on three main aspects in order to understand a culture: topography, religion, and history.

Topography

Guy and Mattock suggest first of all that the topography of a country has an influence on the culture, specifically through its sense of national identity. They suggest the following exercise to illustrate this.

Activity 12.3 Topography

First, draw a simple sketch map of Spain, with its boundaries and show its capital.

Next, do the same for Germany.

Because of geography, politics and history, it was probably very difficult to sketch Germany. It has very few natural boundaries in all directions, and they have constantly changed in modern history right up to the present day. This may tell us something of the national identities of both countries, one having a strong sense of what it means to be Spanish despite strong regional differences. Germany and 'Germanness' is something which perhaps fosters insecurities and doubts, and is not all that clear. The topography of a country is a good starting point. It may give insights into the nature of a national culture. National insecurity may give rise to a need for orderliness and uncertainty avoidance. This approach is slightly contentious, and should be used with caution. It does offer a simple starting point, but should only be considered in connection with other factors such as religion and history, and also with other indicators such as Hofstede's dimensions. The example above, for instance, could be connected with Hofstede's concept of uncertainty avoidance.

Religion

We can find out a lot about a national culture by looking at dominant religions, the proliferations of religions and also the importance of religion (or lack of it) in a secular state. A country where the dominant religion is Muslim may, for example, have particular business practices (for example the Muslim law of banking which forbids the charging of interest on loans for non-productive purposes as this is seen as usury), may have particular attitudes towards women in business, and may have a particular vision of the future ('Insha'allah' or God willing, and a belief in fate rather than a matter of rationally controlling events). Beliefs in animism in some developing countries are also worth looking at in order to understand some of the beliefs, assumptions and practices in countries in which you are doing business.

Mini case 12.3 Animism in Malaysia

Putti and Chia (1990) describe the belief of many Chinese and Malays in Malaysia of the spirit Datuk-kong, the spirit of a kind man who has chosen to stay in this world and who inhabits an old tree or a rock. The spirit first makes its existence known through revealing himself in a dream of a needy person. News spreads by word of mouth. It is this local deity that people turn to when they are in need, and he looks after the well-being of the local people and their fortunes. If anybody were to remove the rock or tree in which the Datuk-kong lives, the offending person would be punished by the spirit.

Following several years studying in the UK and USA, Yahya Ibrahim returns to Kuala Lumpur to pursue a career in engineering. He quickly gains success in the government controlled manufacturing industry, and after a few years is appointed general manager of Intronics, a small electrical motors assembling factory in Port Dickson, some 100 km from the capital.

The outgoing general manager had run the company in a *laisser-faire* manner, and Yahya considered discipline to be poor and the factory generally in a mess. The factory layout was inefficient and machinery was old. Workers would trickle in well after 8.00 a.m., and very few of the managers were at their desks at this

---

229

time. As he left the factory the first evening he noticed that an old tree just outside the main gate was obscuring the view of drivers as they left the factory.

The next morning he called a meeting of the managers and announced several far reaching changes which would turn the present old fashioned company into a model factory of the future. He would hold regular Friday morning meetings with all managers. A 'clocking-in' machine was ordered to improve time-keeping. The production manager, and Lim the engineering manager and deputy to Yahya were asked to work on a plan to re-lay the production lines. Similar changes were made elsewhere. Whilst there were some stifled protests, the workers (who were un-unionized) generally went along with the changes and production rose.

After six months, in the scheduled managers meeting Yahya said that he wanted the 'eyesore' of a tree outside the main gate removed as it obstructs the view of drivers, and could Lim, the engineering manager organize this.

Lim retorted that he must be mad thinking about removing the Datuk-kong tree, containing the spirit who looks after the well-being of the factory. Yahya became angry saying that this was superstitious nonsense. To this Lim replied that it was no such thing, that the daughter of Hassan, the materials manager, was struck down with fever which the doctors could not cure. He prayed to the Datuk-kong and his daughter recovered immediately. Hassan confirmed this.

But Yahya became more angry, demanding that the tree should be got rid of by the next meeting, a week hence.

Lim refused to have the tree removed for several weeks, with the tacit concurrence of the work-force. When Yahya told him to comply or resign, Lim got outside help as nobody in the factory would do the job. He prayed to the Datuk-kong explaining that it was not his decision, but he needed the job to support his family.

Soon after a woman worker fell sick for a week. She recovered, but there was a rumour circulating the factory that in a dream she had tried to pray to the Datuk-kong, but it was no longer around. Sick leave rose. There was a belief that one of the toilets had become haunted and people did not like using it. Of course, these occurrences were all attributed to the Datuk-kong by the factory workers.

Four months after, Lim resigned, as did another thirteen workers who had all been recruited by a rival factory which had started up in the area. Yahya knew that this was the beginning of an exodus and that something had to be done?

Discussion. What can be done? What should have been done? Was Yahya clearly wrong for destroying the tree?

(*Sources*: Putti and Chia, 1990.)

History

The third aspect of the model building process is history. We have already mentioned in connection with topography, the changing political and geographical scene in Germany as part of its history. Guy and Mattock (1991) mention the history of a new life for Europeans settling in the new America, the struggles of succeeding generations, and the pursuit of the Dollar, with a tough win–loose negotiation style. They contrast this with the isolation for generations of the Japanese from both the outside world and from democracy, with echoes of xenophobia and the need for a distinct hierarchy still evident in the lives of Japanese business men.

Guy and Mattock (1991) argue for this model building approach to understanding culture. While it may be interesting to learn tit-bits of cultural information, like receiving a Japanese business card in both hands or not offering an Arab business man something with your left hand, they mean much more if they can be placed in context.

Activity 12.4 Discovering a country's culture

You may like to apply this three aspect approach to cultural model building by looking at a country with which you do business, or are interested in (in many ways this is easier if you apply this to a country which you do not know very much about), and look in turn at each of the three aspects of:

- topography
- religion
- history.

What do each tell you about the country and its culture? How do the three aspects fit together? After your initial research, write a short account of what these three aspects tell you about the culture. Look at the *facts*. What *attitudes* can you derive from these? What *behaviours* are a likely consequence of these attitudes?

Company culture

A manager or business person is not simply a product of his or her national culture, but also of the organizational culture and sub-cultures within the company. Understanding the nature of the organization from which your colleague (or adversary) is drawn and the interplay of different cultures at different levels, is as important as understanding the national cultures (see also Chapter 8 for a discussion of organizational culture). However, consider the follow research findings.

Mini Case 12.4 National culture in multi-national companies

Following Hofstede's (1980) findings on national culture undertaken in IBM which showed that national culture explained fifty per cent of the differences in employee's attitudes and behaviour, Laurent (1983) undertook research in multi-nationals and found that national cultural differences were more pronounced among foreign personnel working in the same multinational organization than among employees working for organizations in their native lands. By studying managers from nine Western European countries and the United States who were working in their home countries, and one multinational corporation with subsidiaries in ten countries, he assumed that he would find that personnel working for the same multi-national company, although from different countries, would be more similar in attitudes to those employees working for organizations in their own countries. Instead he found the differences were greater between managers from the ten countries in the same multi-national, than those in their own countries working for different organizations. It therefore seems that when working away from home in a multi-national company French become more French, Americans become more American, and so on! Laurent went on to replicate this research in two other multi-nationals with the same results.

Discussion. Why do you think this is the case? Although the research did not draw definite explanations, it may be interesting to discuss the possible reasons for this.

Whilst we have considered the analysis of organizational culture in some detail (Chapter 8) Guy and Mattock (1991) set out to explain the interconnectedness of the various aspects of national and organizational culture and their implications for cross cultural encounters by proposing a five-factor model, as follows.

- Language
- Culture
- Hierarchy
- Contact
- Motivation.

These aspects are all interconnected in any cross-cultural encounter.

Language

This is sometimes a major stumbling block if the two parties do not speak a common language. English is often a common language in international business negotiations, although native speakers of English often present a problem to non-native speakers through their use of idiomatic English. This may be the first factor to address.

Culture

Language does not just comprise words, but also cultural meaning. Once we have learnt something of the national, organizational, and professional culture of the other party, we need to have an idea of the connotations of the language and not simply accept the dictionary definition. Hence the use of first name terms may be acceptable in one culture between certain hierarchical levels, but not in others. Similarly, different cultures may think differently. Not simply do we have differences between people of different professional backgrounds (for example science and arts graduates) but also between different broad national cultures.

For example, Southern Europeans with a Catholic and Latin background may present arguments by way of a general proposition, and then work backwards to show the reasons why. Those from a Northern European, Protestant and Germanic or Anglo-Saxon background may present arguments from the bottom up: presenting the facts, drawing conclusions and then presenting a proposition. This may lead to mutual frustrations when the two come together, the one thinking the Latin irrational and impatient, the other thinking the Northerner pedestrian and cold.

Hierarchy

It is not just language differences which cause problems and cultural differences which cause suspicion. The relationship between headquarters and a subsidiary may be based on mutual suspicion, and between a corporate chief executive and those managers under him or her, as may the relationship between managers and shop floor workers. Those at the top of the hierarchy may not trust those towards the bottom to get on with the job, while there may be a suspicion from the bottom that the top is withholding information. These problems may be compounded in a multi-national company between head office and subsidiary. The distinction inherent in the hierarchy may be more distinct than national cultural differences.

The use of language within this hierarchical situation should be used with caution. The use of 'we' to represent the headquarters management when discussing with a subsidiary manager may be interpreted as a 'them' and 'us' distinction to be avoided. Whereas the use of 'we' to include the subsidiary management suggests a team involvement.

Contact

Simply, if your colleague is in another country, contact on a regular basis may be difficult. It will certainly have to be planned. However, this problem is compounded when dealing at different hierarchical levels. For example, there must be a balance between a headquarters top manager maintaining close contact with a subsidiary head, and breathing down his neck! Over-involvement in a subordinate's project may be a demotivating factor. Maintaining contact may be a motivating factor. The attitude towards this type of contact may also be a cultural factor, where a sense of personal space may correspond with a subordinates tolerance of interference. Also, language may act as a barrier to regular contact and the interchange of ideas. Long meetings in a foreign language may be stressful, for example.

Motivation

This factor may be seen to embrace the other four. If the other four factors are in order, then motivation may well follow. Also, it is the job of the management of an international organization to have the motivation to put these four factors in order. But, perhaps the most important aspect of motivation in any organization, international or not, is the creation of a common goal. The following case study illustrates this in a national organization with different cultural interests, but looks at what happens when the national interest is opposed to the company culture.

Mini Case 12.5 Company and national culture in Nigeria

Nigeria is a multi-ethnic society with more than a hundred ethnic groups and different cultures. The three main tribes can be described, albeit rather simplistically, as follows.

- *Yoruba*: values education, respect of elders, preference for male children;
- *Ibo*: deep respect for family members, favouritism to family through action rather than just words;
- *Hausa*: little importance given to formal education, importance attached to wives and children (children being a symbol of wealth).

Common values are loyalty to family and identification with your village and your fellow villagers.

The Bendel Steel Company was established in 1978 by the federal government as a commercial operation with the hope that it would give employment for a thousand Nigerians. Only well qualified managers were recruited, among them both Nigerians and European and Asian expatriates. All Nigerian managers had either worked in another country or obtained qualifications from another country or both, believing that a wider experience and exposure of those recruited would provide a higher level of creativity. The head of human resources was himself a Nigerian who had been educated to masters level in both the UK and USA. He had also worked as a human resources specialist in the United States. He returned to Nigeria at the age of 40 to take up this job. He was now charged with recruiting.

The general manager, with the head of human resources and others from the management team, had formulated a company philosophy around four ideas:

- *Aisojusaju*, or non-favouritism. This went against the national value of favouritism, but was considered the cornerstone of the company policy to foster unity among employees.
- Equal opportunity for all to receive training, promotion and so on, regardless of race, religion, or tribe.
- Commitment to hard work, co-operation, and innovation.
- Commitment to the ethical standards of honesty, truth, and fairness and to respect the rights of all employees.

It was the job of the head of human resources to translate this into practice by recruiting on the basis of this well publicized philosophy and to train new people in the way of this philosophy. As a result of recruiting on the basis of qualifications and experience only, there grew a work-force which over-represented those tribes which favoured education, achievement and industry. There was some recruitment of oversees personnel. Whilst there was a diversity of different types of people working for the company some tribes were under-represented.

Every effort was made to train and develop initiates into the new culture. Despite some drop out, this was very successful. In the next few years performance grew and the company was successful.

Then in 1986 a government directive announced to all its Federal companies that it must give their work-force a 'federal character'. In an attempt to help disadvantaged areas of the country, it required its Federal companies to employ people from all twenty-one states, distributing posts at all levels.

This, of course, was at variance to the philosophy of *aisojusaju* which the company had built up over the years. *Sojusaju*, or discrimination, was actively being encouraged by the government. The work-force, particularly those who were coming up for promotion were upset, the expatriates were no longer sure of their position, the head of human resources was upset as he had nursed and nurtured this culture very successfully over the years, but would probably lose his job if he did not comply. The general manager was torn between honouring the Bendel philosophy and obeying the government. What should be done?

Discussion. Use the five factors to examine this case. Despite the variety of different languages in Nigeria, this is not a problem as English is used extensively as a common second language. What are the different cultural problems? What are the contact problems? What are the hierarchy issues here? Finally, what are the issues of motivation?

(*Source*: Putti and Chia, 1990)

Individual character

In cross-cultural encounters, you speak with an individual, not a company or a nation! At this level we must consider all three aspects of national culture, company culture, and individual character.

Not only should we have an understanding of the other's character (see Chapter 3 for a detailed discussion on this aspect), we should also have an understanding of our own.

Similarly, we should not let our preconceived ideas about a national culture cloud our understanding of the character of, for example, an individual French, English or Chinese person. The following may be applied to both yourself and the other person with whom you are dealing.

Activity 12.5 Understanding individual character

Use the following guide-line to understand both your own and the character of a person you are currently working with, or having business dealings with.

1 *Is there a deep general principle or philosophy which is being applied by the other person? What principle or principles are you applying?*

For example, we saw in the above case study (Mini case 12.5) that an overriding principle of non-favouritism was being applied in recruitment interviews at

Bendel Steel company. It helps to understand if the other person is applying a company principle or one of his or her own derived from a particular business philosophy or even religious conviction. For example, responses to proverbs are a good indication. A positive response to 'Blood is thicker than water' from a person at Bendel, for example, would not bode well for the philosophy instilled within this company. Guy and Mattock (1991) suggest the following test.

Look at the following proverbs and circle a number on the scale to show how central each is to your business and personal life (0 = irrelevant, 5 = essential).

Blood is thicker than water	0 1 2 3 4 5
Time is money	0 1 2 3 4 5
God will provide	0 1 2 3 4 5
My word is my bond	0 1 2 3 4 5
Do as you would be done by	0 1 2 3 4 5.

It is difficult, of course to give this test to the other person. You can certainly gain an idea of your own values, and perhaps you can start to infer these values by carefully listening to and watching the other person.

2 *What type of upbringing is the other person likely to have had, and how does this compare with your own?*

Again this if difficult information to obtain but might well form the subject of small-talk in the bar (depending on whom you are dealing with, and from what cultural background). Upbringing may vary considerably from one person to the next in any particular country, and this may have a substantial influence on that person's outlook. The differences in outlook, for example, of a manager in Britain who spent his childhood in an English public school as a boarder, and one who went to school at the local secondary modern school may be substantial. Other differences may be in other aspects of family background. Some of this information may be obtained in an informal setting.

Ask yourself how this may affect their outlook? Ask yourself how this differs from your own upbringing and outlook on life. You may begin to get a picture of whether this person is a normal (or expected) product of his national cultural background, and whether he or she represents those values and cultural aspects of the organization they work for.

3 *How can I understand the personality of the other person?*

One model we can apply here is the distinction made by a number of theorists from Jung to Eysenck (see Chapter 3) between introvert and extrovert. Can you make this type of distinction? The following checklist is adapted from Guy and Mattock (1991).

	Introvert	Extrovert
Orientation:	inward looking	outward looking
Values:	achievement	status
	fulfilment	respect
	task	people
	knowledge	action
	understanding	domination
	fantasy	fact

While it may not be necessary to categorize somebody as either introvert or extrovert, the checklist will help you to understand the personal values systems of both the other person and yourself.

4 How is the other person viewed by his colleagues, boss and subordinates?

Not only can you determine where in the formal hierarchy the other person is, but also how he is personally regarded. Is he respected, feared or despised? Do his colleagues listen when he or she makes a proposal? Do they look to him or her to take the lead? Is he or she brushed aside by colleagues or boss?

5 How typical are both the other person and you of your own cultures?

Finally you should be prepared to adapt your ideas gained about the country and organizational culture in the light of the individuals with whom you deal. They may well fit a national stereotype, but may also be at variance with it. The other person may well have preconceived ideas about you. You may like to try to work out, from the way he or she has interacted with you, what these preconceived ideas might be, and how accurate they are.

(See also Guy and Mattock, 1991, for a more detailed discussion of many of the aspects covered in this Activity.)

Summary

We have therefore tried to provide a more pragmatic approach to the issues involved in managing cultural differences. This will provide a good starting place for specific issues which we discuss in subsequent chapters, such as international negotiation, decision making, change management and international project management.

We first looked at the barriers to cross-cultural understanding, and named these as cultural misperceptions, misinterpretations and misevaluations. We suggested a numbers of ways these barriers could be broken down. We then turned to the framework provided by Guy and Mattock (1991) in considering the 'constants' of culture, company and character.

These are the aspects of doing business internationally which we must try to understand, without being able to change them. It is only in later chapters where we discuss those aspects of international business behaviour, such as negotiation tactics, which we can affect.

References

Adler, N. J. (1991) *International Dimensions of Organizational Behaviour*, Boston, Massachusetts: PWS-Kent.

Fetterman, D. M. (1989) *Ethnography: Step By Step*, Newbury Park, California: Sage.

Guy, V. and Mattock, J. (1991) *The New International Manager*, London: Kogan Page.

Hofstede, G. (1980) *Culture's Consequences: International Differences in Work Related Values*, Beverly Hills, California: Sage.

Hofstede, G. (1991) *Culture and Organizations: Software of the Mind*, London: McGraw-Hill.

Laurent, A. (1983) 'The cultural diversity of western conceptions of management', *International Studies of Management and Organization*, XIII, 1–2, Spring–Summer, 1983, pp. 75–96.

Putti, J. M. and Chia, A. (1990) *Culture and Management: A Casebook*, Singapore: McGraw-Hill.

13

Cross-cultural negotiation

Objectives

Following this chapter you should be able to:

1 Describe the preconditions for successful cross-cultural negotiations to take place.
2 Demonstrate an understanding of the necessary preparations required for successful cross-cultural negotiations.
3 Demonstrate an understanding of different styles of negotiations across cultures.
4 Describe the qualities of a good negotiator.
5 Demonstrate an understanding of the process of cross-cultural negotiations.
6 Demonstrate an understanding of negotiation tactics and their varieties and different effects in cross-cultural negotiations.

Key concepts

- Preconditions for negotiation
- Preparation for negotiation
- Negotiation styles
- Qualities of effective negotiators
- Negotiation process

Introduction

A dictionary definition of 'negotiation' is '(noun) a discussion set up or intended to produce a settlement or agreement' (the *Collins English Dictionary*). In other words it is a process which involves face to face communication, with a particular objective or objectives to arrive at an agreement. As such this definition could embrace a whole number of different business and management situations, where two or more people get together to make an agreement. This could include the selling of a product or service, agreeing on a joint venture, settling a dispute between, say, management and a trade union, or between head office management and subsidiary management. A complication in negotiations is that the two parties may have different objectives. These objectives may be different from what each requires from the agreement, or different in respect that one party may not even want an agreement. Another complication is that the intended route to be taken by each party to arrive at the objectives may be quite different. The fact that these issues are often compounded in cross-cultural negotiations is often problematic as are a number of related issues. The negotiation styles of negotiators are an issue we look at in this chapter, as is the skills requirement for cross-cultural negotiators. Tactics also play an important role, and it is difficult to assume that the other (foreign) party is going to play by the same rules.

In this chapter we therefore look at the preconditions for success, the necessary preparations for cross-cultural negotiation, negotiation styles across different cultures, the skills and qualities of effective cross-cultural negotiators, the process of negotiation itself, and the employment of tactics in cross-cultural negotiations.

Preconditions for successful cross-cultural negotiations

Preconditions of successful negotiations revolve around factors of situation, people, and objectives. Fisher (1980) for example identifies a number of variables through a study of different cultures which affect the process of negotiation. An understanding of these variables is an essential precondition for successful negotiation and are as follows.

- Cultural conditioning regarding how different negotiators will view the negotiation process. For example, the give and take of negotiation may not follow and may lead to frustration unless there is some understanding of the fact that different perceptions and different rules may well be applied by the other party.

- The use of a third party may be common in some cultures such as Japan where face to face disagreement is seen as an unpleasant situation, and a middle person may be used to resolve the issue.

- Different degrees of trust. Whilst some negotiators may come to the table mistrusting the other party until they can establish an element of trust, other negotiators may come fully trusting the other unless led to believe that the other person is untrustworthy. French negotiators are cited as being of the former case, and Americans of the latter case.

- The extent to which the negotiation is seen as a problem solving exercise. Some negotiators negotiate on the basis that the problem has been solved and they are not prepared to shift their position substantially. Others might see that there is a problem to be solved, and it can be so solved by sitting around the negotiating table.

- The importance of protocol. Negotiators from some cultures may regard negotiations as a time for rhetoric and performance and even a matter of national honour (Mexicans are cited as examples of this).

- Selection of the negotiating team. Some teams may be selected on the basis of technical expertise, others may be selected for their position of power and authority.

- Decision making. There are differences in both perceptions of the decision making process and who makes decisions. This involves factors such as a need to refer to a higher authority, not wanting to negotiate with anybody if they are not of the highest authority, and trade-off practices for making decisions within negotiation.

A precondition of successful cross-cultural negotiation is an ability of each party to enter into the cultural space of the other party. The above points serve as a provisional check-list for doing this.

Preconditions relating to the personal characteristics of the individual negotiator also exist. Casse (1979) points to five skills necessary for the successful negotiator, as follows:

- see the world as others see it, and understand others' behaviour as a result;
- show the advantages of what you are offering in order that the other person is willing to change;
- manage stress and cope with ambiguous situations and unpredictable demands;
- sensitivity to the other person's culture and adjusting proposals in line with perceived constraints and limitations.

Perhaps it is debatable to what extent these are skills which can be learned!

Adler (1991) offers a number of situational factors which should be borne in mind for successful negotiations.

- *Location*. This factor may determine an advantage of access to information to the party who can negotiate on their own premises, and this is particularly so when negotiations take place between companies in different countries. If you negotiate on your own premises you can also remove the other person from telephone calls and interruptions. A neutral location may be selected. Costs of hotels and travel may even increase the pressure to conclude the negotiation as quickly as possible.

- *Physical arrangements*. Sitting around a boardroom table at opposite sides emphasizes a confrontation situation. Sitting at right angles, and facing 'the problem' to be solved rather than the other party engenders cooperation.

- *Participants*. The number of members in a negotiating party is important in cross-cultural negotiation, and Adler (1991) recommends that more is better. This suggests to the other party that the issue is important, and also provides some team members who can be concerned with observing and listening to cultural cues while some are responsible for the discussion itself. The question also of who is represented may be important. For example, should trade unions be included? Should the negotiation be made accessible to the public?

- *Time limits*. It is said that during the Paris Peace talks regarding the negotiated peace in Vietnam, the Americans arrived in Paris and booked their hotel accommodation for a week, whereas the Vietnamese leased a chateau for a year. This indicates the different time expectations of different cultures, with American negotiators working with a sense of urgency ('time is money'). Concessions in negotiations are most usually made towards the time deadline of the party making the concession. This obviously puts time conscious cultures at a disadvantage. It of course helps to know the deadline of the other party.

- *Status differences*. In egalitarian or low power distance (Hofstede, 1991) societies, negotiations are often informal and even on first name terms. However, in some societies like Japan, status differences may be emphasized, and more formality is expected. This would normally mean that negotiators from countries such as the United States or United Kingdom would have to adopt more formality in negotiation than is normally expected in the home situation. Also, in some societies where age connotes seniority, sending a young 'whizz kid' to negotiate may insult the other party.

Activity 13.1 Preconditions for successful negotiation

We have discussed the following factors and preconditions for success in cross-cultural negotiation:

Process factors

1 General cultural conditioning
2 Use of third parties
3 Different degrees of trust
4 Degree to which negotiations are seen as a problem-solving exercise
5 Relative importance of protocol
6 Selection of negotiation team
7 How decisions are made by each party

Person factors

8 Ability to see the world as others see it
9 Ability to show the advantages of what you are offering
10 Ability to manage stress and ambiguity
11 Sensitivity to the other culture and adjusting proposals accordingly

Situational factors

12 Location of negotiation
13 Physical arrangements of negotiation room
14 Number of participants on each side
16 Time limits
16 Status differences between participants.

Referring to the sixteen points above, use them as a check list to state how you would try to ensure the success of your forthcoming negotiations. You represent a company in your home country, wishing to supply products to a company in (a) United States, (b) Russia, (c) Japan. What would you need to know in each case? How would you select your team? What else would you do prior to the negotiations, and during the negotiation to make sure it is successful? Would your approach be different in each case?

We have therefore looked at some of the preconditions for successful negotiating. We will now look at what preparation can be done before entering into a negotiation with a party from another culture. In so doing, we will look in more detail at some of the factors mentioned above.

Preparations for cross-cultural negotiations

Mead (1990) provides four broad areas to consider in preparation for negotiations.

- Background information, including company, industry and cultural information.
- Who the other parties are, what their interests are and why. This includes asking questions on who is representing their interests, what authority the team has to make decisions, why they are negotiating, and the expected balance between co-operation and competition in the negotiation.
- How you intend to negotiate. This includes questions on the composition of your team and its authority, the preparation of issues, and identifying your interests.
- Preparing the logistics: when and where. This includes the investment of time, the itinerary and the location.

Background information

The acquisition of background information is a prerequisite to preparing for negotiation. You must know what you require and from where you can get it. Apart from information on the company, on the industry and on the national business, social and legal structure (which can be obtained from embassy trade offices and libraries, trade missions and other associations) you should also obtain data on the cultural environment including:

- attitudes towards time, relationships, modes of activities and nature; and on power distance, uncertainty avoidance individualism/collectivism and masculinity/femininity values;
- attitudes towards motivation, conflict, decision making and planning;
- face to face negotiation styles;
- attitudes towards culture change;
- values attached to innovation and technology;
- attitudes towards outsiders and members of your culture or nationality;
- religious, ethnic, political and social groupings as well as inter-group conflicts;
- language and language groups.

Who are the other parties and what are their objectives?

You should try to ascertain the situation and interests of the other party in relationship to your own. You will need to find out the following.

- Who is representing the interests of the other company? You should try to find out the size and composition of the other negotiating team, either by a direct approach or by referring to other colleagues or other companies who have had dealings with the other party. Finding out about the various ranks and areas of expertise will give you information on the interests of the other team and their relative authority. If engineers are heavily represented, for example, this may signify the importance placed on the engineering implications of the deal. The age and hierarchical importance of participants also indicate the symbolic importance attached to both age and top management involvement, rather than of technical importance.

- What authority does their team have to make decisions? In other words, are the negotiators the decision makers? The decision makers may be present but not take an active part in the discussions. They may also not be present at all. Limited authority (or claims to limited authority) includes:

  - limited personal authority
  - financial and policy limitations
  - technological limitations
  - legal or political limitations
  - ethical and principled limitations.

You should try to gain information on their decision making process to decide whose interests you have to satisfy. This may involve a collective responsibility (high collectivist society), a supreme personal authority of the chief executive officer (high power distance culture), family veto or consultation, or a final decision resting with the State (People's Republic of China for example).

- Why are they negotiating? What are there objectives? You should try to ascertain the relative importance to them of the issues involved in the negotiation. You should consider:

  - the objectives that they must achieve;
  - the objectives they would hope to achieve;
  - those lesser objectives which would be nice if they could be achieved.

It may be difficult to discover this in an international context as priorities may be quite different to your own. If you are aware, for example, of your own international competition you may be able to discover the other party's alternative to a negotiated agreement. If negotiations break down, can they go to a competitor, or are you the only company which can satisfy their needs?

How do you intend to negotiate?

You should consider the interests of the other party in connection with your own interests. The issues to address are as follows:

- The size of your team and its composition. This is not just a matter of selecting the appropriate expertise within your team, but also thinking about the implications in another culture. For example, should you select women in your team when you are negotiating with a company in Saudi Arabia? Will it be better to select a team with older managers if you are negotiating in China?

- The authority you have to make decisions. You need to be sure of the limits of your authority, particularly when you are working in a foreign country and you do not have ready access to quick and secure communications if you have to seek instructions. A limit to your authority may work to your disadvantage as a sign of weakness and lack of position, but may also work in your favour when you want to defer a decision. For example, when you are not willing to accept new conditions introduced into a negotiation by the other party, you may break off the meeting in order to seek a decision which you are not empowered to make. This may then force the other party to think again!

- Preparing the issues for negotiation. You should consider those things which you are negotiating for and what you can offer in return in order to make sure that as far as possible both parties gain in a win-win situation. Commercial negotiations might involve issues of price of goods, discounts, quantity, quality and technical specifications, delivery and insurance, and so on. They rarely involve just single issues of, say, price. Through creative negotiation, new issues can be raised in order to solve problems. For example, although the price you are asking may be a 'must have' you can look at discounts through quantity and thus maintain your margins. You should prioritize the issues, deciding what to negotiate on and what to avoid.

- Deciding your interests and objectives. After listing the issues on which you are to negotiate, you should decide your interests on each issue. You should decide on those objectives:

  - you must achieve
  - you hope to achieve
  - you would like to achieve, but are less important.

You should compare this with the priorities you expect the other party to have, those areas in which you can co-operate and those in which you expect to compete. You should identify your 'Best Alternative To a Negotiated Agreement' (BATNA) if negotiations break down. In so doing you can decide on what you are prepared to concede to prevent negotiations breaking down. You should not expect to achieve all your objectives. If this happens, you have either asked too little, or the other party is too weak! You should consider carefully whether you want to do business with a 'weak' partner, who may have problems if confronted with difficulties at the implementation stage.

Preparing the logistics

This mainly involves points of where and when the negotiations should be held.

- How much time should you invest in the negotiation. This decision is not simply a commercial one (that is, deciding on the return on the time invested in a negotiation) but also a cultural one where some cultures are more time conscious than others. For example, Americans have got a reputation for being very time aware in negotiations, and wanting to arrive at a deal in order to satisfy the need for quick results. This is often used against then by less time conscious negotiators who will introduce new demands as the deadline approaches. It is probably a good rule not to display impatience.

- What is the schedule, and what is the location? Particularly if you are travelling long distance you should make sure you arrive in plenty of time to go to the negotiation fresh. You should also make sure that the information and authority you take with you is in accordance with the ease, or lack of ease, with which you can communicate with your home base.

Activity 13.2 Preparing to negotiate

We have stressed the importance of preparation, and have outlined four areas to consider when preparing for negotiations, as follows.

Background information

1. The other party's attitude to time, relations, modes of activities, and so on
2. Attitudes to motivation, conflict, decision making and planning
3. Attitudes towards cultural change
4. Values attached to innovation and technology
5. Attitudes to outsiders and your own nationality
6. Religious, ethnic, political, and social grouping and inter-group conflicts

The other party and their objectives

7. The size and composition of the other party, and their roles, rank and expertise
8. The other team's authority to make decisions
9. The reasons why they are negotiating, their objectives, what they must achieve and what they would like to achieve, and their Best Alternative To a Negotiated Agreement

How you intend to negotiate

10. The size of your own team and its composition
11. The authority you have to make decisions
12. The issues you are negotiating and their relative priorities
13. You party's interests and objectives, including what you must achieve and what you hope to achieve, and your Best Alternative To a Negotiated Agreement.

The logistics

14. The time you should spend on the negotiation
15. The schedule and the location.

You are preparing to negotiate with representatives from companies in the three countries listed in Activity 13.1, namely (a) United States, (b) Russia, (c) Japan, again, representing your company in your home country. How do you expect them to negotiate? List four factors which you would expect to affect the way each will negotiate, making sure that your four points are different in each case. You should do this as far as you are able from your existing knowledge of these three cultures, using the fifteen points above as a check-list.

Negotiation styles across cultures

A major factor which must be taken into account both in planning negotiation tactics, and during the course of the negotiations are the different negotiating styles both of individuals and of different cultures. Adler (1991) makes the point that styles of negotiation vary considerably between cultures on key aspects such as the amount and type of preparation, the emphasis on task versus interpersonal relationships, the use of general principles versus specific detail, and the numbers in the negotiating team and their relative influence in the team. The following summaries of different cultural negotiating styles (adapted from Adler, 1991) illustrate this point.

Table 13.1 *Cultural negotiating styles*

	North American	*Arabs*	*Russian*
General negotiating style	rational and appeal to logic	appeals to emotion	appeals to ideals
Counters arguments with . . .	facts	feelings	ideals
Concession making	small, and at early stage to establish relations	made throughout as part of the process	very few made
Response to concessions	usually reciprocate	almost always reciprocates	viewed as weakness and not reciprocated
Relationships	short-term	long-term	not continuing
Authority of negotiators	wide	wide	limited
Starting position	moderate	extreme	extreme
Deadlines	very important	casual	ignored

Source: adapted from Adler, 1991, and based on the research of Glenn *et al.*, 1984.

While it is possible to point to research undertaken into styles of negotiating in different cultures, it is perhaps more valuable to try to assess yourself the negotiating styles of both the other party and of yourself. For this we draw on the work of Casse (1979), reported in Harris and Moran (1987), who distinguishes four negotiation styles: factual, intuitive, normative and analytical.

Activity 13.3 Negotiation styles

For each set of four words (1–12) select the one word that has the most appeal to you in negotiations. For example, in the set of four words in row 1, you may think that it is important to be principled in negotiation rather than appearing charismatic, unemotional, or being factual. You therefore circle 'principled'.

[1]	[2]	[3]	[4]
1 charismatic	principled	unemotional	factual
2 creativity	people	analysis	precision
3 energy	sensitivity	logic	details
4 inspiration	compromise	systematic	information
5 intuition	harmony	cause & effect	experience
6 future	co-operation	planning	the present
7 enthusiasm	praise	statements	well tested
8 exciting	emotions	making sense	patience
9 imagination	agreement	consistency	pragmatism
10 emotions	threats	arguments	low key
11 novelty	value	incisive	realism
12 potential	tolerance	organization	conclusions

Now count up the number of words you have circled in each column, and plot your scores for each on the chart below. You can construct your profile by joining the four points.

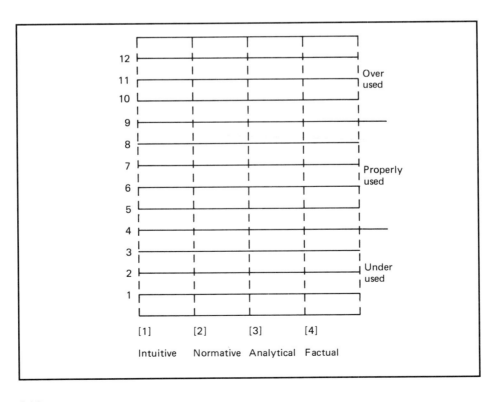

You can now analyse you negotiation style as follows.

- *Intuitive style*: You work on the assumption that imagination can solve any negotiation problem. You tend to focus on the entire situation rather than the details, looking into the future, being creative and imaginative, going beyond facts, and generating new ideas, but sometimes getting the facts (which are not that important to you) wrong.

- *Normative style*: You prefer to judge and assess a set of facts on the basis of a set of principles or values. You tend to be evaluative, approving and disapproving. You propose rewards and incentives appealing to people's feelings. You pursue a 'fair' deal. You focus on people and their reactions and use power and status where appropriate to threaten, to demand, and to require.

- *Analytical style*: You believe that the use of logic leads to the right conclusions. You weigh up different arguments, infer and analyse cause and effects, put things in logical order, and are thorough in your reasoning.

- *Factual style*: You use, and point to facts in an unemotional and detached way. You keep track of what people say, asking them to explain and reminding people of what they have said when appropriate. You look for proof, and tend to document statements.

Other people's negotiation styles

You should also look for clues for the styles which the other party are using. You can do this by listening for key words which may be used.

- Intuitive: Creative, idea, new, tomorrow, essential.
- Normative: Right, wrong, good, bad
- Analytical: Consequently, because, then, therefore, in order to.
- Factual: Define, clarify, facts, explain.

Negotiating with others according to their negotiation style

You should adapt you own style in order to deal with the style of the person you are negotiating with, as follows.

Intuitive:
- focus on the whole situation
- be future oriented
- tap into the imagination of the other person
- be quick in reacting to one idea, then another
- build on the reactions of others.

Normative:
- establish a solid relationship with the other person from the beginning
- show an interest in what the other person is saying
- identify the other person's values and adjust to them

- compromise if necessary
- appeal to the feelings of the other person

Analytical:
- use logic when arguing
- be patient
- analyse the various options available
- look for explanations of cause and effect.

Factual:
- carefully present your facts and be precise
- refer to the past and what is already established
- go from facts to the principles
- take notes

So, instead of making assumptions about the other person's likely style of negotiation by referring to national stereotypes (although this certainly provides a start in your preparations for negotiation) try to look at the individual. First understand your own negotiation styles, and then adjust them to the expectations of the other party.

The qualities of effective negotiators

The qualities of a good negotiator are in some ways influenced by the culture and the type of negotiation styles which are appropriate. For example, Adler (1991) lists the following individual characteristics of negotiators from four different countries which have been identified in research undertaken in 1983 by Professor John Graham at the School of Business Administration, University of Southern California.

While there are similarities between these different cultures, for example the American Taiwanese and Brazilian negotiators are good planners, this is not a quality looked for in Japanese negotiators. Brazilian negotiators are very similar to Americans, but value competitiveness above integrity. The Japanese stress a more interpersonal approach over a rational one and stress listening ability. The Taiwanese emphasize the ability to command respect and to be persistent and determined in their dealings, as well as being an interesting person. Also from this same research:

- Brazilians are more successful in negotiation when they are more deceptive, are self-interested and have high self-esteem and the other party are more honest;

- Americans are more successful when the other party is honest, not self-interested, introverted and can be intimidated by the negotiator's actions;

- Japanese are more successful when they can make the other party more comfortable;

- Taiwanese do better when they are deceptive and where the other party is not self interested and have uninteresting personalities (from Graham, 1983).

Table 13.2 *Characteristics of negotiators from four different countries*

Japanese	Chinese (Taiwan)	Brazilian	American
Dedicated to job	persistence	competitiveness	has integrity
Exploitation of power	ability to win respect	exploitation of power	exploitation of power
Can win respect and confidence	planning and preparation abilities	planning and preparation abilities	planning and preparation abilities
Has integrity	product knowledge	product knowledge	product knowledge
Listening skills	is interesting	can think under pressure	can think under pressure
Has a broad perspective	has intelligence and judgement	has intelligence and judgement	has intelligence and judgement
Verbal expressiveness		verbal expressiveness	verbal expressiveness

Source: Graham, 1983.

The research work into negotiations skills of the Huthwaite Research Group in the United Kingdom (Rackham, 1976) has been widely reported. This looked at the differences between successful and average negotiators during the planning stages and the face-to face stage. The variables were as shown in Table 13.3.

Skilled negotiators therefore spend more time on looking at different options available and possible outcomes, spend more time on reviewing areas of common

Table 13.3 *Successful planning behaviour*

Planning Behaviour:	Average Negotiator	Skilled Negotiator
Time spent planning	same	same
Number of options considered for action per issue	less	more
Attention given to common ground issues	less	more
Consideration of long-term issues beyond the immediate implementation stages	less	more
The use of sequential planning such as critical path analysis as opposed to issue planning which is not linked to sequence and shows more flexibility	sequential	issue
Setting fixed point limits as opposed to setting upper and lower limits in a range	fix point	range

Source: Rackham, 1976.

ground and co-operation, look more towards the long-term issues, define limits as a range, say from £10 to £20 per unit, rather than a fixed point of say £15 in order to give them more bargaining flexibility. They also use issue planning which means that they consider each issue independently, planning the issues to cover, rather than sequential planning of discussing issue *A* then *B* then *C* in an ordered sequence. Again this provides more flexibility in the negotiation process.

Table 13.4 *Successful negotiating behaviour*

Negotiating behaviour:	Average negotiator	Skilled negotiator
Use of irritators (phrases that have little value to the negotiation but which irritate, e.g, 'generous offer')	more	less
Frequency of counter-proposals	more	less
Defensive/attacking behaviour	more	less
Describing verbal behaviour prior to the behaviour such as 'Can I ask a question' and then asking the question and thus fore-warning other party:		
When disagreeing	more	less
All other verbal behaviour	less	more
Active listening through:		
testing understanding	less	more
summarizing	less	more
Asking questions	less	more
Giving information on own feelings (for example on the progress of talks or in response to proposal)	less	more
Argument dilution by providing more arguments per issue or case they are advancing	more	less

Source: Rackham, 1976.

Skilled negotiators therefore avoid using irritators which might detract from the negotiation (for example, 'fair price', 'generous offer', 'reasonable arrangement') use fewer counter-proposals, get less defensive and attack less frequently, and refrain from diluting their argument by using too many (and usually weak) arguments per issue. They use behaviour labelling extensively, providing advanced warning to the other party of what they are going to say (except when disagreeing), they are active listeners, they question frequently and provide accounts of their own personal feelings on the progress of negotiation or specific issues.

The research carried out by the Huthwaite group in Britain relates specifically to British negotiators, and although valuable, no similar research has been undertaken to replicate this internationally as far as the current author is aware. However, consider the research in Mini case 13.1.

Mini case 13.1 Lessons from behind the bamboo curtain

In an article 'Negotiation: lessons from behind the bamboo curtain', Kirkbride and Tang (1990) argue that those skills and abilities in negotiation which are most commonly quoted in the literature as being requisite to successful negotiations, are generally what comes naturally to negotiators from the People's Republic of China. These are:

- *Setting bargaining ranges for the negotiation process.* Setting too specific a limit or setting the minimum and maximum points too close together is often a fault of Western negotiators, but less so with Chinese negotiators, whose culture stresses compromise rather than conflict. The more flexible you are on your bargaining range the more likely you are to arrive at common ground and thus avoid conflict.

- *Seeking to establish general principles early in the negotiation.* These are the key commitments or fundamental elements which underpin an agreement. If you can get the other party to agree on these principles you are likely to gain the advantage in the final settlement. These aspects seem to be an essential part of Chinese negotiations, where much time is spent on establishing these basic principles. Again this may be an attempt to avoid conflict on details at a later stage. General principles may be turned to agreed-upon goals to which the two parties are then committed.

- *Focusing on potential areas of agreement and seeking to expand on them.* Establishing common ground will help to unite the two parties. Chinese negotiators may see 'compromise' as a goal in negotiation, rather than the western view of this being half way to a defeat: of giving in. The Chinese ideal is the development of mutual interest.

- *Avoiding taking the negotiation issues in sequence.* Even though sequential ordering of issues is seen as counter productive, it is often the natural, logical way to progress negotiations in western culture, gaining agreement on each issue as they arise. The Chinese take a more holistic view of negotiations, seeing issues as being connected, and not wanting to make a commitment on any issues until all have been discussed. This may be attributed to a more holistic psychology which sees the wholeness and harmony of nature rather than trying to separate it logically into its parts.

- *Avoiding excessive hostility, confrontation, and emotion.* For example, avoiding defending and attacking behaviour, and avoiding using irritators in negotiation is more productive, and conducive to establishing common principles and common ground. Chinese negotiators adopted lower levels of conflict behaviour than their western counterparts. This may be attributed to the beliefs and doctrines of harmony and conflict avoidance. Generally they are also less 'assertive' and have lower levels of verbal interaction.

- *Giving the other party something to take home.* In Chinese terms this is allowing the other party to gain something from the negotiation and providing 'face'. This is another reason for Chinese negotiators not to be overtly aggressive as this may cause a loss of face. This is generally socially unacceptable.

• *Negotiating as a team*. This often runs counter to Western 'individualism'. The need to stress team work in training programmes indicates that this is something which does not come naturally. The 'collectivism' of Chinese society emphasizes co-operation and collaboration in teams, and runs counter to individual initiative. Chinese negotiating teams are usually large, with roles specifically allocated (for example, negotiator, recorder and analyst). These are usually seen as informal and friendly to begin with, and get more bureaucratic when serious negotiating gets underway. This is in contrast to American teams, where, when the serious substance of the negotiation begins to be discussed, there is a move towards a one-to-one relationship (Pye, 1986).

The process of cross-cultural negotiation

There is no general agreement in the literature on the precise definition of each stage in the negotiation process. Also, when looking at the styles of different negotiators from different cultures, there are different emphases on the various phases of negotiation. Graham and Herberger (1983) distinguish four stages:

• non-task relationship creation
• task-related exchange of information
• persuasion
• concession and agreement.

Adler (1991) views this as a traditional competitive approach which is not always appropriate in cross-cultural encounters. She puts forward a 'synergistic' or collaborative/cultural approach to understanding the various stages of international negotiations, as follows.

• *Preparation*: cross-cultural training; defining interests.
• *Relationship building*: separating the people from the problem and adjusting to their style and pace.
• *Information exchange*: exchanging information about task and participants; clarifying interests; clarifying customary approaches.
• *Inventing options*: for mutual gain which are appropriate to both cultures.
• *Choice of best option*: this should be based on criteria appropriate to both cultures.
• *Agreement*: translating and back-translating agreement; and if necessary renegotiating.

Mead (1990) suggests that this type of sequential approach to understanding the process of negotiation is over-systematic. Different cultures have different regard for the importance of the phases of a negotiation. For example, Americans tend to be keen to get the formalities over with quickly and get to what they see as the heart of the matter, whereas the Brazilians and Chinese (see Graham and Herberger, 1983) emphasize the rapport-building aspects, and perhaps see this as ongoing. Mead (1990) therefore prefers to think of this process in terms of topic areas rather than sequential stages as follows:

- creating a relationship
- finding common ground
- persuasion
- bargaining and conceding
- implementation.

Creating a relationship

Generally speaking the opening moves of the negotiation involve the negotiation of trust between the two parties. If you feel you can believe what the other party says, you are more likely to want to do business with them. This trust involves a belief that the other party will:

- not resort to unethical behaviour such as tapping communications, restricting food and drink, or arranging the room to your disadvantage;
- honour any agreements made and do their best to convince their stake holders to accept the agreement;
- respect confidences and not leak information to outsiders;
- see that it is in their interests to do business with you.

The last point emphasizes that you cannot base a deal on pure trust and empathy but that there must be a real commercial interest in the other party doing a deal with you. Although in most Anglo-Saxon and Western European countries which have a history of large companies, it is usual to trust someone as a representative of a large company with a good reputation. This may not be the case when dealing with other cultures that have a more face-to-face tradition of building up relationships with individuals rather than conglomerates. Also many cultures such as Russia and Japan are more conservative and modest in extolling their own virtues and prior achievements. Therefore, trying to show a good track record may be counter-productive. Prior written evidence, and a reference to 'we' rather than 'I' is usually more productive.

Another point in establishing a relationship through the course of the negotiation and beyond is the balance between creating a short-term relationship and a long-term relationship. While some (usually collectivist rather than individualistic) cultures emphasize the building of a long term relationship, outsiders cannot assume that this will apply to them. While it may be tempting to be persuaded that if you take a lower profit on the first deal, then the relationship so developed will be a long and fruitful one, you must weigh up various factors in deciding whether you maximize your advantage on this (and possibly the only) deal, or whether you are prepared to look more towards the future. The factors you must weigh up are as follows.

- Your personal interests and those of your opposite number. Can you expect them to stay in their present job and with their present company for very long? If not there may be no basis for a long-term personal relationship.

- Is the other party's company likely to stay in the same line of business with the same interests? If not for very long there may be no opportunity to develop a long-term relationship with the company.

- What is the alternative to negotiating future deals? For example, you must have knowledge of the competition and alternative supplies to the ones that you are proposing and how these may change in the future.

- What are the cultural priorities of the other party? Do they place value on a long-term relationship?

Finding common ground

The next area or phase in negotiations which Mead (1990) points to is that of building common ground between the two parties. This involves the following factors.

- Preparation prior to the negotiation in order to identify possible areas of common ground. These areas can then be pushed to the top of the agenda for early discussion.

- Trading information. It is necessary to disclose information about your own interests in order to develop common ground, but a judgement must be made on how much, and when. This depends on the extent to which it is being reciprocated and how damaging the information you might supply could be to your interests in the negotiation.

- Establishing objective criteria. It may be mutually beneficial to establish criteria to settle such issues as the price of goods by reference, for example, to market prices. Objective criteria can also be used to decide upon what issues should be negotiated, what information is relevant to the issues, the value of information supplied and the reliability of technical information. It may be difficult to establish the basis of objective criteria across different cultures. For example, government statistics supplied by the former Soviet state may be mistrusted by an American negotiator.

- Linking issues. The Huthwaite research, discussed earlier (Rackham, 1976), suggests that negotiators who link issues in a non-sequential way tend to be more successful than those who insist on settling one issue before proceeding to the next. This prevents the linking of issues to mutual benefits where it may be difficult to go back to a previous point where it has already been decided. For example it may be useful to link in a previously unsettled decision to an issue presently under discussion as a lever to conclude the discussion (for example, 'we might be able to agree on *Y* if we modify the terms for *X*'). A contentious issue may be best left without settlement, when it may be possible to come back to it in the light of further discussion on other related issues.

- Asking questions. A major tool of the negotiator is question asking, and this can be used successfully to establish common ground, by:
  - checking your understanding of shared interests, and the extent to which you can trust the other person;
  - checking on your understanding of the apparent agreement – this is especially important when dealing with a person of a different culture who may have a different understanding to you;

- checking on the degree to which the other person is bluffing;
- showing that you are interested and are actively listening to the issues raised by the other side;
- demonstrating what points interest you;
- guiding the interaction in the direction you wish it to go, and away from issues you wish to avoid;
- probing, by asking 'why?' to statements in order to get to the real issues (a continued use of 'why?' normally gets to the root issues, but also try a lesser antagonistic 'I'm interested in how you are going to . . . ' and variations of this)

If you fail to get the answer you were looking for following a question, rephrase the question and ask again, as in a cross-cultural encounter this may not be evasion but simply misunderstanding.

Persuasion

This is the aspect of the negotiation where you convince the other party to accept your terms, and is most usefully conducted after developing common ground. Successful persuasion usually involves the following factors.

- *Supporting arguments*. The Huthwaite research (Rackham, 1976) showed that the success in getting your position accepted is not how many arguments you can put up to support it, as this tends to dilute your case, but that one strong argument is sufficient.

- *Counter-proposals*. Again, the Huthwaite research showed that the most successful negotiators give fewer counter-proposals to the other party's proposals, and also they delay these counter-proposals in order to:

  - give them time to think;
  - keep the other party guessing at your reactions;
  - give them time to consider their response in terms of the overall issues involved.

- *Silence*. The use of silence may be differently regarded in different cultures. The Japanese tend to make more use of periods of silence to consider and to understand the other party. This may unnerve people from other cultures who are used to filling in silences. Using silence might be a strength. It may keep the other side wondering what your reactions are and unnerve them. It may prompt them to keep talking and provide further concessions. It could, however, be seen as a sign of weakness in the face of an attack on your essential interests. Knowing when to keep silent is an important aspect of listening skills.

- *Disagreement*. Disagreements in a cross-cultural encounter may simply involve differences in perceptions rather than differences in the substance of the negotiation. Similarly, the seeming absence of disagreement cannot be taken as an expression of agreement (for example the avoidance of the use of 'no' by Japanese negotiators). Disagreements should be explained rather than degenerating in attacking/defending behaviour, particularly when dealing with a 'face-saving' culture such as China or Japan where the protection of the other person's face is as important as protecting one's own face.

- *Threats*. These only work if they are capable of being carried out. So, if you threaten to walk out of the negotiation at a certain time if a point is not settled, you must, otherwise you lose all credibility.

- *Personal attacks*. These may be a result of cultural misunderstandings, an attempt to gain advantage by making the other person lose their temper, an attempt to break off the negotiation, and so on. Decide which it is and consider your response in terms of the interests you have in continuing the negotiation.

- *Avoidance*. You can avoid talking about a topic you do not wish to pursue, as it will lead to conflict or lead away from the main agenda, by:

    introducing a new topic, perhaps by asking a question which leads away from the point;

    returning to previous stages in the negotiation, perhaps by seeking clarification;

    postponing further discussion, saying that this can be looked at later;

    maintaining silence.

    However, avoid using jokes as an avoidance tactic, as quite often jokes are culturally specific depending on a shared sense of incongruity.

- *Making a final offer*. If this really is your final offer, it puts pressure on the other party to meet your terms or break off the negotiation. If it is not your final offer you may loose credibility if they call your bluff.

Conceding and bargaining

You must prepare for the negotiation by working out what you must achieve from the negotiation and what it would be nice to achieve. It also helps if you know the other person's musts, and their Best Alternative To a Negotiated Agreement (BATNA). This will help you to decide what you can concede and what you can get in return. If you make a concession, you should always try to get something in return.

Mini Case 13.2 Negotiating in Iran

In being conciliatory and offering concessions and compromises in negotiations you should always be careful with the words you use when dealing with Iranians. Rather than 'compromise' having the positive connotations it has in English, in Farsi it has a negative meaning such as in 'her virtue was compromised' or 'our integrity was comprised'. The word 'mediator' in Farsi implies a 'meddler', or somebody who interferes without being invited. When UN Secretary General Waldheim went to Iran in 1980 to help in the hostage crisis, Iran national radio broadcasted a translation of his speech which said, 'I have come as a mediator to work out a compromise'. Minutes later his car was stoned by angry Iranians!

(*Source*: Adler, 1991)

Implementation

The conclusion to the discussions may not signify the end of the negotiation in some cultures. In more individualistic cultures, legal proceeding are relied upon to enforce a contract if it is breached, whereas in collectivist societies, pressure of family and close associates are used as a type of peer pressure. If you are outside a particular culture, it may be difficult to enforce a contract.

It is normal in the People's Republic of China for the implementation stage to be regarded as another stage in the negotiation, where there is a continued process of adjustment and discussion. If, in any foreign country, your partner feels that the terms you have gained in the negotiations are too harsh, there may be little incentive to implement the contract. In developing countries where there are frequent changes of government, the political situation may change so that your partner is unable to proceed with implementation.

Activity 13.4 Managing the process of negotiation

We have discussed the various phases of the negotiation process as follows.

Creating a relationship

1 Establishing trust
2 Establishing a balance between a short-term and long-term relationship

Finding common ground

3 Identifying possible common ground before the negotiation
4 Trading information
5 Establishing objective criteria
6 Linking issues in negotiation
7 Asking questions

Persuading

8 Supporting arguments
9 Making counter-proposals
10 Using silence
11 Disagreeing and understanding disagreement
12 Using and coping with threats
13 Coping with personal attacks
14 Avoiding topics
15 Making a final offer

Bargaining and conceding

16 Working out what you must achieve from the negotiation and what your alternatives are

17 Working out what the other party needs to achieve and what their alternatives are

18 Making concessions and getting something in return

Implementing

19 Enforcing a contract.

From the information already given on negotiation in the People's Republic of China, (see particularly Mini case 13.1) which of the nineteen aspects of the negotiation process would you concentrate on in negotiating with the Chinese? Of the aspects which you choose as important, how would you handle them?

Negotiation tactics and their relative effects in cross-cultural negotiations

In the last section we looked at some of the tactical aspects of the process of negotiation and have referred to some differences between cultures. The following tactics are reviewed by Graham (1985) across three different cultures.

Table 13.5 *Use of negotiation tactics across three different countries*

Tactic	Average number of times used in half-hour negotiation		
	USA	*Japan*	*Brazil*
Promise	8	7	3
Threat	4	4	2
Recommendation	4	7	5
Warning	1	2	1
Reward	2	1	2
Punishment	3	1	3
Normative appeal	2	4	1
Commitment	13	15	8
Self-disclosure	36	34	39
Question	20	20	22
Command	6	8	14

Source: Graham, 1985.

Promise. This is a conditional, positive statement which promises a concession in exchange for a concession in return, such that you will lower the price if they will order more units. Brazilians seem to use this tactic less than Japanese or Americans.

Threat. This is a conditional negative which promises a negative response if you refuse to make a concession, such that you will walk out if they do not lower the price of the goods. Brazilians seem to use this less than the other two nationalities.

Recommendation. This is a recommendation that if you do something, then a third party will respond to this in a positive way, such that your government will sanction further deals if they are able to offer your developing country a special concession on price. American negotiators seem to use this less than Japanese negotiators.

Warning. This is a negative warning that a third party will do something you do not desire if you now do something I do not wish – so that if you do not concede on this issue, your national press will get hold of the story telling the nation what a disservice you have done for your country.

Reward. This is an unconditional offer, usually as a reward for previous co-operation, for example offering to meet tomorrow on their premises.

Punishment. This is again an unconditional offer, but a negative one, stating that you will give them something they do not want, such as your refusing to listen to them any more. The Japanese seem to use this less often that the Americans or Brazilians.

Normative appeal. This is appealing to a societal norm, such as suggesting that their competitors have all got this same technology. The Japanese seem to use this more than the other two nationalities.

Commitment. This is an unconditional commitment to do something positive such as making delivery by a certain date. This seems to be used less frequently by Brazilians.

Self-disclosure. This involves providing information about yourself or your company's position, and is used extensively by all three nationalities researched by Graham (1985).

Question. This involves asking a question in order to get more information and is used frequently by all three nationalities.

Command. This is an order to do something, such as demanding that you lower the price. It is used more often by Brazilians than the other two nationalities in the above study.

Graham (1985) also studies the non-verbal tactics used by these three different nationalities. Silences are used most frequently by Japanese negotiators, and hardly at all by Brazilians who tend to argue and make more concessions in response to silences. Americans tend to interpret Japanese silences as a rejection of their proposals, as they do with non-native speakers of English, and tend to jump in with a compromise.

'Conversation overlaps' happen when two or more people are speaking at the same time. Brazilians interrupt each other more readily than do American or Japanese negotiators, frequently speaking simultaneously. When Japanese or American speakers are interrupted one will normally stop speaking. The Brazilian practice may be interpreted as rudeness by the other two cultures.

Facial gazing involves direct eye contact. This is common with Brazilian negotiators, less common with Americans, and is mostly avoided by Japanese negotiators. Frequent and held eye contact may be viewed as over intimate in some cultures, and in the studies reported above, makes American and Japanese negotiators feel uncomfortable. Touching behaviour (not including handshaking) during negotiations also depends on culture, with Brazilian negotiators touching each other on average five times per half hour, whereas there was no contact between American or Japanese negotiators in these studies. Too much touching for American, Japanese and other cultures shows too much intimacy and therefore would make them feel uncomfortable.

Finally, we can refer to some 'dirty tricks' in negotiation tactics of which you should be aware.

Activity 13.5 Dirty tricks

Below are a number of 'dirty tricks' in negotiation which you may encounter. State how you would deal with each.

Ambiguous authority. You are told by the other party that they are unable to make a decision on the current proposal and that they will have to adjourn the meeting and refer it to their boss tomorrow. It is still early in the afternoon.

Stressful situation. You are negotiating in the other party's company offices. The room is too hot, there is no private place to talk, and there is too much touching.

Personal attacks. You were kept waiting before you entered the negotiation rooms. There has been little eye contact throughout. Members of the other party seem not to be listening. They keep interrupting with other business. They challenge your status. They keep asking you to repeat things and make suggestions about you intelligence, and about your personal appearance, asking you if you have been up all night.

Extreme demands. You know the proposal is worth only £50,000, but they keep asking for £200,000.

Refusal to negotiate. You tell them that you are prepared to pay £50,000 and that the £200,000 they propose is far too high. They refuse to negotiate further.

Escalating demands. You finally agree on £75,000. Later they ask for punitive penalties on late delivery. You say you are not happy with this, and so they ask for a further increase in the price of the original proposals. They go through a process of making concessions and then adding new demands, and reopening old demands.

Locking-in tactics. Prior to the start of the negotiation, the other party released a press statement committing themselves to a course of action in the project which had not been agreed to by your party.

Waiting for your deadline. The other party knows that you have a deadline for the negotiations which runs out this evening. You think the deal is almost concluded. They then put up another demand which will substantially reduce your profit margins.

You should consider your responses in line with the other information in the text.

Summary

We have therefore looked at the preconditions of successful cross-cultural negotiations, and the necessity for preparation and the nature of the preparation which should be undertaken. We have seen that the Huthwaite studies showed that both average and skilled negotiators spent the same amount of time on preparation, and therefore this did not indicate an advantage in doing too much preparation. However, we could say that this is a prerequisite to any negotiation, and could speculate that this is even more important in cross-national negotiation where it is essential to have some understanding of the different national culture.

We also looked at the different styles of negotiation and pointed to some cross-cultural differences, although stressed the importance of focusing on the individual's style as well as trying to make assumptions from a limited knowledge of his or her national culture. Following this, we looked at the different skills and abilities for negotiation, stating that those qualities most recognized may be different in different cultures.

We then looked at the process of cross-cultural negotiation, mentioning that we should not regard this as sequential, but rather as inter-related, phases of the negotiation process. Finally we looked at tactics and focused on a study which compared different uses of tactics by American, Japanese and Brazilian negotiators, noting that tactics may be treated differently between cultures, but also non-verbal cues such as eye contact and touching may not be tactical but simply an expression of the culture itself.

References

Adler, N. (1991) *International Dimensions of Organizational Behaviour*, Boston, Massachusetts: PWS-Kent
Casse, P. (1979) *Training For The Cross-Cultural Mind*, Yarmouth, ME: Intercultural Press.

Fisher, G. (1982) *International Negotiation: A Cross-Cultural Perspective*, Yarmouth ME: Intercultural Press.

Glenn, E. S., Witmeyer, D. and Stevenson, K. A. (1984) 'Cultural styles of persuasion', *International Journal of Intercultural Relations*, 1.

Graham, J. L. (1983) 'Brazilian, Japanese and American Negotiations', *Journal of International Business Studies*, 14, 1, Spring-Summer, pp. 47–61.

Graham, J. L. (1985) 'The influence of culture on business negotiations', *Journal of International Business Studies*, 16, 1, Spring, pp. 81–96.

Graham, J. L. and Herberger, R. A. (1983) 'Negotiators abroad – don't shoot from the hip', *Harvard Business Review*, July/August, pp. 160–8.

Harris, P. R. and Moran, R. T. (1987) *Managing Cultural Differences*, Houston: Gulf Publishing.

Hofstede, G. (1991) *Culture and Organizations: Software of the Mind*, London: McGraw-Hill.

Kirkbride, P. S. and Tang, S. F. Y. (1990) 'Negotiation: lessons from behind the bamboo curtain', *Journal of General Management*, 16, 1, Autumn.

Mead, R. (1990) *Cross-Cultural Communication*, Chichester, W. Sussex: Wiley

Pye, L. W. (1986), 'The China trade: Making the deal', *Harvard Business Review*, July/August.

Rackham, N. (1976) 'The behaviour of successful negotiators' (Huthwaite Research Group Report) in Raider, E. (ed.) *International Negotiations: A Training Program For Corporate Executives And Diplomats*, New York: Ellen Raider International.

14

Managing uncertainty: decision making

Objectives

Following this chapter you should be able to:

1 Demonstrate a knowledge of management decision making in an uncertain, multi-cultured and rapidly changing environment.
2 Describe differences between organizations and national cultures in organizational decision making.
3 Describe differences in individuals' decision making styles.
4 Critically explain the central role of values in decision making, and the implications for ethical decision making.
5 Document your own decision-making styles and describe the decision-making processes within an organization.
6 Use specific techniques for management decision making.

Key concepts

- Decision-making styles: autocratic, consultative, participative.
- Vroom–Yetton • Decision Tree
- Decision-making process
- Ethical decision making: Utilitarianism, Formalism
- Donaldson's ethical algorithm

Introduction

This chapter is concerned with decision making at two levels: the individual level (and how individuals make decisions in business situations), and at the organizational level. The latter refers to the structures and processes of decision making which may vary between different organizational and national cultures. At the individual level also, it is possible that different patterns of cognitive processes may reflect different national cultural characteristics.

Decision making is an attempt to manage uncertainty by:

* making sense of ambiguity
* taking risks.

The first aspect, making sense of ambiguity, is by necessity historical: you are working on the information you have of what has happened in the past. The second aspect is future oriented. You are taking a risk because you are applying a perspective based on knowledge of the past, and projecting this to what might happen in the future if a certain course of action is followed. A decision maker will balance the risk of success or failure involved by trying to reduce the uncertainty of what will happen as a result of that decision. So, the more sense which can be made of the historical data, and the more information which can be obtained about the possible risks, the more likely it is that the decision will be a good one.

However, not all decisions are made on the basis of reducing the likelihood that the course of action will fail. Some decisions are more high-risk than others because the likely pay-offs are greater. Sometimes decisions need to be made quickly with little information, because if we put off a decision it will have negative consequences.

Decisions made by foreign exchange dealers have to be made rapidly. The consequences of not making a decision will be that the dealer, at best, does not do a deal and make money, at worst it might mean not selling currency when he or she should and therefore losing vast sums of money. The consequences of taking a wrong decision are largely statistical in this case. Generally, foreign exchange market dealers can afford to be 40 per cent wrong and 60 per cent right in the decisions they make. If the ratio slips in the wrong direction they could quickly find themselves out of a job!

Decisions may often be made as a result of a rational decision-making process.

Insurance companies make decisions on a slightly different basis. They collect statistical historical information on the incidence of, for example, motor car accidents by driver's age and size of car. This allows them to set a premium for each person requiring car insurance based on factors such as the motorist's age and car. They do not know whether this particular person will have an accident and subsequently make a claim against them. They do know, however, that in the whole population of their insured motorists in the age and car size category, that a certain number are likely to have accidents and make claims against them. The premium they charge each motorist, therefore, reflects the total amount of money they expect to pay out, plus an additional amount to cover costs and profits. Decisions made by insurance companies are therefore well researched, and very low in risk.

However, what is seen as 'rational' may differ between individuals and between cultures.

A human resources manager in England must make a decision on who she should recruit from a list of nine candidates. She looks at the candidates past record of employment, educational qualifications and references. She interviews applicants and makes a decision based on these various factors.

The senior manager of a company in Japan recruits a junior manager to the company as he knows his family is connected with his own, and he knows he can rely on the new employee. He would not like to recruit from outside this family group because he could not trust and rely on such an outsider.

Both of the above managers make decisions based on historical information which, for them, reduces the uncertainty of the recruitment decision, reducing the risk of failure. Rationality may, however, be based on different assumptions.

Decisions may also be made on a purely intuitive basis, and not follow any recognized logic. A manager may have a 'gut feeling' that a decision is right to recruit a certain person, even though he has not got a track record, or a suitable background. Decisions may also be taken purely on an 'irrational' basis. There are overriding odds to suggest that if I buy a lottery ticket, I will not win. So, why do people buy lottery tickets? An insurance company, in the description of their decision making process above, would not buy a lottery ticket! Rationality may be subjective as well as objective, therefore. I may feel that it is worth losing the £1 I spend on the ticket, in the hope that I may be the lucky winner of thousands of pounds, even though the odds are against me.

The concept of cost-benefits of a decision on which many (rational) decision-making models are based in the literature, may also be at fault in many instances. These models, as Eiser (1986) tells us, are based on utilitarian theory, which is not always borne out in practice. People have different value systems which can be accounted for by alternative decision models. This aspect is seen as extremely important in considering decision making across cultures and will be explored later in more detail.

Decisions are never made in isolation from the cultural and organizational setting and the perceptions and value judgements of individuals. We can illustrate this by once again referring to the 3Cs context–content–conduct descriptive model outlined in the earlier parts of this text (see for example, Chapter 1) as in Figure 14.1.

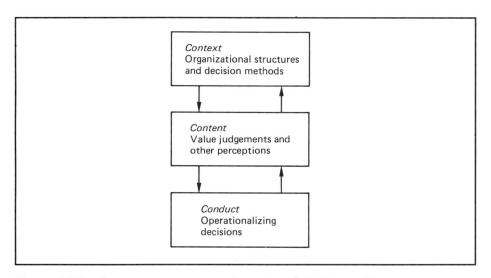

Figure 14.1 *The context, content and conduct of decision making*

Any one of these three factors may be looked on as being influenced by national culture. We could mention briefly the impact of a high power distance (see Hofstede, 1991 and, for example Chapter 2 for an outline of Hofstede's cultural dimensions) on organizational decision making where we would expect a more authoritarian approach to prevail in a high power distance country and a more participative style of organizational decision making in a low power distance society. The degree of collectivism may also influence organizational decision making and we will explore this in more detail later.

The influence of national and organizational culture on the values and perceptions of individuals may be substantial. A contentious, and very important issue which we will explore later is the place of ethical values in national and international business decision making, and the question of ethical relativism: should an international manager accept that there are different approaches to ethical decision making in different parts of the world and do business according to the host country's values, or should he or she conform to a universal standard which transcends national values? We later discuss such issues as corporate bribery and how the international manager may respond to such practices which are commonplace in some countries.

Coming to the last aspect of conduct, it also follows that the way decisions are implemented may differ according to different behavioural practices. However, in this chapter we are mainly concerned with the basis upon which decisions are actually made. We therefore turn first to organizational decision making, to discuss how decisions are made and by whom.

Organizational decision making

Vroom and Yetton (for example, Vroom,1973) describe three basic 'styles' of management decision making in organizations:

- autocratic
- consultative
- participative.

These may be regarded as overriding decision styles in organizations, where a particular company's management can be described as 'autocratic' in its decision making, or 'consultative' in the sense that managers consult those who may have the necessary expertise or those who will be affected by the decision made, or 'participative' in the sense of allowing others to participate in actually making the decision rather than simply being consulted about the decision. This usually involves a degree of industrial democracy.

However, these 'styles' may also be regarded as decision-making 'methods', which may be used from time to time in an organization, depending on a number of variables. Vroom and Yetton describe the factors which determine the best 'style' to adopt as follows:

- the quality of the decision to be made;
- the level of acceptability required by subordinates in order to implement the decision; and,
- the time scale of the decision-making process.

These factors are elaborated into seven questions which form the components of Vroom and Yetton's 'decision tree', which provides the basis of a rational consideration of which type of decision making to adopt in an organization in any particular circumstance. This is adapted in Figure 14.2. The decision tree should be followed, answering yes or no to the following questions.

A Is there a quality requirement in that one solution is more rational than another?

B Do I have enough information to make a decision?

C Is the problem structured through procedures and established practices?

D Is it important that my subordinates accept the decision in order that implementation is effective?

E If I make the decision by myself, can I expect that my subordinates will accept it?

F Do my subordinates share the organizational goals to be attained by solving the current problem?

G Is there likely to be conflict between my subordinates in the preferred solution?

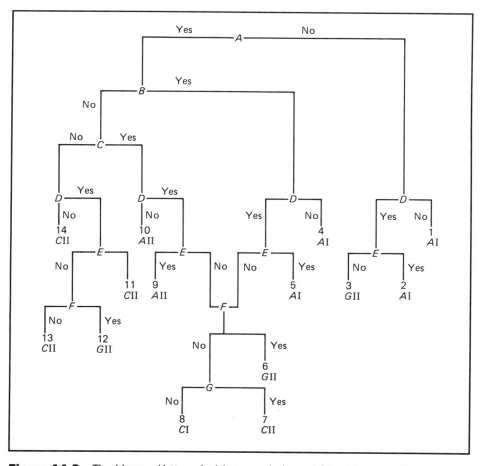

Figure 14.2 *The Vroom–Yetton decision tree (adapted from Vroom, 1973)*

Within the Vroom and Yetton model, questions *A*, *B* and *C* relate to the quality and rationality of the decision required, questions *D* and *E* refer to the acceptance of the decision by subordinates, and questions *F* and *G* refer to the subordinates' commitment to the problem situation and the preferred solution. The decision tree is designed to facilitate a decision about which decision style to use as follows.

Autocratic

AI Solving the problem by making the decision by yourself by what information you have available.

AII Obtaining the necessary information from subordinates and deciding on the solution yourself.

Consultative

CI Sharing the problem with relevant subordinates individually in order to get their ideas, and then making the decision whether or not it reflects the views of your subordinates.

CII Sharing the problem with subordinates as a group, and in so doing getting ideas which you may or may not use in making the decision.

Group or participative

GI Sharing the problem with one of your subordinates and arriving at a joint decision.

GII Sharing the problem with the group and together arriving at a decision.

These preferred decision styles are indicated after each problem type (1–14) in Figure 14.2.

Mini Case 14.1 Understanding Vroom and Yetton's decision tree

You are a junior manager in the international operations department of a company in the head office in London. You have been given the task of looking at a persistent problem of inaccurate and inconsistent data being transmitted to the central computer in London, from the European offices in six different countries. There are differences in error rates between the different offices, and each location has its own methods of collecting data, and collating it. You have little information on these different practices in the six countries, but you do have information on the error rates themselves.

The quality control supervisors are responsible for collection of data in each location, and it is these supervisors (a very dedicated collection of individuals) who are your main contacts in the locations.

> While it is in everybody's interest (not just the headquarters) to ensure that these data are accurate because many important decisions are made as a result of their analyses, the supervisors tend to resent outside interference. Any solution which does not involve the supervisors' active support is likely to fail.
>
> Let us now apply the decision tree to the solution of this problem.
>
> *A* Yes – a quality decision is required as you are relying on the production of accurate data.
>
> *B* No – it seems that the variation in error is dependent on local practices about which you know very little.
>
> *C* No – you do not know what is causing the errors and you have no established procedures to refer to in order to correct the errors.
>
> *D* Yes – you need the acceptance and involvement of the supervisors.
>
> *E* No – the supervisors are very sensitive to outside interference.
>
> *F* Yes – the supervisors are very dedicated to their work and the company.
>
> The preferred decision style in this case is *GII*, a shared group decision.
>
> (This example is adapted from Kolb *et al.*, 1991)

The implication of this type of model of organizational decision making is that the preferred style is a participative one, although for certain decisions this may not be appropriate. There is therefore a time/quality ratio inherent within this type of model, where the consensus model is preferred where a quality decision is appropriate, as you are more likely to get a good decision to which everybody involved will be committed, if all relevant people are involved in the decision-making process. However, because this type of decision making takes time, it is only when the quality of the decision is justified by the time taken, that a participative style of decision making should be used. Where the decision is simply a small one, with no major implications, it is pointless spending a morning, involving a team of ten, on this type of problem.

Other authors, often American, point to the desirability of a prevailing participative style in management decision making. Likert (1967), for example (see Chapter 6 of the current text), with his four management 'systems' of 'exploitative–authoritarian', 'benevolent–authoritarian, 'consultative', and 'participative–group', clearly favours a participative approach to decision making, and produces evidence to suggest that this style is more effective and produces a more effective organization.

Johnson and Johnson (1975) describe seven possible ways decisions can be made in organizations, as follows.

1 By consensus, where, although not necessarily meaning that the decision should be unanimous, all must support it. All participants in this process should be given time to voice their opinion, and a decision is made on the basis that an idea is accepted by the whole group. Each should be able to support it publicly.

2 By majority vote, where, after a full discussion, a vote should be taken on the alternative proposals until one is accepted by a majority. This then becomes the decision of the group.

3 By averaging the opinions of individuals. Normally in a group session, each member should be asked their opinion, but with little or no discussion. The chairperson or manager then makes the decision on the basis of the most popular proposal.

4 By expert member where the decision is delegated to the person with the most appropriate expertise to solve the problem.

5 By authority after discussion. Following a group meeting on the issue where information and opinions are collected, the manager then makes the decision.

6 By minority. This can take a number of forms and would normally comprise some type of executive committee. It can be an elected or appointed subcommittee, or committee, which may represent a wider body of employees (for example in a joint consultation committee comprising management and employee representatives). Such a body might have complete authority to make decisions, such as a management group of a company, or may have to refer decisions back to the body of people they represent (share holders or employees, for example).

7 By authority with no discussion or consultation. The manager may simply make a decision with no reference to anyone else.

These styles or methods of decision making may depend on the circumstance, the organizational culture, and the national culture.

Mini Case 14.2 Consensus decision making in Java and Japan

A Javanese manager's decision-making style in an Indonesian subsidiary of an international company was seen by his superiors as very authoritarian. Decisions which were issued could not be questioned by anyone. When a European took over the position, he instigated a democratic style of decision making. Decisions were discussed in meetings, and often the decision was made by majority vote. This was seen by his subordinates as authoritarian and coercive, with the objection that not all matter could be discussed in the meetings, that often there was a coercion of a minority by the majority, and that the minority that would vote against the decision were also held responsible for the decision (Martyn-Johns, 1977). The decision-making process in Java is that of *musjawarah* or extensive deliberation until everyone agrees on a best decision. This is reached by consensus, taking into account the views of all who wish to express their opinion. Following the achievement of consensus, everyone is bound by the decision. After this stage it is not questioned by anyone because it has been agreed.

The *ringi* system of decision making in Japan involves the initiative of a draft proposal, which may come from a senior level but quite often from the lower levels of the organizations. Plans are drafted at the lower levels of the organization, and are circulated to the various departments. Employees are encouraged to develop their own ideas on this, and propose changes. Through a process of repeated changes at each level as the draft plan is circulated up the organization it finally achieves approval at the appropriate level of seniority. Hence this leads to more involvement of employees giving a sense of commitment to the decision. It also provides access to information at various levels of the organization, thus improving the quality of the decision.

(*Source*: Adapted from Berry *et al.*, 1992)

We now turn more specifically to the cultural differences inherent within decision-making styles and methods.

Cultural differences in organizational decision making

Berry *et al.* (1992) indicate the lack of positive conclusions which can be drawn from the cross-cultural research findings on decision making. This seems to indicate that there are probably few differences in decision-making styles and methods between different countries. Negandhi (1987) concludes that:

> The convergence in organizational practices in general, and decision making in particular, is taking place rapidly. This can be seen from the results of our recent study of United States, German, British, Japanese, and Swedish multinational companies. The results showed that United States management practices concerning decision making are the norms being followed by other nations. Other countries' practices correlated strongly with those of United States practices (Negandhi, 1987, p. 194).

However, Adler (1991) indicates areas where there are cultural differences, by describing five basic steps in decision making, and their cultural variations. These are:

- *problem recognition*: do managers from different cultures see problems in the same way?
- *information search*: do they gather similar types of information in order to investigate the problem?
- *construction of alternatives*: do they construct the same types of solutions?
- *choice*: do they employ the same types of choosing strategies in order to select a solution from different alternatives?
- *implementation*: do they implement decisions in the same ways?

Problem recognition

Adler (1991) tells us that some cultures emphasize solving problems whilst others are more oriented to accepting the situation as it is. So, in the United States managers see situations more as problems to be solved, whereas Thai, Indonesian or Malaysian managers are more likely to attempt to accept the situation for what it is. She refers to an example of a supplier who cannot make a delivery on time. The American manager may look for another supplier who could make the delivery. The Malaysian manager, for example, might accept that there will be a delay in the delivery, and therefore the project will be set back a day or two. Situation-accepting managers would not see a problem in this situation, they would accept that they cannot change every situation which confronts them. This may also be combined with a belief that fate or God will intervene, and these managers are more likely to attribute cause and effect to external circumstances rather than internal attributes which are within their control (see also attribution theory in Chapter 4).

Information search

For the next stage in the decision process Adler (1991) refers to Jung's two modes of information gathering (see Chapter 3 of the current text): sensing and intuition. The former mode is concerned with the collection of facts relevant to the decision and relies more on induction. The latter mode relies more on holistic images and ideas, and on deductive ways of thinking. While she does not present any evidence to suggest that this may involve a cultural distinction, she does cite the example of the different type of decision making during the Israeli–Arab war in 1973. The Americans based their assessment of the outcome on the overwhelming number of troops and arms which the Arab forces had, the Israelis based their predictions on strong beliefs and images of the future.

Constructing alternatives

This stage in the decision-making process is concerned with either looking at an issue historically in order to solve problems or to looking for new ideas for the future. Adler (1991) uses the example of the differing attitudes towards selection and training, in order to adapt an organization for new developments like information technology. A (organizational) culture which stresses the changeability and development of individuals may look towards training in order to develop the work-force for the future. A culture which stresses the permanence of human nature may place an emphasis on initial selection: that it is more important to ensure that you select the right people for the job at the beginning, rather than trying to change them afterwards.

This attitude may also be reflected in other areas of decision-making alternatives, particularly in the type of solution offered in order to solve problems: they may be looking to the known and established or looking to alternatives which break new ground and are innovative. The belief in some African societies that education is tantamount to rejecting the ways of ancestors is indicative of a past orientation.

Choice

This stage involves a number of factors which reflect cultural preferences.

- Are decisions made by individuals or collectively (individualism/collectivism)? Individualist societies such as the United States may see the individual with the primary responsibility to make the final decision. In a collectivist society such as Japan, it is the group or team which makes the decision after much consultation.

- At what level of the organization are decisions made (power distance)? In a high power distance society decisions tend to be made at the top of a specific hierarchy, whereas in a lower power distance society such as Sweden, it is more likely that worker autonomy schemes such as that initiated in the Volvo Kalmar plant will be prevalent, where decisions are taken at a lower level.

- Are decisions made quickly or slowly (time orientation)? Some societies are more time conscious than others. Hence North American and Western European business people may often be frustrated by the time taken to make a decision in other cultures. We have seen (in Chapter 13) that this factor may often be used against negotiators from time conscious societies, by negotiators from Asian, African and South American cultures.

- How much risk is considered too much (uncertainty avoidance)? In high uncertainty avoidance cultures, managers may be unwilling to deviate too much from accepted and proven patterns and alternatives in order to contain the amount of risk involved. This also applies to different industries within the same national cultures. For example, high street banking in the UK is far less risk taking than, for example, stock exchange securities dealers (in the same industry) or than high tech companies launching a new product on to the market.

- Are alternatives considered holistically or sequentially? We have already seen (Chapter 13) that in negotiations, managers from some cultures such as China, are more likely to address and solve problems in a more holistic way, rather than in a sequential way, addressing each issue or sub-issue as it arises and trying to solve it before proceeding to the next.

Implementation

The cultural differences in the implementation stage are largely those already discussed such as whether the speed of implementation is fast or slow, whether responsibility is delegated downwards or managed from the top of the hierarchy, or whether it is a collective or individual responsibility.

Decision making in international organizations

We have so far discussed decision making in organizations, and have looked at some distinctions in the way decisions are made between different types of cultures. We are now going to look briefly at the way cultural differences may influence decision making in companies that operate in more than one country. Hodgetts and Luthans (1991) provide the following examples.

- *British* organizations tend to be decentralized in order that upper level management, often without specific technical knowledge, can delegate decisions with a high specialist content to middle level managers.

- *French* companies tend to have an opposite approach to this where decisions are taken at the top of the organization by managers who are mostly *grande école* graduates who often lack confidence in their lower managers. Decisions therefore tend to be centralized.

- *German* managers tend to focus more on productivity and quality rather than managing subordinates. Management education has a high technical focus, and the legal requirement of codetermination requires managers to consult workers on major decisions. This tends to lead (Hodgetts and Luthans (1991), assert) to centralized, autocratic and hierarchical international German organizations.

- *Swedish* companies are also governed by codetermination laws, but have more of an emphasis on quality of work life and the importance of individuals. Swedish companies are more likely to be decentralized and participative in their decision making.

- *Japanese* companies use decision making by consensus (*ringi*: see above). While this may be time consuming it enables a high degree of commitment to decisions made in this way. This combines a centralized with a decentralized system of decision making, whereby top management exercise a high degree of authority over what decisions are examined at the lower levels.

- *United States* multinationals tend to be highly centralized in their decision making, in order to exercise the necessary control to affect a world-wide strategy: ensuring all units are operating to the overall strategic plan.

Hodgetts and Luthans (1991) further add that there seems to be a tendency of international operations to be more centralized in decision making and to follow the American model.

Values and ethical decision making across cultures

We have seen from the discussion of cross-cultural differences above that cultural 'values' are important to decision making, and particularly so when we consider decisions which are made which cut across national cultures. For example, a Western European business person may do business in a West African country where corporate bribery may be the norm. This involves an interface between two sets of cultural values. The question of what is ethical in this situation (and also, what is good business) is raised.

From a cross-cultural perspective, it may be that the value content of the decision is fundamental to an understanding of decision making. To what extent do individual managers consider (consciously) their value system when making decisions? To what degree is their value system an unconscious influence on decision making? What principles (either consciously or not consciously) are applied when decisions are made? What principle should we follow when the other culture's principles or values are different to our own?

Brady (1990) distinguishes two basic ethical principles upon which decision making may be based: rules and results. This is based on two main schools of thought in ethics: the 'formalism' of Kant (a German) and the 'utilitarianism' of Bentham (an Englishman).

Activity 14.1 Ethical decision making: rules or results

Before we go further in the text, you may like to complete the following questionnaire adapted from Brady's (1990) 'Survey of ethical theoretical aptitudes'.

Complete the following statements by choosing either (a) or (b) and circling your choice.

1 A person's actions in business can be described as being
   a good or bad
   b right or wrong

2 When making ethical decisions you should pay attention to
   a your conscience
   b other people's needs, wants and desires

3 Solutions to ethical problems are usually
   a not easily definable
   b easily definable

4 It is preferable for a society to
   a follow traditions, maintaining its distinctive identity
   b be adaptable and responsive to new conditions

5 I prefer to think about ethical problems by
   a developing workable alternatives
   b making distinctions and clarifications

6 I would try to obtain agreement on ethical matters by
   a working out points of agreement
   b trying to get a workable compromise

7 Telling lies is wrong because
   a it can lead to further problems dependent on the results of the lie
   b it is not right for everyone to lie

8 It is more important to
   a apply the law fairly and impartially
   b seek an improved life for all through benevolent legislation

9 I would prefer to be known as a person who
   a has achieved a great deal
   b is principled and has integrity

10 Ideally the aim of science is to
   a discover truths
   b solve problems

11 Lying is a matter of
   a degree: everyone lies to a certain extent
   b type: that is, you are either a liar or you are not

12 A society should pay attention to its
   a roots and inheritance
   b potential and the future

13 It is more important for me to be
   a a happy person
   b a person of some worth

14 We can describe unethical behaviour as
   a violating a principle of law
   b causing a degree of harm

15 The purpose of government, ideally, is to
   a enable its citizens to have a good and happy life
   b enable its citizens to be fairly and justly treated.

Scoring

Sum the odd (a)s and the even (b)s and subtract 8.

Interpretation

Score = +7 to +5 = strong utilitarian
        +4 to +2 = moderate utilitarian
        +1 to −1 = no preference
        −2 to −4 = moderate formalist
        −5 to −8 = strong formalist

Utilitarianism

The utilitarian approach is predominantly a North American one, and this is reflected in much of the management literature on ethical decision making (for example, Blanchard and Peale, 1988). Here we find the premiss that ethical decision making has a pay-off. If only companies are ethical then they will be prosperous. Ethics is good for business. This stems from the principles of utilitarianism which is based on the premiss of results or outcomes of a decision. We judge a decision to be ethical on the basis of its perceived outcomes. Utilitarianism in its original form was based on the precept of the greatest good for the greatest number of people. Hence, governments could make policy on the basis that its outcome would benefit the greatest number of people (even at the expense of the minority). A business example could be a decision to make a minority of people redundant from a factory, in order for the factory to be run more cost-effectively and therefore benefit the majority who would remain in employment.

A modern day derivative of this theory is cost-benefit analysis which looks at decisions from the point of view of their total costs, both financial and social, and total benefits. Environmental decisions involving such issues as pollution may be decided on this basis, where the costs of pollution control may be weighed up against the potential benefits to the community.

Utilitarianism tends to be a forward looking philosophy. Decisions are made on the basis of looking into the future, to look at future gains and future costs. However, there are problems in this school of thought. The first is the question of justice. It is perfectly justifiable, using these principles, to persecute a minority in the interests of the majority. Democratic systems are often based on this principle in both the national arena and the organizational arena.

The example of Javanese management practices above (Mini case 14.1) illustrates the problem with industrial democracy. The example of the minority being made redundant in favour of the majority, above, illustrates the problem of 'persecution' of minorities.

There is also the question of subjective benefits, or the way people see the benefits which will accrue to them, and the possibility of 'preference manipulation': persuading people that they will enjoy more benefits from a decision than is possibly the case. So, in negotiations, a manager may 'sell' a decision to his or her opposite number by using manipulative persuasion techniques to convince the other negotiating team of the benefits available to them.

Formalism

Formalism is independent of wants and needs, and is based on universal moral principles. Instead of anticipating the results of the decision, you ask the question, Is it right? based on certain established principles. Kant's principle is that of the 'categorical imperative' whereby everyone should act to ensure that similar decisions would be reached by others in similar circumstances. As such, formalism is established

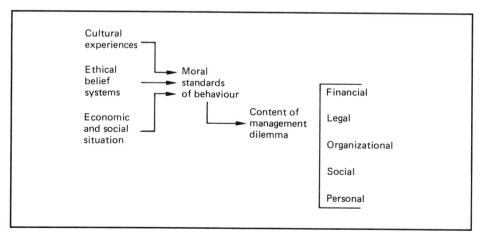

Figure 14.3 *Model of ethical analysis in management decisions (adapted from Hosmer, 1987)*

on the basis of a shared understanding. Everybody (at least within your organization, or within your country) understands the principles of right and wrong which you are applying. This type of decision making principle is backward-looking in perspective as it is based on historically formulated principles. As such it can lead to bureaucratic practice in the following of rules which govern decisions and actions, and can lead to dogmatism. It also tends to ignore individualism.

In discussing international negotiation (Chapter 13) we noted that Russian negotiators were more likely to appeal to overriding normative principles in negotiation, than were their negotiating partners from Western Europe or the United States. It may be that individuals from different cultures have different preferences for one or the other decision principles.

Hosmer (1987), discussing ethics in making decisions about human resources, develops a useful model of 'ethical analysis' of management decisions (Figure 14.3). In order to illustrate this model, let us first consider a particular case.

Mini Case 14.3 Employee drug testing

Our production, both in productivity and quality at some of our factories is low, we suspect because of drug and alcohol abuse.

We know that testing for chemical dependency is an invasion of personal privacy, and that the test can be inaccurate.

We think that less than 20 per cent of the work-force is involved, but that the other 80 per cent will have to go through the indignity of the tests.

Discussion: What is the 'right' thing to do?

Let us now consider this (fundamentally local, rather than international) problem using Hosmer's (1987) model. We must first look at the content of the managerial dilemma: financial, legal, organizational, social and personal content.

The financial content involves the benefits that might accrue from solving the drug problem, against the costs of testing. This may, in fact, dominate the decision.

The legal content involves any legislation which permits or prevents this type of testing. There may also be civil legal action which can be taken arising in compensation claims. This may have financial implications, of course.

The organizational consequences of the proposed action must also be considered. This may involve the positive aspects of a better working environment once the problem is solved, and more job security as a result of more efficient production. It may also have negative implications of low morale as a result of the action.

The social content would involve the implication for this action on the wider society. Perhaps this may result in a better competitive position for the company. It may enhance the reputation of the company in the locality, or it may have implications in the community as a result of charges of invasion of privacy.

The personal content is the impact it will have on the manager or persons making the decision. Will it affect their careers? Will they lose their jobs if this goes wrong?

It is clear that this approach is a utilitarian one, where a calculation of the results of the action is made. Within Hosmer's (1987) model there is a consideration of moral standards of behaviour, prior to the consideration of the dilemmas facing the decision maker. He describes these as the criteria we use to judge our behaviour and that of others. He warns that they tend to be subjective, imprecise and variable between individuals, they also may vary from one situation to another (for example, our attitude towards lying). We can, and should, trace these moral standards back to our ethical systems of belief, which we can clarify as providing guiding principles for our decision making. He identifies five such systems of belief which we summarize in Table 14.1.

These ethical belief systems contribute, with cultural experiences and with prevailing economic and social conditions, to moral standards of behaviour within Hosmer's (1987) model. It may be that different national cultures tend to have a preference for one of these belief systems in decision making. If systems of belief are different between different cultures (that is, incompatible) then a utilitarian approach

Table 14.1 *Five belief systems in ethical decision making*

	Nature of this belief system	*Problems in this belief system*
Eternal law	Moral standards are revealed in religious teachings and represent an eternal law to which we should adhere	The problem of multiple interpretation of this law
Utilitarian theory	Standards are derived from the perceived outcomes of the action	It is easy to justify immoral acts by reference to benefits to majorities at the expense of a minority
Universal theory (formalism)	Standards are derived from the intent of the decision according to universal principles	There are problems in the concept of universality and who judges the morality of principle
Distributive justice	Moral standards are based on the primary of single value of justice. Everyone should act towards the more equitable distribution of benefits as an essential factor in social co-operation	This is dependent on accepting that a more equitable distribution of benefits ensures social co-operation
Personal liberty	Moral standards are based on the primacy of the single principle of liberty. Everyone should act to secure greater freedom of choice, promoting market exchange and social productivity	This is dependent on accepting that a market system promotes social productivity.

Source: Hosmer, 1987.

(that is a more pragmatic approach) may need to be used when considering ethics issues in international decision making. We will consider the problems to which we have alluded on a number of occasions in the last two chapters: corporate bribery.

Activity 14.2 Cultural relativism in ethical decision making

When we do business across cultures should we adhere to our own (national) ethical standards or conform to the standards of our 'hosts'?

Discussion: Is corporate bribery justifiable in cultures where this is normal practice – that is, you do not get the business if you do not do it – and should we follow this practice?

The idea of cultural relativism in ethical decision making is common. The idea goes something like this. All cultures are different and no culture is any better or worse than any other, they are simply different. It is therefore correct to accept a culture, and its values, for what they are, and not to be judgemental. Therefore, if the value system within one culture allows for corporate bribery, then this should be acceptable.

Donaldson (1989) believes this position to be untenable, suggesting that people mistakenly endorse cultural relativism, confusing it with cultural tolerance. He argues:

> If a culture disagrees with the Shiite Moslem practice of having women wear veils, yet owing to its tolerance believes nonetheless that it should refrain from forcing its views on Shiite Moslems, then tolerance counts as a moral, not relativist, value ... were a cultural relativist asked whether culture A's belief in tolerance is any better than B's belief that values should be forced down people's throats, the relativist would be forced to deny it. The relativist would not endorse tolerance over intolerance (Donaldson, 1989, p. 16).

He also claims that cultural relativism requires an absence of any objective grounds for morality, such as a concept of evil and good, for example:

> consider the practice of Japanese Samurai warriors in earlier centuries. A new sword would be tested by murdering a complete stranger. When the sword had been forged, the Samurai would find a stranger in the road, confront him face to face, and without warning swing the sword down in a diagonal arc. If the sword cut neatly from the side of the neck to the waist on the opposite side, it was of adequate quality. If not, it was unfit for a warrior (Donaldson, 1989, p. 17).

While rejecting a moral free-for-all, and the international arena as a moral 'free zone', Donaldson (1989) also does not accept the ethnocentric view of applying the moral values of one country (perhaps the United States) on another. It may therefore be difficult to establish a moral objectivity which can be applied in all countries of the world. Instead, he suggests an 'ethical algorithm' which provides a guide-line for those attempting to answer the question 'Is the practice permissible for the multinational company when it is morally and/or legally permitted in the host country, but not in the

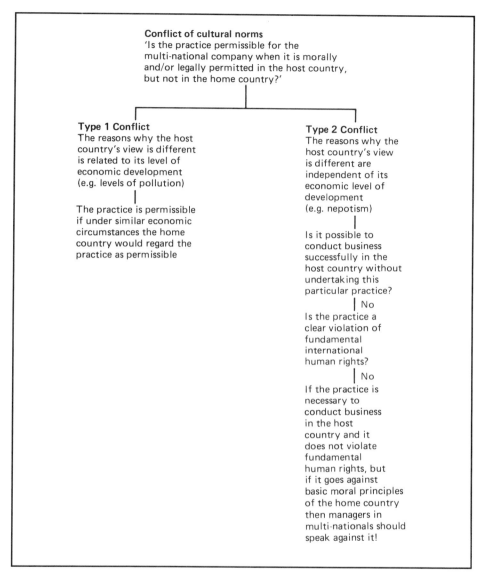

Figure 14.4 *An algorithm for international ethical decision making (adapted from Donaldson, 1989)*

home country?' We will summarize this algorithm in diagrammatic form (see Figure 14.4).

Donaldson (1989) separates these two types of dilemma because practices which purely reflect the level of economic development are easier to empathize with, provided that the home country would do the same thing in similar circumstances (a current debate about the world's rainforests may fit into this type of category, where the local economy is dependent on tree felling and reflects a level of economic development, but still the developed world is telling these countries to halt the level of tree felling).

An issue such as corporate bribery may not be dependent on the level of economic development of a country, although it may be a reflection of low salaries. This is particularly the case where bribery concerns petty officials in some developing countries. It is often the case that business cannot be done without bribery, and it does not seem to contradict any fundamental international human rights. However, managers from multinational companies doing business in such a country may feel that they have to speak out against such practices. From a purely pragmatic point of view, however, this may cause embarrassment to both the company and to the host country's government.

Another view, that of Condon (1981), is that:

- values reflect the culture;
- ethics transcends the culture.

Thus we have an idea that ethical decision making is not culturally relative. That is, we do not have to accept values of the host country which we do not feel are right (as are the implications of Donaldson's theory). However, this is a complex issue. The variables involved seem to be:

Sources of values

Personal values which individuals hold which may result from:

- group values which are held in common by, for example, a peer group;
- religious values which have different relative influences in different societies and for different group and individuals;
- cultural values which are particular to a particular community or nation;
- fundamental human values which may be held in common by all or most countries (for example, not allowing murder)

Types of international values

- ethnocentric: our values are best
- realistic cultural relativism: allowing for differences in values between one society and another (within reason).

Universal ethical values

- declarations of fundamental human rights by such international bodies as the United Nations;
- acceptance of universal values by power and dominance of one or many countries over others, through economic or political power in world affairs.

We could probably think of other aspects of international ethical decision making, but we have tried to cover here most of the relevant factors involved in decision making where the final arbiter may be an individual manager, the executive of a multinational company or a national government. This area is a difficult one to work in, and we have tried here to draw attention to the main points and problems involved.

Management decision-making techniques: cultural implications

The use of specific decision making techniques recommended in the largely Anglo-American literature may not be appropriate in all cultural situations, as Jaeger (1990) points out in connection with 'brainstorming'. This is advocated where there is a need for creativity in solving difficult problems or in making complex decisions. This is carried out in a group where the members share ideas without their being judged or criticized so that divergent and creative ideas are not suppressed. It stresses the importance of intuition in generating non-obvious solutions.

Jaeger (1990) notes the values with which this technique may come into conflict in developing country cultures, as in Table 14.2.

Table 14.2 *Cultural differences between developed and developing countries which may influence success or failure of decision-making techniques.*

Dimension	Developed country	Developing country
Control of outcomes	internal	external
Creative potential	unlimited	limited
Potential to change and develop	unlimited	limited
Time focus	future	past and present
Task orientation	proactive	passive/reactive
People orientation	participative delegative	authoritarian paternalistic
Environment orientation	context independent	context dependent

Source: Jaeger and Kanungo, 1990.

Thus, with a predominantly external locus of control (attributing events to external causes of which you have little or no control) may go against this type of decision making where you are trying to gain control of events. With a belief in a low creative potential of individuals and where individuals have a limited capacity for development, this may not seem a suitable technique for managers to cultivate in developing countries. Similarly with a perspective fixed on the past and the here and now, creative and new ideas may not be easy to develop and accept.

Task orientation is towards the reactive and passive end of the continuum, which again mitigates against taking a proactive approach to solving ideas and generating new ideas, as does a context dependent orientation. The latter is concerned with the degree of abstractness of thought where, in developed countries there is an emphasis on the value of abstract thinking, transcending contextual forces. In developing countries there is more of an emphasis on thinking being relative to environmental forces. Brainstorming, as an abstract form of decision making may well be at odds with this mode of thinking. The process itself of brainstorming may go against the predominantly authoritarian and paternalistic management approach.

Jaeger (1990) also addresses the problem of adopting the Vroom–Yetton model of decision making in developing countries' management practices. Here the alternatives between authoritarian, consultative and participative decision methods may not be alternatives to consider. While the participative method is recommended by Vroom and Yetton to increase the amount of information going into the decision and the amount of commitment which comes out of the decision, this may be inappropriate for a manager in a developing country context who would expect, and be expected to, use a more authoritarian mode of decision making.

Conclusions

We have therefore looked at decision making techniques which have been developed mainly in American- and Anglo-cultures to cater for the needs of a more individualistic, and democratic management style. In this light we looked at the Vroom–Yetton decision tree and its uses. We then pointed to cultural differences which may exist in decision making processes, stating that these may occur in the various decision phases of problem recognition, information search, construction of alternatives, making choices and implementation of the decision. We also focused on differences in organizational decision making in companies in different countries.

Of particular importance for managers operating internationally are the decisions which have to be made based on sometimes conflicting ethical standpoints. How these decisions should be viewed was discussed on the basis of two major different views of ethical decision making: utilitarianism and formalism, and the use of an 'ethical algorithm' for determining how best to address cross-cultural issues of ethical decision making.

Finally, management decision-making techniques were looked at in connection with differences between developed and developing countries, where the wholesale use of western techniques may not be appropriate.

It is likely that as business becomes more and more international, the issues of decision making involving ethical and morale concepts will become even more prominent. It is therefore important that more consideration should be given to this aspect by international managers, and that more research is conducted in this area.

References

Adler, N. J. (1991) *International Dimensions of Organizational Behaviour*, (2nd edn.) Boston: PWS-Kent.

Berry J. W., Poortinga, Y. H., Segall, M. H. and Dasen, P. R. (1992) *Cross-cultural Psychology: Research and Applications*, Cambridge: Cambridge University Press.

Blanchard K. and Peale, N. V. (1988) *The Power of Ethical Management*, Cedar/Heinemann.

Brady, F. N. (1990) *Ethical Management: Rules and Results*, Macmillan.

Condon, J. (1981) 'Values and ethics in communication across cultures: some notes on the North American case', *Communication*, 6, 2, pp. 255–65.

Donaldson, T. (1989) *The Ethics of International Business*, New York: Oxford University Press.

Eiser, J. R. (1986) *Social Psychology: Attitudes, Cognition and Social Behaviour*, Cambridge: Cambridge University Press.

Hodgetts, R. M. and Luthans, F. (1991) *International Management*, New York: McGraw-Hill.

Hofstede, G. (1991), *Culture and Organizations: Software of the Mind*, London: McGraw-Hill.

Hosmer, L. T. (1987) 'Ethical Analysis and Human Resource Management', *Human Resource Management*, Fall, 26, 3, pp. 313–30.

Jaeger, A. M. (1990) 'The applicability of Western management techniques in developing countries: a cultural perspective', in Jaeger and Kanungo (1990).

Jaeger, A. M. and Kanungo, R. N. (eds.) (1990) *Management in Developing Countries*, London: Routledge.

Johnson, D. W. and Johnson, F. P. (1975) *Joining Together: Group Theory and Group Skills*, Englewood Cliffs, New Jersey: Prentice-Hall.

Kolb, D. A., Rubin, I. M. and Osland, J. (1991) *Organizational Behaviour: An Experiential Approach*, Englewood Cliffs, New Jersey: Prentice-Hall.

Likert, R. (1967) *The Human Organization*, Tokyo: McGraw-Hill Kogakusha.

Martyn-Johns, T. A. (1977) 'Cultural conditioning of views of authority and its effects on the business decision-making process with special reference to Java', in Poortinga, Y. H. (ed.), *Basic Problems in Cross-cultural Psychology*, Lisse: Swets and Zeitbirger, pp. 344–352.

Negandhi, A. R. (1987) *International Management*, Boston: Allyn and Bacon.

Vroom, V. (1973) 'A new look at managerial decision making', *Organizational Dynamics*, Spring.

Section 6
Managing in a Changing Environment

We now focus specifically on the management of change in a changing and ambiguous environment.

We first look at the management of change in organizations, its implications, problems, and how these might be overcome. Here we focus on both structural change and cultural change.

The chapter on project management is intended as an example of an international management process which focuses on change across cultures and which is becoming more and more important as organizational structures have to adapt to the international marketplace. It is also intended as a means by which the reader may draw on much of the work in this text, in order to explore the many issues and problems of using a management method on an international basis.

15

Managing change

Objectives

Following this chapter you should be able to:

1 Explain the significance of change to international managers, and the importance of successfully managing change, and the implications for the organization and the individual.
2 Demonstrate an understanding of the problems of change in organizations, and how these problems may be overcome.
3 Use specific techniques to manage change in organizations.

Key concepts

- Force Field Analysis
- Organizational design: differentiation, integration.
- Cultural change

Introduction

In this chapter we look both at change generally within organizations, and the implications for the individuals working within such change environments, and organizational structural change, based on organizational theory. Previously, we have dealt with the question of individual or personal change through a consideration of learning (Chapter 10), and career development (Chapter 11). Here we concentrate more on the implications of working in a fast moving, international environment, where change may be both temporal (across time) and lateral (across space: particularly across cultures, both organizational and national).

We look specifically at force field analysis which focuses on the constraining forces and the compelling forces of organizational change, particularly in the attitudes and behaviour of individuals. The management of change is considered here to involve the identification of such factors, and the weakening of dragging forces and the strengthening of pushing forces within the organization.

We then focus on organizational design which aims to manage the balance between differentiation of task functions and the integration of diversity in order to affect change.

Finally we discuss cultural change and outline a number of techniques for affecting change in this area, and then look at some of the national cultural implications for change management by reference to the different attitudes towards management and organizations in different countries. These attitudes and subsequent behaviours comprise much of the subject matter in the current text.

There is no doubt that the manager working at an international level has to cope with a changing environment, and it is perhaps one of the major attributes required of the 'global manager'. Not only do they have change thrust upon them (with which they then must cope or manage), but also they must be innovators or change agents. They must lead from the front, rather than being involved in 'damage limitation' at the rear end of change!

The subject of change management is broad ranging encompassing many of the subjects mentioned above and covering most of the dimensions contained in the other chapters of this text. By necessity we must here restrict our coverage of this important issue. We look at some 'classical' approaches to managing change, principally through 'force field analysis' and then through structural analysis. We then look at organizational cultural change, and the implications of national culture for change strategies.

In order to outline the coverage of this subject area, we can briefly describe the focus of organizational change by references to the descriptive framework of context–content–conduct. In the model shown in Figure 15.1, the direction of change is towards the motivations and attitudes of individuals who are required to live with and manage the change process.

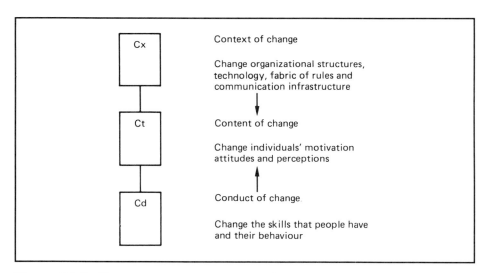

Figure 15.1 *The context–content–conduct of change*

We can best illustrate this by using the example of three separate consultants going into an organization to investigate a performance problem in order to change the relevant factors involved. We do this by also referring to the three schools of thought previously outlined in Chapter 9. The responses of the three consultants may be as follows.

Consultant 1: 'We need to look at the structure of the organization. The hierarchical structure hampers communication and prevents people showing initiative and performing' (a structuralist approach).

Consultant 2: 'We need to carry out an attitude survey, ask people what motivates them, what their objectives are, how these can be matched with company objectives. If we can motivate them, they will perform' (a phenomenological approach).

Consultant 3: 'We need to train people in basic skills. We can do a training needs analysis which will show us the skills gap between what they currently have and what they need. If they are competent they will perform' (a behaviourist approach).

We perhaps need to combine these approaches if we are to change the way people work in organizations, by:

- enabling attitudes towards change to 'unfreeze' (content);
- providing the organizational support and structure for change (context);
- developing appropriate skills and knowledge and styles of working of the individuals concerned (conduct).

We are first going to look at the 'unfreezing' of change by a consideration of a well known management technique: force field analysis (Lewin, 1951).

Force field analysis

One of the most important factors in a change situation is that of the attitudes of the individuals involved in it. People tend to resist change because of:

- loss of security or status, for example as a result of redundant skills which are no longer applicable to new techniques or tasks or new technology;
- inconvenience, as a result of disruption to comfortable and familiar patterns of acting;
- distrust or uncertainty, suspecting the real reasons for change;
- disparaging of old ways of working, or rubbishing the techniques and skills which were previously highly valued, and perhaps which were acquired over a lengthy apprenticeship, but have now become redundant or lowly valued.

From a survey of top level executives in companies world-wide, Vandermerwe and Vandermerwe (1991) report the percentage respondents mentioning the following obstacles to implementing strategic change:

92 per cent   The fear factor and human resistance
82 per cent   Complacency and a low sense of urgency
75 per cent   Insufficient time set aside
73 per cent   Poor communication
62 per cent   Leaving systems and technology too late.

Lewin (1951) suggests that change may be facilitated by a process of: 'unfreezing', introducing the change, and 'refreezing' as follows.

Unfreezing: A sense of dissatisfaction should be created with the *status quo*. People should be shown that there is a need for change. If you can show, for example, that an old production method is preventing people obtaining job satisfaction as it may be boring, and that a new system would improve both their production, their job satisfaction, and be a cleaner and less physically demanding job, then people may begin to feel uneasy with the old system and yearn for the new.

Changing: The people involved in the change should have an opportunity for direct discussion with the change makers to sort out any problems. Training, advice, the appropriate equipment, and assistance as necessary should all be provided.

Mini Case 15.1 Implementing change in a securities handling department

During the latter half of the 1980s the UK Stock Exchange and the banking and finance industry in the City of London introduced a number of technology changes aimed at reducing the paper work involved in transactions in company shares (securities) handling. One such securities handling department of a major bank was in the forefront of these changes, introducing computer handling of many of the transactions involved and linking directly to the Stock Exchange. The new computer system was introduced at the beginning of one year, and over a period of twelve months was tested and the system refined and developed.

The Chief Manager of the department was very pleased with the work of his staff when the current author spoke to him. They had worked very hard to get the system running properly. However, when I consulted the staff themselves, it was a different story! They were very unhappy about the situation. They felt that production had gone down. There were many 'bugs' in the system which created a lot of frustration.

When I spoke to the Chief Manager again, I conveyed these feelings that the staff felt they were not doing very well, and that morale was quite low. He said, again, that he was very pleased with their performance.

It gradually emerged during the course of these discussions that the department, over the last twelve months had been treated as a 'test-bed' for the new computer system, whereas the staff assumed that the system had been introduced fully developed, and that it was their fault that the system was not running. After suggesting to the Chief Manager that he should convey the information he had given to me to his staff, a number of regular communication meetings were set up, in order to keep staff fully informed about the changes and so that they could discuss any problems.

This was a case where those involved in the change had not had direct discussions with the change makers, and had not, therefore, fully appreciated their role in the change process.

Refreezing: The new behaviour required as a result of the change should become part of the regular behaviour of the individuals concerned. An environment should be created which reinforces the desired change. The gains made by training, for example, may be short-lived if not reinforced by management in the office giving positive feedback when the appropriate behaviour is enacted successfully (see also, learning theory in Chapter 10).

A criticism of this conceptualization of the change process is that it is essentially linear with a start and finish point, whereas in practice change may be a continuous phenomenon in the modern technological world. Refreezing as a concept may be outmoded, unless we regard this as simply a reinforcement or support of the change process itself. Rather than reinforcing a particular set of behaviours in the work place, we are supporting an attitude to change and development. This is akin to the idea of learning to learn discussed in Chapter 4 of the current text (see also Argyris and Schon, 1978). Vandermerwe and Vandermerwe (1991) posit perhaps a modified version of Lewin's stage approach to change which reflects the need to regard change as continuous. These stages are: creating strategic discomfort; providing and managing focus; energizing and mobilizing people; and maintaining momentum.

Resistance to change may be regarded as an attempt to regain control over one's environment. Resistance may be reduced by:

• creating an awareness of the need for change;
• involving people in determining what the changes should be, although this is not always feasible when the change is imposed by a higher authority;
• communicating the changes, and the rationale behind them;
• dealing honestly with people's concerns, creating a forum for discussion and consultation;
• giving people a role in introducing the change – some form of group participation may be appropriate;
• reducing the level of uncertainty and ambiguity as much as possible by being consistent: if you say something is going to happen, make sure it does happen! (see also Kanter, 1991, for another view on building commitment to change).

Force field analysis (Lewin, 1951) looks at the counter-balances between forces which push for change, and forces which resist change in any situation, on the basis that for each action there is an equal and opposite counter-action. We can illustrate this by Figure 15.2.

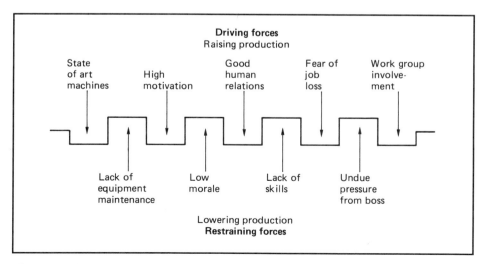

Figure 15.2 *Force field analysis*

The central line in Figure 15.2 represents a state of equilibrium, with the various pushing and pulling forces exerting pressure. If the change is forced, this equilibrium may shatter. Change can be affected by weakening the forces on the restraining side, and strengthening the forces on the driving force side. The following case study will help you to use this analysis in practice.

Case Study 15.1 The Urbanian subsidiary I

Introduction to the case

Urbania is a fictitious country. The fact that it does not exist holds one major advantage to the study of this case: you cannot hold any preconceived ideas of the culture of the country. You cannot make the assumption that you know how managers act within this particular culture. You have to come to this country's culture completely fresh, not knowing anything about it. The culture is simply as we later describe it within the context of the organization. While the country is fictitious, the events described in this case study are based on fact. This applies equally to the case study in the next chapter, which also involves the Urbanian subsidiary.

Background

A large UK bank operating on an international level has recently bought out the remaining shareholders of an Urbanian consumer credit company in which it has had a major shareholding for a number of years.

We list the major cultural and organizational variables under the three headings: Context, Content and Conduct.

Context

Social/cultural environment:
Urbania is a republic with a strong bureaucratic tradition, but values free trade and enterprise.

Organization:
UK Bank – 100,000 employees world-wide with 65,000 in UK domestic banking, 200 branches in the UK.
Subsidiary – 3,000 employees in Urbania only, in 20 branches. Head office is in the capital city.

Customer base and type of relationship with customers:
The subsidiary's business is transaction related rather than relationship related as in the UK bank. Representatives work hard to obtain customers who in turn obtain loans from the company offering the best deal. The UK bank relies on customer loyalty.

Management structure and systems:
The UK bank relies on traditional 'checks and balances' in its business, operating bureaucratic systems such as 'dual control'. It reacts slowly to change, but needs to respond to rapid changes in the finance industry. The subsidiary has to respond quickly, and is more 'competitive' in its approach. However, the administrative staff are often overwhelmed with bureaucratic paperwork as the legal system is complex.

Communication structures and media used:
The staff of the subsidiary work on a commission basis and are often out of the office. Keeping in touch with them is difficult, and is mainly a one-way process of sales reports sent into the office by representatives. However, each branch manager must hold a monthly meeting with all staff to give feedback and keep them up to date with company matters. The parent bank relies on a mass of memoranda and newsletters of all kinds, directed at the largely office-based staff. Recently office 'quality circles' have been established to get ideas from staff on how to improve the quality of customer service.

Explicit and implicit 'rules' within the company:
The parent bank is overtly hierarchical with privilege given to each grade of management. Dress is formal, and time-keeping is strict. In the subsidiary at branch level, relations with managers and dress is very informal. The top management is very remote and staff and branch managers are very loyal and deferential to top managers. Their word is law in the company. This contrasts with the parent, where it is normal to be cynical towards top management. For example, the introduction of quality circles was treated with much derision, few people taking it very seriously.

Content

World view:
The subsidiary recruits people with a serious outlook which values hard work, but representatives 'know their place': they are deferential to authority. While they can earn a good living, they have no illusions about progressing through the organization. This requires 'breeding', knowing the right people and having the right social manners. In the parent there is a view, treated by some people a bit cynically after not progressing their career in the bank, that anyone can rise to become Group Chief Executive.

Objectives and goals:
The subsidiary values independence, and wants to demonstrate its profitability to the parent in order to retain its independent functioning. The parent recognizes the subsidiary's potential, but is worried by its 'cavalier' attitude towards business, which does not befit a 'bank'.

Motivation of individuals:
Subsidiary staff are motivated by money. Bank staff are as well, but are also motivated by their privileges of rank such as company cars and size of office.

Congruity of perceptions and objectives:
There is a great deal of cynicism in the parent bank, and much conflict with the views expressed by top management. One of the problems is lack of promotion, although many people stay for a forty-year career. In the subsidiary, there is not so much 'in-fighting' and politics. People are too busy dealing with customers and reaching monthly sales targets, rather than looking internally, and looking after their own careers (people do not really expect a career). Staff and managers generally accept the top management view.

Styles of management:
Bank management styles and attitudes are predominantly rational and logical, focusing on planning and a 'classic' approach to management functions. The management training courses provided reflect this approach. The subsidiary's management style is more intuitive, business driven, and far more instinctive than the predominant style in the parent bank. No courses in management are provided, but sales courses are provided.

Language:
Subsidiary – Urbanian
Parent – English.

Conduct

Technical knowledge of individuals:
The subsidiary has specialist representatives with a good knowledge of their subject and their products. Branch managers are drawn from the most successful representatives. The parent's staff and managers are regarded as generalists.

Skills level of managers:
The nature of skills varies between the companies, reflecting the different styles and requirements. Neither are particularly highly skilled managers.

Effectiveness of managers and operations:
The branches of the subsidiary generally meet the stretching sales targets set by head office. The branches of the parent have a complex set of targets, usually met, but also capable of being manipulated. The branch managers are usually complaining that targets are too stretching.

Profitability of companies:
The bank is the top performing bank in the UK in terms of profit. The subsidiary makes reasonable profits, and there is much room for improvement.

Language ability:
The subsidiary's managers speak Urbanian and no English accept a few senior managers, although these rely on interpreters when dealing with the parent. No top manager in the parent speaks Urbanian. They use agency interpreters.

First change initiative

The parent bank now wishes to provide the opportunity for managers of its wholly owned subsidiary to pursue careers within the group, with the vision that one may become the future Group Chief Executive. The parent bank's policy is that by providing the same type of development programme for the Urbanian subsidiary, it will help to integrate the company into the group.

Managers in the subsidiary do not believe the corporate 'myth' prevalent in the parent bank, that any junior clerk can become the future chief executive. Also, the subsidiary values its independence and resents interference in its internal affairs. It particularly does not want the parent forcing top management on them from England – they have assumed this is the corollary of sending Urbanian managers to the UK.

Few of the Urbanian managers speak English, and any corporate messages concerning group policy and identity are selectively filtered down the hierarchy to fit the views of the Urbanian top management.

Discussion: Look back on the various aspects of the subsidiary and its relationship with the parent, and state what are the restraining forces in this situation, and what are the forces pushing for change.

Second change initiative

The UK board of directors of the parent bank decide that they should be doing far more to try to bring the subsidiary closer to the parent, particularly regarding the development of management potential. Accordingly Jim Watts, currently Systems Manager in the UK Information Technology Department, is appointed project manager to introduce a new computerized personnel system into the subsidiary, which via modem link can feed into the UK personnel system. This will allow the Group Personnel Department to identify early management potential in the Urbanian subsidiary, and channel it into the Group's management development programme. It will also allow Group Personnel to keep a close eye on the subsidiary's manpower needs, and provide appropriate 'talent' to the subsidiary if this is needed.

So, with a small project team of translators/interpreters, personnel specialists, systems analysts, and programmers, Jim Watts reports to the Urbanian Managing Director. Jim learns that the subsidiary currently has only a paper-based personnel record system at branch level, and a computerized system at head office. The records system only allows for information about employees' start dates, previous and current positions, and personal information such as date of birth and home address. The personnel specialists advise Jim that a more sophisticated record system is needed which also provides details on training undertaken, sickness records, and potential (based on the annual staff appraisal system already in operation). This will allow for more detailed manpower planning and the identifying of potential high-fliers who might be nominated for management development courses.

The system would be based on networked computers in each branch office, operated by the administration manager in each branch and linked via modem to the subsidiary's head office. The benefits to the branch administration managers should be obvious as they will be able to plan their human resources better, and more systematically nominate staff for training courses. Head Office in turn would be able to track manpower and identify high fliers. The system would then link in with that of the UK, would be bilingual and available to analysis by Group Personnel. The project team quickly develop plans for the system (their brief is for speed of implementation and therefore they do not have time to visit any branch offices, but they consult with the subsidiary's personnel officer) and present their plans to the subsidiary's Managing Director who approves the plan.

Implementation is equally as fast. Soon the system is up and running. Computer terminals are in each branch, and each administration manager is given a half-day training session on using the system.

The subsidiary Managing Director sends out a personal letter saying how important the system is to the personnel function and in developing synergy with the parent bank. He asks everybody for their support in effectively using the system.

Many of the twenty administration managers reply to this letter, offering their support and co-operation.

Three months later no administration manager has sent any data to the mainframe at Head Office, and only an estimated five have used the system locally.

Subsequently Jim Watts discovers that only 60 per cent of managers ever regularly complete an appraisal form on their staff.

Discussion: What is the situation which Jim is faced with and what can he do about it? If he could start again, what should he do to identify obstacles and increase the chances of the initiative succeeding?

Currently five out of twenty administration managers use the system. In six months time you want all of them to use the system. Work through the following force field analysis.

Force field analysis:

1 If it is possible within a group, first 'brain-storm' the driving forces and the restraining forces in this situation, by moving quickly from one person to the next. Take each aspect at a time. Individuals should 'pass' if they have not got an immediate contribution. No idea should be evaluated or discussed at this point, but simply written down. (You can do this individually, by writing down as many ideas as you can, without yet making a judgement about their value.)

2 Next look at the items for 'restraining force' and 'driving force', and select those that can be influenced or controlled, listing them on the Force Field Worksheet below.

Force Field Worksheet

Worse state Nobody using system	Present state 5 out of 20 using system	Desired outcome 20 out of 20 using system

Driving forces	Restraining forces

3 Next, design an action plan for removing restraining forces and strengthening driving forces and include, as far as possible, the following:

- what must be done;
- the timetable;
- those who can contribute;
- responsibility for each part, or action;
- how the various parts are co-ordinated;
- what the requirements are for feedback and evaluation.

Managing change through organizational design

We next focus on another management technique for organizational change which addresses the needs for structural adaptation and redesign. We describe the approach of Lawrence and Lorsch (1967) in seeing organizations as a balance between 'differentiation' and 'integration'. A familiar example of the importance of this balance is in the relationship between the sales department and the production department. The sales department is concerned with selling as many units as possible to customers (a differentiated function), but without good communication, co-ordination and co-operation between the sales department and the production department (integration), sales may get ahead of production. The production manager will get annoyed because production cannot keep pace with sales, and the sales manager will get frustrated as he cannot service his or her customers quickly. This will lead to further bad feeling between the sales and production departments, with a possible loss of customers and revenue. Thus there is a need for a differentiation of sales and production functions, but there is also a need to integrate the work of these two functions through co-ordination and co-operation.

Thus, 'differentiation' means that different people or organizational units do different things within the organization, and 'integration' is the necessary state of collaboration existing between these different parts of the organization in order to get the job done. Organizational design addresses these two (opposing) factors: the level of differentiation needed; and, the amount of integration needed. We can depict these two organizational variables by Figure 15.3.

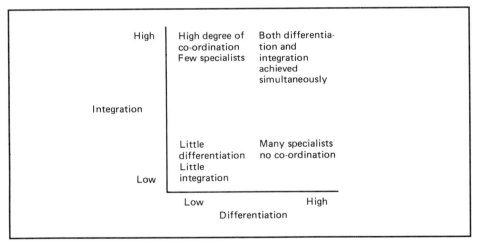

Figure 15.3 *Differentiation and integration in organizational design (adapted from Lawrence and Lorsch, 1967)*

Planned change can be affected by a consideration of these two factors. As a general rule, the more dynamic the business environment in which the organization is operating, the more differentiation is required. The higher the level of integration the better performance of the organization.

The business environment can be characterized by:

- *complexity (homogeneity–heterogeneity) or simple versus complex*: this characterizes the differences and complexities in the environment. For example we could describe the current European market place as complex (see Chapter 9 for a discussion on this).

- *dynamism (the rate of change)*: this involves both the rate of change and the degree of unpredictability of change. Seasonal changes in the market are fairly predictable although they may represent a rapid rate of change. Thus companies which produce products for Christmas can predict the rate of change. This alone does not constitute a dynamic business environment. It is only when the changes are not very predictable, indicating a higher level of risk taking in decision making, that we can describe an organization's environment as dynamic. The changing fortunes of the computer industry, with rapid product innovation, foreign competition, and changes in usage of computers indicate a very dynamic marketplace.

It is in this way that Miles (1980) describes the business environment and its implications for levels of differentiation and integration, as in Figure 15.4.

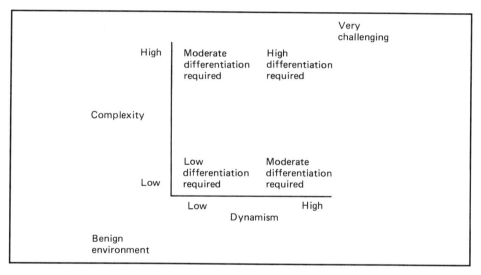

Figure 15.4 *Implication to organizations of complexity and dynamism in the business environment (adapted from Slevin, 1989)*

The more complex the technical or commercial environment, the more likely it is that specialist functions will have the necessary knowledge to make sense of the complexity. It is unlikely that generalist teams will have the necessary high level of differentiated specialization and expertise. If the situation is very dynamic as well, specialists are more likely to be able to keep abreast with and respond to these changes than are teams of generalists.

Managing differentiation

There are a number of ways in which the need for differentiation may be managed within an organization:

- Recruit specialists from outside the organization in order to acquire the necessary levels of expertise in differentiated functions. Whereas in previous years bank employees had been developed as generalists, 'zigzagging' from one function to another every two-and-a-half to three years as they pursued their careers upwards, UK banks found an increasing need to recruit specialists in mid-career in order to meet a growing competition among banks, and respond to a more complex rapidly changing business environment in the mid-1980s.

- Acquire specialized units. Again the UK banks found that there was a need for the acquisition of specialized companies in order to perform specialist functions such as share dealing, insurance brokerage and consumer credit dealing in a very complex marketplace.

- Manage and develop specialists and specialized functions within the organization. More career bankers in the UK clearing banks began to assume more specialized careers towards the end of the 1980s, rather than being regarded as generalists who could work in any function within the bank. There was a corresponding increase in specialized training courses in order to develop these specialists.

- Integrate specialist units and individuals. Much of the integration of retail banking specialist functions such as personal and business lending, share dealings, insurance and mortgage lending, was achieved through the activities of the bank branches which provided a 'shop window' for the specialized services. Business could then be passed to the specialized units. However, integration at the corporate level was often problematical where it was sometimes difficult to blend the very different organizational and business cultures represented by the various specialized subsidiaries. Hence, in at least one case, the main (Group) board of directors' control of such functions as merchant banking and share dealings became a case for national concern and a major embarrassment for the parent bank, as described in Mini Case 15.2.

Mini Case 15.2 The Blue Arrow Affair

While it is not possible here to go into the full details of this case, the following extracts from Donaldson (1992) provide some insight into the problems experienced by National Westminster Bank and its subsidiary County NatWest, and its stockbrokers Phillips and Drew: possibly a case of lack of integration and lack of, or inappropriate, management controls.

> In August 1987 the Blue Arrow employment agency made a takeover bid for the firm Manpower, with a £837 million rights issue planned. That September, the rights issue was recognized as unsuccessful, and the balance of shares were placed with investors. A press statement was released claiming the rights issue to have been a success, however. In October, in the Stock Market crash, there was a £65 million loss on NatWest's Blue Arrow involvement (Donaldson, 1992, pp. 252–3).

The subsequent Department of Trade and Industry report, reported in the *Guardian*, 21 July 1989, criticized the dealings as follows.

> The Stock Market was deliberately misled through the concealment of important information, the Companies Act broken and there may have been insider trading ... the Report is unprecedentedly critical of Britain's biggest High Street Clearing Bank and its dealings in the City.

While Blue Arrow were cleared of involvement in these actions, the case led to prosecutions of key people in County NatWest and the subsequent resignations of NatWest main board members.

Discussion: To what extent is it possible for a traditional British high street bank, with its typical culture of caution and restraint, to exercise control on a subsidiary with a culture of quick deals and higher risk decision making?

Managing integration

Slevin (1989) describes five states of organizational integration, namely:

D – Dis-integration
U – Unstable
I – Instantaneous integration
II – Process integration
III – Composite integration.

He defines these in terms of three key variables:

- information exchange
- agreement on decision
- agreement on decision making authority.

Disintegration. This state exists where there is no information exchange between the organizational units involved. This is not necessarily negative where there is no need for two units to communicate, for example, in the case of two different subsidiaries in two different countries. However, this is negative where this state affects performance. For example, a stock part available at our southern office could have been supplied to a customer had the northern office known about it. As a consequence of not having a good information system, the sale was lost. Information exchange is essential to effective management.

Unstable. This state exists where there is information exchange, but no agreement on decisions nor on the decision making authority. This often results in conflicts, tension and possibly a change in status through, for example, a communication breakdown (to a state of disintegration) or progresses to another state of integration. An example is where there are many memoranda and heated exchanges between the production department and the sales department because the salesmen work on a commission basis and they obtain customers' orders with which the production department cannot fulfil.

I – Instantaneous integration. Here there is information exchange, agreement on decisions, but no agreement on the decision making authority. This therefore only provides a short-term solution which is costly on communication, short lived and may arise again. A great deal of time is used in getting consensus in participative management situations, leading often to high motivation levels, but when the environment becomes unpredictable, time pressures are great, there can be much resentment of 'dictatorial' management and lack of recognition of authority.

II – Process integration. Here there is information exchange, no agreement on decisions, but agreement on the decision-making authority. For example, a dispute between two departments might be resolved by both their superiors, where both departments accept the decision making authority (perhaps the General Manager) but do not accept the decision. The same problem of conflict still exists between the departments. In this situation, the recognized authority for making decisions is there, but if the staff do not agree with the decisions on a regular basis, then there will be a fall off in morale and motivation. This state of organizational integration may be efficient, but should be used sparingly.

III – Composite integration. In this state of organizational integration, there is information exchange, agreement on decisions and agreement on the decision making authority. Where a decision is made with the agreement of the two departments (for example), and the authority to enforce that decision is recognized, usually there will be a mutual understanding between the two departments. A fully integrated organization, with clear lines of authority which are understood and accepted with the basis of agreement on decisions, often indicates a situation where there will be effective decision making and high motivation to carry out decisions.

Although the highest state of integration is not always required, there are certain indicators of integration problems which Slevin (1989) points to, which may indicate a need for change.

- A lack of information exchange between departments, subsidiaries, or other organizational units, so that activities cannot be co-ordinated.
- Wasteful use of information exchange, for example, too many memoranda, or meetings. There may be an information overload or dilution, which may reduce the level of integration.
- A lack of agreement on decisions, often typified by complaints about decisions.
- Units working at cross-purposes, a lack of information exchange, political differences and a lack of shared goals.
- A lack of awareness of who is the decision-making authority, or where the power realities do not parallel the organization chart.

Instantaneous integration is appropriate where the problem is non-routine, where it is a one-time agreement and where the agreement of subordinates is necessary. Process integration may be appropriate where the problem is routine, where repetitive decisions are necessary, and where agreement on any specific decision is not necessary for its implementation. Composite integration is necessary where the maximum amount of organizational integration is required, where a final and continuing resolution of a problem is required, and where consensus and a clear decision-making authority is necessary for implementation. The problems of trying to achieve this higher state of integration are that it requires a high degree of commitment to the organizational goals, and it may be costly, in terms of time, to achieve.

Change management through organizational differentiation and integration

The steps towards the required level of integration through a process of organizational design are described by Slevin (1989), and outlined in Figure 15.5.

Specific devices, tools or techniques which can be used to affect integration are:

- setting organizational goals and obtaining commitment to them, providing a commonality of interest and fostering integration;

- management information systems, which provide a source of and means of obtaining management data for integration purposes, providing information exchange;

- providing a clear hierarchy and delegation of responsibilities with adequate controls in place, and clear definitions of roles and rules;

- developing project teams and matrix structures in order to obtain higher levels of co-operation between specialists, departments and subsidiaries all working towards specific objectives.

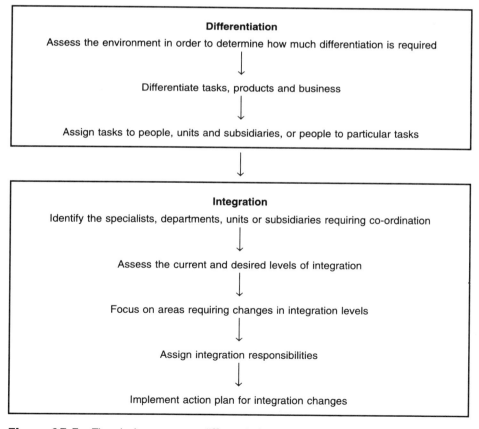

Figure 15.5 *The design process: differentiation and integration (adapted from Slevin, 1989)*

Case Study 15.2 The Urbanian subsidiary II

Before reading this case study, you need to refer to Case Study 15.1, on page 296, for the background.

The original board of the subsidiary had sold out to the parent bank as it recognized that without a substantial inflow of funds it would not be able to compete effectively with some of the multi-national finance companies which were gradually winning more and more of the subsidiary's market share.

The parent had seen it as an opportunity to extend its influence and presence in the continent. Previously it had only a small representative office in Urbania through its UK credit finance subsidiary. The aim was for the Urbanian subsidiary to merge with the UK subsidiary, but only after the parent had developed firm controls over the Urbanian subsidiary. It did not want the problems of control which it had experienced with the UK credit finance subsidiary because of differences in culture (particularly the sales culture of the credit finance industry as opposed to the 'relationship' approach of the parent bank).

The parent had tried to solve these problems in the UK by 'imposing' a Chief Executive on the UK subsidiary. This made the Chief Executive's job both a lonely one as well as a thankless one. They were now keen to look on the new acquisition in Urbania as an opportunity for getting things right and not repeating past mistakes.

However, the new acquisition had caused 'ripples' in the UK subsidiary. They could not understand why they were not involved in the acquisition right from the start. The UK subsidiary board of directors was consulted originally but the parent had engaged a firm of consultants to advise on the acquisition. It would seem logical to them for the UK subsidiary to acquire the Urbanian company, as they were in the same business.

The parent had not communicated the intention for the eventual absorbing of the Urbanian subsidiary into the UK subsidiary 'group'.

Much of the business of the consumer credit industry is conducted through a third party. In the case of the UK subsidiary, the dealership network of the major car manufacturer in the UK is used to sell one of the main products of the company: consumer credit for car purchase via sales or leasing arrangements. The UK subsidiary had a good relationship with the dealership network and regularly trained new dealer managers in the products they sold on a commission basis on behalf of the UK subsidiary.

The UK subsidiary's route into the continent was via the dealership network which was to extend into Urbania and neighbouring countries. Through this 'third party' the UK subsidiary would have a significant presence in the continent without the need of a branch network.

The acquisition of the Urbanian subsidiary by the parent had somewhat confused the issue. Among other activities the Urbanian subsidiary had now begun talks with the new dealership network of the UK car manufacturer in Urbania. This has both confused the dealership and has angered the UK subsidiary.

Many meetings have subsequently taken place between the UK subsidiary and representatives of the dealership network to try to resolve the issues, but what can the subsidiary do? It does not really know itself how the problem has arisen!

The Chief Executive of the UK subsidiary has spoken to the parent bank's General Manager of Related Banking Services Division (the main board level manager responsible) about the acquisition of the Urbanian subsidiary, and has been told that as far as possible the Urbanian subsidiary is being left to make its own decisions about how it conducts business in Urbania. Certain administrative and personnel controls are imposed, but the subsidiary is free to pursue its own objectives for the time being.

Clearly the Chief Executive of the UK subsidiary was not happy with this. He explained to the General Manager that this may cause a loss of faith by the dealership in the UK subsidiary and perhaps a loss of business. The General Manager suggested that the Chief Executive should approach the Managing Director of the Urbanian subsidiary informally to discuss the problem to see what could be worked out.

Meanwhile, in Urbania, the Urbanian subsidiary's Managing Director was grappling with another problem. The main aim of the takeover by the parent bank was to provide much needed funds for an expansion of the branch network in order to compete more effectively. Increasingly, the subsidiary was finding that this solution was too simplistic. That over the last twelve months, competition had increased to an extent that not only was it necessary to have a good geographical coverage across the country, but it was necessary to compete on quality of service to customers. This required highly trained specialists who could respond to specific customers' needs, both personal business and industrial business, where the subsidiary was increasing its business with the dealership networks of two major car manufacturers. It lacked the specialization and training in this area. Where could they get this training and specialized knowledge?

A problem had occurred between the sales representatives who had gone out to various local motor dealers and had got them interested in doing business with the Urbanian company. Unfortunately, the administration staff had no idea how to put this into effect, as they had no training in this type of work.

In the UK the Dealer Services Director of the motor manufacturer with whose dealership network the UK subsidiary had been doing business for years, was sitting in his office perplexed. He had received numerous telephone calls from his dealers in Urbania asking about the Urbanian subsidiary's approaches to them. He had no control over the dealership as they were mostly independent chains of motor dealers having no other relationship with the manufacturer other than holding a franchise to sell their cars. But good relations with them were essential. Also, the manufacturer could make strong recommendations to the dealerships about which consumer credit finance company to use. Yesterday he had a visit from a rival consumer credit finance company with an internationally based organization with strong co-ordination from the UK centre, and a network of branches in Urbania.

Discussion: What are the problems? Use the techniques of organizational design to solve the problems in a way which is likely to be acceptable to all parties. You should take the position of an independent consultant, using the following worksheet.

Change through organizational design worksheet

First, list the target organizational units.

1

2

3

4

5

6

On the following matrix describe the current relationship between units and the desired relationship in terms of the degree of integration required, using the following guide-lines:

D – low level or lack of information exchange. Use only when no interaction is required.

U – information exchange, but no agreement. Never use this as it is unstable.

I – information exchange and agreement on decisions on a short term basis, but no agreement on decision making authority. This involves consensus and agreement and provides a short-term solution. Use only when one time agreement is necessary. This may become crisis management.

II – information exchange, no agreement on decisions, but agreement on decision making authority. This identifies responsibility for decision making. Use when decisions must be made, but it may generate over-bureaucratization.

III – information exchange, agreement on decisions and on decision making authority. Consensus and high morale is a feature of this. Use when implementation issues are important and decision quality is crucial. It takes a lot of organizational time.

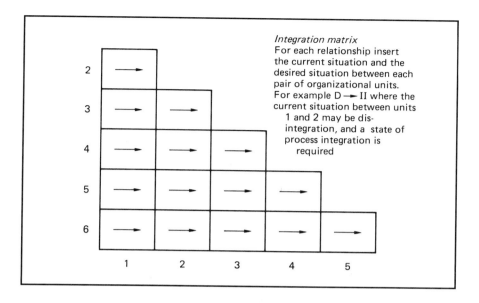

Now describe the problems, where they exist, between organizational units, and a suggested cause of action which may be taken.

Target units	Problem outline	Action required
and		
and		
and		
and		
and		
and		
and		

Worksheet material adapted from the work of Slevin (1989).

Organizational culture change

Organizational culture has been discussed at some length previously in this text (see Chapter 8) and we have looked at the work of Schein in this area. Here we briefly summarize his (Schein, 1989) ideas on 'mechanisms' of organizational culture change, which we can describe as follows. These represent different paths to cultural change which organizations might follow.

Natural evolution

Where an organization is not under too much environmental stress, and often where the founders have been around for a long time, the organization will evolve a culture of what works best. This may also involve what Schein calls a 'general evolution' to the next stage of the organizations development through diversification and growing complexity. Elements of the culture which act as 'defence mechanisms' may persist especially if the company has been successful. Sub-cultures will also emerge around the growing number of different sub-units of the organization. This is all part of the process of 'differentiation' discussed above, and what Schein (1989) calls 'specific evolution'.

Self-guided evolution through organizational therapy

This is based on the assumption that culture is partly a defence mechanism, and if the organization can discover its own strengths and weaknesses, by gaining insight by, usually, an outside consultant acting as a catalyst to 'unfreeze' the organizational culture, then dramatic changes can occur. This involves assumptions and techniques found in organizational development, and reflects many of the views of Lewin as we discussed above.

Managed evolution through hybrids

This is an approach which is useful where the culture needs to change, but the organization is in danger of loosing its identity. Rather than bringing new people in from outside the culture, key people from the existing culture, who recognize there is a need to change, are used in positions of authority so that change can be affected. In this way, there is less likely to be the type of resistance from insiders that might be experienced if outsiders were brought in.

Planned change and organizational development

Through a process of growth and increasing complexity, differentiation may lead to a growth of sub-cultures which may even take on the guise of warring factions, pulling in different directions. Organizational development addresses these differences through, usually, a consultant increasing self-insight and developing change programmes to reduce the conflict. This invariably involves some form of culture change.

Technological seduction

This works on the basis that technological changes disrupt behaviour patterns, and also force you to look at underlying assumptions. The introduction of personal computers to strata of management, or the introduction of electronic mail may force a reconsidering of the way business is undertaken, changing behavioural patterns, and affecting a change in the culture.

Change through scandal, explosion and myth

The distinction made by Argyris and Schon (1978) between an organization's 'espoused theories' and 'theories in use' provide the basis for this mechanism. As an organization matures there often grows a gap between the cultural assumption of the organization as they are publicly espoused, and the practices that actually occur. An espoused theory that individual staff preferences are taken into account when considering a geographical move, might be countered in practice by individuals being taken off the promotion ladder if they do not accept a certain posting. Schein (1989) uses the example of the manager who was posted overseas against his will, and committed suicide. He left a letter which was leaked to the press explaining that the company had not taken his feelings into account and let it be known to him that if he did not accept the assignment he would be passed over for promotion. Other such revelations may take the form of 'whistleblowing' where actual practice in a company does not live up to the high ethical standards espoused by the company. Such exposures often lead to a reconsidering of assumptions and consequent cultural changes.

Incrementalism

This is a gradual approach to cultural change, where change is not implemented in one go, but incrementally, so that it is hardly noticed, and may take place over several years. An example of this is to gradually put people into key positions in the organization who have different attitudes and assumptions. Thus through recruitment and selection policies, the organizational culture will slightly move over the years, where it reaches a stage when all or most of the key positions are filled by decision makers who act on different assumptions to the old culture.

Coercive persuasion

Schein (1989) describes this as a process used in a mature culture where there is a need to turn around a culture. By firstly making it difficult for key personnel to leave by using the right incentives, the change agents (perhaps senior managers) can consistently challenge old assumptions, thus making it difficult to sustain the old assumptions. By being supportive and by rewarding any evidence that the key person is shifting to the new assumptions, psychological 'safety' is provided for the key person. With sufficient psychological safety, members of the group can gradually give up their old cognitive defences.

Turnaround

This involves a capable and determined turnaround individual or team who can use all the above mechanisms, providing an unfreezing, and the necessary psychological safety to reduce resistance. The turnaround agent must have a clear idea of where the organization needs to go, a model of how to change the culture, and power to implement the model. Fundamentally, it is the willingness to coerce which Schein regards as crucial.

Reorganization and rebirth

This is unusual, and involves the complete destruction of the group which is the carrier of the old culture and its replacement by a new group and a new culture.

Organizational change and national culture: some conclusions

Laurent (1989) asserts that managers from different cultures have different assumptions about such things as the nature of management, authority, organizational structure, and relationships within organizations. In turn, these assumptions shape value systems and management practices which reinforce the original assumptions. Of note is the cultural assumption of organizations being seen as instrumental (for example to achieve economic objectives) and being seen as social systems. Hence the North American view of the organization might be as a set of tasks to be achieved through a problem solving hierarchy, and in Latin countries as a collectivity of people managed through a formal hierarchy.

In the latter case positions may be defined in terms of status and levels of authority, rather than in the former case where they might be defined in terms of function. In the instrumental view authority is there to accomplish tasks, and in the social view tasks are seen as a way to establish authority. Hence the United State gave birth to 'organizational development' through an instrumental view of organizations. Approaches to organizational change in the Latin countries favoured institutional approaches ('institutional analysis') dealing with the social intricacies of the human collectivity. Organizational development has tended not to deal with power relations in organizations, while institutional analysis has emphasized this issue.

Laurent (1989), therefore favours a contingency approach to organizational change. If organizations reflect their national cultures, so too should change strategies.

While there may not be too many difficulties in conceiving of change as a transition from position *A* to position *B* (perhaps to total quality, valuing customers or personnel), it is the means of getting to *B* which will reflect the national cultural perspective, by the different ways of managing and the different views of organizations. In the case of the multi-national organization, the means used to achieve ends which may be agreed internationally, should be the subject of decentralization, by which means national units can find their own pathways to achieving the desired state.

In this chapter we have looked at three fundamental approaches to change management: force field analysis, organizational design, and cultural change management. Force field analysis analyses the change situation as pushing and pulling forces, where the mechanisms of change concentrate on decreasing the dragging forces and strengthen the pushing forces. Organizational design looks at the balance in the structure of an organization between differentiation and integration, where change is directed towards achieving the desired level of differentiation to successfully respond to and manage environmental pressures, and to obtain the required degree of integration within this situation.

Cultural change management addresses a number of issues concerned with organizational culture and a number of techniques and approaches were described which meet the requirements for cultural change in different circumstances.

Finally, we said that change strategies must be considered in line with particular approaches to management and organizations which may be prevalent in specific national cultures, and which form much of the subject matter of this text.

References

Argyris, C. and Schon, D. (1978) *Organizational Learning*, Reading, Massachusetts: Addison-Wesley.

Donaldson, J. (1992) *Business Ethics: A European Casebook*, London: Academic Press.

Kanter, R. M. (1991) 'Managing the human side of change', in Kolb, Rubin and Osland (eds.), *The Organizational Behavior Reader*, Englewood Cliffs, New Jersey: Prentice-Hall.

Laurent, A. (1989) 'A cultural view of change' in Evans, P, Doz, Y. and Laurent, A. (eds.) *Human Resource Management In International Firms: Change, Globalization, Innovation*, Basingstoke, Hampshire: Macmillan.

Lawrence, P. R. and Lorsch, W. J. (1967) *Organization And Environment*, Cambridge, Mass.: Harvard University Press.

Lewin, K. (1951) *Field Theory in Social Science*, London: Harper and Row.

Miles, R. H. (1980) *Macro Organizational Behaviour*, Glenview, Ill: Scott Foresman.

Schein, E. H. (1989) 'Organizational culture: what it is and how to change it', in Evans, Doz and Laurent (eds.) cited above.

Slevin, D. P., (1989) *The Whole Manager*, New York: AMACOM, American Management Association.

Vandermerwe, S. and Vandermerwe, A. (1991) 'Making strategic change happen', *European Management Journal*, 9, 2.

16

Managing international projects

Objectives

Following this chapter you should be able to:

1 Demonstrate an understanding of the principles of project management in an international context, drawing on many of the theories, principles and techniques previously discussed in this text.
2 Apply these principles in a management situation.

Key concepts

- Project and line management
- Factors of project management
- Project phases
- International project competences

Introduction

This chapter provides both a consolidation of much of the work in this text and the introduction of new ideas and information on the human and organizational aspects of project management. It is possible that many readers of this text will be, or will become project managers in an international career, or will work in 'project mode' from time to time in their jobs. The differences between 'line' and 'project' management will be discussed as will the different pressures associated with each. The problems of cross-cultural and cross-professional management are also looked at in this context. A focus of this chapter is a case study where the reader is asked to analyse and address a practical application of project management.

We are mainly concerned here with the practicalities of successful project management in the international context, drawing on many of the principles discussed in preceding chapters such as

- social perception and effective inter-cultural communication;
- team work;
- leadership;
- organizational structure and culture;
- managing cultural differences;
- change management.

Other issues which should be borne in mind are motivation, learning, power and influences. We will allow the reader to draw on these sources, and apply them to the case study.

However, this is not primarily a text on project management (the interested reader may like to refer to Anderson *et al.* 1987, for example for a more detailed discussion of the operational aspects of project management) as we focus on the human aspects of managing projects. These aspects are fundamental to the success of any project, and the understanding of the management of difference, as applied to both different cultures and different professions, is an essential aspect of project management.

A trend towards project management

Project management is not simply regarded here as an interesting application of previously expounded theory, it is regarded as very much the future of management and particularly of international management. There are many predictions about the ways in which organizations are evolving (principally in the West).

Bennis (1966) saw, in the 1960s and 1970s a move from the more bureaucratic organization, to one based more on functional autonomy and learning. He stressed:

- an ability to learn from experience;
- developing methodologies in organizations from improving the learning process;
- an ability to use feedback on performance, developing a process orientation and to be self analytical;
- the ability to manage your own destiny.

In the 1980s Handy talked about the dispersed organization as a shift from the centralized administration to a decentralized and dispersed professionalism. This would be characterized by:

- independence and autonomy for professionals;
- flat organizational structures;
- a career in your profession rather than in one organization;
- a preference for networking rather than working through hierarchies;
- a need to train the next generation, so that organizations become schools as well as places in which to work;
- fixed term contracts;
- flexible time contracts to allow for the fact that many professionals will be self-employed elsewhere;
- personal and portable pensions rather than company pension schemes.

Hodge and Anthony (1988) see similar directions in organizational evolution, drawing conclusions that there will be a tendency to bigger and more complex organizations to cope with increased complexities in the environment, but that they will be more highly differentiated with a tendency towards autonomous sub-units. They predict trends towards:

- temporary organizations set up for specific purposes and with a limited life span;
- minimum status differentials where people are judged on their competences rather than on the status of their position;
- professional managers with highly developed specialized expertise;
- flexibility and adaptability of organizational structures;
- decentralization and delegation ensuring quicker response time and better management of complexity by having decision making closer to the organizational operation (although the use of computer technology produces the counter-trend of centralized control);
- complexity involving differentiation of functions;
- greater social sensitivity, having to sense and adapt to social and environment trends and to be accountable to the wider community;
- goal directedness, focusing more on specific organizational missions and task objectives.

Inherent within these assumptions is that:

> Organizations of the future will likely be more temporary arrangements than they are today ... They will exist for a certain purpose and will cease to exist once that purpose has been achieved ... Project and matrix management will be more commonly used within organizations (Hodge and Anthony, 1988, p.654).

'Line' and 'project' management

It is therefore likely with an increase in complexity, specialization and flexibility that we will see more managers working in 'project' mode, and particularly international operations developing project teams for specific purposes to work across national boundaries and to manage a variety of professions. While many of the competences required of project managers are similar to those required of line managers, there are some differences. Essentially, while line managers certainly work to tight schedules and for specific objectives it is based on a 'business as usual' approach. Project managers, on the other hand, have a 'one-off' finite deadline. Principally, project managers need to be able to:

- convert business objectives to project objectives;
- obtain value for money through planning and controlling both physical and human resources over a set period of time;
- integrate complex effort and multi-professional groups of people, often across cultural divides;
- communicate with all levels of management, upwards and across;
- react to continual change;
- accelerate innovation and change;
- restructure new teams and develop attitudes, and facilitate working relationships, often in a very short space of time;
- work with and satisfy the needs of clients.

318

Mini Case 16.1 Developing project members

One of the key aspects of training project members is the attitudinal transformations which former line workers must make, before they are effective in 'project mode'.

In the current author's experience of project management in a major UK bank, bank employees were brought on to a specific project, or to work in a department where the work was project based (such as training and development, marketing, or information technology), from several years experience in a 'line' position.

There previous positions were invariably concerned with processing work, under normal 'day's work' constraints: certain work within, for example a bank branch, has to be completed by the end of the day's business. In these line jobs there tends to be a concentration on process rather than on specific objectives and results. For example, the movement of paper from the in-tray to the out-tray is important, and is seen as a certain measure of job effectiveness.

Coming into project work from this type of job, the member of staff invariably felt guilty! Often they would sit at their desks, perhaps working at a particular problem, or perhaps they would spend considerable time just researching a specific issue: but they were not producing any visible signs of output.

This feeling was apparently quite prevalent (the current author checked this over an extensive period in many project areas within the bank), and was also a problem. Often the member of staff would apply for a transfer back to a line job after a few weeks or a couple of months.

The problem was not just confined to project members, but also to new (and not so new) project managers, who themselves may have had years of experience in a bank line job, and would expect to see some movement in paper from their project team. They would sometimes also impose unnecessary controls on their project members like expecting them to be in the office, when they would have been better employed being with the 'client' or tracking down much needed information.

Discussion: The best solution that the current author could offer to this problem was making the new project member or manager aware of this problem: a feeling or attitude which is extremely common. How would you deal with this problem?

Project management across cultures

Project management, both across professional divides and national boundaries is complex. Its complexity can best be understood by reference to the context-content-conduct model described earlier in this text (Figure 16.1).

The project manager's job is to manage across these systems in order to meet specific business objectives within a finite period of time. This is not a 'matrix' structure, although this (Figure 16.1) describes the structural links that often form the

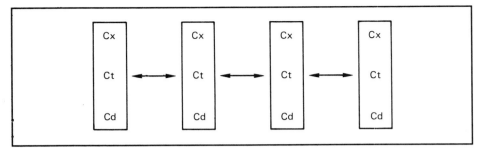

Figure 16.1 *Managing across cultural systems*

bases of project management. It describes the cultural systems which have to be bridged if project management is to work. These are:

- *Context (Cx)*. The organizational arrangements which need to be forged in order to get an effective team working in its environment. This often has to be with regard to existing organizational arrangement.

- *Content (Ct)*. The perspectives, motives and objectives which need to be forged together, with people from different professional, organizational or national cultures, usually through shared goals and commitment to these goals.

- *Conduct (Cd)*. The selection of appropriate skills and knowledge, and appropriate task training and use of specific skills throughout the project.

These cultural systems, which may be represented in individuals within the project team, or by groups or different stake-holders in the project, need to be integrated in some way in order to co-ordinate the various aspects of the project to make it a success. Let us look at this in the context of the key factors in project management (with acknowledgement to Slevin, 1989).

Key factors of project management

The following factors of project management are described by Slevin (1989).

Project mission

There is a need initially to define the project's goals in line with the business objectives, in order to make clear where it is going and how it can benefit the organization. There should be:

- a clearly defined mission;
- an clear indication that the project is necessary and why;
- a conviction that the project can succeed;
- a reference to specific goals and objectives.

Top management support

The project will be likely to fail unless it has the full support of your top management. This is particularly important in order to secure the support of the rest of the organization. This applies mainly to a project which is internal to an organization. When the project is undertaken for another organization (for example you may be a consultant working for a client), then the support of this organization's top management is essential. You should obtain such support, or you should ensure that your client has it (unless your client in this case is the top management). You must therefore ensure that:

- the top management are convinced that the project is necessary;
- they are convinced it will succeed;
- they have communicated this to everyone concerned;
- they fully understand your (the project manager's) role in the project, have confidence in you, and will support you in a crisis.

Project plan

All activities should be scheduled along with the resources required. There must be ways of monitoring progress in line with specific stage deadlines. You should consider if:

- the plan is workable;
- the amount of time, money, and people allocated is sufficient;
- the organization will carry through the plans;
- the funds are guaranteed;
- there is flexibility in the plans allowing for over-running of the schedule.

Client consultation

The client should be clearly identified, usually as the one who will be 'using' the completed project (but this may vary, and identification of the client, particularly with 'inside' projects, is often easier said than done: see the case study below). Close consultation with the client is necessary. For 'outside' projects you should:

- know the client and what he or she requires;
- schedule regular meetings with the client (you should 'take the client with you' at all stages).

For 'inside' projects you should:

- identify the key people who must support the project in order for it to succeed;
- identify what 'political' action is required in order to get client acceptance, and support from key people;
- ascertain whether the client is accepting or resisting.

Recruitment, selection, and training of project personnel

There must be careful consideration of what skills are required, both technical and project team skills. In considering personnel for the project you should:

- consider whether you can recruit from outside or within your organization, or whether you will have to accept those you are offered;
- consider whether you can work well with them, perhaps by previous experience or through what you know of them as team members;
- consider whether you can trust them and delegate to them;
- consider whether their technical skills as well as their team skills are adequate.

Technical tasks

Technical tasks must be matched to the right people, and the right technology should be available to fulfil the tasks. As a check-list list you should:

- assign correct tasks to the right people;
- document the required technology and make sure it works adequately for the job;
- ensure the team understands the technology, the tasks and their place in achieving project objectives;
- ensure you have the provision to change or update the technology as the project develops.

Client acceptance

This is usually the 'bottom-line' which should be backed up with perceived and tangible benefits, and involves good communication. This involves:

- developing a selling strategy at an early stage in order to sell the project to the client;
- developing a relationship so that you can negotiate with the client where necessary;
- having 'trouble shooters' in place within your team, to overcome problems in the early stages and before they fully develop.

Monitoring and feedback

Throughout the project key individuals should have feedback on progress. This requires having the necessary monitoring procedures in place in order to ensure quality, and regular feedback. You should:

- regularly request feedback from team members;
- assess the performance of team and team members;
- update the project team on developments and problems;
- establish formal feedback channels;
- make sure the monitoring system is actually working with accurate information rather than being told what you want to hear or what the team members want you to hear.

Communication

This is the key factor in all the other factors, and is what makes the main difference between a successful or unsuccessful project. You should ensure that:

- you have clearly communicated the project goals to the team;
- there are feedback channels for team members to communicate with you;
- there is provision for written status reports from you to the team;
- team members are keeping lines of communication open to the organization and the client;
- both you and the team know to what extent the project is secret or open to the organization (or to the public or press);
- you control rumours about the project.

Trouble-shooter

All team members should act as 'look-outs' for problems. This presupposes that the team comprises of people with the necessary technical expertise to diagnose and fix problems as they occur. Therefore:

- all members should monitor the project;
- the team should utilize its capabilities to solve problems quickly, as they arise;
- there should be a capacity to identify potential problems which can kill the project;
- problems should be identified as those that can be left (as they will get better or disappear), or those where immediate action should be taken.

These factors of project management are summarized in Figure 16.2.

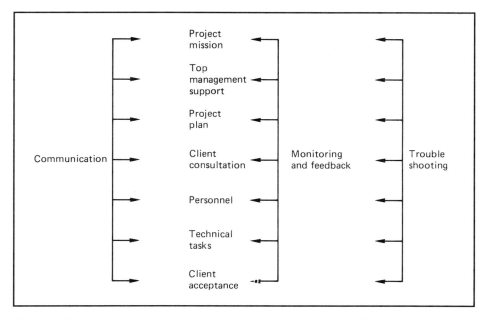

Figure 16.2 *A model of project management (adapted from Slevin, 1989)*

Project phases

The model of project management presented above represents aspects which are not necessarily sequential. Projects are managed through various phases. These are as follows.

1 Conceptualization and initiation. These involve:

- identifying the business needs;
- the setting of goals and specific objectives in line with business needs;
- gaining support for the project from key stake holders, by
- identifying and communicating the benefits of the project.

2 Planning. The planning process involves:

- scheduling, usually by well established methods such as critical path analysis;
- budgeting;
- allocating resources;
- recruiting, team building and training.

3 Execution and control. These involve:

- the actual work being undertaken;
- the ongoing monitoring of the work;
- the performance being verified, usually by reference to the achievement of objectives for each stage of the project, and by means of quality control.

4 Termination and audit. The following questions should be answered:

- Was the project successful? Did it meet the requirement of the client?
- Can it now be 'handed' to the client? Is the client's team sufficiently trained for the take-over?
- What now happens to the project team? Do they go on to another project? Is the team responsible for follow-up work on the completed project? Is the team disbanded?

A case of project management in a cross-cultural context

The following case both illustrates some of the points outlined above and asks the reader to specifically identify the areas which signify success or failure. You should refer to Chapter 15 for background information on the Urbanian case. We regard here, project management as another technique of change management. The Case 16.1 below, continues where the Case 15.1 finished.

Case Study 16.1 The debit card project

The debit card had been a great success in the UK in the late 1980s and early 1990s, and the parent bank had implemented a successful project with two other banks in the UK in establishing a joint debit card scheme.

The debit card is a piece of plastic which largely gets rid of the necessity to use a cheque in payment for goods to retailers who have joined the scheme. The transaction is recorded on an 'on-line' device connected to the retailer's tills and 'sent' to the mainframe at the bank where the customer's current account details are kept. The customer's account is then automatically debited with the amount of the transaction.

For the bank, money is earned through charging the retailer for the service. The customer is happy because of the convenience of not having to write a cheque. The retailer is happy because he is providing the customer with a quick and efficient service.

As a result of the parent bank's success in Urbania, firstly through its consumer credit company, and now through its newly acquired retail bank network, it wishes to be the first bank to establish in Urbania a debit card scheme. It has already approached the two others banks in the UK who are involved in the UK scheme, but they were not interested in pursuing this in Urbania as they felt they had not got the established 'presence' through their very small Urbanian subsidiaries.

The chief instigator of the initiative was John Steele, Head of Plastic, in the UK parent. He had established a strong project team for the UK initiative and wanted the senior project manager, Fred Stone to head the Urbanian project.

John Steele had already secured the support of the UK board of directors who had promised the necessary backing and finance. He had approached the Urbanian board of directors who had at first expressed certain reservations about the project, saying that Urbania had not been used to using plastic, had a strong tradition of cash transactions, but none the less had begun to use credit and charge cards. However there was certainly not the popular use of plastic in Urbania as there was in the United Kingdom.

John Steele had finally persuaded the Urbanian board, using the argument that the scheme would be 'ahead of its time' and 'a leader in the market place'. They had promised their support of the project and the assignment of resources to it.

The project's mission was set. The bank would gain advantage by being the first to offer debit cards in Urbania. This would establish the Urbanian subsidiary as a market leader in the eyes of its customers and potential customers.

Fred Stone was briefed. He worked hard in putting together a strong project team with the necessary technical and team skills. Some of these were from the original UK project team. He flew to Urbania to talk to potential team members in the subsidiary. While they seemed less committed to the project than their UK counterparts, they none the less had the necessary skills to be an effective part of the international team.

Job descriptions had been written for each team member (something which seemed a little odd to the Urbanians as they were not used to working to written descriptions of their jobs). Appraisal procedures were explained to each team member (again a bit odd to the Urbanians, because although they had periodic interviews with their line managers, they had no idea about formal appraisals of their work).

Each team member understood their role, understood the goals of the project, and had received initial training in team and project skills. Tests of their technical competences had been carried out.

With a great deal of enthusiasm for the success of the project, Fred Stone introduced himself to the board of the subsidiary, explaining how he was going to conduct the project, and that he had an excellent team to implement the project. He had produced a Work Breakdown Analysis, a Critical Path Analysis, a GANTT chart and other necessary planning aids. He explained all these to the board who were delighted with Fred's attention to detail and his enthusiasm. The subsidiary board, still stating their one reservation about the project, promised their support to this project which would be funded entirely by the UK parent. They promised any additional resources which the project might require, and promised that they would communicate to all those concerned in the subsidiary bank in order to make sure everyone co-operated.

The project plans were finalized soon after the meeting with the subsidiary's board of directors. Resources were allocated, making sure that they were sufficient and certain. Non-critical activities were provided with 'slack time' to enable transfer of these resources (both physical and human) if need be. Budgets were agreed and contingency plans were made just in case the project schedule did not work out exactly.

The project involved the employment of a number of specialists from different parts of the bank, as well as members from the two countries. These included:

- project engineers, architects, and quantity surveyors;
- information technology specialists;
- operational management specialists;
- 'bank' personnel from 'the line' who were new to project work, but who were regarded as being very 'close' to the business of banking;
- marketing and sales specialists, who were used to working with the retail trade in the UK.

So, a good 'spread' of specialists were included, although each of them had different backgrounds and working cultures and did not communicate easily with one another. Also, the communication was difficult between the English and the Urbanians, although they all spoke English.

However, all the technical tasks went smoothly. The sales force had to sell the concept to large retailers in Urbania; and this was running very slowly. Without a 'product' to show the retailers, it was very difficult to get them to 'buy into' the scheme. At least the premises and technical work was going well, and the facility to offer the service would be available within six months.

Despite the problem with the sales, the project went on. It was really a matter of making sure that everything was in place ready to begin the scheme and offer a tangible product to the customers. There was no problem with resources, and Fred had not gone back to the subsidiary's board since the beginning of the project, but had kept in touch with John Steele, and had reported progress.

Regular meetings with the team had begun to get a bit difficult. This was not just due to pressure of work, but also to the time taken in getting agreement within the team with such different views and outlooks. Eventually, Fred relied on contacting individuals to see how they were progressing with the project.

Regular appraisals of staff were also difficult, mainly through lack of co-operation from the Urbanians.

Then a number of problems began to occur. The premises team had run over budget on the conversion of the premises for information technology installation. Fred contacted John Steele who said there were no additional funds available and that he would have to manage with what he already had. He quickly communicated this to the premises team leader by telephone and told him to do the best he could.

Another problem was one Fred should have heard about weeks ago, but he had just learned that the Urbanians on the team were getting very cynical about the likely success of the project. They completely lacked motivation, were frequently absent from work, and were holding up the project. The main causes seemed to lie in their belief that the product was not right for Urbania, and the lack of team work between UK and Urbanian project members. Plans were being changed without project members being told why and the teams were not very happy. Despite suggestions for improving things, these suggestions were not passed upwards by the team leaders to Fred Stone.

There seemed to be no mechanism for solving problems as they arose. The team members had tried to help by passing information upwards, but had stopped when no feedback was given to them.

The outcome was that the project was completed six months after schedule. Eventually, additional funds had been obtained, from the subsidiary, once they had discovered what was happening, and only to 'save face' with the customers, particularly the retailers who had already 'signed up' for the scheme.

The end result was a facility for administering the scheme. This involved both support to retailers and to card holders. Fifty per cent of the people employed in this facility were involved in 'authorization' work. This work involved answering a telephone where retailers were telephoning for authorization of the transactions where the amount of the transaction was above the 'floor limit' of the retailer. Very few retailers had been 'signed up' for the scheme, and there was very little work to do for the authorizations clerks.

The sales team is still working hard to 'sign up' additional retailers. All current account holders of the subsidiary bank were sent debit cards. However, although they can also use these as cheque guarantee cards, there are few retailers at which they can use them as debit cards in Urbania.

Discussion:

1 What went wrong with the project?

2 Use the project implementation analysis (Activity 16.1 below) to help you to analyse the situation.

3 Refer back to previous chapters. Can you use any of the principles, theories or techniques discussed to improve the situation in this project, and to help manage it, if it were re-run?

Analysing and developing international projects

Slevin (1989) makes the distinction between strategy and tactics in project management, and makes the point that it is important to get both right. Strategy involves: the mission, top management support and project planning. Tactics refer to: client consultation, personnel recruitment and training, identification of tasks, gaining client acceptance, monitoring and feedback, communication and trouble shooting.

Projects are often characterized by a weakness in either strategy or tactics, and this may lead to different types of error, as can be seen in Figure 16.3.

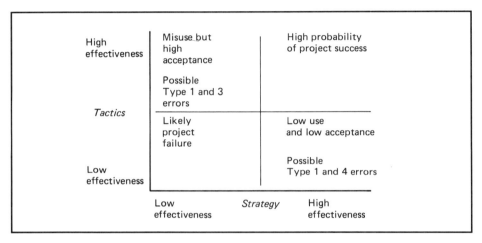

Figure 16.3 *Project strategy and tactics effectiveness (adapted from Slevin, 1989)*

The error types to which Slevin (1989) refers are:

- type 1: failing to take an action when one should be taken;
- type 2: taking an action when one should not have been taken;
- type 3: taking the wrong action or solving the wrong problem;
- type 4: solving the right problem but the solution is not used.

In summary, we can say that strategy helps to correctly identify and address issues and problems, whereas tactics make sure the solutions found are actually accepted by those who are going to use the outcome of the project. Both are equally important in international problems. The following Activity (Activity 16.1) provides a check-list which should be used to analyse Case 16.1 above.

Activity 16.1 Analysing and developing international projects

Use the following check-list to address the issues in Case 16.1 or to analyse and develop any international project.

Strategy

Project mission

1 Is there a clearly defined mission in line with both organizational aims and business requirements?
2 Is there a clear indication that the project is necessary and have the reasons been communicated?
3 Do all stakeholders hold a conviction that the project can succeed?
4 Have specific goals and objectives been identified for the project?
5 Are there any differences in market conditions, culture or attitudes in the countries involved in the project?

Top management support

6 Are the top management in both parent and subsidiary involved in the project, convinced that the project is necessary?
7 Are they convinced it will succeed in the context of the markets and cultures involved?
8 Have they communicated this to everyone concerned?
9 Have they fully understood your (the project manager's) role in the project, have confidence in you, and will support you in a crisis?
10 Do the subsidiary top management feel that the project is being imposed on them?
11 Who is responsible for the necessary finance (subsidiary, parent, or both)?

Project plan

12 Is the plan feasible and workable in the environment within which it will be carried out?
13 Is the amount of time, money and people allocated sufficient?
14 Will the parent and subsidiary organizations involved carry through the plans?
15 Are the funds guaranteed?
16 Is there flexibility in the plans allowing for over-running of the schedule?

Tactics

Client consultation

17 Have you clearly identified who the client is and what he or she requires?
18 Have you scheduled regular meetings with the client in order to take him or her with you throughout the progress of the project?
19 Have you clearly identified the key people in both parent and subsidiary as appropriate, who must support the project in order for it to succeed?
20 Have you identified what 'political' action is required in order to get client acceptance, and support from key people, and have you enlisted 'local' help in this if you are working in a foreign subsidiary?
21 Have you ascertained whether the client is accepting or resisting, and have you worked out a strategy to deal with a resisting situation?

Project personnel

22 Have the team got previous experience in working in an international environment? If not what can be done?
23 Is the team sufficiently trained in project work? If not what should be done?
24 Is the team sufficiently motivated? If not why not? What can be done?
25 Are the technical skills of the team sufficient? If not what should be done?
26 Are their team skills adequate? If not what should be done?
27 Will the international team work together well? If not, what can be done to develop synergy?
28 Are there any attitudinal, cultural or other problems which may clash with the project mission or may cause disharmony in the team? What are these problem areas and what can be done?

Technical tasks

29 Have the correct tasks been assigned to the right people?
30 Has the required technology been acquired and does it works adequately for the job?
31 Does the team sufficiently understand the technology, the tasks and their place in achieving project objectives?
32 Is there the provision to change or update the technology as the project develops?

Client acceptance

33 Has the project been 'sold' to the client at each stage?
34 Has a relationship developed with the client so that the client can be negotiated with as necessary?
35 Are there 'trouble shooters' in place within the team, to overcome problems with the 'client organization' in the early stages and before they fully develop?

Monitoring and feedback

36 Is feedback regularly requested from team members?
37 Is it appropriate to assess the performance of the team and team members within the different cultures involved? If not how is it possible to monitor performance?
38 Is the project team regularly updated on developments and problems?
39 Have formal feedback channels been established and do they work?
40 Is the monitoring system actually working with accurate information being received rather than what the team members want the project leader to hear?

Communication

41 Are there any language or other communication problems within the team?
42 Have the project goals been clearly communicated to the team and are they understood?
43 Is there provision for written status reports from the project leader to the team? When is this necessary?

44 Are team members keeping lines of communication open to the organization and the client?

45 Does the team know to what extent the project is secret or open to the organization?

46 Are rumours about the project controlled?

Trouble shooter

47 Are all team members involved in monitoring the project?

48 Does the team have the capabilities to solve problems quickly, as they arise?

49 Are problems being correctly identified and dealt with?

Overall project performance

50 Has the project been completed on time?

51 Has it been completed within its budget?

52 Does it show clear benefits to the user/client?

53 Is the end result being used by the client or end user?

54 Has the project had a positive impact on the organization (for example its reputation, building international synergy, etc)? Specify.

You should now refer to Figure 16.3 and identify whether the main problems are with strategy or tactics of the project and which types of errors have occurred.

Summary

We have therefore looked at international project management as an application of many of the principles which have been discussed in this text. By way of summary we can refer to some of these principles, and the chapters in this text to which the reader might again like to refer.

We have seen that there is a need for project managers to have certain competences and abilities. We can relate these abilities to specific areas of international organizational behaviour previously mentioned, as follows.

Convert business objectives to project objectives. This is a broad competency in the international context which involves an ability to understand the international marketplace, the international organizational structures involved through which you must work, the political aspects of such organizations, the potentially different cultural perception of the business issues and possible strategies for addressing them. The ability to negotiate across cultural divides is important as is the necessity to formulate change strategies.

Obtain value for money through planning and controlling both physical and human resources over a set period of time. The whole aspect of managing resources in an international context involves the understanding of cultural differences, the ability to lead an international team, and negotiation skills.

Integrate complex effort and multi-professional groups of people, often across cultural divides. Advanced team building skills are required together with leadership, negotiation and decision making abilities. An understanding of the importance of learning in individual development, together with a concept of career is also important.

Communicate with all levels of management, upwards and across. This involves both advanced communication skills as well as a good understanding of organizational structure, power, and politics.

React to continual change, and accelerate innovation and change. The skills of change management and decision making are perhaps the most directly pertinent facets.

Restructure new teams and develop attitudes, and facilitate working relationships, often in a very short space of time. Team skills and leadership skills are most important here.

Work with and satisfy the needs of clients. Negotiation skills are fundamental to this type of relationship.

We stated that there is a growing trend towards project management as a way of achieving specific objectives in an international situation, and as an approach to organizing across national borders. The international manager should ensure that he or she should be well placed to work in project mode!

References

Anderson, E. S., Grude, K. V., Hough, T. and Turner J. R. (1987) *Goal Directed Project Management*, London: Kogan Page.

Bennis, W. (1966) *Changing Organizations*, London: McGraw-Hill.

Handy, C. (1984), *The Future of Work*, Oxford: Blackwell.

Hodge, B. J. and Anthony, W. P. (1988) *Organizational Theory* (3rd edn.), Boston: Allyn and Bacon.

Slevin, D. P. (1989), *The Whole Manager*, New York: AMOCOM, American Management Association.

17

Conclusions: becoming an effective global manager

Now that we are at the end of this text, we should be in an excellent position to see international management development in the light of those aspects of organizational behaviour we have discussed in previous chapters. Particularly in the latter half of this text we have deliberately taken a developmental approach, focusing on the role and nature of the European manager in the global marketplace, looking at both learning and career development, and then focusing on relevant international management skills such as negotiation, decision making and managing change.

Reaching the top: cultural perceptions

Within a global marketplace, international managers must by necessity be in competition for top international jobs in multi-national companies with their counterparts in Europe, North America, and Japan and other areas. However Adler (1991) remarks that what is a relevant management attribute for reaching the top in one country may not be seen as relevant in another. Drawing on the research of Derr and Laurent (Derr, 1986, Laurent, 1986; Derr and Laurent, 1987), she identifies national differences as follows:

North American: must be seen to have ambition and drive within companies which value entrepreneurs.

French: must be labelled as high potential, and be able to manage power relationships and to work within an organizational system, which is seen as a hierarchy of levels of power, depending on their place within it.

German: believe in creativity as essential for success, within an organization which is viewed as a co-ordinated network comprising individuals who make decisions based on their professional expertise.

British: creating the right image and getting noticed, seeing interpersonal skills important within the organizations which is viewed as a network of relationships where things are achieved by influencing others by negotiation and communication.

So, while, for example, German and Swiss companies value highly technical expertise and creativity, French and British companies may see managers with these qualities as pure technicians. Similarly, French and British companies may view the qualities of entrepreneurship valued by the North Americans, as disruptive.

For a manager pursuing a career internationally, this may have consequences as to the way his or her potential for development is seen by particular companies in specific home bases. For the multi-national company developing its managers across a number of companies, this may also have implications for the way they select top management talent and how they develop management potential within and between the various countries within which they operate.

The different operating practices and international personnel policies of multi-national companies will also reflect on the regard for international management development. Permutter (for example in Chakravarthy and Permutter, 1985) identifies four different policies of multi-national companies.

1 *Ethnocentric*: executives from the home country are developed for the key positions in all countries where the multi-national operates, such is the case with many Japanese multi-nationals.

2 *Polycentric*: executives from the local countries within which the multi-national operates are developed for key positions in their own country, particularly in cases where expatriation is too expensive to operate such as in the Far East and Australasia.

3 *Regiocentric*: Executives within a particular region are developed for posts anywhere in that region, for example in the case of companies positioned within the European Community. Gillette is a particular example of this approach.

4 *Geocentric*: the best people anywhere in the world are developed for key posts anywhere in the world, as in the case of IBM (see also Hodgett and Luthans, 1991).

It is perhaps the latter position which has the most implications for our former point: that different national cultures may perceive differently those factors which signify top management potential. Also, the fact that multi-nationals have different policies regarding the development and deployment of key managers has implications in itself for the way 'international' managers are developed.

How do multi-national companies develop global managers?

In an address to the Financial Times Conference: Creating a Euro-workforce in the 90s, in 1990, T. W. Liardet, Head of Management Resourcing and Development of Shell International, outlined the benefits seen by the company of an international management development system, as follows.

* to enable a balance and breadth of global management understanding at senior levels of management;
* to enable the development of managers in depth as well as in breadth;
* to gain top management involvement by ensuring that they know the global resources of the organization;
* to test high potential managers by throwing them in at the deep end;
* to encourage a drive for change by developing new ideas;
* to facilitate a cultural and functional interchange in order to encourage managers to take a fresh look at problems and issues;

- to stimulate individuals' career development by providing challenges and encouraging 'rebirth';
- to promote and effect the cohesion of the organization: the corporate glue.

International management development is therefore seen as a natural process for managers aiming for top management. The process of international development described by Liardet in Shell consists of four stages as follows.

First stage within the operating company: initial training and testing takes place, together with the development of professional expertise. There is inter-functional posting within the immediate operating company, and managers are ranked in terms of their performance and potential in the local pool of junior managers.

Second stage within the region: the higher ranked staff from the local pool progress to this stage where they are posted within the region to facilitate their broadening. There is professional development training provided, and testing for management ability. Ranking of performance and potential is then undertaken within this wider, regional pool.

Third stage across regions and in central office locations: only the highest ranked staff from the regional pool go through to this stage, where postings are inter-regional and in central offices, and professional and general management development is undertaken at group level. Ranking of performance and potential is here undertaken at full international level. Only then do the most outstanding individuals go through to the fourth stage.

Fourth stage at group level: general group management.

From a survey of international management by a research group at Ashridge Management College in England, Barham and Oates (1991) report on an approach to international management development taken by the Hongkong and Shanghai Bank. The fundamental approach taken to international development within a management career is different to that seen in Shell.

Hongkong and Shanghai Banking Corporation has a dual career structure for its managers. It recruits graduates who specifically choose a career within their own country (resident officers) or who choose an international career (international officers). Both categories of management recruits undergo the same six months executive development programme, with a combination of technical and interpersonal skills, with the opportunity to develop cultural sensitivity and synergy. Drawing recruits from all over the world on the same programme with as many as ten different nationalities living and working together over this initial six months, often provides contacts which last a working life-time.

The training programme is divided into four stages. The first is an orientation and team-building process over a two-day seminar designed to develop cultural awareness. This provides the basis for understanding how cultural background shapes individuals' values, attitudes and behaviour, and the way people from other cultures perceive them. The second stage is a ten day outdoor development course designed to build team skills, cultural understanding and synergy and situations which require trust, participation, and interpersonal skills. This is held in the Hong Kong New Territories.

The next stage is a one week course in interpersonal skills development. The fourth stage is an international assignment in order to gain experience in a branch as well as working in a different culture, reinforcing the learning undertaken in the first three stages. The main aim of this is to develop cultural awareness and sensitivity.

So, the approach of the Hongkong and Shanghai bank is to expose management trainees at an early stage in their career to cross-culture differences, which will stand them in good stead for the remainder of their careers, whether they are working internationally or domestically. This is in contrast to the approach of Shell, which is to provide a wider geographical exposure for managers as they progress up the career ladder.

Different approaches to becoming an effective global manager

We can therefore point to different national differences in regard to what it takes to get to the top in international management, and differences between multi-nationals in their regard for developing managers internationally. We can also point to different emphases in advice given to managers for becoming more global or international managers. Barham and Oates (1991), for example, suggest that managers wishing to become more international should:

- think globally and develop their global expertise by broadening their understanding of the global business environment, and developing their knowledge of their own industry in the international arena, seeking out best practices and reading appropriate literature;

- develop their global networks both inside and outside their company through, for example, conferences;

- develop their global leadership skills and values through learning as much as they can about cultural differences generally and specifically about the environment in which they do business; developing understanding about their own culture; improving linguistic skills; learning about different ethical points of view.

Phillips (1992) points to the competences required of international managers as:

- *technical skills and experience*: being competent in their own job;

- *people skills*: being able to relate to others people by understanding their needs through cultural empathy; by developing teams across cultures; by empowering others; and communicating with a wide range of people;

- *intellectual skills*: being able to analyse and process information in a creative way, drawing on best practices in local situations, recognizing that there is more than one way to do this;

- *emotional maturity*: by being open-minded, patient and mature enough to be adaptable, sensitive to others, aware of their own strengths and limitations; by being able to work independently often with little or no local infrastructure; having confidence in themselves and being able to demonstrate this through their own creativity and management of change; and being able to deal with pressure and stress factors.

While the current text does not pretend to teach the international managers all these attributes and skills, we can hope that it provides a good start in considering some of the issues, and will give readers a push in the right direction towards becoming an effective global manager.

References

Adler, N. J. (1991) *International Dimensions of Organizational Behaviour,* (2nd edn.) Boston: PWS-Kent.

Barham, K. and Oates, D. (1991) *The International Manager*, London: Business Books.

Chakravarthy, B. S. and Permutter, H. V. (1985), 'Strategic planning for a global business', *Columbia Journal of World Business*, Summer, pp.5–6.

Derr, C. B. (1986) *Managing the New Career*, San Francisco: Jossey-Bass

Derr, C. B. and Laurent, A. (1987) 'The internal and external careers: a theoretical and cross-cultural perspective', Working Paper, University of Utah and INSEAD.

Hodgett, R. M. and Luthans, F., (1991) *International Management*, New York: McGraw-Hill.

Laurent, A. (1986) 'The cross-cultural puzzle on international human resource management', *Human Resource Management*, 13, 2, Summer, pp.91–102.

Phillips, N. (1992) *Managing International Teams*, London: Pitman.

Bibliography

Adler, N. J. (1991) *International Dimensions of Organizational Behaviour*, (2nd edn.) Boston: PWS-Kent.

Agor, W. H. (1985) *Agor Intuitive Management Survey*, Bryn Mawr, Penn.: Organization Design and Development Inc.

Agor, W. H. (1986) 'The logic of intuition: how top executives make important decisions', *Organizational Dynamics*, 1986, 14, 4, pp.5–18.

Agor, W. H. (1987) *How To Use and Develop Your Intuitive Powers For Increased Productivity*, Bryn Mawr, Penn.: Organizational Design and Development Inc.

Aiken, L. R. (1988) *Psychological Testing and Assessment*, (2nd edn.) Boston: Allyn and Bacon.

Alderfer, C. P. (1972) *Existence, Relatedness and Growth: Human Needs in Organizational Settings*, New York: Free Press.

Alston, J. P. (1985) *The American Samurai: Blending American and Japanese Managerial Practice*, Berlin: Walter de Gruyter.

Anderson, E. S., Grude, K. V., Hough, T. and Turner J. R. (1987) *Goal Directed Project Management*, London: Kogan Page.

Argyle M., (1967) *The Psychology of Interpersonal Behaviour*, Harmondsworth: Penguin.

Argyle, M., Furnham, A. and Graham, J. A. (1981) *Social Situations*, Cambridge: Cambridge University Press.

Argyris C. and Schon, D. (1978) *Organizational Learning*, Reading, Massachusetts: Addison-Wesley.

Barham, K. and Oates, D. (1991) *The International Manager*, London: Business Books/The Economist Books.

Barsoux, J.-L. and Lawrence, P. (1990) *Management In France*, London: Cassell.

Bartlett, C. A. and Ghoshal, S. (1989) *Managing Across Borders: The Transnational Solution*, London: Hutchinson.

Bennis, W. (1966) *Changing Organizations*, London: McGraw-Hill.

Bennis, W. (1991) 'The four competences of leadership', in Kolb, D. A., Rubin, I. M. and Osland, J. S. (eds.) *The Organizational Behaviour Reader* (5th edn), Englewood Cliffs, New Jersey: Prentice-Hall.

Berger, P. L. and Luckmann, T. (1966) *The Social Construction of Reality*, New York: Doubleday.

Berry, J. W., Poortinga, Y. H., Segall, M. H., and Dasen, P. R. (1992) *Cross-cultural Psychology: Research and Application*, Cambridge: Cambridge University Press.

Blake, R. R. and Mouton, J. S. (1985) *The Managerial Grid III*, Houston: Gulf.

Blanchard, K. and Peale, N. V. (1988) *The Power of Ethical Management*, Cedar/Heinemann.

Blau, P. (1964) *Exchange and Power in Social Life*, New York: John Wiley.

Blauner, R. (1964) *Alienation and Freedom: The Factory Worker and his Industry*, Chicago: University of Chicago Press.

Bottomore, T. B. and Rubel, M. (eds.) (1961) *Karl Marx: Selected Writings in Sociology and Social Philosophy*, Harmondsworth: Penguin.

Bournois, F. and Chauchat, J.-H., (1990) 'Managing Managers in Europe', *European Management Journal*, 8 1.

Bowditch, J. L. and Buono, A. F. (1990) *A Primer On Organizational Behaviour*, New York: John Wiley.

Boyatzis, R. E. (1982) *The Competent Manager*, New York: John Wiley.

Brady, F. N. (1990) *Ethical Management: Rules and Results*, Macmillan.

Brianas, J. (1986) 'Management styles: a matter of statistical probability', *Training and Development*, October.

Brown, J. A. C., (1954) *The Social Psychology of Industry*, Harmondsworth: Penguin.

Burgoon, M. and Ruffner, M. (1978) *Human Communication*, New York: Holt, Rinehart and Winston.

Burns, J. M. (1978) *Leadership*, New York: Harper and Row.

Burns, R. B. (1979) *The Self Concept*, London: Longman.

Campbell, J. P. (1970) *Managerial Behaviour, Performance and Effectiveness*, New York: McGraw-Hill.

Campbell J. P. and Pritchard, R. D. (1976) 'Motivational theory in industrial and organizational psychology', in Dunnette, M. D. (ed.), *Handbook of Industrial and Organizational Psychology*, Chicago: Rand McNally.

Carr, J. B. (1979) *Communicating and Relating*, Menlo Park, California: Benjamin/Cummings Publishing.

Casse, P. (1979) *Training For The Cross-Cultural Mind*, Yarmouth, ME: Intercultural Press.

Cattell, R. B. (1965) *The Scientific Analysis of Personality*, Harmondsworth: Penguin.

Chakravarthy, B. S. and Permutter, H. V. (1985) 'Strategic planning for a global business', *Columbia Journal of World Business*, Summer, pp.5–6.

Cicourel, A. V. (1964) *Methods and Measurement in Sociology*, New York: The Free Press.

Clutterbuck, D. and Crainer, S. (1988) 'The Corporate Sages', *Business*, September.

Cockerill, T. (1989) 'The kind of competences for rapid change', *Personnel Management*, September.

Cohen, A. R. and Bradford, D. L. (1989) 'Influence without authority: the use of alliances, reciprocity and exchange to accomplish work', *Organizational Dynamics*, 17, 3, Winter, pp.4–17.

Condon, J. (1981) 'Values and ethics in communication across cultures: some notes on the North American case', *Communication*, 6, 2, pp.255–65.

Constable, C. J. (1988) *Developing The Competent Manager in a UK Context*, Report for the Manpower Services Commission, Sheffield: Manpower Services Commission.

Cooley, C. H. (1902) *Human Nature and the Social Order*, New York: Charles Scribner's Sons.

Cronbach, L. J. (1990) *Essentials of Psychological Testing*, (5th edn.) New York: Harper Collins.

Dahl, R. A. (1957) 'The concept of power', *Behavioural Science*, 2, pp.201–18.

Davison, S. 'International competencies – are they useful as models?' (unpublished)

de Boer, C. (1978) 'The polls: attitudes towards work', *Public Opinion Quarterly*, 42, pp.414–23.

de Bono, E. (1970) *Lateral Thinking*, Harmondsworth: Penguin.

Deal, T.E. and Kennedy, A.A. (1982) *Corporate Culture: The Rites and Rituals of Corporate Life*, Reading, MA: Addison-Wesley.

Derr, C. B. (1986) *Managing the New Career*, San Francisco: Jossey-Bass.

Derr, C. B. and Laurent, A. (1987) 'The internal and external careers: a theoretical and cross-cultural perspective', Working Paper, University of Utah and INSEAD.

Donaldson, T. (1989) *The Ethics of International Business*, New York: Oxford University Press.

Donaldson, J. (1992) *Business Ethics: A European Casebook*, London: Academic Press.

Dowling, P. J. and Schuler, R. S. (1990) *International Dimensions of Human Resource Management*, Boston: PWS-Kent.

Dunnette, M. D. (ed.) (1976) *Handbook of Industrial and Organizational Psychology*, Chicago: Rand McNally.

Durkheim, E. (1915) *The Elementary Forms of the Religious Life* (Trans. Swain, J. W.) London: Allen and Unwin.

Eiser, J. R. (1986) *Social Psychology: Attitudes, Cognition and Social Behaviour*, Cambridge: Cambridge University Press.

Ewen, R. B. (1988) *An Introduction To Theories of Personality*, (3rd edn.), Hillsdale, New Jersey: Lawrence Erlbaum Associates.

Eysenck, H. J. (1953) *The Scientific Study of Personality*, London: Methuen.

Eysenck, H. J. (1971) *Race, Intelligence and Education*, London: Temple Smith.

Fetterman, D. M. (1989) *Ethnography: Step By Step*, Newbury Park, California: Sage.

Fiedler, F. (1967) *A Theory of Leadership Effectiveness*, New York: McGraw-Hill.

Fisher, G. (1982) *International Negotiation: A Cross-Cultural Perspective*, Yarmouth ME: Intercultural Press.

Fleishman, E. A. and Quaintance, M. K. (1984) *Taxonomy of Human Performance*, New York: Academic Press.

Folberg, J. and Taylor, A. (1984) *Mediation: a comprehensive guide to resolving conflicts without litigation*, San Francisco: Jossey-Bass.

French, J. R. P. and Raven, B. (1959) 'The bases of social power', in Cartwright, D. (ed.) *Studies in Social Power*, Ann Arbor: Institute for Social Research.

Freud, S. (1940) *Outline of Psychoanalysis*, (standard edn. 1969 vol 23), London: Hogarth Press.

Ghiselli, E. E. (1971) *Explorations in Managerial Talent*, California: Goodyear.

Gibb, C. A. (1954) 'Leadership' in Lindzey, G (ed.) *Handbook of Social Psychology*, Reading, Massachusetts: Addison-Wesley.

Gladwin, T. N. and Walters, I. (1980) *Multinational Under Fire: Lessons in the Management of Conflict*, New York: John Wiley.

Glaze, T. (1989) 'Cadbury's dictionary of competence', *Personnel Management*, July.

Glenn, E. S., Witmeyer, D. and Stevenson, K. A. (1984) 'Cultural styles of persuasion', *International Journal of Intercultural Relations*, 1.

Goffman, E. (1959) *The Presentation of Self in Everyday Life*, (1971 edn.), Harmondsworth: Penguin.

Gould, R. L. (1979) *Transformation*, New York: Simon and Schuster.

Graham, J. L. (1983) 'Brazilian, Japanese and American Negotiations', *Journal of International Business Studies*, 14, 1, Spring-Summer, pp.47–61.

Graham, J. L. (1985) 'The influence of culture on business negotiations', *Journal of International Business Studies'*, 16, 1, Spring, pp.81–96.

Graham, J. L. and Herberger, R. A. (1983) 'Negotiators abroad – don't shoot from the hip', *Harvard Business Review*, July/August, pp.160–8.

Guy, V. and Mattock, J. (1991) *The New International Manager*, London: Kogan Page.

Handy, C. (1976) *Understanding Organizations*, Harmondsworth: Penguin.

Handy, C. (1984) *The Future of Work*, Oxford: Blackwell.

Harre, R., Clarke, D. and DeCarlo, N. (1985) *Motives and Mechanisms*, London: Methuen.

Harris, P. R. and Moran, R. T. (1987) *Managing Cultural Differences*, Houston: Gulf Publishing.

Harrison, R. (1972) 'How to describe your organization', *Harvard Business Review*, Sept/Oct.

Hastorf, A. H., Schneider, D. J. and Polefka, J. (1970) 'The perception process' in Corner, J. and Hawthorne, J. (eds.) *Communication Studies*, London: Edward Arnold.

Hayes, J. and Allinson, C. W. (1988) 'Cultural differences in the learning styles of managers', *Management International Review*, 28, 3.

Heider, F. (1946) 'Attitudes and cognitive informations', *Journal of Psychology*, 21, pp.107–12.

Heider, F. (1958) *The Psychology of Interpersonal Relations*, New York: Wiley.

Hersey, P. and Blanchard, K. (1977) *Organizational Behaviour: Utilizing Human Resources*, Englewood Cliffs, New Jersey: Prentice-Hall.

Herzberg, F., Mausner, B. and Snyderman, B. (1959) *The Motivation to Work*, New York: Wiley.

Hilgard, E. R. and Bower, G. H. (1967) *Theories of Learning*, New York: Appleton.

Hodge, B. J. and Anthony, W. P. (1988) *Organizational Theory*, (3rd edn.) Boston: Allyn and Bacon.

Hodgetts, R. M. and Luthans, F. (1991) *International Management*, New York: McGraw-Hill.

Hofstede, G. (1980) *Culture's Consequences: International Differences in Work Related Values*, Beverly Hills, California: Sage.

Hofstede, G. (1980) 'Motivation, leadership and organization: Do American Theories Apply abroad?' *Organizational Dynamics*, Summer, pp.42–63.

Hofstede, G. (1984) *Culture's Consequences: International Differences in Work-Related Values*, (abridged version), Beverley-Hills CA: Sage.

Hofstede, G. (1989) 'Organising for cultural diversity', *European Management Journal*, 7, 4.

Hofstede, G. (1991) *Cultures and Organizations: Software of the Mind*, London: McGraw-Hill.

Hogan, R. C. and Champagne, D. W. (1987) *Personal Styles Inventory*, Organizational Design and Development Inc, USA.

Homans, G. (1958) 'Social behaviour as exchange', *American Journal of Sociology*, 63, pp.597–606.

Honey, P. and Mumford, A. (1982) *The Manual of Learning Styles*, Maidenhead: Peter Honey.

Hosmer, L. T. (1987) 'Ethical Analysis and Human Resource Management', *Human Resource Management*, Fall, 26, 3, pp.313–30.

House, R. J. (1971) 'A path-goal theory of leadership effectiveness', *Administrative Science Quarterly*, 16 pp.321–38.

Hughes-Weiner, G. (1986) 'The "learn-how-to-learn" approach to cross-cultural orientation', *International Journal of Intercultural Relations*, 10, pp.485–505.

Hui, C. H. (1990) 'Work attitudes, Leadership and Managerial Behaviour in Different Cultures', in Brislin, R. W. *Applied Cross-Cultural Psychology*, Newbury Park: Sage.

Hunt, J.G. (1991) *Leadership: A New Synthesis*, Newbury Park: Sage.

Jackson, T. (1984) 'Interpersonal Communication: Education and Training in Business Studies', Unpublished Masters Thesis, Keele University.

Jackson, T. (1991) *Measuring Management Performance*, London: Kogan Page.

Jackson, T. (1992) 'Management Performance', Unpublished Doctoral Thesis, Henley the Management College, Brunel University.

Jacobs, R. (1989) 'Getting the measure of management competence', *Personnel Management*, June.

Jaeger, A. M. (1990) 'The applicability of Western management techniques in developing countries: a cultural perspective', in Jaeger and Kanungo (eds.) 1990.

Jaeger, A. M. and Kanungo, R. N. (eds.) (1990) *Management in Developing Countries*, London: Routledge.

Jalali, F. A. (1989) 'A cross-cultural comparative analysis of the learning styles and field dependence/independence characteristics of selected fourth-, fifth-, and sixth-grade students of Afro, Chinese, Greek and Mexican-American heritage', unpublished doctoral thesis, St John's University, New York, quoted in Cushner, K. (1990) 'Cross-cultural psychology and the formal classroom' in Brislin, R. W. (ed.) (1990) *Applied Cross-Cultural Psychology*, Newbury Park, California: Sage.

Johnson, D. W. and Johnson, F. P. (1975) *Joining Together: Group Theory and Group Skills*, Englewood Cliffs, New Jersey: Prentice-Hall.

Johnson, T., Feigenbaum, R. and Welby, M. (1964) 'Some determinants and consequences of teacher's perceptions of causation', *Journal of Educational Psychology*, 55 pp.237–46.

Jung, C. G. (1921) *Psychological Types*, (Collected Works, Vol 6, 1976) New Jersey: Princeton University Press.

Kakabadse, A., Ludlow, R. and Vinnicombe, S. (1987) *Working in Organizations*, Harmondsworth: Penguin.

Kanter, R. M. (1991) 'Managing the human side of change', in Kolb, Rubin and Osland (1991), *The Organizational Behavior Reader*, Englewood Cliffs, New Jersey: Prentice-Hall.

Katz, D. and Kahn, R. L. (1978) *The Social Psychology of Organizations*, (2nd edn.) New York: John Wiley.

Kelley, H. H. (1967) 'Attribution theory in social psychology', *Nebraska Symposium on Motivation*, 15, pp.192–238.

Kelley, H. H. (1973) 'The processes of causal attribution', *American Psychologist*, 28, pp.107–28.

Kelly, G. A. (1955) *The Psychology of Personal Constructs Vols. 1 and 2*, New York: Norton.

Kelly, L. and Worthy, R. (1981) 'The Role of Culture in Comparative Management: A cross Cultural Perspective', *Academy of Management Journal*, 24, 1, pp.164–73.

Kelly, L., Whatley, A. and Worthley, R., (1991) 'Self-appraisal, life goals, and national culture: an Asian-Western Comparison', *Asia Pacific Journal of Management*, 7, 2 pp.41–58.

Keltner, J. W. (1973) *Elements of Interpersonal Communication*, California: Wadsworth.

Kim, U. (1990) 'Indigenous psychology: science and application' in Brislin, R. W. (ed.) (1990) *Applied Cross-cultural Psychology*, Newbury Park, California: Sage.

Kirkbride, P. S. and Tang, S. F. Y. (1990) 'Negotiation: lessons from behind the bamboo curtain', *Journal of General Management*, 16, 1, Autumn.

Kline, P. (1986) *A Handbook of Test Construction*, London: Methuen.

Kline, P. (1988) *Psychology Exposed: Or the Emperor's New Clothes*, London: Routledge.

Kolb, D. A. (1976) *The Learning Styles Inventory*, Boston, Mass: McBer and Co.

Kolb, D. A., Rubin, I. M. and Osland, J. S. (1991) *Organizational Behavior: An Experiential Approach* (5th edn.), Englewood Cliffs, New Jersey: Prentice-Hall.

Kotter, J. (1982) 'What effective general managers really do', *Harvard Business Review*, 60, 6, pp.156–67.

Kotter, J. (1990) *A Force For Change*, New York: Macmillan.

Laurent, A. (1983) 'The cultural diversity of western conceptions of management', *International Studies of Management and Organization*, XIII, 1–2, Spring-Summer, pp.75–96.

Laurent, A. (1986) 'The cross-cultural puzzle on international human resources management', *Human Resources Management*, 13 2, 1986, pp.91–102.

Laurent, A. (1989) 'A cultural view of change' in Evans, P., Doz, Y. and Laurent, A. (eds.) *Human Resource Management In International Firms: Change, Globalization, Innovation*, Basingstoke: Macmillan.

Lawrence, P. R. and Lorsch, W. J. (1967) *Organization And Environment*, Cambridge, Mass.: Harvard University Press.

Leavitt, H. J. (1965) 'Applied organizational change in industry' in March J. G. (ed.) *Handbook of Organizations*, Chicago: Rand McNally.

Lee, R. and Lawrence, P. (1991) *Politics at Work*, Cheltenham: Stanley Thornes.

Lessem, R. (1989) *Global Management Principles*, London: Prentice-Hall.

Leung, K. and Wu, P.-G. (1990) 'Dispute processes: a cross-cultural analysis', in Brislin, R. W. (ed.) *Applied Cross-Cultural Psychology*, Newbury Park: Sage.

Levinson, D. J. (1986) 'A concept of adult development', *American Psychologist*, 41, 1, January, pp.3–13.

Lewin, K. (1951) *Field Theory in Social Science*, London: Harper and Row.

Likert, R. (1967) *The Human Organization*, Tokyo: McGraw-Hill Kogakusha.

Lonner, W. J. (1990) 'An overview of cross-cultural testing and assessment' in Brislin, R. W. (ed.) *Applied Cross-Cultural Psychology*, Newbury Park: Sage.

Luft, J. (1961) 'The Johari Window', *Human Relations and Training News*, January, pp. 6–7.

McCalman, J. (1989) 'Performance organizations in the 1990s: flexibility for manufacturing management', *European Management Journal*, 7 3.

McClelland, D. R. (1961) *The Achieving Society*, Princeton, NJ: Van Nostrand.

McClelland D. C. (1987) *Human Motivation*, Cambridge: Cambridge University Press.

Maccoby, M. (1976) *The Gamesman*, New York: Simon and Schuster.

McCormick, E. J. and Ilgen, D. (1985) *Industrial and Organizational Psychology*, London: Allen and Unwin.

McGoldrich, B. (1984) 'Inside the Goldman Sachs Culture', *Institutional Investor*, January, pp.53–67 and cited in Hodge and Anthony (1988) *Organizational Theory*, (3rd edn.) Boston: Allyn and Bacon.

McGregor, D. (1960) *The Human Side of Enterprize*, New York: McGraw-Hill.

Mainguy, W. (1988) 'Leadership qualities: Europe's CEOs are surveyed by Management Centre Europe', *European Management Journal*, 6, 3.

Malinowski, B. (1927) *Sex and Repression in Savage Society*, New York: Harcourt Brace.

Martyn-Johns, T. A. (1977) 'Cultural conditioning of views of authority and its effects on the business decision-making process with special reference to Java', in Poortinga, Y. H. (ed.), *Basic Problems in Cross-cultural Psychology*, Lisse: Swets and Zeitbirger, pp.344–352.

Maslow, A. H. (1954) *Motivation of Personality*, New York: Harper and Row.

Mead, G. H. (1934) *Mind, Self and Society*, Chicago: University of Chicago Press.

Mead, R. (1990) *Cross-Cultural Communication*, Chichester, W. Sussex: Wiley.

Merton, R. K. (1949) *Social Theory and Social Structure*, Glencoe, Illinois: The Free Press.

Miles, R. H. (1980) *Macro Organizational Behaviour*, Glenview, Ill: Scott Foresman.

Miller, D. (1986) 'Configurations of strategy and structure', *Strategic Management Journal*, pp.55–76.

Miller, D. T. and Ross, M. (1975) 'Self-serving biases in the attribution of causality: fact or fiction?' *Psychological Bulletin*, 82, pp.213–25.

Morgan, R. G. T. (1979) 'Analysis of social skills: the behaviour analysis approach' in Singleton, W. T., Spurgeon, P. and Stammers, R. B. (eds.) (1980) *The Analysis of Social Skills*, New York: Plenum Press.

Morse, N. C. and Reimer, E. (1956) 'The experimental change of a major organizational variable', *Journal of Abnormal and Social Psychology*, 52, pp.120–9.

MOW (Meaning of Working) International Research Team (1987) *The Meaning of Working*, London: Academic Press.

Murray, H. A. (1938) *Explorations in Personality*, New York: Oxford University Press.

Myers, M. T. and Myers, G. E. (1982) *Managing By Communication: An Organizational Approach*, New York: McGraw-Hill.

Nadler, D. A. and Tushman, M. (1991) 'A congruence model for diagnosing organizational behavior', in Kolb, D. A., Rubin, I. M. and Osland, J. S. (eds.) *The Organizational Behaviour Reader* (5th edn), Englewood Cliffs, NJ: Prentice-Hall.

Negandhi, A. R. (1987) *International Management*, Boston: Allyn and Bacon.

Newcombe, T. (1953) 'An approach to the study of communication acts', *Psychological Review*, 60.

Olie, R. (1990) 'Culture and integration problems in international mergers and acquisitions', *European Management Journal*, 8, 2, June.

Ouchi, W. G. and WIlkins, A. L. (1985) 'Organizational Culture', *Annual Review of Sociology*, 11, pp.457–83.

Paranjpe, A. C. (1984) *Theoretical Psychology: The Meeting of East and West*, New York: Plenum.

Parsons, T. (1949) *The Structure of Social Action*, Glencoe, Illinois: The Free Press.

Parsons, T. (1951) *The Social System*, Glencoe, Illinois: The Free Press.

Parsons, T. (1964) *Structure and Process in Modern Societies*, Glencoe, Illinois: The Free Press.

Pascale, R. T. and Athos, A. G. (1981) *The Art of Japanese Management*, New York: Simon & Schuster.

Perlmutter, H. (1954) 'Relations between self-image, image of the foreigner, and the desire to live abroad', *Journal of Psychology*, 38, pp. 131–7.

Peterson, R. B. and Shimada, J. Y. (1978) 'Sources of management problems in Japanese-American joint ventures', *Academy of Managerial Review*, 3, pp.796–804.

Phatak, A. V. (1992) *International Dimensions of Management*, (3rd edn.), Boston: PWS-Kent.

Phillips, N. (1992) *Managing International Teams*, London: Pitman.

Polanyi, M. (1967) *The Tacit Dimension*, New York: Doubleday.

Porter, L. W. and Lawler, E. E. (1968) *Managerial Attitudes and Performance*, Illinois: Dorsey Press.

Prien, E. (1981) 'The function of job analysis in content validation', *Personnel Psychology*, 30, pp.167–74.

Putti, J. M. and Chia, A. (1990) *Culture and Management: A Casebook*, Singapore: McGraw-Hill.

Pye, L. W. (1986) 'The China trade: Making the deal', *Harvard Business Review*, July/August.

Rackham, N. (1976) 'The behaviour of successful negotiators' (Huthwaite Research Group Report) in Raider, E. (ed.) *International Negotiations: A Training Program For Corporate Executives And Diplomats*, New York: Ellen Raider International.

Rackham, N., Honey, P. and Colbert, M. *et al.* (1971) *Developing Interactive Skills*, Northampton: Wellens Publishing.

Radcliffe-Brown, A. R. (1952) *Structure and Function in Primitive Society*, London: Cohen and West.

Reading, B. (1992) *Japan – The Coming Collapse*, London: Weidenfeld and Nicolson (abstracted in *Sunday Times*, 3 May 1992).

Reddin, W. J. (1970) *Managerial Effectiveness*, London: McGraw-Hill.

Renwick, G. (1985) *Malays and Americans: Definite Differences, Unique Opportunities*, Yarmouth, ME: Intercultural Press.

Revans, R. (1965) *Science and the Manager*, London: MacDonald.

Ribeaux, P. and Poppleton, S. E. (1978) *Psychology at Work*, Basingstoke: Macmillan.

Rogers, C. R. (1951) *Client Centred Therapy*, Boston, US: Houghton Mifflin.

Rogers, E. M. and Agarwala-Rogers, R. (1976) *Communication in Organizations*, New York: The Free Press.

Rotter, J. B. (1966) 'Generalized expectancies for internal versus external control of reinforcement', *Psychological Monographs*, 80, 1, whole No 609.

Schein, E. H. (1965) *Organizational Psychology*, Englewood Cliffs, New Jersey: Prentice-Hall.

Schein, E. H. (1978) *Career Dynamics: Matching Individual and Organizational Needs*, Reading Massachusetts: Addison-Wesley.

Schein, E. H. (1985) *Organizational Culture and Leadership*, San Francisco: Jossey-Bass.

Schein, E. H. (1989) 'Organizational culture: what it is and how to change it', in Evans, Doz and Laurent (eds.) *Human Resource Management in International Firms*, Basingstoke: Mamillan.

Schmidt, S. M. and Kochan, T. A. (1972) 'Conflict: towards conceptual clarity', *Administrative Science Quarterly*, 17, pp.359–70.

Schutz, A. (1972) *Phenomenology of the Social World*, London: Heinemann.

Silverman, D. (1970) *The Theory Of Organizations*, Aldershot: Gower.

Skinner, B. F. (1953) *Science and Human Behaviour*, New York: Macmillan.

Slevin, D. P. (1989) *The Whole Manager*, New York: AMOCOM, American Management Association.

Smiley, T. (1989) 'A challenge to the human resource and organizational function in international firms', *European Management Journal*, 7, 2.

Smith, P. B., Misumi, J., Tayeb, M., Peterson, M. and Bond, M. (1989) 'On the generality of leadership styles measured across cultures', *Journal of Occupational Psychology*, 62, pp.97–109.

Springer, S. P. and Deutch, G. (1981) *Left Brain, Right Brain*, New York: Freeman.

Stewart, D. (1986) *The Power of People Skills*, New York: John Wiley.

Sullivan, J., Peterson, R. B., Kameda, N. and Shimada, J. (1981) 'The relationship between conflict resolution approaches and trust: a cross-cultural study', *Academy of Management Journal*, 24, pp.803–15.

Talbot, R. P. and Geyer, R. L. (1991) 'Comparing cross-cultural thinking preferences', *National Productivity Review*, Spring, pp.181–93.

Tannenbaum, R. and Schmitt, W. H. (1973) 'How to choose a leadership pattern', *Harvard Business Review*, May/June.

Taylor, F. W. (1911) *Scientific Management*, New York: Harper & Row.

Thurley, K. and Wirdenius, H. (1989) *Towards European Management*, London: Pitman.

Tichy, N. M. and Devanna, M. A. (1986) *The Transformational Leader*, New York: Wiley.

Tijmstra, S. and Casler, K. (1992) 'Management learning for Europe', *European Management Journal*, 10, 1, March.

Toch, H. and MacLean, M. S. (1967) 'Perception and communication: a transactional view', in Sereno, K. K. and Mortensen, C. D. (eds) *Foundations of Communication Theory*, New York: Harper and Row.

Tolman, E. C. (1932) *Purposive Behaviour in Animals and Men*, California: University of California Press.

Triandis, H. C. (1990) 'Theoretical concepts that are applicable to the analysis of ethnocentrism', in Brislin, R. W. (ed.) *Applied Cross-Cultural Psychology*, Newbury Park: Sage.

Turnipseed, D. L. (1988) 'An integrated, interactive model of organizatinal climate, culture and effectiveness', *Leadership and Organizational Development Journal*, 9, 5, pp.17–21.

Tyler, E. B. (1871) *Primitive Culture*, cited in Levi-Strausss, C. (1963) *Structural Anthropology* (trans. Jacobson, C. and Schoel, B. G.) Harmondsworth: Penguin.

Vandermerwe, S. and Vandermerwe, A. (1991) 'Making strategic change happen', *European Management Journal*, 9, 2.

van Dijck, J. (1990) 'Transnational management in an evolving European context', *European Management Journal*, 8, 4.

van Maanen, J. and Barley S. R. (1985) 'Cultural organization: fragments of a theory', in Frost, P. J., Moore, L. L., Louis, M. R., Lindberg, C. C. and Martin, J. (eds.), *Organizational Culture*, Newbury Park, CA: Sage, pp.31–53.

Vroom, V. (1973) 'A new look at managerial decision making', *Organizational Dynamics*, Spring.

Vroom, V. H. (1964) *Work and Motivation*, New York: Wiley.

Waterman, R. H., Peters, T. J. and Philips, J. R .(1980) 'Structure is not organization' reproduced in Kolb, D. A., Rubin, I. M. and Osland, J. S., (eds.) (1991) *The Organizational Behaviour Reader*, (5th edn.) Englewood Cliffs, NJ: Prentice-Hall.

Williams, A., Dobson, P. and Walters, M. (1989) *Changing Culture*, London: Institute of Personnel Management.

Wolfe, D. M. and Kolb, D. A. (1991) 'Career development, personal growth, and experiential learning', in Kolb, D. A., Rubin, I. M. and Osland J. S. (1991) *The Organizational Behaviour Reader*, (5th edn.) Englewood Cliffs, NJ: Prentice-Hall.

Ziller, R. C. (1973) *The Social Self*, New York: Pergamon.

Ziller, R. C., Long, B. H. Remana, K. and Reddy, V. (1968) 'Self esteem: a self-social construct', *Journal of Consulting and Clinical Psychology*, 33, pp.84–95.

Index